THE INSTITUTIONALIZATION OF EDUCATIONAL CINEMA

THE INSTITUTIONALIZATION OF EDUCATIONAL CINEMA

North America and Europe in the 1910s and 1920s

Edited by Marina Dahlquist and
Joel Frykholm

Indiana University Press

This book is a publication of

Indiana University Press
Office of Scholarly Publishing
Herman B Wells Library 350
1320 East 10th Street
Bloomington, Indiana 47405 USA

iupress.indiana.edu

 The paper used in this publication meets the minimum requirements of the American National Standard for Information Sciences—Permanence of Paper for Printed Library Materials, ANSI Z39.48-1992.

Manufactured in the United States of America

Cataloging information is available from the Library of Congress.

ISBN 978-0-253-04519-5 (hb)
ISBN 978-0-253-04520-1 (pb)
ISBN 978-0-253-04522-5 (web PDF)

1 2 3 4 5 24 23 22 21 20 19

Contents

Acknowledgments

Six of the essays included in this collection are revised versions of papers presented at an international symposium at Stockholm University in May 2013 titled "The Institutionalization of Educational Cinema." The editors would like to thank all participants of the symposium—that is, Zoë Druick, Oliver Gaycken, Lee Grieveson, Frank Kessler, Nico de Klerk, Sabine Lenk, Paul S. Moore, and Greg Waller—for contributing to the vivid, critical, and constructive discussions during which the seeds for this volume were planted. We're equally thankful to the scholars who joined in somewhat later to take the topic in new and exciting directions. We would also like to express our gratitude to the Department of Media Studies at Stockholm University, both for financial, practical, and other forms of support that made the symposium possible and for covering the costs of copy editing an earlier draft of this manuscript. Many thanks to Erika Stevens, who carried out the aforementioned copy editing with great skill and diligence and whose perceptive comments on the contents were extremely useful. Insightful remarks from the anonymous readers of a later draft also helped us improve the quality of the volume considerably. Thanks go as well to Bart van der Gaag for helping out with the images and for other kinds of technical support throughout the process. Finally, our sincere appreciation goes to Janice Frisch and her coworkers at Indiana University Press for all their efforts in making this book a reality.

THE INSTITUTIONALIZATION OF EDUCATIONAL CINEMA

Introduction

Marina Dahlquist and Joel Frykholm

The pedagogical usefulness of motion pictures has long been recognized as a defining quality of the medium—particularly during the formative decades of cinema. Indeed, ideas about film's potential to educate have been crucial for the development of cinema as a cultural institution, arguably just as important as various conceptions of film as a form of art, science, industry, or entertainment. For example, when reformers in the early years of the twentieth century began voicing concerns about films' allegedly undesirable fictional representations and their effects on impressionable audiences—including women, children, immigrants, and the working classes—many of the same reformers also suggested that a unique educational potential held the key to the medium's entire raison d'être. From the very first years of cinema, the widely shared faith in the educational value of moving images translated into a plethora of *practices* when it came to film production and programming. Even if the dissemination of motion pictures to a mass public happened largely as a result of the discovery and development of their commercial potential as a cheap but attractive amusement, commerce was just one manifestation of many ideas about the proper social and cultural uses of the new technology.

Acknowledging the diversity of cinema and the complexity of its past may seem de rigueur to present-day film scholars. But this was not always the case. Until quite recently, much cinema scholarship was centered on a standard film form—the narrative feature film—and the standard film experience or situation that is theatrical moviegoing. Generally, if not exclusively, there has been a bias in favor of a conception of cinema as art or entertainment and a concomitant historiographical tendency toward linearity, canon construction, and artist idolization. The ongoing scholarly exploration of educational cinema, and other strands within the domains of "nontheatrical cinema," can be thought of as a challenge to these norms, biases, and processes of inclusion and exclusion. Through the rediscovery of previously neglected "other" cinemas, "orphan" films, and exhibition contexts outside and beyond the purpose-built commercial movie theater, the field of cinema studies has expanded, adding nuance, richness, and complexity to the historical understanding of cinema at large. As a result, cinema scholars have gained a new and deeper insight into the wider cultural histories of cinema and the social and political roles cinema has played historically.[1] This is not to imply that cinema historians no longer hold any biases or no longer have to delineate, restrict, and select—only that their area of study and their approaches are becoming increasingly diverse.

This collection of essays, which offers new research on educational cinema in North America and Europe in the 1910s and 1920s, can be seen as a continuation of the ongoing scholarly efforts to expand the terrain of cinema studies and historical research of film. The book's aim is to offer a twofold contribution to the study of educational cinema. First, it recasts the history of educational cinema in terms of its *institutionalization*. Second, it offers a more distinctly *international* approach to the topic than has typically been the case, by highlighting patterns of transnational influence as well as connections and movements between the local and the global. Along these lines, the essays explore how, why, and to what extent an "institutionalization" of educational cinema occurred in the 1910s and 1920s and whether there is an overarching narrative of how educational cinema coalesced into a relatively autonomous and enduring institution. If so, what were the elements of its institutional stability? How, or to what extent, were durable methods of production, distribution, and exhibition established? What types of lasting networks of organizations, individuals, companies, and government agencies were created? What genres and types of film came to dominate the field? How did local, national, and international initiatives connect in processes of institutionalization? In sum, the project's overarching questions concern the wider developments and larger patterns of educational cinema in the 1910s and 1920s, in different local, national, and transnational contexts. Naturally, these questions are not formulated from scratch but instead are posed in dialogue with booming research initiatives undertaken during the last ten years or so—work that has made it possible to discern some general patterns and formations of educational cinema nationally and internationally.

This collection brings attention to a remarkable but under-researched phase in the history of educational cinema; namely, the period that came after an early experimental phase that was characterized by initial debates over the educational value of moving images and an exploratory search for successful practices, but before 28 mm and later 16 mm film stock enabled more widespread and structured uses of motion pictures within educational and amateur contexts. Roughly speaking, the pioneering efforts and debates were about the discursive construction of the field of educational cinema while the later developments of small-gauge formats concerned the technical standards of the field. By contrast, this book is about the range of cultural practices that shaped educational cinema as an institution, and about the ways educational cinema fit into a larger institutional matrix. Or, to put a finer point on the agenda, the period this book explores is distinguished by the ways in which discourses, cultural practices, technical standards, and institutional frameworks coevolved according to patterns that transformed educational cinema from a convincing idea into an enduring institution. This is the process we refer to with the book's primary keyword: *institutionalization*. The term appears throughout the volume but is not meant to imply a faithful adaptation from sociological institutionalism, institutional economics, organizational studies, or some other field where it has been theorized and operationalized. This is by choice. The basic idea for the book has been to deploy *institutionalization* as a heuristic for generating new approaches to the history of educational cinema rather than to pinpoint the precise meaning of the term itself.

This is not an attempt to let us off the editorial hook. Indeed, to give an idea *why* the idea of institutionalization is heuristically useful, we want to take this opportunity to say something more about what the term might mean and to give the reader an impression of how recurring themes, ideas, and issues in the various chapters feed into the notion of an institutionalization of educational cinema. A primary understanding of the idea of institutionalization points toward a stabilization of sorts—the coalescing of various one-off experiments or isolated initiatives into a field characterized by regularized modes of production, distribution, and exhibition. A more concrete dimension of this process can be traced to the various practices that gradually, through trial and error, establish the norms and conventions of the field and its modes of operation. Such practices, and their relevance with regard to a possible process of institutionalization, take center stage in the chapters that follow.

In the aforementioned sense, *institutionalization* refers to the ways in which educational cinema can be thought of and studied as an institution in its own right. An alternative interpretation suggests that the process of institutionalization has more to do with the ways in which educational cinema was incorporated into various *other* institutions, such as schools, libraries, and industries. The essays in this volume offer plenty of examples of this sense of institutionalization too, according to which the educational potential of motion pictures was contained within other institutions and reanimated for these different institutions' specific purposes and agendas—for their target audiences, users, and constituencies.

But how does a plausible narrative of the process of institutionalizing educational cinema square with the apparent diversity of production models, modes of representation, distribution methods, and exhibition contexts and the wide spectrum of vested interests? Take, for example, this reflection on the power of motion pictures, penned by the American Library Association's Gerald McDonald in 1942:

> Films introduce a world we never saw, a life we never lived, and people we never knew. They show glimpses of beauty to be treasured and of ugliness which men must strive to obliterate. They can speak directly to many who are not accustomed to obtaining ideas from the printed page. They quickly summarize a subject, raise an issue, or pose a problem. They furnish a speedy method of communication to large groups, and provide them with a common experience. They provide a visual imagery to be applied to the things people read. They can clarify job techniques for the worker, picture the living past for the historian, and extend the range of the eye for the scientist. They have in them the power to open study on vital problems, to revitalize democracy, and to develop a more responsible citizenship.[2]

This multiverse of uses and functions of film is mirrored by the many topics that may be, and have been, included under the banner of "educational film." For instance, the cover to George Kleine's oft-cited *Catalogue of Educational Motion*

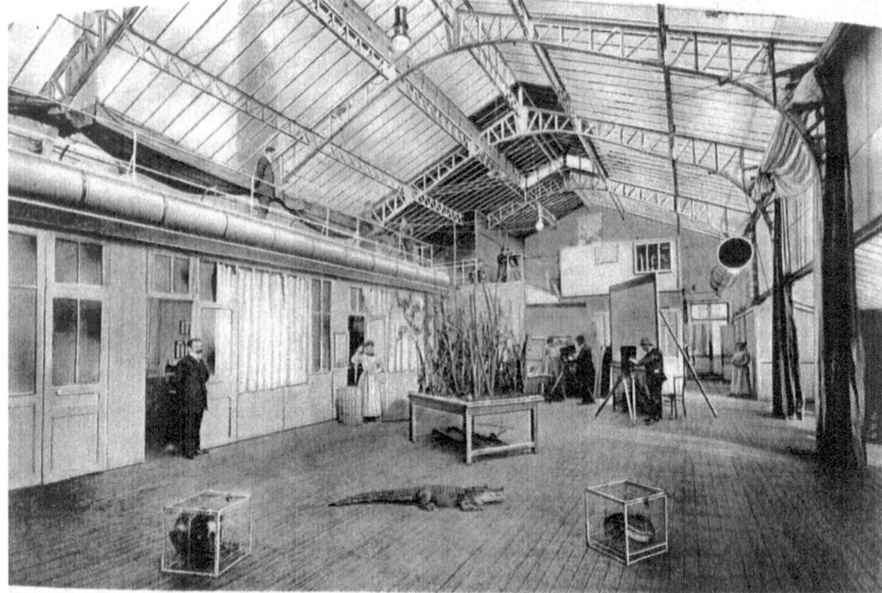

L'atelier de prise de vues scientifiques.

Fig. 0.1. Production of scientific films at Pathé Frères' studio.

Picture Films, issued in 1910, listed the categories of travel, history, surgery, zoology, botany, railways, aeronautics, ethnology, naval, geography, geology, microscopy, agriculture, military, mining, and kindergarten.[3] In 1921, *Educational Film Magazine*, the "International Authority on the Non-theatrical Motion Picture Field," stated that it was "covering motion pictures in the following departments": accident prevention; Americanization; aviation; child welfare; education; forestry; agriculture; biography; civics and government; community; cultural; current events; geography; history; home economics; health and sanitation; industry; juvenile; literature; pedagogy; recreational; religion; scenic; science; sociology; travel, welfare; and women.[4] Catalogs and periodicals such as the ones referenced here established different kinds of subcategorizations while also expressing a preference for the term *educational* as the main header. But the distinction between terms such as *educational film* (as popularized by Kleine and others in the United States around 1910), *scènes instructives* (as utilized by Pathé Frères), *popularized science*, and so on is not self-evident.

The differentiation of and between terms points to a panoply of attempts throughout the history of educational cinema to properly categorize and label groups of motion pictures and match them with their most suitable exhibition sites. Consider, for the categories of pictures already mentioned, the miscellaneous lot of potential audiences and exhibition venues: public, private, and parochial primary and secondary schools; universities and colleges; technical schools; job training courses; night schools; churches; clubs; factories; YMCAs; PTAs; women's clubs; granges; corn clubs; farm discussion groups; national, state, and local governments; community centers; fairs and expositions; hospitals; prisons; charitable institutions; fraternal organizations; and labor unions (to name a few).[5] Venues and their audiences were catered to through a variety of distribution schemes, drawing on a range of sources with differing terms and conditions. People who ventured into the field did so for a variety of reasons and with different sets of interests. For commercial distributors and entrepreneurs, educational cinema represented a business opportunity. For Progressive-era reformers, educational cinema was a means to encourage "uplift," self-improvement, or the dissemination of liberal values. For industries and businesses, it was a means to advertise, create goodwill, and instruct as well as control the labor force. For the state, educational cinema provided a platform from which it could boost patriotism, spread and uphold state ideology, reproduce the dominant values of liberal democracy and capitalism, or maintain colonial power.

The question is whether this seeming mishmash of practices, policies, politics, and participants and the negotiations of competing interests in educational cinema can be subsumed under terms like *institutionalization* and *institution.* A snapshot of the situation from around 1923 indicates that the question merits further investigation. In that year, Eastman-Kodak launched its 16 mm safety film system, which was gradually established as a technical standard for the nontheatrical field. Around the same time, an increasing number of production companies that specialized in educational film and other nontheatrical genres had emerged. Furthermore, associations that worked to promote and encourage interest in the use of motion pictures as an educational tool (e.g., the National Academy of Visual Instruction in the United States) came to the fore, as did various periodicals devoted specifically to educational film (e.g., *The Educational Screen*, to cite another example from the US context). Starting in the 1910s and the early 1920s, schools and universities began to inaugurate departments of visual instruction, some of which acted not only as distributors of educational film but also set up production facilities. Some universities instigated research into the effects and efficiency of visual instruction and/or inaugurated teacher-education courses in visual instruction.[6] An increasing number of other cultural institutions, including museums and public libraries, began to embrace motion pictures and put them into use.[7]

Institutionalization might not be the only word that captures these larger developments of the field, and we are aware of the risk of invoking grand historical narratives that might not respect the complexity of what really happened. But the chapters that follow have convinced us that educational cinema did in fact develop into something more durable and autonomous in the 1910s and 1920s—with its own technical standards, its own companies and agencies, its own associations and periodicals—reconfiguring its position vis-à-vis other cultural and social institutions. The chapters in this collection jointly sketch the contours of a process of institutionalization that unfolded quite similarly in many places. Widespread recognition of the social urgency of moving images gave rise to reform discourses characterized by the intertwining of negative and positive aspects, the latter of which generated (a) pursuits to achieve a general embrace of the *idea* of educational cinema and (b) a wide range of *practices* oriented around educational uses of motion pictures—practices that became increasingly geared toward the overarching goal of establishing a durable *infrastructure* for educational cinema, which, in turn, turned out to be predicated on finding the proper *institutional support* for the field. Let us turn to the chapters included in the volume in order to add some flesh to this admittedly skeletal figure.

Jan Olsson's opening essay outlines a trajectory of educational cinema in Sweden that moves from initial debates about the educational power of moving images via a series of more or less successful initiatives and experiments to a point, circa 1921, at which "the many strands of film education, its many practices and discourses within many organizations and agencies, not least the censorship board, dovetailed within the framework of SF" (Svensk Filmindustri [SF] was the film company that had secured an all but monopolistic control of the Swedish film industry at this juncture). The Swedish case matches the general blueprint of the process of institutionalization that this introduction has presented, but for the moment let us focus on one specific element that takes center stage in Olsson's analysis: reform discourses. As mentioned already, we might think of the early and widespread acknowledgment of the social significance of moving images not only as the point of origin for educational cinema but also as a generator for discourses of reform that took aim at the new medium. We know from earlier research that these discourses contained negative and positive sides (what Jennifer Peterson has called the two "wings" of reform discourse), where the former was represented by various ideas about how to limit the potentially dangerous impact of moving images on (some) audiences and the latter by various ideas about how to make use of them for socially beneficial purposes.[8]

Olsson's analysis recalls this framework but recasts it specifically in terms of an "intertwining of positive and negative aspects of cinematic education." The "intertwining" is key here. As Olsson shows, "ideas and practices concerning positive learning via moving pictures [ran] parallel to the efforts to curtail the destructive lessons that cinema allegedly was teaching when operating unchecked." As things turned out in Sweden, concerns regarding the supposedly negative impact of motion pictures—a cultural form perceived of as a "school of crime," or more generally as a hothouse for all kinds of sensational representations—yielded the most concrete results in the form of the inauguration of a state-operated censorship bureau in 1911. But, as Olsson shows, "initiatives to create didactic films branched out from regular censorship activities, which were to classify, ban, or clear films—with or without cuts." And the people who clamored for censorship, or were involved in its implementation from 1911 onward, were oftentimes the most prominent advocates of educational cinema. For instance, an influential pedagogue such as Marie-Louise Gagner would "simultaneously [voice] enthusiasm for cinema's didactic potential and criticism of the current offerings' sensational representations."

Sabine Lenk and Frank Kessler's chapter about the "Kinoreform" movement in Germany maps a discursive terrain similar to that of Sweden's, but here, different groups of pedagogues and reformers seem to have been more inclined to emphasize either the negative *or* positive dimension of cinema's educational potential, manifested in a split between "ultras" and "liberals." Lenk and Kessler focus on the latter's efforts to establish educational cinema as a sustainable practice, first through a campaign to set up "Reformkinos" and later, after the war, through the inauguration of distribution centers that would facilitate a steady stream of educational films and other visual instruction aids into schools.

An intertwining of negative and positive reform discourses was key to the emergence of educational cinema in the British Empire and the Netherlands too, as the essays by Tom Rice and Floris Paalman show. Paalman notes that the "schoolbioscoop" (school cinema) appeared as a "reaction" to a "discourse from the 1910s regarding the social danger of cinema." Similarly, in Great Britain, "anxieties around social behavior—whether attributed to the images on screen or the experience of cinemagoing—were well established by 1917 and motivated much of the discourse on film and education." As was common in Sweden, the United States, and many other places, British reformers conceived of cinema as a potential training ground for criminal behavior—one of the examples that Rice references is an influential 372-page survey compiled and issued in 1917 by the National Council of Public Morals that "focused on the effects of film on behavior (a link between cinema and juvenile crime) and also on the physical effects of cinemagoing."

If negative reform discourses were fueled by alarmist ideas about the morally and socially degenerative effects of sensationalist motion pictures and spending time in the shady venues in which they were screened, the positive flip side found nourishment in utopian (or, in hindsight, potentially dystopian) aspirations of wielding the educational power of moving images for the purpose of creating better citizens—or better human beings more generally. In the case of Britain, Rice argues that educational cinema was motivated by a "desire to create productive imperial citizens" and thus "imbricated with . . . wider pedagogical imperatives to shape and manage populations."[9] He details how films like *One Family* (in which a geography lesson in the form of moving images doubles as promotion for the British Empire) were designed to work toward that end. Marina Dahlquist's essay about the Rockefeller Foundation's use of motion pictures in health-awareness campaigns brings the dialectics between the social and the sanitary to the foreground. For the Rockefeller Foundation (as well as other Progressive-era reformers), social progress hinged on the eradication of sanitary evils. As one Rockefeller slogan put it: "Better milk, better babies, better citizens." Movies were presumed to be an indispensable instrument for promoting this agenda, as Dahlquist's chapter details. A "better citizens" theme also runs through Zoë Druick's essay about the role the University of Alberta's extension division played in the establishment of educational cinema in Canada. In this case, motion pictures were believed to be especially useful for connecting with citizens who hailed from eastern Europe and the Ukraine for the ultimate purpose of better assimilating these immigrant populations. Here, again, the project of shaping and managing populations (which Druick theorizes via the Foucauldian notion of "governmentality") seems to have provided an overarching rationale for initiatives in educational cinema.

Tom Rice points out that the development of educational cinema in Great Britain was still largely "on the level of discourse" in 1917. The pattern was similar elsewhere: the recognition of the pedagogical potential of moving images did not necessarily generate successful practices. In the United States, the enthusiastic reception of *Catalogue of Educational Motion Picture Films* issued by George Kleine in 1910 offers the most notable manifestation of how the idea of educational cinema was gaining traction. However, as Oliver Gaycken's analysis of the catalog shows, Kleine's failure to deliver on the catalog's promise in actual practice—few of the more than one thousand motion pictures listed were actually available to put into use—demonstrates the gap between discourse and practice that Rice also identifies.

These two examples may serve to illustrate a larger point that Gregory Waller makes in his essay; namely, that institutionalization may be "understood both as involving certain actions and practices (successful or unsuccessful) and also as discursively constructed as a necessity, opportunity, goal, or solution to particular problems." Applying this to the "blueprint" of institutionalization that we are making a case for, we would argue that the widespread support for the *idea* of educational cinema was a necessary—albeit not sufficient—condition for its institutionalization. And we would add that the discursive construction of the field gave rise to a plethora of practices. Jan Olsson's essay indicates that early practices and initiatives in the sphere of educational cinema revolved around the problem of connecting the right types of motion pictures to the right types of exhibition sites and audiences within the right type of pedagogical framework. Categorization of the film material seems to have been crucial in many places, including Sweden, where the key distinction was between "value films" for the general audience and school films that catered exclusively to the educational sector.

If, as Olsson suggests, a "double ambition" to cover both of these groups of films, audiences, and venues characterized the institutionalization of educational cinema in Sweden, in Germany it involved a shift of focus from theaters to schools, according to Lenk and Kessler (Paalman notes a similar shift in the case of the Netherlands). As Lenk and Kessler put it: "The second Reformbewegung was about bringing film into the schools instead of bringing teachers and pupils into film theaters." As in Sweden, the differentiation of exhibition venues for educational cinema mirrored a division of "educational film" into subcategories, for example *Unterrichtsfilm* (classroom films), *Lehrfilm* or *Instruktionsfilm* (a "broader class of instructional films"), *Schulfilm* or *Schulungsfilm* (instructional films for specialized contexts and audiences), and *Kulturfilm* ("popular science subjects and other broadly educational topics for a large nonspecialized audience").

Tom Rice's chapter also highlights the variety of contexts and exhibition spaces for educational film, but from the perspective of how one particular film—*Black*

Cotton—was repositioned "from public exhibition to commercial cinema and then to the classroom." For Rice, this illustrates "the uncertain place of educational film within Britain during the 1920s." Uncertainty with regard to classification of films as well as exhibition venues is also a key theme in Katy Peplin's chapter. Peplin shows how the motion pictures produced by the Ford Motor Company blurred the boundaries between categories such as education, advertising, and propaganda. She suggests that a closer look at the exhibition sites for these films challenges neat distinctions between theatrical and nontheatrical cinema as well as the notion that educational films existed only in the classroom.

As already indicated, and as the reader will learn from the chapters that follow, if the myriad attempts to find a winning combination of film, venue, and audience had one common denominator, it was that practices rarely lived up to the high hopes and general exuberance that characterized the discursive imaginings of the field of educational cinema. Setbacks were frequent, and results often disappointing. Several of the essays point to infrastructural obstacles, including a lack of equipment at key exhibition sites (e.g., schools) and a lack of suitable films, two problems that tended to reinforce each other. Tom Rice's assessment of a situation in Great Britain that persisted well into the 1920s seems to apply more broadly across the period and places covered in this book: "Herein lies a central conundrum. . . . In order to justify further investment in projectors and equipment in schools, councils wanted to see more established and suitable educational films, while producers wanted to see more schools and venues equipped for film before investing in further productions."

Lenk and Kessler similarly identify several practical impediments to the solid and secure establishment of educational cinema in Germany in the 1910s. But they also suggest that the various ideas, initiatives, and practices promoted by German motion picture pedagogues and reformers nonetheless "raised awareness about the potential of educational films not only for teachers . . . but also for the cinema industry." The same goes for the aforementioned catalog issued by George Kleine in 1910. Gaycken's analysis demonstrates that even if the "material infrastructure" was inadequate for making widespread practical use of the catalog feasible, it nevertheless "constituted a significant achievement, particularly in terms of its archival zeal and rhetorical force, which serve as emblems of arguments for cinema's particular suitability as a medium of visual education."

Moreover, discourses, however hyperbolic, and practices, however fledgling, often brought about a concrete result that was crucial to the institutionalization of educational cinema; namely, the formation of networks and associations of likeminded people. In Sweden, for example, the Cinematographic Society (Kinematografiska Sällskapet) was established in April 1918, gathering together "representatives from the censorship board, the school museum, the industry, the press, and leading pedagogues" who shared the ambition to explore "a larger scope for film education with multiple partners involved," as Olsson puts it. Lenk and Kessler's chapter identifies a number of networks—local and regional, formal and informal—and associations, such as the Kinematographische Studiengesellschaft e. V. (eingetragener Verein, i.e., registered association; the cinematographic studies association), that were instrumental in the formation of educational cinema in Germany. Dahlquist's chapter shows that educational health films produced in the United States in the 1910s were often the result of collaborations between "municipal, medical, and philanthropic institutions and the film industry." The campaigns that used such motion pictures in the 1910s and 1920s usually engaged an extended network of partners, including boards of health, educational authorities, private organizations such as the Rockefeller Foundation, and so on. Similarly, but with regard to a different case and context, Druick's chapter makes visible "the networks of institutions and individuals that crystalized at the University of Alberta and then went on to make their mark on the national film and media scene." Druick notes that "Alberta was in sync with American land-grant universities, which were experimenting with film and educational broadcasting in the teens and twenties." One experiment was George Kleine's attempt in the 1920s to mobilize a network of extension divisions at state universities across the United States to establish a nationwide nontheatrical motion picture distribution system that he believed would ultimately secure nontheatrical cinema's status as an autonomous cultural sphere in film. Joel Frykholm's study of the experiment documents an initially enthusiastic but increasingly awkward and ultimately doomed attempt to forge a network of institutions that included the film industry (Kleine, the motion picture distributor), the educational sector (the network of extension divisions), the automobile industry (Henry Ford), and, more abstractly, the "market." In this case, it is the anatomy of failure that offers support—in negative form—for the idea that successful networking was key to the institutionalization of educational cinema. The connection between networks and institutionalization is highlighted in Waller's chapter as well. He argues that the forging of networks, particularly in the shape of formalized associations that set out to give "structure, order, and direction to the field of educational cinema," can be understood in terms of "centralization and professionalization," which we may in turn think of as one facet of a process of institutionalization. Waller's primary example is the National Academy of Visual Instruction, founded in 1920. This association (and its leading figure Professor William H. Dudley) likewise features heavily in Frykholm's chapter, because the bulk of the membership consisted of extension divisions and bureaus of visual instruction at the state universities involved in Kleine's ill-fated experiment.

In short, each in their own way, all of the chapters bring the formation of various vital networks into view. These networks were not only instrumental in the institutionalization of educational cinema through their mere emergence (as we have just argued) but also through their activities. Particularly important in terms of the aforementioned "raising of awareness," and for the future institutionalization of educational cinema more generally, were the many surveys and mappings of educational films, the film industry, its audiences or educational cinema culture at large that the various networks, associations, and committees produced. The practice of mapping emerges as another recurring motif in the essays included in this volume. The subsection in Tom Rice's chapter called "Catalogs and Committees: Toward an Educational Cinema" offers plenty of examples from the UK context alone. As Rice's subtitle suggests, we can think of the various surveys of educational cinema as a preamble to, or step on the way toward, the actual emergence of the field. In the case of Great Britain, the turning point happened sometime in the second half of the 1920s, when there was near-universal acknowledgment of the educational power of motion pictures, particularly when the state recognized that imperial interests could be bolstered via the use of educational film. At this juncture, educational cinema shifted focus from "catalogs and committees" to efforts to establish a durable infrastructure for the field, for example via state-supported efforts to organize film libraries.

The lack of a material infrastructure was a key problem for advocates of educational cinema in the tentative phase of its institutionalization, giving rise to more concentrated efforts to solve this key problem. In the most general sense, an "infrastructure" for educational cinema would include all the basic components required for it to function as a regularized practice, which potentially includes anything from a reliable railroad system to projectors, to exhibition sites, to support industries—and so on. Druick articulates a similar finding in her chapter, when she frames the wider context of the medium in terms of a "material network of human and nonhuman actors. Libraries of films, labs, projectors, railways, roads, cars, generators, auditoria, and so on are all necessary corequisites for the circulation of film." For Druick, *distribution* stands out as the most vital scholarly entry point: "Its relationship to infrastructure and networks, the material forces and forms that are the actual intermediaries or relays between production and exhibition, clearly makes it central to the cinema circuit." Druick's case study deals with the University of Alberta's Department of Extension, which "became a national leader in establishing film and slide libraries and in extending the reach of both educational and nontheatrical cinema into the population at large" and provided a model "when the ideas of nontheatrical film work were more widely adopted and gained momentum at a national level in the 1930s."

The centrality of distribution issues in general, and the key role of university extension divisions in the efforts to build an infrastructure for educational cinema in particular, is emphasized in chapters by Frykholm and Waller. Frykholm's essay details how George Kleine's forays into nontheatrical cinema in the 1920s were predicated on the conviction (or hope, rather) that if only a smooth-running distribution system could be established on a national scale, an enormous market for educational film and other genres outside of the mainstream would be activated. He joined forces with the extension education circuit in the United States precisely because these institutions were already spearheading the field of nontheatrical film distribution. A case in point was the Bureau of Visual Instruction (BVI) at Indiana University's Extension Division, one of the five primary objects of study in Waller's chapter. Waller describes a distribution operation of significant scope, with a capacity to reach a wide range of exhibition sites and audiences across Indiana, but he also emphasizes that "efficiently dispatching motion pictures . . . was by no means the sole function of the BVI." It also issued circulars about the educational value of film, offered courses in visual instruction, and even set up film production facilities on campus.

The BVI at Indiana University was a member of the National Academy of Visual Instruction (NAVI), an organization that we mentioned in our discussion about the role of networks in processes of institutionalization. Waller's analysis of NAVI indicates that, although NAVI's ambitions touched on a multitude of issues related to visual instruction, a top priority was solving the problems that hampered the distribution of educational motion pictures, perceived by some as the "fundamental question (or opportunity) facing the field." NAVI's solution, according to Waller, was hinted at in its 1921 national map of "distributing centers," which "[rendered] the field of visual instruction in the United States as essentially a terrain strategically covered by state universities, with no commercial competition." In his work with extension divisions George Kleine had a similar idea of the field; although, whereas he sought to remodel their distribution operations according to market logics, NAVI was, as Waller puts it, "much more inclined to stake its faith in the academy than the market." Kleine's experiment failed and NAVI toned down its initially high-flying aspirations, but these examples seem to vindicate Druick's emphasis on distribution as a key focus, specifically with regard to historical efforts to build a solid infrastructure for educational cinema.

For Kleine, building an infrastructure for production, distribution, and exhibition of educational motion pictures promised the liberation of educational cinema—or the "nontheatrical" sphere at large—from its dependence on other institutions, most notably the government and the commercial film industry (tensions between "nontheatrical" cinema and Hollywood are also addressed in Peplin's essay on Ford). Indeed, Kleine's pivotal role in the history of educational cinema in the United States is less due to successful practices than to his pioneering and persistent envisioning of educational cinema as an autonomous film cultural formation from the release of his 1910 catalog onward. As Frykholm's essay argues, however, Kleine was steeped in a form of business-oriented ethos that blinded him to the possibility that the "market" was also an institution rather than a natural order. The construction of an *infrastructure* for educational cinema was predicated on the proper *institutional* recognition and support—be it from the market, the government, the film industry, the education system, or some other institution or set of institutions. In other words, the formation of educational cinema as an institution in its own right hinges on its integration into other institutions, blurring these two meanings of the term *institutionalization*.

The essays included in this volume rarely reach a point where educational cinema finds truly secure institutional frameworks and establishes durable infrastructures—at least not permanently. Rather, the essays tend to focus on the phase that we have referred to in this introduction as "experimental" and that roughly overlaps with, for instance, Druick's notion of a "transitional period" of film education, Lenk and Kessler's "'second step' toward the institutionalization of cinema as a pedagogical tool," and Paalman's "second stage of institutionalization." We want to make clear, therefore, that we regard this phase as constitutive to the process of institutionalization, not just as some chaotic prestage to an imagined final state of institutionalized status. Indeed, what would such a finalized situation look like? What would the "end point" of the institutionalization of educational cinema be? Waller's chapter identifies what is probably the most plausible candidate: the regularized use of motion pictures throughout the educational system. But Waller convincingly argues that institutionalization should be conceived of as a continuous and multivalent process. The essays in this volume support this view to the extent that they prove that the history of educational cinema cannot be reduced to the gradual move toward the universal usage of moving images in the classroom—or to some other equally one-dimensional conception of the term, for that matter. Indeed, they highlight the diversity of educational cinema and its character as a "multi-sited enterprise," as Waller writes.

Yet as our survey of the recurring themes across chapters is meant to convey, it is possible to discern some broad patterns in the ways that educational cinema developed in most places, albeit not necessarily exactly in the same way at the exact same time. We can discern such patterns not because institutionalization signifies one master narrative to which all histories and cases of educational cinema must conform but because it is a useful tool for tracing how a variety of discourses, practices, and specific institutional frameworks interacted—in different ways in different places—to generate the cultural formation we discuss as educational cinema.

Institutionalization, as our choice of keyword, is intended to account for the tension between diverse practices and generalized patterns of development. We could reformulate this agenda in terms of a dynamic between the local and the global. Along these lines, Paalman's chapter suggests that institutionalization should be thought of as a process of the local "embedding" of certain global phenomena, which creates a kind of feedback loop between the local and the global. Indeed, the chapters in this volume confirm what earlier research has already shown; namely, that the idea of educational cinema had global reach from the very start and that the notion of instructive cinema found a multitude of applications in various places across the globe. Local, national, and international efforts seem to work in tandem from the early years of educational cinema when it comes to pedagogical notions as well as to production and distribution. Pathé Frères offers an obvious case in point: while Pathé was one of several companies (including Gaumont, Éclair, and Urban) that contributed to the filmic popularization of science in the early 1910s, Pathé was the leading company when it came to sheer production volume, the range of explored subjects, and—not least—the international reach of distribution, which placed the company at the nexus of local film cultures and the global film trade.

If Pathé stands out as an early apex of the globalization of educational film (and cinema in general), there are numerous other examples of transnational exchange and influence within Europe as well as between different countries in Europe and North America. The pioneering efforts to institutionalize school cinema in

Germany served as a model for similar movements in Sweden and other countries as well as a source of inspiration for advocates of visual education in the United States and elsewhere. Charles Urban's promotion of educational film in the United Kingdom through cataloging and categorization was directly imitated by American distributor George Kleine in 1910. The people and institutions that would shape the later developments of educational cinema in the British Empire did so with at least one eye constantly open to the formations of educational cinema in France, Russia, and the United States.

These are just a few examples that signal the importance of acknowledging the international dimensions of educational cinema and of trying to further explore the dynamics among local, national, and global. While this collection does not include any explicitly comparative analyses, and while there is no attempt to cover all corners of the world, by bringing together thematically oriented case studies of educational cinema in different countries in Europe and North America, the book makes differences as well as similarities visible when it comes to federal, municipal, and private agencies; public discourses; and notions of pedagogy. Hopefully it will invite further comparison and further elaborations of transnational approaches to educational cinema.

Taken together, the essays that follow offer multiple viewpoints on the ways in which a widely shared faith in the educational power of moving images and their capacity to spread ideas, knowledge, and information was transformed into a number of concrete investments, projects, and ventures carried out by various agents on local, regional, national, and international levels in the 1910s and 1920s. They map a cultural shift that resulted from the continual efforts during this period to establish educational cinema as an integrated part of the educational system, as a vital component of other institutions, and as an institution in its own right. Whatever the merits and limitations of our own conceptual framework, we hope that the volume will inspire further exploration and further scholarly discussion concerning the history of educational cinema.

Notes

1. This is far from an exhaustive bibliography, but the following sources give an overview of research on educational, nontheatrical, and "useful" cinemas in the last fifteen to twenty years: Charles Acland and Haidee Wasson, eds., *Useful Cinema* (Durham, NC: Duke University Press, 2011); Devin Orgeron, Marsha Orgeron, and Dan Streible, eds., *Learning with the Lights Off: Educational Film in the United States* (New York: Oxford University Press, 2012); *Film History* 15, no. 2 (2003); *Film History* 19, no. 4 (2007); and *Film History* 25, no. 4 (2013). The surge in scholarly interest in these topics also manifests itself at various conferences, workshops, and symposia (e.g., the biannual Orphans symposium; Domitor 2010 / "Beyond the Screen"; and Domitor 2008 / "Peripheral Early Cinema"). Proceedings of the two Domitor conferences mentioned here are available in Marta Braun et al., eds., *Beyond the Screen: Institutions, Networks and Publics of Early Cinema* (New Barnet, UK: John Libbey, 2012); and François de

la Bretèque et al., eds., *Domitor 2008: les cinémas périphériques dans la période des premiers temps = Peripheral Early Cinema = los cines periféricos de los origenes = els cinèmes periferics dels orìgens* (Perpignan: Presses universitaires de Perpignan, 2010). In recent years, work on educational and nontheatrical cinemas has been published and presented not only for specialized scholarly constituencies in niche conferences and periodicals but also in prestigious mainstream outlets such as *Cinema Journal*. See, for example, Lee Grieveson, "The Work of Film in the Age of Fordist Mechanization," *Cinema Journal* 51, no. 3 (2012): 25–51, and Paul Monticone, "'Useful Cinema,' of What Use? Assessing the Role of Motion Pictures in the Largest Public Relations Campaign of the 1920s," *Cinema Journal* 54, no. 4 (2015): 74–99.

2. Gerald D. McDonald, *Educational Motion Pictures and Libraries* (Chicago: American Library Association, 1942), 106–7.

3. George Kleine, *Catalogue of Educational Motion Picture Films* (Chicago: Bentley, Murray & Co., 1910). The *Catalogue* is available at MoMA (New York City), the New York Public Library, the Margaret Herrick Library (Beverly Hills), and the UCLA Library, and also reproduced on reel three of *Early Rare British Filmmakers' Catalogues* (London: World Microfilm Publications, 1982).

4. The slogan and the examples are from the letterhead of *Educational Film Magazine* stationery. See Leona Block (editor of the Industrial Department of Educational Film magazine) to George Kleine, September 29, 1921, George Kleine Papers, Library of Congress, Manuscript Division, Washington, DC, box 18, file "Educational Film Magazine, 1921."

5. These examples are culled from McDonald, *Educational Motion Pictures and Libraries*.

6. A standout example of early research into the effects of visual instruction are the studies conducted at the University of Chicago in the early 1920s. See Frank N. Freeman, ed., *Visual Education: A Comparative Study of Motion Pictures and Other Methods of Instruction* (Chicago: University of Chicago Press, 1924). On the inauguration of teacher education courses in visual instruction from 1918 (when the first official credit course in visual instruction was offered at the University of Minnesota) and into the 1920s, see Paul Saettler, *The Evolution of American Educational Technology*, 2nd. ed. (Greenwich, CN: IAP, 2004), 149–61.

7. For a brief overview of how museums began to make use of motion pictures from "a very early point in the development of motion pictures," see Haidee Wasson, *Museum Movies: The Museum of Modern Art and the Birth of Art Cinema* (Berkeley: University of California Press, 2005), 78–81. See also Alison Griffiths, *Wondrous Difference: Cinema, Anthropology, and Turn-of-the-Century Visual Culture* (New York: Columbia University Press, 2001), especially part 3. On the history of motion picture uses by public libraries, see Jennifer Horne, "A History Long Overdue: The Public Library and Motion Pictures," in Acland and Wasson, *Useful Cinema*, 149–177.

8. Jennifer Peterson, "'The Knowledge Which Comes in Pictures': Educational Films and Early Cinema Audiences," in *A Companion to Early Cinema*, ed. André Gaudreault et al. (Chichester, UK: Wiley-Blackwell, 2012), 279–80.

9. The use of motion pictures for the purpose of managing and shaping populations also feature as a theme in Lee Grieveson's work on educational cinema. See, for example, Grieveson, "Work of Film in the Age of Fordist Mechanization."

Bibliography

Acland, Charles, and Haidee Wasson, eds. *Useful Cinema*. Durham, NC: Duke University Press, 2011.

Braun, Marta, et al., eds. *Beyond the Screen: Institutions, Networks and Publics of Early Cinema*. New Barnet, UK: John Libbey, 2012.

Bretèque, François de la, Michel Cadé, Jordi Pons i Busquet, and Angel Quintana, eds. *Domitor 2008: Les cinémas périphériques dans la période des premiers temps = peripheral early cinema = los cines periféricos de los origenes = els cinèmes periferics dels orìgens.* Perpignan: Presses Universitaires de Perpignan, 2010.
Film History 15, no. 2 (2003).
Film History 19, no. 4 (2007).
Film History 25, no. 4 (2013).
Freeman, Frank N., ed. *Visual Education: A Comparative Study of Motion Pictures and Other Methods of Instruction.* Chicago: University of Chicago Press, 1924.
Grieveson, Lee. "The Work of Film in the Age of Fordist Mechanization." *Cinema Journal* 51, no. 3 (Spring 2012): 25–51.
Griffiths, Alison. *Wondrous Difference: Cinema, Anthropology, and Turn-of-the-Century Visual Culture.* New York: Columbia University Press, 2001.
Horne, Jennifer. "A History Long Overdue: The Public Library and Motion Pictures." In *Useful Cinema*, edited by Charles R. Acland and Haidee Wasson, 149–177. Durham, NC: Duke University Press, 2011.
Kleine, George. *Catalogue of Educational Motion Picture Films.* Chicago: Bentley, Murray & Co., 1910.
McDonald, Gerald D. *Educational Motion Pictures and Libraries.* Chicago: American Library Association, 1942.
Monticone, Paul. "'Useful Cinema,' of What Use? Assessing the Role of Motion Pictures in the Largest Public Relations Campaign of the 1920s." *Cinema Journal* 54, no. 4 (2015): 74–99.
Orgeron, Devin, Marsha Orgeron, and Dan Streible, eds. *Learning with the Lights Off: Educational Film in the United States.* New York: Oxford University Press, 2012.
Peterson, Jennifer. "'The Knowledge Which Comes in Pictures': Educational Films and Early Cinema Audiences." In *A Companion to Early Cinema*, edited by André Gaudreault, Nicolas Dulac, and Santiago Hidalgo, 279–80. Chichester, UK: Wiley-Blackwell, 2012.
Saettler, Paul. *The Evolution of American Educational Technology.* 2nd. ed. Greenwich, CN: IAP, 2004.
Wasson, Haidee. *Museum Movies: The Museum of Modern Art and the Birth of Art Cinema.* Berkeley: University of California Press, 2005.

MARINA DAHLQUIST is Associate Professor of Cinema Studies at Stockholm University. She is editor of *Exporting Perilous Pauline: Pearl White and the Serial Film Craze* and coeditor (with Doron Galili, Jan Olsson, and Valentine Robert) of *Corporeality in Early Cinema: Viscera, Skin, and Physical Form* (Indiana University Press, 2018).

JOEL FRYKHOLM is Research Associate at Stockholm University, Department of Media Studies, Section for Cinema Studies. He is author of *George Kleine and American Cinema: The Movie Business and Film Culture in the Silent Era.*

1 Platforms for Learning

Jan Olsson

By capturing modernity in action and in motion, the Lumière cameramen and their colleagues opened novel avenues for seeing and learning about the world in all its diversity. Almost from day one, moving pictures were inextricably linked to powerful steam locomotives, which became the emblematic machine of the filmstrip, while the lively panorama on the platforms—as people alighted or boarded the cars—offered additional dynamism and excitement.

Wolfgang Schivelbusch, Lynne Kirby, and other scholars have taken us inside the cars to analyze the perceptual networks and associations that were called up when literary travelers depicted their experiences of the moving landscape, a means of educating the viewer in the early days of cinema.[1] Similarly, the early experiences of film screenings inspired attempts at literally coming to terms with the program offerings' genres and their implications for entertainment and education. Some of the accounts of early film technologies were bleak and pessimistic, like those of O. Winter and Maxim Gorki, while Howard B. Hackett's perennially quoted enthusiasm for the Eidoloscope veered toward the sentiment that the whole gamut of modernity's experiential fabric was waiting to be scooped up for eager eyes. Apart from film footage of boxing, he expected that the screen would depict "circuses, suicides, hangings, electrocutions, shipwrecks, scenes on the exchanges, street scenes, horse-races, football games."[2]

This dynamic panorama of sensational scenes caused pedagogues to become skeptical of film education, although they hoped the voracious film camera would instead shift its focus and offer beneficial lessons and wholesome vicarious experiences for its audiences. In fact, in the era of newsreels Hackett's shipwrecks were rarities, although rail traffic's recurrent disasters generated frequent examples of modern gore swiftly brought to the screens. The rich train imaginary—albeit from an unmediated scene to be discussed soon—also functioned as a figurative emblem and backdrop for the negative views of film education, particularly in the Swedish context.

Before the newsreels became a staple of the screen around 1912, attaching the camera to moving vehicles of many kinds produced a cornucopia of spectacular phantom rides and vicarious experiences for those spectating from armchairs or the less plush benches in theaters. On its own terms, and outside the phantom-ride genre's framing of mobility, cinema turned into a machine that allowed viewers to visit faraway places vicariously, teaching its patrons—*teaching* is the operative keyword for this text—about life in those distant locales by conveying indirect experiences and camera impressions that added to the viewer's repertoire of insights beyond his or her corporeal reach. This form of learning about places outside the immediate physical realm figured into the debates about the positive and negative aspects of cinematic education that were almost on par with those about learning in the haptic realm—the unmediated experiences within reach, touch, and sight.

Notions of cinema as an involuntary, almost automatic form of instruction bolstered pedagogues' hopes that cinema's educative power would encourage positive learning to counterbalance the putative detrimental knowledge absorbed by children under the irresistible sway of the medium. The instructional might of moving pictures was perceived as both the operational default and harmful due to the nature of the signifying materials, which, critics claimed, all too often rendered representations that were unsuitable for young audiences—mainly depictions of gore, crime, or erotic motifs.

This text will analyze the dialectics of the ideas and practices concerning positive learning via moving pictures in parallel with the efforts to curtail the destructive lessons that cinema was allegedly teaching when operating unchecked. The focus is on Swedish discourses and practices, particularly children's viewing habits, and leading up to and then spinning off from censorship issues. First, however, in round-trip fashion, a couple of discursive snapshots from the United States and a return to the role of trains.

The cultural fascination with trains and their screen representations in the late nineteenth and early twentieth centuries figured in critiques of many concerned activists who raised concerns about cinema in the early nickelodeon era. *The Great Train Robbery* (Edison Manufacturing Company, 1903), as *the* pioneering, sensationalist story film, was regularly flogged in media debates in the Chicago press, long before the much-discussed campaign in the columns of the *Chicago Tribune* in the spring of 1907 against what was perceived as the negative education offered by the nickel shows.[3] The fascination with gangs and criminality that cinema's critics wanted to safeguard children from at this time, and again, specifically in Chicago, focused on the immense media coverage of the exploits by the so-called Car Barn Bandits. In 1903, the production year of *The Great Train Robbery*, three very young men gunned down Frank Stewart, a clerk at the Chicago City Railway. After a spectacular chase in the wake of a spree of crimes including a tally of eight murders, the bandits were hanged in 1904. In this context, a Chicago alderman, Linn H. Young, "asserted that the natural tendencies of such exhibitions [live curiosities, objects from crime scenes, and images and films depicting crimes] were to corrupt the morals and minds and poison the imaginations of boys and of persons naturally susceptible to criminality and imbued with a spirit of so-called adventure."[4]

According to an article in the *Los Angeles Times* in 1906, the influence of Porter's film was still vividly present, along with much lore concerning the Chicago gang. The article stated, "Nearly all the recent films relate to crime. There are many pictures of safe-cracking. There are even train robberies. The most famous picture ever taken was a big train robbery."

In a companion piece that further elaborated on the catchphrase "schools of crime" in relation to film exhibition, Fred R. Bechdolt offered a blueprint for coming debates about negative film-based instruction: "As a school of crime the penny arcades and 5-cent theater educates two classes of pupils. These are boys and ignorant men. Its curriculum includes highway robbery, thuggery and murder. Its graduates, if given freedom in exercising their acquired talents, swell the ranks of a peculiar class of reckless crooks very similar to yeggmen. Notable among these crooks are such men as the Chicago car-barn bandits and the San Francisco gas-pipe thugs."

In Bechdolt's account, dime novels and the yellow press, in cahoots with penny arcades and nickelodeons, are perceived to "breed in these young hoodlums a desire for fame and a spirit of adventure. The films are especially conducive due the vividness of the moving images, and the criminal deeds have a heroic slant."[5] The sentiments of this succinct account and its terms and analysis permeated much of the activism, in Sweden as well as the United States, around cinema as a form of negative education that idealized criminal exploits and presented their operating methods in the form of a manual, as it were, especially when using close shots or enlargements in the contemporary vernacular.

Next Stop, Sweden

As standing film theaters emerged as conspicuous fixtures in the Swedish cityscape, especially in Stockholm, pedagogical professionals, in league with concerned journalists, initiated a critical debate about cinema's roles and functions in relation to audiences that, in their perception, consisted to a large extent of schoolchildren. Like Bechdolt, appalled by gruesome representations and false idealization of violence, the pedagogues argued for a mission for future cinema beyond current practices. Such a cinema was to be based on an ideal of positive and worthwhile education alongside wholesome entertainment that was outside "the spirit of adventure."

In Sweden, the first organized expressions of misgivings regarding cinema had been voiced by late 1905 in Gothenburg and Stockholm, more or less simultaneously, albeit independently. In Gothenburg, an editorial offered a blueprint for the coming years' activism that, as it turned out, would eventually usher in national censorship in 1911. The editorial called for an informal but vigilant coalition of the press and the pedagogical professionals to keep cinema in check, stating, "It's the fourth estate's duty to stop cinema from going astray."[6] Cinematic activism in fact did develop along those lines, and the most dedicated newspaper was the conservative *Stockholms Dagblad*. The most active group of concerned educators was Pedagogiska Sällskapet (the Pedagogical Society) in Stockholm, most prominently the member Marie-Louise Gagner.

The Swedish discourses and practices concerning cinema and education pivoted on issues of regulation and focused on children both before and after national censorship was instituted. The establishment of a formal body for national censorship in late 1911 stands as the critical moment for summing up the debates on negative film education. These debates dated back to the creation of standing theaters in 1905 and continued until a diverse set of initiatives—more or less emanating from the censorship board—situated cinema as a potentially positive influence on the curriculum both within and outside the regular film exhibition and eventually operating within the fold of the film industry. Via the censorship body, the government took a firm, institutionalized stance on film culture. Initiatives to create didactic films branched out from regular censorship activities, which were to classify, ban, or clear films—with or without cuts—for the market according to the legal framework. This chapter follows the work of leading spokespersons as they simultaneously lobbied for educational film and argued against many aspects of regular film programs from 1908 to 1911—and especially against the gradual dominance of sensational feature films. As it happened, these activists were appointed as the first generation of censors by the government, and in this capacity they also took on the larger issue of educational film.

Training in the Dark

In late 1907, Marie-Louise Gagner published a text on children and cinema that paved the way for a key rally in February 1908 organized by the Pedagogical Society. Gagner's text posits a widespread craving for exciting perceptual experiences—both direct and mediated ones—as Chicago alderman Young and Bechdolt had done. She uses a railroad-related short story by Herman Bang as her point of departure, which underwrites the fascination with trains, tracks, and forceful speed in the contemporary cultural imaginary.

"In 'The Screw (Skrufven),'" wrote Gagner, "Herman Bang depicts a young country boy who, out of vanity and a desire for exhilarating experiences [the spirit of adventure] commits a crime; he manipulates the screws between the tracks. An express train derails and gas canisters under the cars explode, causing a conflagration. According to Bang, this desire for exhilarating experiences is the decease of our age." Gagner suggested that cinema offers vicarious experiences along similar lines. A few years later, social activist Jane Addams elaborated on related notions in her book *The Spirit of Youth and the City Street* and even titled one chapter "The Spirit of Adventure."[7] Addams had been part of an alternative initiative for film exhibition at Hull House in Chicago in 1907 after the *Tribune* campaign, but the exhibition quickly failed because the children allegedly fancied sharper films and more sensational types of screen adventures than the tame fare found at Hull House.

Many of the spectacular crimes depicted on film—and criticized both in Chicago and Stockholm—took place within a vehicular matrix because speed in shifting forms provided novel opportunities for circumventing the law. Brisk tempo in different guises seemingly also correlated with the spirit of adventure. To "passively" view fast-paced exploits on the screen reconfigured timeworn notions of corporeality. It was therefore not happenstance that many pedagogical activists promoted physical education and favored film programs featuring sporting bodies, as will become evident.

Gagner's train of thought—which simultaneously voiced enthusiasm for cinema's didactic potential and criticism of the current offerings' sensational representations and, not least, their underlying spirit of excitement—echoed in the activist discourse more or less everywhere during the early nickel-show phase. On the one hand, as Gagner wrote, "what a superb educative site [the film theaters] could be." But on the other hand, "alongside the excellent images from different countries and cities, and the depictions from industries and businesses, there are always the sensational, idiotic, and indecent titles." Such titles would pander to young persons enthused by the type of spirited adventures and excitements depicted in Bang's story, albeit in indirect form via representations. It is worth mentioning, however, that the protagonist in Bang's story is twenty years old, somewhat challenged, and perhaps not an ideal foil for Gagner's purposes and her concerns about children's film preferences. For its part, Bang's text doesn't mention cinema.

From Activists to Censors

In the wake of the 1908 rally featuring Gagner as a speaker, protests against film culture's inroads were regularly lodged in the Swedish press.[8] These texts were underpinned by empirical audience data, often systematically collected, as well as observations about film content, predominantly gleaned from printed program brochures and poster texts. To coordinate the activities, the Pedagogical Society instituted a film committee in Stockholm. The committee, as a first measure, managed to convince local film theaters to have their offerings inspected by teachers and thus approved by way of informal censorship.

The pedagogical groups' persistence, complaints, and initiatives soon garnered support from the parliament and forced the government to formally investigate whether cinema ought to be somehow regulated beyond the level of the local police. Even the industry's first trade organization, Svenska Filmsförbundet (the Swedish Film League), asked the government for nationally imposed regulations instead of having to cope with the inconsistencies of local inspections by the police.[9] A government committee of three investigators, known as Biografkommittén, was appointed in late 1909. The participants were Swedish Biograph's CEO Charles Magnusson from the film industry; Marie-Louise Gagner, from the pedagogical circles; and, finally, lawyer and police administrator Per Cronvall. When he was appointed as government investigator, Magnusson was a recent hire at Swedish Biograph, a company that dominated the Swedish film market after relocating to Stockholm from small-town Kristianstad in 1911–12. The company owned theaters across Sweden, albeit not in Stockholm, and was also a leading distributor.

Gagner was a pioneering activist for regulation of educational film; Walter Fevrell became chairman for the Pedagogical Society's film committee after having

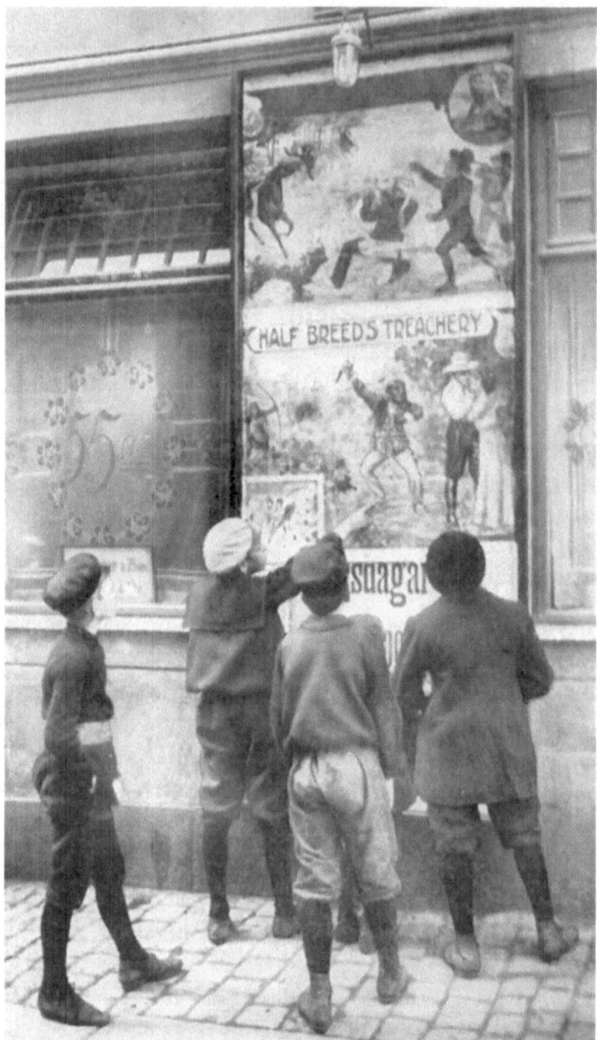

Fig. 1.1. Young boys studying a film poster outside a Stockholm theater in 1912. From the author's collection.

finished his doctoral dissertation on second-language teaching. His first text on film was published in February 1909 and tied in with Gagner's talk from the 1908 rally.[10] From this moment on, Fevrell dominated the critical discourse; Gagner seemingly considered her role as investigator incompatible with activism. Her last texts were published on November 10 and 14, 1909, and mainly focused on cinema's live acts, which she described as often vulgar and indecent. On November 20, she was appointed government investigator. Both Gagner and Fevrell, however, received government grants for studying film culture abroad and its educational organizations relevant to cinema, especially in Germany.[11] German film regulations, especially localized censorship in Berlin, were much studied by the Swedish pedagogues.[12] A consequence emerging from Gagner's final interventions was that her and others' complaints about the live acts that several theaters at that time had added to their programs led to a ban so that no live performances besides music accompanying the films were allowed.

Fevrell, in his first writings on film, compared his impressions from a film program he had attended with the regulatory framework the local police in Stockholm had adopted. He concluded that the police did not police according to the letter of the law and that children were exposed to scenes that might cause fear and horror. According to the regulations, children were not allowed to attend screenings of such films. His text was based, as was the discourse at large, on mappings of children's movie habits put in the context of synopses from sample titles and theater visits to illustrate the mismatch between vulnerable audiences and the "lessons" they were "exposed" to.

In a series of articles over the following years, penned in parallel to the government investigators' work and as features gradually began to take over the market, many of them Danish, Fevrell relayed Gagner's line of reasoning when arguing against sensationalized titles.[13] He attacked individual exhibitors—for example N. P. Nilsson, Stockholm's dominant figure in the exhibition field—as well as specific theaters and their programs. Nilsson was singled out for showing sensationalist Danish films such as *Ved fængslets port* (Nordisk, 1911).[14] Nilsson responded film by film, as did another exhibitor after Fevrell had critically analyzed one of his programs at Metropol. The exhibitor's account of his programming practices and audience responses suggests they were similar to those of the educational programming offered in 1907 by Chicago's Hull House. In both cases, the young audiences preferred the regular, "sharper" titles. According to Axel Frölén, Metropol's owner, he had started out by offering free shows with scientific themes and "nature images" to neighboring schoolchildren and their teachers. None of the invited children returned for new programs due to the lack of sensations, he claimed. As profit dropped, Frölén had to adapt his programming to keep pace with his competitors' offerings, "only to be attacked by the pedagogical committee." Frölén closed his response with hopes for impartial censorship that would regulate the market in order to level the field.[15]

One of Stockholm's schools, Borgarskolan, offered a public lecture series on diverse topics. In early 1909, the school began to offer lectures combined with screenings of both lantern slides and films on travel topics. One of their most frequent lecturers initially was Alexis Kuylenstierna. After pursuing a military career, Kuylenstierna had worked as a foreign correspondent for the Swedish newspaper *Dagens Nyheter*. In his 1912 book, titled (in translation) *Adventures among Turks and Arabs*, and other orientalist writings, Kuylenstierna wrote under the pseudonym "Mustafa." His talks accompanied by film were mainly devoted to the Far East, including China and Japan. Count Claës Lewenhaupt, explorer and hunter, was another frequent film lecturer; his talks predominantly showcased vistas around the Mediterranean. Walter Fevrell's first appearance in this series, which then had its home at Viktoria-Salen, took place on December 9, 1911. At the time, he was the head of the new censorship board and later a consultant for the programming. Borgarskolan's film lectures would stay on the market for several decades.

When Biografkommittén presented their findings to the government in 1910, the investigators—Magnusson, Gagner, and Cronvall—proposed the creation of a national body with the mandate to inspect and classify all films, old and new, on the commercial market. The government's subsequent bill was adopted by the parliament, and Statens Biografbyrå (the National Board of Film Censors) began its work in the fall of 1911. From December 1, all films shown in Swedish theaters had to be inspected and classified. The board operated with three categories: white, which meant the film was prohibited from screening; yellow, which allowed patrons fifteen years and older, with or without cuts; and red, which applied to films allowed for all audiences.

Staffing the new agency with the former pedagogical activists had lasting repercussions for Swedish film culture. Walter Fevrell led the agency, Marie-Louise Gagner became the second censor, and Jakob Billström, also known from the critical debates, was attached as a medical and psychological expert. In addition, Gustaf Berg, with a background as a journalist at *Svenska Dagbladet*, was hired on a temporary basis to help handle the initial film deluge. Berg had written on film matters under pseudonyms, mainly as "G- -g." At the end of 1912, over seven thousand three hundred titles had been inspected. Berg replaced Gagner as censor in 1913. Gagner continued to have an affiliation with the board, however, even after she returned to teaching and pursuing other pedagogical and literary interests. Berg took over the leadership of the board when Fevrell stepped down in 1914. Fevrell continued to publish frequently on film and was in charge of the Swedish School Museum's film library between 1917 and 1920; the museum was founded in 1908. Berg left the censorship agency and joined the industry in 1918 to become a literary consultant for the Skandia film company.[16] As Skandia merged with Swedish Biograph to form Svensk Filmindustri (SF) in late 1919, Berg ended up in the new corporation. By then he was the leading voice in the Swedish film debate, not least in *Filmbladet*, which commenced publication in 1915. In 1921, Berg became the head of SF's new educational wing, the division for school and educational cinema. The division lasted for decades and over the years built an extensive library of several thousand educational titles that were offered in regularly published catalogs. In this role, the dynamic Berg turned into the unrivaled authority in the field as educational cinema became institutionalized, not least when the company started a journal in 1924, *Tidskrift för Svensk skolfilm och bildningsfilm*; it was published up until 1942.

Hiring the leadership from the pedagogical film movement to become censors indicated the government's perception of a need to regulate the market along the lines suggested by the film committee. The censorship agency became a clearinghouse for the market by way of its inspections of films. It also became central to

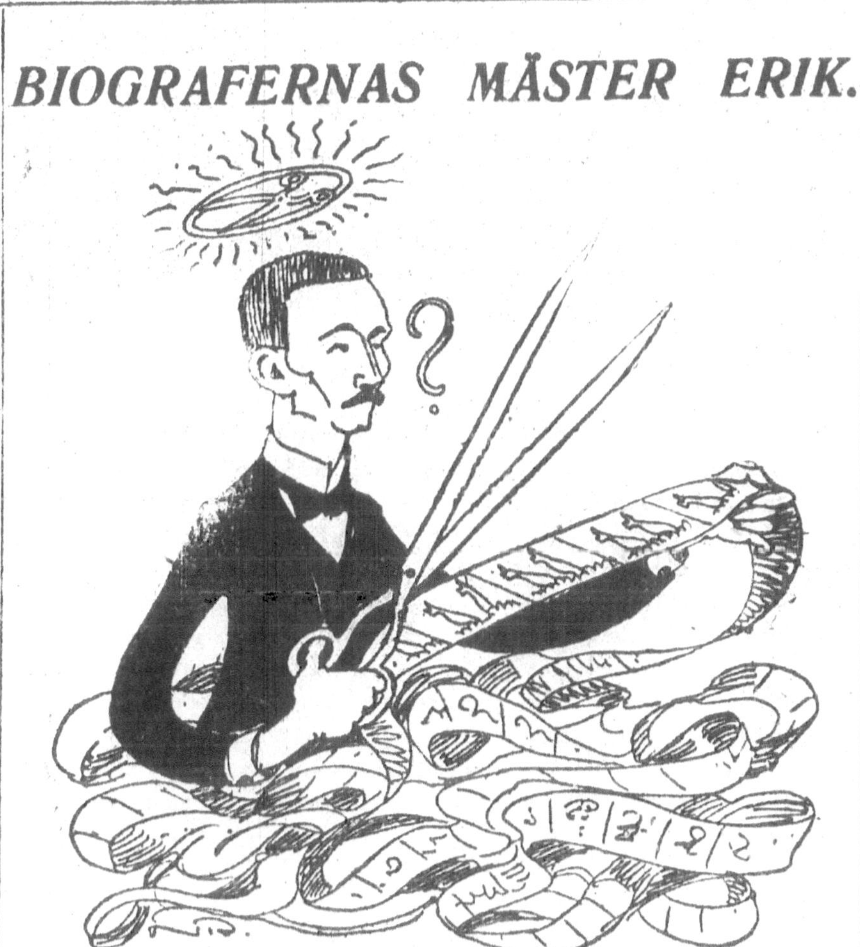

D:r Walter Fevrell, som åter lyckats ådraga sig svenska folkets uppmärksamhet genom sina underliga klipp i biografernas films, är till yrket lärare och har som sådan öfvat sig i 0 års tid, dels i landsorten, dels i Stockholm. Sina speciella förutsättningar för att censurera biografbilder har han förvärfvat dels genom att vara ordförande i en biografkommitté inom Pedagogiska sällskapet, dels genom att studera censurförhållandena i Berlin och Köpenhamn. Det förefaller som om han lärt mest i Berlin.

Fig. 1.2. Fevrell with scissors in hand. Cartoon published in *Dagens Nyheter*, January 10, 1912, 8. The caption reads: "Dr. Walter Fevrell has again attracted the Swedish population's attention due to his weird cuts in the theaters' films. He is a teacher and has practiced for nine years in Stockholm as well as elsewhere in Sweden. He has acquired his special qualifications for censoring films as chairman in the Pedagogical Society's film committee, and by studying censorship in Berlin and Copenhagen. He has seemingly learnt most in Berlin."

Swedish film discourse, in particular for initiatives with bearing on educational cinema; for example Fevrell's role as advisor for the film programs presented in Borgarskolan's lecture series.[17]

The new censors had a mandate to deal with the emerging dominance of sensational features—especially the Danish productions—by bans and cuts if these representations overstepped regulations; not an easy matter to determine in many cases. Unyielding censorship in this regard was in line with Fevrell's critical newspaper interventions in the period leading up to his new job.

Not only Danish films were casualties of censorship. A German film featuring Asta Nielsen, *In dem grossen Augenblick* (Deutsche Bioscop, 1911), became the first big censorship case. Nielsen made pleading protests in a published letter addressed to Gagner and then arrived in Stockholm for a private screening for invited journalists and others.[18] The Swedish producers affected by outright bans latched on to Nielsen's method of private screenings and thus managed to inspire much brouhaha in the press. The French company Pathé Frères, established in Sweden in 1910, had its first Swedish feature, *Tvenne bröder* (1912) banned; a similar fate befell Victor Sjöström's first film for Swedish Biograph, *Trädgårdsmästaren / Världens grymhet* (1912), and Sweden's leading producer, Frans Lundberg, had multiple titles butchered by cuts and still others banned. Lundberg elected to shut down his Malmö-based business. Stockholm's leading exhibitor, N. P. Nilsson, died in 1912. In 1911, he had been targeted in Fevrell's articles for screening Danish titles, and, when his son took over, the company's small production of domestic features came to a halt. Censorship practices had a clear impact on the domestic production structure at a time of large market transitions, and the government backed all the censors' decisions when film companies filed formal complaints hoping to have bans overturned.

Educational Film Initiatives

Alongside Borgarskolan's film lectures, Brunkebergsteatern, owned by Biograf AB Victoria, began to offer educational or nonsensational screenings in November 1910. After the censors began their work, the theater elected to show only red titles—universally approved films. By late 1909, Victoria had advertised its plans to start a reform theater.[19]

Walter Fevrell did not limit his activities to serving as the head of the censorship board. In addition, he sought to influence the market by lectures and exhibition initiatives. Branching out to participate and influence came naturally to a pedagogue who was accustomed to teaching and instructing. These ambitions were even more pronounced for Berg. His background in journalism facilitated his many interventions in the press prior to his role as head of SF's school film division.

Fevrell's first talk in Borgarskolan's lecture series at Viktoria-Salen, on December 9, 1911, focused on physical education and was titled "Ling and the Youth's

Physical Education." Pehr Henrik Ling (1776–1839) was the Swedish pioneer for physical education. After the talk, Fevrell showed a film program including surfing in Hawaii, pictures from the military academy at Karlsberg, gymnastics from Stockholm, a sporting event from Karlshamn, Boy Scout activities in England, and Swedish winter sports. Fevrell argued for physical education as an essential part of the schools' regular curricula in many of his texts, where he proposed it would serve as an antidote to passive activities. He would return to Borgarskolan six years later for two film lectures on physical education.

Fevrell was invited to speak at a conference in Gothenburg devoted to popular education a few months after his first film lecture. Again, he balanced cinema's detrimental influence in its current guises with its potential for worthwhile, truly vivid education beyond what lantern slides could offer in this respect. He also mentioned a new type of salon projector that would greatly facilitate film exhibition in all kinds of venues. Fevrell kept the developer's name, Pathé, under wraps but formed a partnership of sorts with the Swedish branch of the company when he began a travel tour in the fall.[20] In October, his pioneering educational tour was announced in an interview.[21] Here Fevrell described himself as an enthusiast for cinema's educational possibilities for all kinds of topics, and, with the Pathé projector, the Pathé K-O-K (later marketed as Pathéscope in the United States) on the market in two sizes, the medium was not highly portable and thus not suited for screening tours. One projector was developed for domestic settings, the other for public halls. The films were in 28 mm rather than the theatrical format of 35 mm, and the stock was not flammable. While criticizing Pathé's comedies, Fevrell nevertheless praised the company's many other useful titles and newsreels. His travel topic for the tour was physical education and lifesaving, plus a newsreel. When he started his tour in Norrköping with two shows at the Worker's Institute, he had to improvise because the films didn't arrive in time for the opening program on October 13.[22] Overall, however, Fevrell's tour clearly demonstrated that novel opportunities for film education beyond the film theaters were available. Shortage of film stock hampered the market as World War I began, cutting short the initiative.

While Fevrell was on the road, the Pedagogical Society organized yet another rally in Stockholm headlined "The Youth and the Dangers of Film Theaters." While still concerned about some films and programs, the tone and focus were different in the era of censorship. Apart from discussing a possible concession system to limit the number of theaters by regulating the right to open such venues, the speakers again hoped that the press would continue to monitor critically the developments and assist in raising the level of programming via a review system while refraining from advertising that was too lavish. The adopted resolution from the meeting again sought to balance the pros and cons of educational cinema while seeking universal support for the work of the censors. According to the minutes, "The meeting acknowledges the great importance of picture theaters as means for education and entertainment. We therefore express our conviction concerning the necessity of strict control to protect the young patrons. It's our hope that all government and municipal agencies will support the important and precarious work carried out by the censorship board."[23] The latter formulation came in the wake of the intense debates after a series of films had been banned and later screened informally for the press—Asta Nielsen's *In dem grossen Augenblick*, Pathé's *Tvenne bröder*, and Victor Sjöström's *Trädgårdsmästaren / Världens grymhet.*

Fevrell's next feud came rather unexpectedly; he was again advertised as lecturer in Borgarskolan's series in early 1913, this time with Claës Lewenhaupt. What complicated matters was the status of the new venue, the Odeon, which was owned by Stockholms Hanverksförening (the artisan guild's society), and the public nature of the event. In Marie-Louise Gagner's last campaign installments in November 1909, she had taken aim at theaters adding live acts to the film programs. Hers was not the only voice of protest, and local regulations in Stockholm soon excluded such performances. This clause was still on the books after the censorship board began its work. In addition to having the films inspected and cleared, cut, or banned, the exhibitors needed permission from local authorities when using a venue for film projection. Such resolutions from the police stipulated safety measures of many kinds and prohibited live acts in conjunction with film apart from in schools, which meant lectures. So when the Borgarskolan lectures moved to the Odeon—which wasn't a regular film theater—for public lectures in tandem with screenings several times a week and advertised Fevrell and Lewenhaupt as lecturers for the first program, trouble ensued, with several installments of intense polemics in the press. This was due to the "live acts"—that is, lectures combined with screenings of film. As schools were exempted from this rule, the interpretation of the nature of the program became the critical issue. Neither the school nor the owner of the Odeon had secured permission to offer films with live acts (i.e., lectures), instead considering this to be a school event—a lecture illustrated with films. The key question was, Could such an event be considered a school event—as a screening with lectures—when the event took place outside the school's premises?[24] The police authorities stopped the inaugural screening, but "allowed" the organizers to test the legal framework by running the show the following day. The police's intention was to refer the matter to the courts for a clarifying ruling. Several of the regular exhibitors filed complaints against what they considered a nonschool event and the press teemed with interventions. The polemics between Fevrell and Brunkebergsteatern's Lars Bergström were particularly harsh. Bergström alleged that Fevrell was skewing the competition by favoring Pathé, which was outside the mandate of someone who was the head of a government agency. Bergström relented somewhat, after a reply from Pathé in which Siegmund Popert clarified that his company hadn't approached Fevrell or sought his support in this matter.[25] Emotions were high on both sides, as Bergström, in harsh terms, had previously criticized how the censorship board operated. Borgarskolan eventually lost the case in the police court and thus applied for permission for its lectures-cum-screenings at the Odeon as well as the Viktoria-Salen for the 1913–14 semesters, while Fevrell continued to argue against the court's decision that a permission was needed. This "cultural film theater" remained part of Borgarskolan's lecture activities for decades.[26]

Cine-Education: Idealism Industrialized and Institutionalized

Walter Fevrell returned to film activities in 1916 after having left the censorship board in 1914. He was then in charge of the Swedish School Museum's new film department and had given a lecture with films to demonstrate the museum's ambition of putting film on the curriculum. The inspiration for Fevrell's efforts was yet another Pathé projector that could operate without the intense heat from electrical carbon arc light. It was instead outfitted with a light bulb as the light source, which was better suited to the school milieu. The films were regular 35 mm on nitrate stock. The museum unfortunately only had a single projector at its disposal and didn't expect to be able to acquire more due to the war, and several schools in and outside Stockholm rented the full outfit during 1917. Under Fevrell's leadership, the museum began to offer full programs on a variety of topics, starting with only five but soon totaling more than thirty. These screenings were supported not only by Pathé but also by Swedish Biograph, Sveafilm, and Edv. Nerliens AB. The first test screening took place on March 12, 1916, at Whitlockska skolan adjacent to the museum. It featured a single film on floating timber down the Torne. Soon thereafter, the museum received a donation of the Swedish films that had been screened at the San Francisco Exhibition in 1915. Three programs were offered in the spring of 1917: *Nature, People, and Industries in Norrland*; *Blood Circulation, Blood Cells, et cetera*; and *Swimming and Lifesaving*.[27] Later in 1917, the museum could offer ten full programs and two years later, thirty-five; the work was then, for a short time, conducted together with Kinematografiska Sällskapet (the Cinematographic Society).[28] Each program included seven hundred to nine hundred meters of film. The museum continued to expand its film library throughout the 1920s but handed over the administration of its school film rental department to the publishing firm and school equipment vendor Norstedts & Söner in 1930. In 1928, the museum's film library consisted of 495 titles. The museum had supplied films for a large number of classroom screenings: 1920 (233), 1923 (1,100), 1926 (1,800), and 1929 (2,700). The screenings reached 290,000 students in 1929.[29]

The museum's activities tied in with a larger agenda envisioned for cinema's cultural role, marked by the formation of the Kinematografiska Sällskapet in April 1918. The initiative came from Gustaf Berg, shortly before he stepped down as head of the censorship board. The inaugural meeting took place within the board's premises.[30] Members from all walks of cinema joined together at a juncture when Fevrell's museum activities had seemingly inspired notions of a larger scope for film education, with multiple partners involved. Representatives from the censorship board, the museum, the industry, the press, and leading pedagogues came together. The society's board consisted of, among others, Gunnar Bjurman (later head of the censorship board); Borgarskolan principal Per Fisciher; journalist Magnus Wester (later editor of the short-lived *Kinematografisk tidskrift*); Swedish Biograph CEO Charles Magnusson; Marie-Louise Gagner; Walter Fevrell; Gustaf Berg; Dagmar Waldner (later the society's archivist/librarian); and Skandia CEO Nils Bouveng.[31]

The organization and its brochure, *Kinematografisk tidskrift*, which was published sporadically in 1921–23, was absorbed organically by SF's Division for School Film led by Gustaf Berg and its ambitious catalog, later also a journal. The merger that formed SF in late 1919 consolidated the film competition within a single corporation that almost completely dominated the market. Prior to the formation of SF, Swedish Biograph and Skandia had been asked to form a joint company for film education as part of the deliberations within the society.[32]

During 1919, the society organized film lectures all over Sweden; 18,800 patrons attended these screenings.[33] The society's focus was on so-called value film (*värdefilm* or *bildningsfilm*) for the general audience, a category picked up from German screen initiatives and their focus on *Bildung*. For its part, the museum screenings during 1917–30 exclusively catered to the educational world with school films. School films and value films (later bildningsfilm) mirrored the double ambition that was reflected in the name of the periodical later published by SF's School Division, *Tidskrift för svensk skolfilm och bildningsfilm*. During their tenures, both the society and the museum were awarded small grants from the government.[34] When SF inaugurated its school film enterprise, the pedagogical market largely ended up a commercial activity within the industrial behemoth of Swedish film. Still, the museum kept up its efforts throughout the 1920s.

The Kinematografiska Sällskapet was invisible after 1922 but wasn't formally dismantled until 1932. What it managed to do was bring together all the key players, from Walter Fevrell to Mauritz Stiller, as well as the two rival industrial factions, Swedish Biograph and Skandia—and perhaps even marginally contributing to the big merger. Their respective CEOs were part of the society's board. Since Gustaf Berg took the initiative to organize the society just prior to joining Skandia, it was logical that he would lead the educational division when SF elected to shepherd and institutionalize the school-film business as well as the values films. This meant regular and professional resources for film education and enlightenment via the screen, because Berg sought to supply films to schools and to make valuable films at large available for exhibition outside the classroom—the latter screenings often hosted by some form of projector-equipped school authority or lecture institution, Borgarskolan not least.[35] SF's educational catalogs reflected this dual purpose. Apart from the large number of nonfiction titles under an array of headings, Berg later added many feature titles from Swedish Biograph, Skandia, and SF under a category introduced in Catalog No. 3 (1923–24), Literary Films. This illustrates the comprehensive vision for film education bringing together lessons from the many "genres" of nonfiction as well as the insights from features branded as "literary films." This latter category gradually turned more and more elastic as many new SF titles were added to the roster. Borgarskolan screened several "literary films" from 1921 and on. In the fall of 1925, for example, the school's lecture series presented Carl Th. Dreyer's *Prästänkan* (Svensk Filmidustri, 1920), Victor Sjöström's *Tösen från Stormyrtorpet* (Swedish Biograph, 1917), and Mauritz Stiller's *Sången om den eldröda blomman* (Swedish Biograph, 1919).

The many strands of film education and its many practices and discourses within organizations and agencies, not least the censorship board, dovetailed within the framework of the SF. An activist phase (1907–11) was followed by national censorship regulations (from late 1911). Long-lasting pedagogical screening initiatives (from 1909 and on), and museum efforts (1916–30) undertaken together with trade organizations (1918–21) were eventually scooped up—or survived in the margin (the Swedish School Museum)—and consolidated by the industry alongside its traditional film business in 1921. Censorship was still in play for many decades, and its leadership continued to exert influence in larger public debates about film.

The Swedish discourses on film education centered on children's positive or negative learning. Once censorship was in place and the industry firmly established, most obviously marked by the formation of SF, the activists' efforts found a broader framework via the company's educational branch and its tireless front figure, the former censor Gustaf Berg. He was still in charge in the early 1940s, when the company elected to phase out 35 mm copies for 16 mm gauge, which facilitated schools' and other institutions' use of film as a part of the curriculum. The longevity of Berg's tenure was seemingly somewhat accidental as SF had reached an agreement in 1928 to sell its educational department to the Norstedts & Söner publishing group. The contract was finalized, but the deal fell apart in the last minute over some minor technicalities at a time when SF also was considering giving up its film production. In a sense the company was therefore stuck with an educational department it otherwise would have gladly sold.[36] Instead, Norstedts & Söner acquired the Swedish School Museum's film collection in 1930, as mentioned above. The introduction of sound changed the prospects for both feature films and film education at SF.

In many ways, Gustaf Berg embodies the institutionalization of Swedish screen education and its inroads from the days of train wrecks, crimes, and sensations to wholesome film learning across the curriculum's many tracks. Berg's illustrious career merits a comprehensive study.

Notes

1. Wolfgang Schivelbusch, *The Railway Journey: The Industrialization of Time and Space in the 19th Century* (New York: Urizen Books, 1979); Lynne Kirby, *Parallel Tracks: The Railroad and Silent Cinema* (Durham, NC: Duke University Press, 1997).

2. O. Winter, "The Cinematograph" [1896], reprinted in *Sight and Sound* 51, no. 4 (Autumn 1982): 294–96; Maxim Gorki, "The Lumière Cinematograph," [1896], reprinted in *The Film Factory*, ed. Richard Taylor and Ian Christie (London: Routledge, 1988), 25–26; Howard B. Hackett, *New York World*, May 28, 1895, 30.

3. See Lee Grieveson, *Policing Cinema: Movies and Censorship in Early Twenty-Century America* (Berkeley: University of California Press, 2004), and Jan Olsson, "Pressing Matters: Media Crusades before the Nickelodeon," *Film History* 27, no. 2 (2015): 105–39.

4. "Ask Law against Crime Displays," *Chicago Tribune*, December 8, 1903, 3.

5. Fred A. Bechdolt, "Five-Cent Theaters Schools of Crime," *Los Angeles Times*, December 21, 1906, 2:1.

6. Ragnar Fehr, "Folknöje på afvägar," *Göteborgs Handels- och Sjöfartstidning*, November 25, 1905, A2.

7. Marie-Louise Gagner, "Barnen och biografteatrarna," *Idun* 20, no. 49 (1907): 607–8. Herman Bang's short story "Skrufven" was published in the Stockholm newspaper *Svenska Dagbladet*, October 3, 1907, 5. Jane Addams, *The Spirit of Youth and the City Street* (New York: Macmillan, 1909).

8. Her talk was published as "Barn och biografföreställningar," in *Verdandi* 26, no. 4 (1908): 154–68.

9. Jan Olsson, *Sensationer från en bakgård* (Stockolm/Lund: Symposion, 1988), 11–12.

10. Walter Fevrell, "Biograferna och ungdomen," *Svenska Dagbladet*, February 8, 1909, 9.

11. Marie-Louise Gagner, "Stockholmsbiograferna och barnen," *Stockholms Dagblad*, November 10, 1909, 9–10. The day before, another newspaper had published a critical article on the live acts under the heading "Varietébiografer," *Nya Dagligt Allehanda*, November 9, 1909, 5–6.

12. Gagner filed a report to the government after her study trip to Germany and also published part of it as an article: "Biografväsendet i Tyskland," *Stockholms Dagblad*, November 14, 1909, 5. Fevrell's study trip took place in 1911; for an account, see his "Biografernas kontroll, bildningsnivå och ekonomi," *Stockholms Dagblad*, April 2, 1911, 8. The local film "censor" in Malmö, pedagogue Frans Hallgren, was also awarded a grant for studying German film culture. He published the first comprehensive film book in Sweden in 1914 (Frans Hallgren, *Kinematografien—Ett bildningsmedel* [Lund: Lindstedts Bokhandel, 1914]). Hallgren never figured into the national debate but played a significant role owing to his censorship practice prior to the national institution. Fevrell emphasized the inspiration from Germany concerning the Swedish legal framework in his in-depth overview of his career as head of Statens biografbyrå (Walter Fevrell, "Statens biografyrå och kinematografiens utveckling i vårt land," *Arkiv för pedagogik* 7, no. 1–2 [1919]: 111–27).

13. For detailed accounts of the polemics prior to the establishment of the censorship board, see Jan Olsson, "I offentlighetens ljus—Några notiser om filmstoff i dagspressen," in *I offentlighetens ljus: Stumfilmens affischer, kritiker, stjärnor och musik*, ed. Jan Olsson (Stockholm: Symposion förlag, 1990); Jan Olsson, "Svart på vitt: film, makt och censur," *Aura: Filmvetenskaplig tidskrift* 1, no. 1 (1995): 14–46; Roger Blomgren, *Staten och filmen: Svensk filmpolitik 1909–1993* (Stockholm: Gidlunds förlag, 1998); Marina Dahlquist, "Upplysning," in *Film och andra rörliga bilder—En introduktion*, ed. Anu Koivunen (Stockholm: Raster förlag, 2008), 40–55.

14. This film was eventually banned by the censors when the regulatory framework kicked in.

15. Walter Fevrell, "Biografeländet fortfar," *Stockholms Dagblad*, December 3,1910, 8; Frölén's response, "Biografcensuren," *Dagens Nyheter*, December 6, 1910, 8.

16. His former colleague Marie-Louise Gagner wrote a highly laudatory piece as Berg resigned—"Gustaf Berg," *Filmbladet* 4, no. 6 (1918): 274–75. Berg had penned an equally panegyrical piece when Gagner turned fifty: "En femtio-åring," *Filmbladet* 4, no. 1 (1918): 1–3.

17. Walter Fevrell, "Biografen i folkbildingens tjänst," *Tidskrift för det Svenska Folkbildningsarbetet* 1, no. 1 (1912): 14–18.

18. See Jan Olsson, "'Dear Miss Gagner!'—A Star and Her Methods," in *Stellar Encounters: Stardom in Popular European Cinema*, ed. Tytti Soila (London: John Libbey, 2009), 219–31.

19. "En reformerad Stockholmsbiograf planerad," *Dagens Nyheter*, November 28, 1909.

20. For an account of Fevrell's talk, see "Fjärde allmänna folkbildningsmötet," *Göteborgs Handels- och Sjöfarts-Tidning*, July 20, 1912, 11.

21. "Doktor Fevrell på turné," *Afton-Tidningen*, October 1, 1912, 1.

22. "Biografen som undervisningsmateriell," *Norrköpings Tidningar*, October 14, 1912, 3.

23. "Pedagogerna slå vakt om biografcensuren," *Dagens Nyheter*, November 2, 1912.

24. For Fevrell's interpretation of the legal framework, see his letter (appearing in the column "Ordet Fritt") to the editor of the journal *Biografen* 1, no. 3 (1913): 12, as well as his article in *Aftonbladet*'s film issue from March 9, 1913, "Biografen i uppfostrans och undervisningens tjänst."

25. Siegmund Popert, "Öppet brev till redaktör Lars Bergström, Stockholm," *Svenska Dagbladet*, March 14, 1913, 11–12.

26. Olof Rabenius, *Stockholms Borgarskola under hundra år 1836–1936: En minnesskrift* (Stockholm: Borgarskolan, 1936), 162–63. Strangely enough, the film activities aren't mentioned in the latest account of the Borgarskolan's history, Sven Kärde and Sten Söderberg, eds., *Kunskapskällan för alla: Stockholms Borgsrskola 1836–1971* (Stockholm: Sällskapet för befrämjande av Stockholms Borgarskola, 1975).

27. Walter Fevrell, "Svenska skolmuseets skolkinematografiska förevisningar våren 1917," *Svensk Läraretidning* 36, no. 30 (1917): 486. For the general background for the initiative, see Walter Fevrell, "Svenska skolmuseets kinematografiska förevisningar," *Svensk Läraretidning* 36, no. 23 (1917): 377–79.

28. Walter Fevrell, "Meddelande Om Svenska Skolmuseets Kinematografiska Förevisningar," *Tidskrift för det Svenska Folkbildningsarbetet* 6, nos. 7–8 (1917): 245–46; Walter Fevrell, "Svenska Skolmuseet och Svenska Kinematografiska Sällskapets Filmförevisningar," *Svensk Läraretidning* 38, no. 41 (1919): 733. See also Walter Fevrell, "Kinematografien, biograferna och Svenska Skolmuseet," *Filmbladet* 4, no. 22 (1918): 442–43, 448.

29. Hjalmar Berg, "Meddelandet från Svenska skolmuseet: Svenska skolmuseets filmavdelning," *Svensk Läraretidning* 49, no. 9 (1930): 193–94.

30. "Svenska kinematografiska sällskapet," *Svenska Dagbladet*, April 18, 1918, 8; "Svenska Kinematografiska sällskapet," *Filmbladet* 4, no. 9 (1918): 157–58, 167; "Svenska kinematografiska sällskapet," *Filmbladet* 4, no. 21 (1918): 414–15; "Svenska kinematografiska sällskapet, *Filmbladet* 5, no. 9 (1919): 156.

31. Walter Fevrell, "Skolkinematografien," *Svensk Läraretidning* 38, no. 13 (1919): 234. When Waldner was appointed as librarian, she had published frequently on film pedagogical matters, for example her book *Filmen som kulturfaktor—En inblick i kinematografiens värld* (Stockholm: Ivar Hæggström, 1915), which comes with a very extensive bibliography, especially concerning German literature on film pedagogy. Her first journal essay regarding film issues was published in 1913 (*Det nya Sverige* 7, no. 6, 365–74), and in 1914, she offered an in-depth account of the pedagogical film efforts in Germany: "Kinematografien som bildningsmedel. Vad man gjort och gör i utlandet för filmens utveckling," *Social tidskrift* 14, no. 11 (December 1914): 460–65.

32. "Svenska Bio och Skandia i bolag?" *Svenska Dagbladet*, July 1, 1919, 1.

33. "Kinematografiska sällskapets verksamhet," *Aftonbladet*, October 27, 1920, 8; see also "Kineamtografien ger god hjälp åt pedagogiken," *Dagens Nyheter*, November 4, 1920, 4.

34. A proposal for adopting the German methods as well as using the Swedish School Museum's film collection as the foundation for an educational film archive was presented by P. Wikert in his article "Filmen i undervisningens tjänst," *Svenska Dagbladet*, January 26, 1921, 9–10. Soon thereafter, SF started its educational division.

35. See Principal Sven Nilsson account, "Stockholms Borgarskola och bildningsfilmen," *Tidskrift för svensk skolfilm och bildningsfilm* 4, no. 37 (1927): 1085, as well as his similarly titled update in *Tidskrift för svensk skolfilm och bildningsfilm* 4, no. 41 (1927): 1197–99. Gustaf Berg wrote a glowing profile on Nilsson's predecessor, Per Fischier, in *Tidskrift för svensk skolfilm*

och bildningsfilm 6, no. 63 (1929): 1682, as well as an obituary in *Tidskrift för svensk skolfilm och bildningsfilm* 10, no. 106 (1934): 2714.

36. See documents in AB Svensk filmindustris arkiv at Centrum för näringslivshistoria, Stockholm. Folder Ö4:4 "Svensk filmindustri. Övrigt 1921–65."

Filmography

The Great Train Robbery (Edison Manufacturing Company, 1903).
In dem grossen Augenblick (*The Great Moment*, Deutsche Bioscop, 1911).
Prästänkan (*The Parson's Widow*, Svensk Filmidustri, 1920).
Sången om den eldröda blomman (*The Song of the Scarlet Flowers/Flames of Life*, Swedish Biograph, 1919).
Trädgårdsmästaren/Världens grymhet (*The Broken Spring Rose*, Swedish Biograph, 1912).
Tvenne bröder (*Two Brothers*, Pathé, 1912).
Tösen från Stormyrtorpet (*The Girl From the Marsh Croft*, Svensk Filmidustri, 1917).
Ved fængslets port (*Temptations of a Great City*, Nordisk, 1911).

Bibliography

Addams, Jane. *The Spirit of Youth and the City Street*. New York: Macmillan, 1909.
Berg, Gustaf. "En femtio-åring." *Filmbladet* 4, no. 1 (1918): 1–3.
———. "Profil." *Tidskrift för svensk skolfilm och bildningsfilm* 6, no. 63 (1929): 1682.
———. "Per Fischier bortgången." *Tidskrift för svensk skolfilm och bildningsfilm* 10, no. 106 (1934): 2714.
Berg, Hjalmar. "Meddelandet från Svenska skolmuseet: Svenska skolmuseets filmavdelning." *Svensk Läraretidning* 49, no. 9 (1930): 193–94.
Blomgren, Roger. *Staten och filmen: Svensk filmpolitik, 1909–1993*. Stockholm: Gidlunds förlag, 1998.
Dahlquist, Marina. "Upplysning." In *Film och andra rörliga bilder—En introduktion*, edited by Anu Koivunen, 40–55. Stockholm: Raster förlag, 2008.
Fevrell, Walter. "Biografen i folkbildingens tjänst." *Tidskrift för det Svenska Folkbildningsarbetet* 1, no. 1 (1912): 14–18.
———. "Kinematografien, biograferna och Svenska Skolmuseet." *Filmbladet* 4, no. 22 (1918): 442–43, 448.
———. Letter to the editor. *Biografen* 1, no. 3 (1913): 12.
———. "Meddelande Om Svenska Skolmuseets Kinematografiska Förevisningar." *Tidskrift för det Svenska Folkbildningsarbetet* 6, nos. 7–8 (1917): 245–46.
———. "Skolkinematografien." *Svensk Läraretidning* 38, no. 13 (1919): 234.
———. "Statens biografyrå och kinematografiens utveckling i vårt land." *Arkiv för pedagogik* 7, no. 1–2 (1919): 111–27.
———. "Svenska skolmuseets kinematografiska förevisningar." *Svensk Läraretidning* 36, no. 23 (1917): 377–79.
———. "Svenska Skolmuseet och Svenska Kinematografiska Sällskapets Filmförevisningar." *Svensk Läraretidning* 38, no. 41 (1919): 733.
———. "Svenska skolmuseets skolkinematografiska förevisningar våren 1917." *Svensk Läraretidning* 36, no. 30 (1917): 486.

Gagner, Marie-Louise. "Barnen och biografteatrarna." *Idun* 20, no. 49 (1907): 607–8.

———. "Barn och biografföreställningar." *Verdandi* 26, no. 4 (1908): 154–68.

———. "Gustaf Berg." *Filmbladet* 4, no. 6 (1918): 274–75.

Gorki, Maxim. "The Lumière Cinematograph" [1896]. Reprinted in *The Film Factory*, edited by Richard Taylor and Ian Christie, 25–26. London: Routledge, 1988.

Grieveson, Lee. *Policing Cinema: Movies and Censorship in Early Twenty-Century America*. Berkeley: University of California Press, 2004.

Hallgren, Frans. *Kinematografien—Ett bildningsmedel*. Lund: Lindstedts Bokhandel, 1914.

Kärde, Sven, and Sten Söderberg, eds. *Kunskapskällan för alla: Stockholms Borgsrskola 1836–1971*. Stockholm: Sällskapet för befrämjande av Stockholms Borgarskola, 1975.

Kirby, Lynne. *Parallel Tracks: The Railroad and Silent Cinema*. Durham, NC: Duke University Press, 1997.

Nilsson, Sven. "Stockholms Borgarskola och bildningsfilmen." *Tidskrift för svensk skolfilm och bildningsfilm* 4, no. 37 (1927): 1085.

———. "Stockholms Borgarskola och bildningsfilmen." *Tidskrift för svensk skolfilm och bildningsfilm* 4, no. 41 (1927): 1197–99.

Olsson, Jan. "'Dear Miss Gagner!'—A Star and Her Methods." In *Stellar Encounters: Stardom in Popular European Cinema*, edited by Tytti Soila, 219–31. London: John Libbey, 2009.

———. "I offentlighetens ljus—Några notiser om filmstoff i dagspressen." In *I offentlighetens ljus: Stumfilmens affischer, kritiker, stjärnor och musik*, edited by Jan Olsson. Stockholm: Symposion förlag, 1990.

———. "Pressing Matters: Media Crusades before the Nickelodeon." *Film History* 27, no. 2 (2015): 105–39.

———. *Sensationer från en bakgård*. Stockholm: Symposion, 1988.

———. "Svart på vitt: film, makt och censur." *Aura: Filmvetenskaplig tidskrift* 1, no. 1 (1995): 14–46.

Rabenius, Olof. *Stockholms Borgarskola under hundra år 1836–1936: En minnesskrift*. Stockholm: Borgarskolan, 1936.

Schivelbusch, Wolfgang. *The Railway Journey: The Industrialization of Time and Space in the 19th Century*. New York: Urizen Books, 1979.

"Svenska kinematografiska sällskapet." *Filmbladet* 4, no. 9 (1918): 157–58, 167.

"Svenska kinematografiska sällskapet." *Filmbladet* 4, no. 21 (1918): 414–15.

"Svenska kinematografiska sällskapet." *Filmbladet* 5, no. 9 (1919): 156.

Waldner, Dagmar. *Filmen som kulturfaktor—En inblick i kinematografiens värld*. Stockholm: Ivar Hæggström, 1915.

———. "Kinematografien i folkbildningsarbetets tjänst." *Det nya Sverige* 7, no. 6 (1913): 365–74.

———. "Kinematografien som bildningsmedel: Vad man gjort och gör i utlandet för filmens utveckling." *Social tidskrift* 14, no. 11 (December 1914): 460–65.

Winter, O. "The Cinematograph" [1896]. Reprinted in *Sight and Sound* (Autumn 1982): 294–96.

JAN OLSSON is Professor of Cinema Studies at Stockholm University. He is coeditor (with Marina Dahlquist, Doron Galili, and Valentine Robert) of *Corporeality in Early Cinema: Viscera, Skin, and Physical Form* (Indiana University Press, 2018), author of *Hitchcock à la Carte* (Duke University Press, 2015) and coeditor (with Kingsley Bolton) of *Media, Popular Culture, and the American Century* (Indiana University Press, 2011).

2 The Kinoreformbewegung in Germany

Creating an Infrastructure for Pedagogical Screenings

Sabine Lenk and Frank Kessler

Introduction

In our article "Kinoreformbewegung Revisited" we presented the performance of educational screenings in Germany before 1914, as promoted and also organized by the Kinoreformbewegung (cinema reform movement).[1] The latter was in fact not a homogenous movement but rather an amalgamation of different social and political interest groups (teachers, clergymen, medical doctors, lawyers, functionaries, and the like) with diverging motivations and aims. That article contextualized these initiatives by looking at underlying pedagogical principles in line with the ideas of reform pedagogy and based on research in psychology around 1900, focusing on concepts of learning and memory that, as we have argued, must have had an impact on the Kinoreformers—at least those who were themselves teachers. A central figure in this context was Hermann Häfker, an author and theorist advocating the use of film as an educational tool.

In our earlier studies, we focused on the theoretical principles on which the educational programs performed by Häfker and others were based but did not touch on an equally important aspect of the Kinoreform (cinema reform): its organizational infrastructure and the networks that were set up in order to promote its ideas. Thus, for example, the teacher Hermann Lemke in Strokow not only organized reform screenings in his hometown but also published a bulletin (*Lichtbildkunst in Schule, Wissenschaft und Volksleben* [The art of projection in teaching, science and life of the people]).[2] To promote the use of film in class, Lemke set up the Kinematographische Reformpartei (cinema reform party) in Berlin in October 1907, created two associations that supported his initiatives, tried to open a Reformkino (reform cinema), and sent letters requesting financial support to the Ministries of Education in Saxony and Prussia in order to buy projection equipment for schools.[3] There were many similar cases of reform activism in Germany.[4]

This chapter focuses on strategic and practical questions that the Kinoreformbewegung faced and will look in particular at the following:

- The historical process of institutionalizing the use of film prints and projectors in teaching in general before and after 1914 in Germany, concentrating on the developments in the western part of Germany as an example of best practices

- The discussions in this region, prior to 1914, regarding practical issues such as the best location and the appropriate films for maximizing the educational benefits the moving image had to offer

The chapter reveals that educational screenings organized before 1914—with some exceptions—were generally local initiatives based on the efforts of a small group of enthusiasts and often took place at irregular intervals. Therefore, even the sum of all these efforts cannot be understood as institutionalization. Nevertheless, the period from 1907 (or 1903) until 1914 appears to be a kind of "test phase." It introduced everything that was needed for the institutionalization of educational film that would take place in the 1920s: the principal educational actors in the new field joined forces and the pedagogical and psychological principles were conceived of and put into writing—not only to create a common ground for the reform work proper (which aimed at uplifting commercial movie theaters in all respects) but also to establish the parameters that all parties involved were obligated to accept. These were aimed at the film business, especially cinema owners, who should agree to subscribe to the high ideals of the mostly conservative Kinoreformers. The ideals were also applied to the films, which, in order to be selected, had to respect certain ethical and moral standards and have educational value. The ideas circulating in the 1910s and 1920s had a profound impact on how, for many decades, German intellectuals perceived cinema both as a form of entertainment and as a pedagogical tool.

The Kinoreformbewegung at the Beginning of World War I

To begin with, this section will briefly discuss the situation the Kinoreformers encountered around 1914, when they prepared the field for the introduction and the institutionalization of film in German schools, which took effect only after the war's end.

The achievements of the heterogeneous Kinoreformbewegung were considerable, given the relatively short time they had been working toward their goal of improving both the films themselves and the venues in which they were shown.[5] Around 1914, the Kinoreformers can be said to have been organized into two major groups that, in many ways, took opposite positions.

The "ultras" (i.e., ideologically ultraconservative reformers), focused on the movie theater as a dangerous institution in essence and considered the cost-benefit analysis of cinematography a negative one. They more or less regarded the commercial picture houses as places of evil. They were in favor of rigid censorship to protect the "people" (*Volk*) from trash and pulp films (*Schund- und Schmutzfilme*), demanding that children and adolescents be banned from entering movie theaters. They also wanted to reform the film industry, which they accused of thriving on patrons' attraction to filthy subjects and scandalous images.[6] According to Thomas Schorr, the ultras did not acknowledge any positive effects a film screening could have.[7] During the war, they continued their campaign for restrictions and were finally successful. In May 1920, a general censorship law (*Reichslichtspielgesetz*) was approved by voters, and two offices in Berlin and Munich started to censor films. They had achieved what they wanted: the government created a solid infrastructure that worked on its own to prevent the negative effects of cinema. It follows that this group no longer had a purpose and disintegrated over time. This chapter will not further examine the ultras, but their influence on early cinema reform was nevertheless important for the formation of the second group, the "liberals."

The "liberals" (i.e., reformers working toward change rather than restriction) agreed with their conservative colleagues with regard to the danger of trashy films and unclean movie theaters, but otherwise maintained highly positive ideas on the cinematograph as such. They tried to make teaching more efficient and saw the use of film in class as one possible way to obtain this goal. They developed concepts for instructional films (*Lehrfilm*) and introduced film screenings as a pedagogical tool for religious and social education (in parishes and municipalities, and in institutions for popular education and workers' cultural associations). They created local networks for school screenings and asked the municipal authorities to open and finance Reformkinos for the intellectual benefit of the inhabitants, thus a form of "Kommunales Kino" avant la lettre, since this movement of "municipal cinemas" first emerged in the early 1970s in Germany.[8]

The Forms of Educational Cinema; or, How and to What Extent Did "Educational Film" Turn into "Educational Cinema"?

This section will first consider the main object of this study: the institutions presenting educational film screenings. Then, it will turn to the films to understand what, in the 1910s, was considered an educational movie.

The Collaboration with Commercial Cinema Owners

As schools did not have the necessary technical infrastructure to show films, interested teachers often worked together with cinema owners to organize programs with documentary films suitable for the instruction of pupils, who were brought to the theater in groups. These screenings were similar to the *Mustervorstellungen* (exemplary film shows) that reformers organized in the evenings for adults. These shows were different from the ordinary theatrical ones with regard to both content (they were specially selected films) and presentation (films were accompanied by educational lectures). Before 1914, Mustervorstellungen generally combined a commercial structure (the cinema with its rented films and paid projectionists) with a noncommercial intention (the education of people and pupils).

The directors of commercial cinemas were apparently not too enthusiastic about such cooperations, as they expected to lose money. Even as late as 1917, the journalist Alfred Rosenthal, writing for the influential trade journal *Der Kinematograph*, stated that reform elements in a film screening would meet with protest from audiences looking for distraction.[9] But the Prussian *Kultusministerium* (ministry of education and culture) had issued a decree on March 8, 1912, that film screenings were subject to the same regulations as all other forms of entertainment. Subsequently, Berlin's city council, following an initiative of the city's education department and the local teachers' association, decided on December 5, 1912, that children under six years old were not allowed to enter movie theaters and that children ages six to sixteen would only be admitted to special screenings for the young. Similar regulations were implemented all over Germany.[10] In Trier, as early as 1911, children of parents living on welfare risked losing financial support for their children should they be found in a cinema.[11] So exhibitors often had no choice; they agreed for financial reasons to organize special screenings for schools or, as was the case in Trier, to label afternoon shows as special programs for the youth, even if schools were opposed to this practice.[12] Elsewhere, cultural organizations such as the literary-oriented Goethe-Bund were highly in favor of this kind of cooperation and encouraged their local branches (e.g., the *Bremer Kinoausschuß* [committee for issues concerning cinema in Bremen]) to engage in such initiatives.[13] The reform pioneer Hermann Häfker had declared as early as 1908 that "cinema owners who want to invite the youth should ask experienced educators for advice."[14]

For instance, exhibitors in Berlin, Bremen, and Cologne collaborated with schools, even though they earned less on school screenings. Thomas Schorr suggests that this might have had an unforeseen effect: "Without intending it, they paved the way toward screenings in schools, because larger groups became aware of the attraction and efficiency of educational films."[15] Even though Schorr refers to the year 1920, his assumption might also be valid for the educational programs prior to 1914. Still, most reformers did not trust commercial exhibitors: "In the first instance, privately owned cinemas, which are businesses, want to make money. This, however, is often incompatible with a true reform of the cinema."[16] With but a few local exceptions, permanent collaborations almost never occurred. The cinema industry did not expect much good from the reformers, calling the pedagogues "the most unbearable and arrogant people under the sun. They interfere in all areas and claim leadership as if they were the only legitimate representatives of the intelligentsia."[17] So in spite of several local initiatives, the model of organizing screenings for pupils in commercial venues did not have a future.[18] Practical problems aside, the generally rather hostile relationships between exhibitors and Kinoreformers from 1907 onward prevented a productive cooperation in the long run. In addition, neither the industry nor the school administrations really supported the efforts toward collaboration.

However, for the education of adults—*Volkserziehung*—local initiatives continued during the war and on into the 1920s, often based on specific circumstances that helped to overcome the antagonism between cinema owners and liberal Kinoreformers. One case in point is Fritz Genandt, owner of several movie houses in Düsseldorf and a highly regarded personality in his hometown. At the beginning of the 1920s, he organized reform screenings with Dr. Wilhelm Winker, the director of the municipal library; Hermann Boss, the director of the municipal *Bild- und Filmstelle* (rental center for educational lantern slides and films); and a teacher (*Studienrat*), Dr. Richard Rein. The series was entitled *Akademische Kurse* (Academic classes) and presented travelogues and films about natural phenomena.[19] This example is typical for Germany's *Bildungsbürgertum* (the educated elite), a group of eminent men united under an academic or scientific banner, who initiated events that increased their or their institution's prestige and might even bring some personal rewards.

The most important result from the collaboration between cinemas and schools was that it raised awareness about the potential of educational films not only for teachers, some of whom were already interested in the new medium, but also for the cinema industry. Producers and exhibitors understood that an educational film could create substantial revenues: in the beginning of the 1920s in Cologne, twelve film theaters formed a network and screened educational films. Their initiative taught them that one single film could reach up to thirty thousand spectators.[20]

Films in Schools

Film screenings in schools were uncommon before 1914. The reasons are easy to understand: the high flammability of the nitrate carrier, the enforced security laws, and also the pedagogues' wish to be able to stop the film in order to show a still image, which was not possible with the existing equipment.[21] Also, the available films produced by Pathé, Gaumont, and other commercial companies were hardly suitable for a traditional curriculum, as they had originally not been made for teaching. This fact increased the fear of losing control over the didactic process and the structure of the lecture to be taught.[22] In addition, many teachers were convinced that their way of teaching was flawless and that to project films in the classroom would mean more work for them, not to mention that hardly any of them were capable of handling a projector even if a school had been willing to invest in such equipment. Last but not least, the relatively small group of men and women interested in using film likely faced prejudice and resistance from their more conservative colleagues as well as from the headmasters and the higher levels of the school administration.

Into the mid-1920s, although the pedagogical value (*Prädikat "volksbildend"*) of films produced by the Universum Film-Aktien Gesellschaft (UFA), then the leading German production company, was recognized by teachers during a Berlin meeting on "Film als Kultur- und Bildungsfaktor" (film as a cultural and educational factor), the ultras did not cease their attacks on moving pictures.[23] So Thomas Schorr's thesis that before the First World War most members of the Kinoreformbewegung had agreed, albeit to different degrees, that film was "an educational tool of extraordinary complexity with regard to its effects and scope" does not seem entirely convincing.[24] The conservatives among the teachers continued to perceive film as undesirable; it is therefore not surprising that after the war, the first schools to have projection rooms were not the classical higher-education schools (*Gymnasium*) but lower-level ones such as elementary schools, secondary schools, and vocational schools (*Kaufmännische Lehranstalten*), as one can see in Düsseldorf.[25]

Musterlichtbildbühnen before 1914

A third form of educational cinema was the *Reformkinematograph* or *Musterlichtbildbühne*, a local, noncommercial screening facility financed by private sponsors, municipalities, or other interest groups. Those among the Kinoreformers who believed in the educational value of film and worked toward a transformation of the cinematographic institutions in order to bring out the beneficial effects of moving pictures had to look for allies and create an infrastructure. First of all, they needed venues for the screenings and turned not only to parishes but also to owners of inns or restaurants who were willing to cooperate. They set up associations of like-minded people such as the Kinematographische Studiengesellschaft e. V. (cinematographic studies association) and founded institutions such as the Lichtbilderei G.m.b.H., M. Gladbach, an organization promoting the use of still and moving images (*Lichtbilder*) that published reform-oriented manuals, flyers, and books that were distributed among the clients to spread the reformers' ideals. Even more importantly, the catholic Lichtbilderei made available its collections of film and lantern slides to be used for the Mustervorstellungen.

Establishing a reform community and, with its support, opening a commercially independent theater was in fact the first step to turning the irregular and at best periodical screenings of educational films (Mustervorstellungen) into something that could be called an educational cinema (Reformkino). The reformers had no doubt that the municipalities were their preferred partners: "But can running a cinema be part of a municipality's tasks? There is hardly any doubt today that schools or cultural and educational institutions are under a municipality's responsibility, as well as all initiatives serving the same ends, such as theaters, uplift entertainment soirées for the people and youth work. The cinema, too, can and must become an excellent educational instrument in the hands of the local authorities."[26] Arguably, the Musterlichtbildbühnen that were set up locally were the most important attempt to institutionalize educational screenings. And even though their financial viability may have been too fragile in the long run, they can be considered the first step toward the institutionalization of educational cinema that occurred after the war.

Building Networks

In order to explain this process, this section concentrates on the case of the region today known as North Rhine–Westphalia, for which there is ample documentation. The starting point is the following statement: "Currently, every day there are about three-and-a-half-million Germans who rush into Germany's four thousand cinemas; that means twenty-four million per week, more than a third of the nation. Given the aesthetic and moral status of cinema in Germany, and, facing the moral flatness of our people, we are justified to say *periculum in mora* [danger is looming]!"[27] Even though the figures given here may be exaggerated, this statement clearly shows that cinema had become an important element of society and that its popularity alarmed German authorities. The author was (probably) Franz Bergmann, a civil servant (*Verwaltungsanwärter*) in the small town of Eickel who also worked as an academic assistant (*wissenschaftlicher Hilfsarbeiter*) for the association of municipalities in Rhineland-Westphalia (Verband Rheinisch-westfälischer Gemeinden), based in Cologne. He attended two conferences on cinema organized by the Kinokommission des Westfälischen Landgemeindetages, a commission for issues regarding cinema founded on June 5, 1912, during a meeting of regional representatives of the towns, province, clergy, unions, and so forth (a group known as the Westfälischer Provinzial-Landgemeindetag, a regional body in Westphalia). Bergmann stated that the participants were men of "almost all professions" and all religious denominations.[28] The first meeting took place just one week after the founding of the commission, which shows the importance the mayors and other influential personalities attached to this issue. The head of the commission was Amtmann Karl Berkermann, also from Eickel, and probably Bergmann's superior.

The starting point of the discussion was the "idea of no longer criticizing to no avail its many excesses of all kinds, but rather to put the undeniable advantages and educational value of the cinematograph at the service of the people—particularly the schools and for the protection of the youth."[29]

The following decisions were reached during the first meeting in Dortmund, on June 14, 1912:

1. Practical action is to be taken as soon as possible.
2. The best answer to the *Kinofrage* (cinema question) is the establishment of hygienically, ethically, and morally irreproachable cinemas, with the finances being the municipalities' responsibilities.
3. The intention is to create a large network of film theaters in order not only to be able to influence film production but also to reform commercial cinemas.
4. Minimum measures to be taken, besides more censorship, are:
   a. the promotion of cinematography's cultural value for society
   b. propaganda for the organization of municipal Reformkinos
   c. "petitions to the Royal Government to give financial support to promote reform efforts, in particular the creation of Reformkinos in the service of the protection of the youth and to provide a basis for efficient German film factories"
5. An office for cinema-related questions at the municipality of Erkel is to be established (the responsibility for technical questions lay with the Lichtbilderei G.m.b.H. in M. Gladbach).
6. An official journal (which was to become *Bild und Film*, published by the reform-oriented Lichtbilderei) is to be published.[30]

This whole process demonstrates the pragmatic and goal-oriented attitude of the reformers: they would bring together influential people of different professions and denominations and give them the practical task of establishing an institution in accordance with (conservative) bourgeois values.[31] Then the reformers would help them apply for state money if their hometown did not have the means to support them, report to the public on a regular basis about the successful operations to also stimulate others, create an institution to turn to in case of questions or for technical assistance, and finally, would create a specialized journal to let people in the region and elsewhere know who is "part of the winning team."

Once a solid sociopolitical basis had been established and the Musterlichtbildbühnen had started to run successfully, the screening practice was put to a test: as there were no forerunners, the newcomers had to learn how to run a reform cinema year-round, where to get appropriate films and good lecturers, and how to entice audiences to return. Often one or two men, such as Adolf Sellmann (Hagen) or Hermann Häfker (Dresden), were the driving forces behind these enterprises. However, they would have failed without a network of local or regional dignitaries supporting them, whom they brought together from time to time to create a stimulating atmosphere during their meetings. They knew that the battle was not won yet—those dignitaries might quickly lose their enthusiasm for the cause. As Lorenz Pieper, head of the Lichtbilderei, would say: "It is often the case today that energetic reform initiatives shine brightly in some places, but these lights might be blown out just as fast."[32]

In the beginning, the Kinokommission was very successful. It sent flyers to all public authorities and other interest groups to promote the creation of Reformkinos, and it contacted dignitaries personally. The two offices in M. Gladbach and Eickel were often solicited for help by individuals, associations, and official representatives.[33] From June to October 1912, the commission met with enormous approval from politicians and members of parliament, union workers, the national and international press, and several Reformkinos were opened or planned, sometimes as traveling cinemas.[34] Another success was that the Kinokommission received funding for its propaganda from the *Minister der geistlichen und Unterrichtsangelegenheiten* (the minister for spiritual and educational affairs).[35] On top of that, the commission tried to push the municipalities to ask for fewer or no taxes at all for the screening of educational films.[36]

Adolf Sellmann initiated the next step—organizing training courses for teachers, clergymen, public servants, or leading members of associations, through which they learned about cinema and its educational, technological, legal, and economic aspects.[37] Sellmann's goal was to increase the use of cinema in schools and other institutions. The first workshop took place in Eickel, on February 26, 1913.[38] It was attended by 450 participants from all parts of Westphalia and the Rhineland. Among the attendees were members of the regional governments, mayors, heads of police, school inspectors, and even bishops—a testament to the prestige the commission had gained.[39]

The commission's activities thus were a mixture of propaganda and networking; it provided support and training for active reformers, organized events, and built powerful alliances to reach its goals. It was successful, but only for a few months. Setbacks occurred as well. In 1912, the movement wanted to extend into the countryside because while villages did not have the means to financially support museums, theaters, and libraries, having a cinema was affordable as long as its hall could also be used for meetings, lantern shows, lectures, and so forth.[40] Alternatively, Sellmann suggested, one could set up a traveling cinema to be able to screen films throughout a region.[41] To the commission's great disappointment, there were not enough towns in Westphalia that wanted to contribute to the financing of the suggested mobile screening facility. So the Kinokommission had to ask those interested in organizing a program to contact commercial exhibitors, even though the reformers profoundly distrusted them.[42] The commission's reservations vis-à-vis the association of regional cinema owners (Verein der Lichtbildtheaterbesitzer von Rheinland und Westfalen) was answered by skepticism and resentment, which certainly did not make things easier.[43] At the second meeting of the commission in Dortmund on December 11, 1913, the presentation of the projects still sounded optimistic and positive, but at its third gathering in Hagen on January 7, 1914, the members were disappointed by the lack of interest the municipalities showed about the reform movement: "The municipalities would have benefited from the reform movement because of the additional tax income. But this was said to be the reason for their lack of enthusiasm. They were happy to receive more money but did not feel compelled to use it in accordance with the goals of the reform."[44] This attitude is understandable, as the income from amusement taxes (*Lustbarkeitssteuer*) was considerable.[45]

Interestingly, several members of the commission insisted that the efforts had not been in vain, because the initiative had established special contacts with members of the working class.[46] As cinemas before the First World War were believed to be frequented mainly by workers and women, the bourgeois officials were especially keen on educating this segment of the Volk. The commission members were equally proud of the fact that the reform had become known abroad—Hungary and Sweden were said to have closely followed their work.[47]

The disappointment, however, did not stop them in their efforts to institutionalize the Kinokommission by asking municipalities and the ministry of culture and education for financial support in order to create a permanent office (*Geschäftsstelle*) in Hagen and to appoint Sellmann as its new director.[48] One will never know whether this first phase of the reform movement would have been able to create a network of Musterlichtbildbühnen all across the country. The war put an end to its efforts. Nevertheless, one can say with certainty that these two years helped to establish the idea that film could be an educational tool.

Up to this point, many smaller towns had bought projectors that were used by associations and organizations for the youth.[49] The Lichtbilderei had bought slides and films and had published a catalog of about seven hundred educational films. In addition, it planned to propose weekly programs of scientific films for Reformkinos. Their length was one thousand meters (i.e., a running time of about fifty minutes), each at six pfennig per meter, per day.[50] It is thus possible that a special distribution system for these programs did exist already before the war. When, during and after the war, a new group of reformers—including the director of the municipal library of Stettin, Dr. Erwin Ackerknecht—relaunched the movement, the fight was more-or-less won.[51] Very quickly, old and new associations pushed for the opening of more *Gemeindekinematographen* (municipal film theaters). But it was the highly respected, eloquent, persevering, and persuasive people engaged in the Kinokommission—with their efficient networks and contacts up to the highest local or regional level—who had prepared the field between 1912 and 1914. As the report about the last meeting before the war, in January 1914, stated: "From the various reports, one could get the impression that the groundwork for the reform had been laid almost everywhere, and that actually a lot more had been achieved than the public was aware of."[52]

What Is an "Educational Film"?

In the 1910s, pedagogues determined the parameters for the *Reformkinematographen*. They knew that in order to get the necessary financing they would have to start with a low budget and to reach the broadest audience possible. As Adolf Sellmann wrote: "These institutions need to function a) in the interest of schools (science and geography lessons), b) for the benefit of youth welfare (images from near and far, industry, economic life, sports, games, military, navy, aviation), c) to entertain and edify the community."[53] To address these different audiences, the movement needed films that corresponded to the various interests they wanted to cater to. So while the main suppliers to the German film market, in particular the French firms, did not produce films for teaching purposes, the travelogues, craft and industry, or popular science films they put on the market seemed at least appropriate enough, even though their original purpose was to amaze audiences with picturesque, exotic, strange, and fascinating views of the marvels of the world.

On January 14, 1914, Pathé Frères invited teachers from the Düsseldorf elementary schools to attend a screening at the Schadow Lichtspiele, one of the city's biggest movie theaters. Their goal was quite obviously to demonstrate that the company produced films that could be used for educational ends or—in the words of the firm's representative that a teacher named H. Runge related—"how cinematography could be of service to schools."[54] According to Runge, the initiative was a blatant failure. In his review of the presentation, he lists five points he considers crucial for a school screening:

1. A close connection with the school's curriculum
2. A limited amount of material
3. A pedagogical organization of the material
4. The use of both still and moving images in order to create a calm and successful demonstration process
5. An explanatory lecture by a teacher

Runge concluded: "The Pathé screening did not fulfill a single one of these conditions."[55] There clearly was some kind of a misunderstanding, as Pathé claimed in a reply that it had no intention to re-create a pedagogical setting in its screening but rather to present its product to potential clients.[56] Yet this dispute illustrates that, even early on, pedagogues demanded a different kind of film for teaching purposes, as mentioned earlier. In special screenings for a larger audience, such as the ones organized by Häfker, travelogues or other films offered by commercial production companies could be used, albeit in connection with lectures or recitations and supplemented by slides. However, teaching films had to be structured differently so that they could be integrated into a curriculum-driven didactic concept.

The field of "educational films" that is so often referred to thus benefits from being subdivided into different types of films serving different purposes. A German online dictionary for film studies initiated by Hans Jürgen Wulff helps to distinguish several categories, even though there also is some overlap.[57]

- *Unterrichtsfilm*: a term introduced in 1921 by Professor Hans Amman from Munich, which refers to films used in the classroom that were made specifically for that purpose
- *Lehrfilm* (also *Instruktionsfilm*): a term referring to a broader class of instructional films serving didactic ends in all kinds of educational contexts
- *Schulfilm / Schulungsfilm*: films produced specifically for teaching or instruction, mainly to demonstrate complex technical or other processes in their various phases, for schools, professional training, military drill, and the like
- *Kulturfilm*: term referring to a special series of films produced by UFA from 1918 onward, which present popular science subjects and other broadly educational topics for a large, nonspecialized audience[58]

This last category may correspond most with the nonfiction films produced by commercial firms before 1914, which were also made to be shown in cinemas as part of an entertainment program and not—at least not in the first instance—in an educational setting. But obviously, they were appropriate for the Reformkinematograph. Adolf Sellmann lists in particular the "heimatkundliche Filme"—films about local or regional landscapes, customs, costumes, festivals or crafts, and industries.[59] An important point here is the representation of the nation as *Heimat* and as a form of identity politics. In Germany, "*féeries* and fairy tales" were often considered suitable subjects as well, probably because they presented traditional popular stories everyone had grown up with.[60]

As for instructional films, Adolf Sellmann had specific ideas too. For the population in the countryside, he suggested asking the agricultural administrations or the ministry to fund films showing model farms and all aspects of agriculture: various plants and crops and their cultivation, animal husbandry, machines, and techniques, as well as farming in other countries and their costumes, customs, and festivals. According to Sellmann, such films should address not only the rural population in general, and more particularly pupils in agricultural schools, but also urban dwellers, who should learn to appreciate rural life and work.[61] Sellmann added that people from the countryside should be shown films warning them about the pitfalls of big-city life to prevent them from falling prey to the many dangers waiting for them there.[62] So, in addition to practical instruction, these educational films should also address issues of social hygiene and serve identity politics. By showing their audiences how people lived and worked in various parts of Germany, the films contributed to the construction of "Germanness" as the common denominator binding together the diversity depicted in them.

According to Schorr, in 1917 an elementary school teacher from Munich, Franz Schönhuber, was the first to put into writing a precise didactic concept for what was later called Unterrichtsfilm, which could be translated as "classroom films." Just like H. Runge in Düsseldorf, Schönhuber insisted on a direct connection between the curriculum and the accompanying lecture as well as on the technical possibility to interrupt a screening to stay on a still image, quite probably in order to make sure that the teacher always maintained control of the lesson. Also, he asserted that close attention should be paid to the structure of the film, in particular its scientific value and pedagogical quality. For Schönhuber, films were particularly useful in geography and the natural sciences—for the latter because they can make visible all that is difficult to observe in natural processes and for the former because they can illustrate basic concepts and the way maps are drawn, as well as demonstrate the beauty of the German Heimat. So, once more, the cinematograph should function in the service of identity politics. Schönhuber even suggests that films should be used to systematically educate the older pupils to ensure that they are citizens aware of their Germanness.[63]

The Kinoreformbewegung before 1914 and Its Consequences

When war broke out, the reform efforts stopped.[64] Some of the reformers became soldiers, and those who stayed at home had to organize the daily life of a community threatened by the consequences of the war years: hunger, poverty, homelessness, high unemployment, crime, the need to care for numerous physically and psychologically handicapped people, and so forth. Then followed the revolution (1918–19), the occupation of parts of the country by foreign armies (1918–25), and the hyperinflation years (1921–23). Despite the precarious political and economic situations, some municipalities provided funding for what one could call a "second step" toward the institutionalization of cinema as a pedagogical tool: the creation of local Bild- und Filmstellen as archives and distribution centers for slides, films, and equipment and the installation of projection facilities in schools.

The constellation of the "second wave" was not very different from the first one: one person or a small group as crystallization point (in Düsseldorf, Hermann Boss), a network of influential allies in the town or the region (in Düsseldorf, *Arbeitsgemeinschaft für Jugendlichtspiele* [a working group dedicated to films for the youth],

Association *Lichtbildkultur* [culture of the projected image], the *Schuldeputation* [council for the local schools]), financial supporters (in Düsseldorf, the company Eduard Liesegang, a manufacturer of film and slides projectors), and so forth.[65]

The regional Kinokommission of the Westfälische Landesgemeindetag, thus an administrative body of the region of Westphalia, was "replaced" by the nationally oriented Zentralinstitut für Erziehung und Wissenschaft (the central institute for science and education) in Berlin in 1915 and the Deutsche Ausschuss für Lichtspielreform (German board for cinema reform) in Stettin in 1917, which both lobbied the German parliament.[66] In similar fashion to its predecessor, the Deutsche Ausschuss für Lichtspielreform organized educational congresses with political representatives and workshops for teachers; it also founded committees and created a network of towns, still pursuing largely the same goals.[67]

But this time the reformers had one more ally. Before the war, only *regional* ministries were involved, and they concentrated mainly on organizing in order to protect viewers from "Schund und Schmutzfilme." But on March 3, 1920, the *national* Ministerium für Wissenschaft, Kunst und Volksbildung (the ministry for sciences, arts, and public education) published a decree urging the municipal authorities and schools to buy projectors and prints of films. No financial aid was given, but this official initiative signaled to everybody that moving images were an approved pedagogical instrument suited for schools.[68] And this was worth money. As a result, Düsseldorf, for instance, decided that from October 1, 1921, onward, teaching institutions should have projection facilities. Less than two years later, in July 1923, seventeen elementary schools (Volksschule) and three schools for higher education (Gymnasium) were fully equipped. And the city had its own Bild- und Filmstelle, founded on April 1, 1922, that was even provided with a small, but annual budget.

In conclusion, one can say that the four years of the First World War did not put an end to the Kinoreform. They were rather an interruption, which permitted a shift in focus.[69] The second Reformbewegung was about bringing film into the schools instead of bringing teachers and pupils into film theaters. It had become a movement to promote classroom film use. Several *gemeinnützige* (noncommercial) Musterlichtbildbühnen, often founded as *Kulturfilmbühnen*, referring to the Kulturfilme produced by UFA, still existed in bigger cities (the most famous ones were the Urania theaters), but the goal was no longer to reach into the villages to address the rural population, as had been the case in Westphalia before the war. Former suppliers such as Pathé and Gaumont were replaced by the UFA and its *Kulturfilmabteilung* (department for educational films), new centralized media archives were created, and the distribution system for prints from and to the schools was optimized. And even the German film industry had changed its attitude, now cooperating willingly with the teachers they had despised for so long.[70]

The efficiently organized and socially embedded reform movement before the war tried to set up an infrastructure for educational film screenings, aiming to establish a network of reform theaters. While this project failed—not only because of the war—it appears, in hindsight, that it was the necessary starting point for the second and decisive step: the definitive institutionalization of the educational cinema in Germany during the Weimar Republic.

Notes

1. Frank Kessler and Sabine Lenk, “Kinoreformbewegung Revisited: Performing the Cinematograph as a Pedagogical Tool,” in *Performing New Media, 1890–1915*, ed. Kaveh Askari et al. (New Barnet: John Libbey, 2014), 163–73.

2. The journal *Lichtbildkunst in Schule, Wissenschaft und Volksleben*, edited by Hermann Lemke and published in fifteen issues from 1912 to 1914 by Schultechnik (Storkow/Mark). It was renamed in 1913 and continued as *Volk und Film: Zeitung für ethische und sociale Kinematographie und künstlerische Filmdramatik.*

3. Rudolf W. Kipp, *Bilddokumente zur Geschichte des Unterrichtsfilms* (Grünwald: Institut für Film und Bild in Wissenschaft und Unterricht, 1975), 102–5. According to Kipp, Hermann (in Hamburg in 1903) and Lemke had already started researching how to use the cinematograph as didactic tool (13).

4. On the Kinoreformbewegung see also Uli Jung, “Kinoreformer: Nicht fiktionale Filme für Bildungszwecke,” in *Geschichte des dokumentarischen Films in Deutschland*, Band 1: *Kaiserreich 1895–1918*, ed. Uli Jung and Martin Loiperdinger (Stuttgart: Reclam, 2005), 333–40.

5. Helmut H. Diederichs, in the fourth chapter of his habilitation thesis, “Ästhetische Theorien der Kinoreformer (1910–1915),” shows to what extent the ongoing debates about cinematography among reformers led to theoretical ideas about the aesthetics of the new medium. See Helmut H. Diederichs, “Frühgeschichte deutscher Filmtheorie: Ihre Entstehung und Entwicklung bis zum Ersten Weltkrieg” (habilitation thesis, Johann Wolfgang Goethe University, 1996), 143–56.

6. Thomas Schorr, “Die Film- und Kinoreformbewegung und die deutsche Filmwirtschaft: Eine Analyse des Fachblatts ‘Der Kinematograph’ (1907–1935) unter pädagogischen und publizistischen Aspekten” (PhD diss., Bundeswehr University Munich, 1990), 116.

7. Ibid.

8. Some towns had *Musterkinos* (cinema that serves as an example, exemplary cinema) as early as 1909 (Ernemann Reformkino, Dresden), 1910 (Kosmographia, Dresden; Reform-Kino, Braunschweig; Reformkino in Klett’s Gesellschaftshaus, Hamburg), 1911 (Reformtheater, Bremen; Urania-Lichtspiele, Königsberg), 1912 (Gemeindekino, Eickel; Germania Saal, Hagen; Musterlichtbildbühne, Altona), and 1914 (Urania, Stettin). Most of them closed before the war, but Stettin and Berlin (Urania since 1888) had permanent ones. Bremen later reopened another one (January 10, 1917). See also Schorr, “Film- und Kinoreformbewegung,” 154, as well as Paul Ferd Siegert, *Bürgerliches Selbstverständnis, Kinoreform und früher Schulfilm: Eine kulturwissenschaftliche Analyse* (master’s thesis, Leuphana University of Lüneburg, 1995), 104, 112, 119. *Bild und Film*, the official journal for the Lichtbilderei organization, indicates even more towns with reform cinemas: “Osterfeld, Bottrop, Hamborn, Sterkrade, Horst, Hagen und eines Wanderkinos für den Landkreis Beckum.” See also Franz Bergmann, “Bericht über die erste Sitzung der Kinokommission des Westfälischen Landgemeindetages am 14.06.1912 in Dortmund: Der Westfälische Landgemeindetag und die Kinoreform,” *Bild und Film* 3–4 (1912): 84–86, accessed September 8, 2014, http://www.lwl.org/westfaelische-geschichte/portal/Internet/finde/langDatensatz.php?urlID=1291&url_tabelle=tab_quelle.

9. Alfred Rosenthal, quoted in Schorr, "Film- und Kinoreformbewegung," 155.

10. See also Amelie Duckwitz, Martin Loiperdinger, and Susanne Theissen, "'Kampf dem Schundfilm!'—Kinoreform und Jugenschutz in Trier," in *KINtop: Jahrbuch zur Erforschung des frühen Films* 9, ed. Frank Kessler, Sabine Lenk, and Martin Loiperdinger (Frankfurt/Main: Stroemfeld, 2000), 53, 61; Alice Schmerling, *Kinder, Kino und Kinderliteratur: Eine Untersuchung zum Medienumbruch in der Kinderkultur und der Weimarer Republik* (PhD diss., University of Cologne, 2007), 76.

11. Duckwitz, Loiperdinger, and Theissen "Kampf dem Schundfilm," 54.

12. See also ibid.; Schorr, "Film- und Kinoreformbewegung," 144–45.

13. See also Schorr, "Film- und Kinoreformbewegung," 154.

14. Hermann Häfker, "Für Kinder!," *Der Kinematograph* 72, May 13, 1908, accessed May 4, 2013, http://www.soziales.fh-dortmund.de/diederichs/texte/haefgesv.htm.

15. Schorr, "Film- und Kinoreformbewegung," 183.

16. "Bericht über eine Besprechung der Kinokommission des Westfälischen Landgemeindetages anläßlich der Eröffnungsfeier des Gemeindelichtspielhauses in Eickel: Kinokommission des Westfälischen Landgemeindetages," *Bild und Film* 3 (1912–13): 70–71, accessed September 8, 2014, http://www.lwl.org/westfaelische-geschichte/portal/Internet/finde/langDatensatz.php?urlID=1298&url_tabelle=tab_quelle.

17. *Der Kinematograph*, December 17, 1913, quoted in Adolf Sellmann, "Der Kampf um den Kino," *Bild und Film* 5 (1913–14): 97–100, accessed June 3, 2012, http://www.lwl.org/westfaelische-geschichte/portal/Internet/finde/langDatensatz.php?urlID=1307&url_tabelle=tab_quelle. This article seems to have grieved the pedagogues very much, as the quotation is repeated several times, among others in "Kinematographenbesitzer und Lehrerschaft," *Allgemeine deutsche Lehrerzeitung* 2 (1914): 16–18, accessed September 8, 2014, http://www.earlycinema.uni-koeln.de/documents/view/24. See also B., "Bericht über die zweite ordentliche Sitzung der Kinokommission des Westfälischen Landgemeindetages am 11.12.1912 in Dortmund: Die Kinokommission des Westfälischen Landgemeindetags," *Bild und Film* 4 (1912–13): 93–96, accessed September 8, 2014, http://www.lwl.org/westfaelische-geschichte/portal/Internet/finde/langDatensatz.php?urlID=1299&url_tabelle=tab_quelle.

18. Schorr ("Film- und Kinoreformbewegung," 79–81) states that up to 1908, *Der Kinematograph* supported the reformers. Nevertheless, when the growing film industry became a financially important client (for example by paying for large advertisements), the journal concentrated on them and stopped cooperating with the reform movement.

19. Sabine Lenk, *Vom Tanzsaal zum Filmtheater: Eine Kinogeschichte Düsseldorfs* (Düsseldorf: Droste, 2009), 130–31.

20. See also Schorr, "Film- und Kinoreformbewegung," 183.

21. See also ibid., 187.

22. This fear continued to be expressed by teachers. See also Eef Masson, *Watch and Learn: Rhetorical Devices in Classroom Films after 1940* (Amsterdam: Amsterdam University Press, 2012), 88–91.

23. See also Schorr, "Film- und Kinoreformbewegung," 193. See also Paul P. Foster, "German Activities with Educational Films," *Moving Picture Age*, May 1921, 15, 30. We thank Greg Waller for sending us this article.

24. See also Schorr, "Film- und Kinoreformbewegung," 115.

25. See also Lenk, *Vom Tanzsaal zum Filmtheater*, 24.

26. "Das Gemeindelichtspielhaus in Eickel: Der erste Gemeindekino im Ruhrkohlenbezirk," *Bild und Film* 2 (1912): 53–54, accessed September 8, 2014, http://www.lwl.org/westfaelische-geschichte/portal/Internet/finde/langDatensatz.php?urlID=1303&url_tabelle=tab_quelle.

27. B., "Bericht über die zweite ordentliche Sitzung."

28. Franz Bergmann, "Bericht über Entstehung, Ziele und Zwecke der Kinematographenkommission des Westfälischen Landgemeindetages: Die Kinokommission des Westfälischen Landgemeindetages," *Bild und Film* 1 (1912–13): 21–23, accessed September 8, 2014, http://www.lwl.org/westfaelische-geschichte/portal/Internet/finde/langDatensatz.php?urlID=1297&url_tabelle=tab_quelle.

29. Bergmann, "Bericht über die erste Sitzung der Kinokommission."

30. See ibid.

31. The background of the men who were to participate was well defined. They had to come from all the relevant groups in society, from local and regional political institutions and administrations as well as from religious, cultural, economic, and professional associations. ("Bericht über den Instruktionskurs der Kinokommission des Westfälischen Landgemeindetages am 26.02.1913 in Eickel: Instruktionskurs der Kinokommission des Westfälischen Landgemeindetags in Eickel," *Bild und Film* 6 [1912–13]: 142–45, accessed September 8, 2014, http://www.lwl.org/westfaelische-geschichte/portal/Internet/finde/langDatensatz.php?urlID=1301&url_tabelle=tab_quelle).

32. "Bericht über den Instruktionskurs."

33. Bergmann, "Bericht über Entstehung," 21–23.

34. Ibid.

35. B., "Bericht über die zweite ordentliche Sitzung."

36. Ibid.

37. See also "Bericht über eine Besprechung der Kinokommission."

38. A second one was planned for Easter 1914 in Hagen. See also "Bericht über die dritte Sitzung der Kinokommission des Westfälischen Landgemeindetages am 07.01.1914 in Hagen. Kinokommission des Westfälischen Landgemeindetages," *Bild und Film* 5 (1913–14): 108–11, accessed September 8, 2014, http://www.lwl.org/westfaelische-geschichte/portal/Internet/finde/langDatensatz.php?urlID=1300&url_tabelle=tab_quelle.

39. "Bericht über den Instruktionskurs."

40. Adolf Sellmann, "Beschaffung von Kinematographen durch die Landgemeinden (Referat auf dem 4. Westfälischen Landgemeindetag in Münster am 15. Juni 1912.)," *Bild und Film* 3–4 (1912), 86–88, accessed September 8, 2014, http://www.lwl.org/westfaelische-geschichte/portal/Internet/finde/langDatensatz.php?urlID=1304&url_tabelle=tab_quelle.

41. Sellmann, "Beschaffung von Kinematographen." See also Bergmann, "Bericht über Entstehung."

42. B., "Bericht über die zweite ordentliche Sitzung."

43. See also Sellmann, "Der Kampf um den Kino."

44. "Bericht über die dritte Sitzung der Kinokommission."

45. According to Sellmann, each cinema in Hannover had payed about 112,000 marks to the city in taxes and for electricity. Adolf Sellmann, "Kino und Stadtverwaltungen," *Bild und Film* 2 (1912), 51–53, accessed June 17, 2019, http://www.lwl.org/westfaelische-geschichte/portal/Internet/finde/langDatensatz.php?urlID=1305&url_tabelle=tab_quelle.

46. "Bericht über die dritte Sitzung der Kinokommission."

47. Ibid.

48. Ibid.

49. Ibid.

50. See also B., "Bericht über die zweite ordentliche Sitzung." The catalog was titled *Belehrende Filme für Schule und Volk*. These weekly programs thus cost sixty marks per day, while school programs of the same length could be rented at fifteen marks.

51. See also Erwin Ackerknecht, *Zur deutschen Lichtspielreform*, Berlin-Schöneberg: Gebhardt, Jahn u. Landt, 1917.

52. "Bericht über die dritte Sitzung der Kinokommission."

53. Sellmann, "Beschaffung von Kinematographen."

54. H. Runge, "Schulvorstellung Pathé," *Bild und Film* 6 (1913–14): 135, http://goobiweb.bbf.dipf.de/viewer/image/ZDB975774786_0003/157/.

55. Ibid., 136.

56. See also Runge's reaction to Pathé's reply in an open letter to "Firma Pathé Frères & Co., Filiale Düsseldorf," *Bild und Film* 8 (1913–14): 196–98, accessed June 17, 2019, http://goobiweb.bbf.dipf.de/viewer/image/ZDB975774786_0003/228/.

57. See also Hans-Jürgen Wulff, ed., *Lexikon der Filmbegriffe*, accessed June 17, 2019, http://filmlexikon.uni-kiel.de/.

58. For more information on the last point, see Hans-Michael Bock and Michael Töteberg, eds., *Das Ufa-Buch* (Frankfurt/Main: Zweitausendeins, 1992), 66.

59. Sellmann, "Beschaffung von Kinematographen."

60. For example, Hermann Häfker, in "Für Kinder!," declared fairy tale films suitable for children. A typical Reformkino program in 1913 could be composed of several travelogues and expedition films in combination with some entertaining ones. ("Die Gründung eines Reformkinos in Hagen. Reformkino in Hagen i. W.," *Bild und Film* 7 [1912–13]: 168–170, accessed September 2014, http://www.lwl.org/westfaelische-geschichte/portal/Internet/finde/langDatensatz.php?urlID=1302&url_tabelle=tab_quelle).

61. See also Adolf Sellmann, quoted in "Bericht über den Instruktionskurs."

62. Ibid.

63. Franz Schönhuber in *Der Kinematograph* 562 (1917), quoted in Schorr, "Film- und Kinoreformbewegung," 158–59.

64. Hermann Häfker, *Der Kino und die Gebildeten: Wege zur Hebung des Kinowesens* (M. Gladbach: Volksvereins, 1915) is the last book publication of the first generation of Kinoreformers.

65. See also Lenk, *Vom Tanzsaal zum Filmtheater*, 24–25, 78–80.

66. See also Schmerling, *Kinder, Kino und Kinderliteratur*, 89–90.

67. See also Schorr, "Film- und Kinoreformbewegung," 145, 153–55.

68. See also ibid., 182.

69. Teacher Walter Günther, looking back in 1924, stressed that the movement had changed and declared that the issues that the Kinoreform had addressed before the war were no longer relevant and the word, if used at all, was now used differently (Walter Günther, "Die Kinoreformtagung in der Wiener Urania 15. bis 18.05.1914," *Der Kinematograph* 90 [1924], quoted in Schorr, "Film- und Kinoreformbewegung," 192).

70. See also Schorr, "Film- und Kinoreformbewegung," 192.

Bibliography

Ackerknecht, Erwin. *Zur deutschen Lichtspielreform*. Berlin-Schöneberg: Gebhardt, Jahn u. Landt, 1917.

Bergmann, Franz. "Bericht über die erste Sitzung der Kinokommission des Westfälischen Landgemeindetages am 14.06.1912 in Dortmund: Der Westfälische Landgemeindetag und die Kinoreform." *Bild und Film* 3–4 (1912): 84–86. Accessed September 8, 2014.

http://www.lwl.org/westfaelische-geschichte/portal/Internet/finde/langDatensatz.php?urlID=1291&url_tabelle=tab_quelle.

"Bericht über die zweite ordentliche Sitzung der Kinokommission des Westfälischen Landgemeindetages am 11.12.1912 in Dortmund: Die Kinokommission des Westfälischen Landgemeindetags." *Bild und Film* 4 (1912–13): 93–96. Accessed September 8, 2014. http://www.lwl.org/westfaelische-geschichte/portal/Internet/finde/langDatensatz.php?urlID=1299&url_tabelle=tab_quelle.

"Bericht über eine Besprechung der Kinokommission des Westfälischen Landgemeindetages anläßlich der Eröffnungsfeier des Gemeindelichtspielhauses in Eickel: Kinokommission des Westfälischen Landgemeindetages." *Bild und Film* 3 (1912–13): 70–71. Accessed September 8, 2014. http://www.lwl.org/westfaelische-geschichte/portal/Internet/finde/l.ngDatensatz.php?urlID=1298&url_tabelle=tab_quelle.

Bock, Hans-Michael, and Michael Töteberg, eds. *Das Ufa-Buch*. Frankfurt/Main: Zweitausendeins, 1992.

"Das Gemeindelichtspielhaus in Eickel: Der erste Gemeindekino im Ruhrkohlenbezirk." *Bild und Film* 2 (1912): 53–54. Accessed September 8, 2014. http://www.lwl.org/westfaelische-geschichte/portal/Internet/finde/langDatensatz.php?urlID=1303&url_tabelle=tab_quelle.

Diederichs, Helmut H. "Frühgeschichte deutscher Filmtheorie: Ihre Entstehung und Entwicklung bis zum Ersten Weltkrieg." Habilitation thesis, Johann Wolfgang Goethe University, 1996. Accessed June 17, 2019. http://publikationen.ub.uni-frankfurt.de/frontdoor/index/index/docId/4924.

Duckwitz, Amelie, Martin Loiperdinger, and Susanne Theissen. "'Kampf dem Schundfilm!'—Kinoreform und Jugendschutz in Trier." In *KINtop: Jahrbuch zur Erforschung des frühen Films* 9, edited by Frank Kessler, Sabine Lenk, and Martin Loiperdinger, 53–63. Frankfurt/Main: Stroemfeld, 2000.

Foster, Paul P. "German Activities with Educational Films." *Moving Picture Age*, May 1921.

Häfker, Hermann. *Der Kino und die Gebildeten: Wege zur Hebung des Kinowesens*. M. Gladbach: Volksvereins, 1915.

———. "Für Kinder!," *Bild und Film* 7 [1912–13]: 168–170. Accessed September 2014. http://www.lwl.org/westfaelische-geschichte/portal/Internet/finde/langDatensatz.php?urlID=1302&url_tabelle=tab_quelle.

———. "Für Kinder!" *Der Kinematograph* 72, May 13, 1908. Accessed May 4, 2013. http://www.soziales.fh-dortmund.de/diederichs/texte/haefgesv.htm.

Jung, Uli. "Kinoreformer: Nicht-fiktionale Filme für Bildungszwecke." In *Geschichte des dokumentarischen Films in Deutschland*, Band 1. *Kaiserreich 1895–1918*, edited by Uli Jung and Martin Loiperdinger, 333–40. Stuttgart: Reclam, 2005.

Kessler, Frank, and Sabine Lenk. "Kinoreformbewegung Revisited: Performing the Cinematograph as a Pedagogical Tool." In *Performing New Media, 1890–1915*, edited by Kaveh Askari et al., 163–73. New Barnet: John Libbey, 2014.

"Kinematographenbesitzer und Lehrerschaft." *Allgemeine deutsche Lehrerzeitung* 2 (1914): 16–18. http://www.earlycinema.uni-koeln.de/documents/view/24.

Kipp, Rudolf W. *Bilddokumente zur Geschichte des Unterrichtsfilms*. Grünwald: Institut für Film und Bild in Wissenschaft und Unterricht, 1975.

Lenk, Sabine. *Vom Tanzsaal zum Filmtheater: Eine Kinogeschichte Düsseldorfs*. Düsseldorf: Droste, 2009.

Masson, Eef. *Watch and Learn: Rhetorical Devices in Classroom Films after 1940*. Amsterdam: Amsterdam University Press, 2012.

Runge, H. "Firma Pathé Frères & Co., Filiale Düsseldorf." *Bild und Film* 8 (1913–14): 196–98. http://goobiweb.bbf.dipf.de/viewer/image/ZDB975774786_0003/228/.
———. "Schulvorstellung Pathé." *Bild und Film* 6 (1913–14): 135–37. http://goobiweb.bbf.dipf.de/viewer/image/ZDB975774786_0003/157/.
Schmerling, Alice. "Kinder, Kino und Kinderliteratur: Eine Untersuchung zum Medienumbruch in der Kinderkultur und der Weimarer Republik." PhD diss., University of Cologne, 2007. http://kups.ub.uni-koeln.de/2792/.
Schorr, Thomas. "Die Film- und Kinoreformbewegung und die deutsche Filmwirtschaft: Eine Analyse des Fachblatts 'Der Kinematograph' (1907–1935) unter pädagogischen und publizistischen Aspekten." PhD diss., Bundeswehr University Munich, 1990.
Sellmann, Adolf. "Beschaffung von Kinematographen durch die Landgemeinden (Referat auf dem 4. Westfälischen Landgemeindetag in Münster am 15. Juni 1912.)." *Bild und Film* 3–4 (1912): 86–88. http://www.lwl.org/westfaelische-geschichte/portal/Internet/finde/langDatensatz.php?urlID=1304&url_tabelle=tab_quelle.
———. "Der Kampf um den Kino." *Bild und Film* 5 (1913–14): 97–100. http://www.lwl.org/westfaelische-geschichte/portal/Internet/finde/langDatensatz.php?urlID=1307&url_tabelle=tab_quelle.
Siegert, Paul Ferd. "Bürgerliches Selbstverständnis, Kinoreform und früher Schulfilm: Eine kulturwissenschaftliche Analyse." Master's thesis, Leuphana University of Lüneburg, 1995. Accessed September 8, 2014. http://dok.uni-lueneburg.de/texte/Kinoreform.pdf.
Wulff, Hans-Jürgen, ed. *Lexikon der Filmbegriffe*. Accessed June 17, 2019. http://filmlexikon.uni-kiel.de/.

SABINE LENK is a researcher in the Belgian Excellence of Science project "B-Magic. The Magic Lantern and Its Cultural Impact as Visual Mass Medium in Belgium (1830–1940)" at Antwerp University and Université libre de Bruxelles. She is author of *Vom Tanzsaal zum Filmtheater: Eine Kinogeschichte Düssedorfs*.

FRANK KESSLER is Professor of Media History at Utrecht University, the Netherlands, and Director of the Research Institute for Cultural Inquiry. He is coeditor (with Jean-Marc Larrue and Giusy Pisano) *of Machines, Magie, Médias* (Presses universitaires du Septentrion, 2018), author of *Mise en scène* (caboose, 2014), and coeditor (with Nanna Vergoeff) of *Networks of Entertainment* (John Libbey, 2008).

3 One Family

The Movement of Educational Film in Britain and Its Empire

Tom Rice

In the 1930 Empire Marketing Board (EMB) film *One Family*, a young London schoolboy turns up late for his geography lesson. "Is everywhere the empire?" he asks from the back of the classroom. "You'll learn all about it when you grow up" replies his teacher, pointing at a map. "That's what they always say; I shall have to find out for myself," concludes the boy, a refrain repeated as he rests his head on his desk.[1]

What follows is a lengthy sequence in which the boy, bored by his classroom geography lesson, falls asleep on his desk and starts to dream. Rejecting traditional forms of pedagogy, the boy (and by extension the viewer) heads to Buckingham Palace with a London policeman. From there, he sources ingredients for the king's Christmas pudding, extracting from the colonies and dominions products that he brings back to London as he embarks, through the medium of film, on a fantasy tour of the British Empire.

One Family offers here a gentle critique of established forms of education, in that the classroom geography lesson—pointing at a map and shouting out countries and products—fails to inspire the young scholar. It is no coincidence that the boy is in a geography lesson and that the subject is the British Empire. Discussions about the pedagogical function of film within British education during the interwar period prioritized film's potential for teaching geography and, more specifically, the products, places, and histories of the British Empire. Indeed, the efforts to retool film as an educational device in Britain between the wars were motivated by a desire to promote and uphold the empire. As Scott Anthony has eloquently argued, this was the moment when public relations came to the fore within Britain, founded and motivated—like much educational and instructional cinema—by a desire to create productive imperial citizens.[2] Educational cinema became imbricated with these wider pedagogical imperatives to shape and manage populations. In Britain, this form of pedagogy was, perhaps uniquely, repeatedly occupied with empire, geography, and economics.

A closer examination of *One Family* reveals the imperial interests motivating British nonfiction cinema during this formative period. It was produced by British

Instructional Films (BIF), which was founded and run by the arch-imperialist Bruce Woolfe in 1919, directed by Walter Creighton (who had previously organized the Wembley Tattoo at the 1924 Empire Exhibition), sponsored by the EMB, and exhibited at the Imperial Institute. In short, British cinema of the 1920s was colonial cinema, and the emergence of a British educational and nontheatrical cinema—whether specifically designed and adapted for classroom use or serving a broader, general pedagogical function—was inherently tied to its colonial projects.

Ultimately, however, *One Family* interested neither cinemagoers nor schoolchildren; viewers evidently decided that even the dullest geography lesson was preferable to sitting through this imperial pageant. The film was a spectacular critical and commercial failure, and even as late as 1950, *One Family* was discussed in the House of Commons "as the greatest flop you ever saw in your life."[3] Yet it is this spectacular failure that marks it as a significant moment in British cinema. The EMB had commissioned *One Family* and a John Grierson film on herring fishing, *Drifters*, as its first two productions. Grierson's *Drifters* achieved critical acclaim and presaged the British documentary movement, yet *One Family* represented a more prosaic form of fictionalized documentary, one largely founded on earlier cinematic forms and pageants. Indeed, the film's spectacular critical and commercial failure—it was described by filmmaker Harry Watt as "abysmally vomit-making" and its box office earnings reportedly failed to cover the costs of the band hired for the film's premiere—helped to consolidate Grierson's reputation and his position at the head of the EMB Film Unit.[4] The documentary aesthetics of *Drifters*, as opposed to the full-length fictional framework of *One Family*, were championed as the celebrated prestige form for state-sponsored imperial filmmaking.

Yet this is only a partial view, and one that obfuscates the wider uses and forms of nonfiction film throughout British cinema history. First, the largely traditional vision of empire within *One Family* provides a significant counter to the image of modern Britain promoted within the more liberal prestige documentaries of the 1930s. Sir Arthur Elton noted the "very old fashioned" nature of *One Family*—"society ladies playing Britannia, and the Empire cake, Buckingham Palace and so forth"—while John Grierson suggested that its reliance on symbols belonged to the Victorian era.[5] This representation of empire—one that foregrounded London as the heart of the empire, and the colonies and dominions as producers for Britain—largely endorses a dominant strand of economic imperialism and, in its form, combines elements of the general promotional or illustrative film with the directly pedagogical. The film's structure comprises a series of brief instructional films, showing, for example, the production and export of fruit from South Africa, raisins from Australia, and butter from New Zealand. These shorts attempt to incorporate the still-dominant form of colonial nonfiction film (the short geography film about a colony and its products) within a semifictionalized prestige production. This mode is also evident in director Walter Creighton's other work. One of his next projects was for Cadbury's, producing shorts from the Gold Coast that included a picture showing the industrial processes of cocoa production and another that, through shots of abandoned castles, celebrated Britain's role in bringing peace, prosperity, and education to the area.[6]

The success of *Drifters*, allied with Grierson's vision and genius for self-promotion, has relegated *One Family* to the margins of a British film history, which largely understands nonfiction through the celebrated British documentary movement. This process was evident as early as 1936. In his foreword to *Documentary Film*, Paul Rotha explained that he had initially intended to consider cinema as a "factor in modern education" but decided that the "educational movement should be considered separately from the documentary movement." Rotha's construction of these two distinct categories—the "so-called general illustration film" and the "direct teaching, or instructional" film—and his statement that he placed a "higher value" on the former, illustrates a hierarchy in nonfiction cinema that has largely relegated the classroom or instructional film to a critical wasteland.[7]

Yet the British documentary movement was merely one strand of British nonfiction film, and what's more, the canonical films of this movement, such as *Drifters* or *Song of Ceylon* (1934), were a misleadingly tiny proportion of British nonfiction output in this period. While *Song of Ceylon* is now widely celebrated, there is invariably very little mention of the four short instructional films produced simultaneously from this material for the Ceylon Tea Propaganda Board, which were available nontheatrically through the EMB's Empire Film Library.[8] A history of British nonfiction cinema should not only privilege the celebrated, unusual, and spectacular successes but also consider equally those films that reappear on nontheatrical catalogs that appear entirely unremarkable. The plethora of instructional, nonfiction films—often critically invisible in histories of British documentary—not only constitute a significantly overlooked part of British nonfiction history but also help determine the form and function of moving images within British education.

This chapter charts the movement of educational film both within Britain and its empire. The end of the Great War marked the territorial apogee of the British Empire, a moment when Britain could claim to govern almost a quarter of the globe. Yet this also marked a point of rupture for this splintering, unsustainable mass of people, lands, and ideologies. While state and commerce looked to use film to maintain and monetize the empire, the discourses surrounding the possible educational uses of film highlight Britain's increasingly fragile cultural power. The rise of American film recognized by the British state as a threatening form of cultural imperialism—and indeed, of more innovative and effective political cinemas, most notably in Soviet Russia, manifested the importance of film in national education. This chapter will examine some of the prevailing discourses between 1913 and the 1930s, positioning educational film within the institution of empire. As the opening example of *One Family* shows, such a history challenges the understanding of nonfiction cinema in Britain by foregrounding often-overlooked instructional and educational films. In exploring the attempts to use and place educational film—the nontheatrical exhibition sites and distribution networks—the chapter locates educational cinema both in Britain and across its empire and, what's more, reveals a pedagogical form frequently beholden to the economics of empire.

Catalogs and Committees: Toward an Educational Cinema

For all the attention paid to the British documentary movement, there remains surprisingly little scholarship on the related establishment of directly educational, instructional, and nontheatrical film in Britain. Writing in 1931, John Grierson suggested a possible reason for this: that there was nothing of consequence to report. Instead, Grierson wrote disparagingly of a succession of short-lived committees dating back to 1917, made up of figures from the fields of education and social service but notably devoid of "those with a knowledge of cinema and industry."[9] "Here and there a committee is formed," he explained, "with names on the letter headings powerful enough in their own estate to launch a fleet of a thousand films. But nothing considerable is launched save always a catalogue; a catalogue which, I am afraid, has become the jest of all who pursue the obscure history of our educational film work." Grierson saw these catalogs as relics, listing films that were hopelessly outdated, often unobtainable and of no educational value. By 1931, he had concluded that "the educational and social films worth retrieving could, in fact, be catalogued by a single clerk in an afternoon."[10] Furthermore, for Grierson, these perceived failings at home were exacerbated by developments overseas. "Russia, France, Germany, the United States and Canada, have taken the matter seriously to the point of creating vast services of supply and distribution," he wrote, "but England, with her very special need of modern method, and intensive instruction in modern method, has let the occasion go by."[11]

Yet these perceived failings—the rejected schemes or forgotten films, lengthy reports, and inconsequential meetings—warrant far closer study, as this was a period when the place and function of film within education was partially configured. In her invaluable, seminal account of British cinema, Rachael Low outlines the numerous attempts to promote and foreground film as an educational tool within Britain during the 1920s.[12] A starting point, as John Grierson noted somewhat dismissively, is often the survey conducted by the National Council of Public Morals, which was published in 1917 as a 372-page book entitled *The Cinema: Its Present Position and Future Possibilities.* The report focused on the effects of film on behavior (a link between cinema and juvenile crime) and also on the physical effects of cinemagoing. In one striking example that highlighted these related fears in reference to cinema space and colonial interaction, the report noted that "immorality is frightfully prevalent" within the London picture houses around Westminster and Victoria. "The district is the centre for colonial troops," the report noted, further highlighting the recent increase in cases of prostitution brought before the Westminster Police Court. These involved women as young as fourteen, who "go to the picture shows in the districts, and that is where they sometimes meet our colonials."[13]

These anxieties around social behavior—whether attributed to the images on screen or the experience of cinemagoing—were well established by 1917 and motivated much of the discourse on film and education. The first International Cinematograph Exhibition, which was held in Olympia in 1913 and invited representatives from all the world to see what "England—the film clearinghouse of the world—was doing," had featured an "educational side." The event displayed the latest educational shorts from around the world and included talks from Henry Wakefield, the bishop of Birmingham, and Canon Edward Lyttelton, the headmaster of Eton, who were invited to discuss the merits (or otherwise) of the motion picture. Canon Lyttelton's address was, one would imagine, not exactly what the organizers had in mind. Rather than outlining the educational potential of film within schools, Lyttelton condemned the effects of the picture palaces on children, concluding that he had "never known any development of education in his lifetime where more caution was required." Supporting legislation, he urged local councils to investigate the effects of films on young viewers and suggested that children in elementary schools would "suffer nothing but harm" if they were allowed to go to more than one of these shows a week.[14]

The regulation and establishment of new picture palaces throughout the country, at that moment of boom, was often tied to these discourses. As one example of many, in 1913 the town council initially opposed plans for a purpose-built cinema in St. Andrews, Scotland, because the proposed site, next to the university and cathedral, "might impair the ancient character of the street." The provost of St. Andrews eventually supported the move, but only after he was persuaded that the cinema could be "a place for education."[15]

By 1913, there were already some attempts to introduce film for specifically educational purposes. For example, the London Education Committee proposed, without success, its introduction into two schools in 1913. A year later, the board of education acknowledged that the use of film within schools had "not even reached the experimental stage." When it did tentatively explore the possibilities of using the cinematograph in education, the board again focused on the physical "dangers" of watching films, most notably the effects on eyestrain (which also constituted one of the five major sections of the 1917 report conducted by the National Council of Public Morals). The board's memorandum, like many that followed, surmised that the cinematograph "may be destined to play a most important part in the educational developments of the future" but concluded that "limited demand" and "excessive cost," both in supplying specialist films and equipment in schools, would make its use "impossible even if desirable."[16]

These questions about the pedagogical potential of film, while inherently tied to regulatory anxieties around film morality, social behavior, and the physical "dangers" of film, were prevalent by 1917, even if they largely remained on the level of discourse. T. P. O'Connor, the first president of the Board of Film Censors and part of the 1917 commission for the National Council of Public Morals, acknowledged in the same year that "there was one side of the possibilities of the cinematograph which had not yet been fully developed and that had to do with the cinema as an educator. . . . If instead of learning geography in the usual way boys and girls were taught by the cinematograph, geography instead of being a disagreeable study would be both interesting and instructive." O'Connor envisaged a day in the not-too-distant future when all public schools would use the cinema in their teaching. O'Connor's choice of subject here is significant. The board of education had also suggested that film would work best in the teaching of nature and geography, "especially such subjects as the differences in the manners, customs, and modes of life of people in various lands."[17]

There were some specific attempts, at this early stage, to bring the empire into schools. Flora Campbell-Patterson, an actress and president of the Incorporated Educational-National Film Body, submitted a proposal to the Carnegie Trust in 1917. Adopting the tagline "I claim that the SCREEN is the blackboard of the future and that its VALUE in COLONISATION is unparalleled," Campbell-Brown sought to bring educational films into schools, to create educational film libraries across the empire, and to send cinematographers around the empire to produce suitable films. Campbell-Brown referenced advances in educational film within the United States, France, and Germany and stressed, somewhat presciently, that the United Kingdom must not "lag behind." Her proposal was ultimately rejected and serves as evidence not only of the individual attempts to promote educational film, particularly in relation to the empire, but also of a lack of institutional support for such schemes.[18]

A brief look at the myriad schemes launched between 1917 and 1931—the committees and catalogs that Grierson critiques—illustrates this increasing interest in film pedagogy if not always an organized national response to the subject. The National Council of Public Morals followed its 1917 commission with a further scientific study in 1919 (published in 1925 as *The Cinema in Education*) while individual and often unconnected initiatives appeared throughout the country. Mary Field, a hugely significant and overlooked figure in British cinema, who was then serving as the education officer at BIF, outlined some of these schemes in a lecture to schoolteachers in Manchester in 1927. These included the "Battersea Experiment," a weekly screening of two educational films presented in the town hall alongside a comedy and an adventure film to eleven hundred children.

Field noted a similar scheme in Liverpool and a further experiment in London to carry "a kinema machine" around scattered schools. She also acknowledged, as Grierson did, that England had now fallen behind five other countries (the United States, France, Italy, Germany, and Russia) both in "general cultural education" and within schools. She credited these foreign successes to wealthy patrons in America, state initiatives in France after 1921 that provided free films to schools, legislation in Italy that set aside money for films concerning health and hygiene, and the initiatives of teachers and parents' unions in Germany that organized morning screenings for children during school hours. "No-one knew precisely what was happening

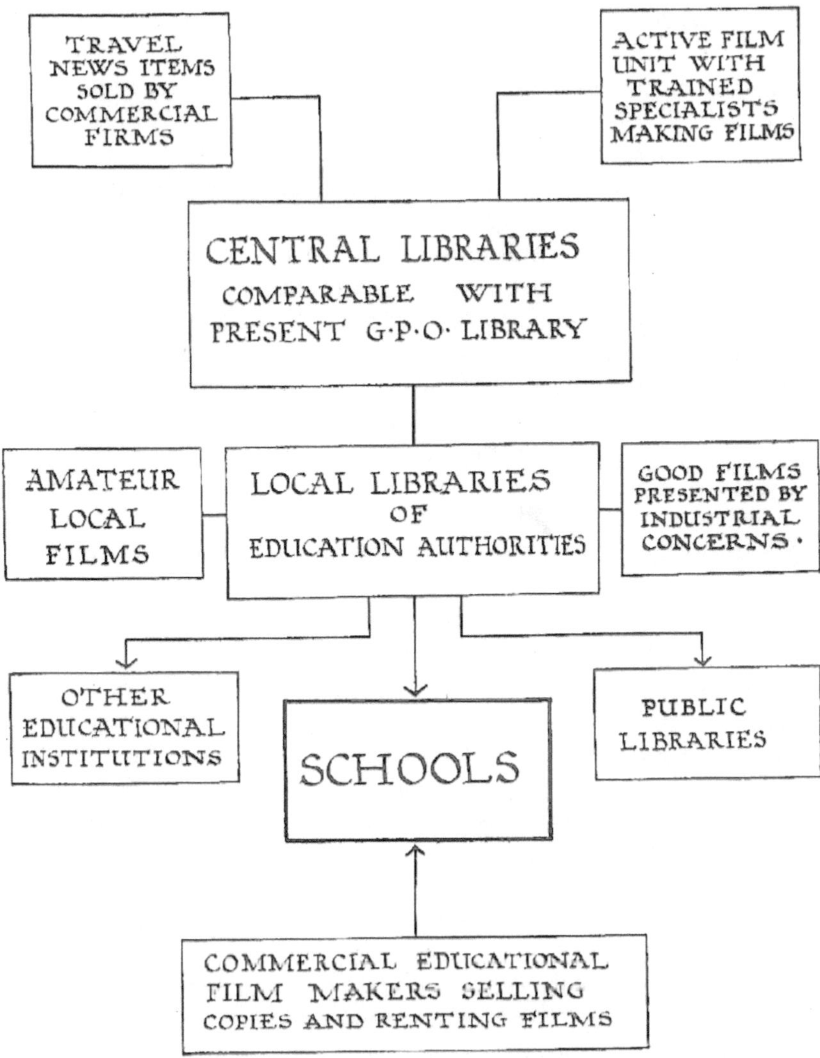

Fig. 3.1. Schoolteacher W. H. George outlined a plan for the use of films in schools in his 1935 book, *The Cinema in School* (London: Sir Isaac Pitman and Sons, Ltd, 1935), 37.

in Russia," but Field noted that the government had recently ordered "2000 kinema machines for installation in schools and colleges."[19]

There are also examples of individual enthusiasts and teachers—for example, Ronald Gow in Altrincham and W. H. George in Chesterfield—making and renting films for schools.[20] George went on to publish *The Cinema in School* in 1935, which also compared the work in Britain unfavorably with advances in other countries. "In Russia, teachers are trained in film usage and they are expected to be as conversant with the film as with books and apparatus." While breaking down the discussion into specific sections ("The teaching film" and "What role does the teacher play?"), George singled out the work of the British documentary movement for praise, perhaps unsurprisingly, since Grierson had provided a foreword for the book. On Basil Wright's Jamaican-filmed "Banana Symphony," George determined that "no teacher with insistent dinning achieves as much, nor does any song-plugging get home like this poetic film style." For his part, Grierson emphasized the potential of film in teaching "civics"—in effect creating citizens and showing how communities should operate. His reasoning here was largely economic, as he recognized that much of the money for educational film came "from the Gas, Light and Coke Co., the General Post Office, the Electrical Department Association and the various industrial firms and departments which provide the actual money and the actual movie."[21]

Despite the initiatives of individuals, corporations, local councils, and education departments, progress within the United Kingdom was often seen to be slow and lacking the state organization evident in France or Russia. The Education Committee of the London County Council concluded in 1926 that it was "doubtful whether the cinematograph has made much progress in its use for educational purposes."[22] By 1929, the latest Conference on Educational Film was reporting that there were "over 3000 films of an educational and instructional character at present available from some 300 to 400 different sources," further claiming, somewhat ambitiously, that about five hundred schools and educational institutions were regularly using films. Yet what was lacking, the report suggested, was an institutionalized system for educational films within Britain. "It seems desirable," the report concluded, "to form an authoritative body of all those who use film for teaching, to act as a central office for all matters relating to educational cinema."[23] Indeed, by 1932 when the Commission of Educational Films, a working group formed from the conference, published its findings in the influential *The Film in National Life*, it concluded that "these successive calls for constructive action have had little result. Conferences have realized that great constructive use can be made of the film and have said so. But there has been no permanent organization to put the agreed principle into practice. It has been nobody's business to keep the interest alive."[24]

It may be tempting to follow Grierson's line here and characterize this as a period of more talk than action, of committees and catalogs, but there are significant caveats to this. First, the talk was not without consequence, at least in shaping the ways in which film would be seen within education and public relations in Britain.

In particular, there remained a significant imperialist bent to these discussions, as education was invariably coarticulated with imperialism in interwar Britain. For example, both the 1923 and 1927 Imperial Education Conferences discussed film. The former produced the *Report on the Use and Value of the Cinematograph in Education*, which urged the board of education to use film in the teaching of science, nature, geography, and scientific and industrial processes. While dismissing suggestions that film stifles imagination, it did propose follow-up discussions on whether the interest generated in class when teaching with film might render all other lessons "insipid." The bigger concern was a financial one. The president of the board of education remained unconvinced by the feasibility of film within the classroom, particularly at a "cost not out of proportion to its value."[25] Herein lies a central conundrum that characterized this period. In order to justify further investment in projectors and equipment in schools, councils wanted to see more established and suitable educational films, while producers wanted to see more schools and venues equipped for film before investing in further productions.

During the 1920s, there was certainly a state acknowledgment of the importance of cinema, more generally, in promoting the empire. Prime Minister Stanley Baldwin noted the "danger to which we in this country and our Empire subject ourselves if we allow that method of propaganda [film] to be entirely in the hands of foreign countries." Baldwin saw the problem more in terms of advertising, as a way of restoring "trade and national prosperity." "On the production side I have no fears," he wrote in 1927, "on the selling side we must modernize our methods and make use of the great developments which have taken place recently in the art of advertising."[26] There were notable state initiatives that utilized film to promote British industry and imperial trade, most notably from the Empire Marketing Board (1926–33) and the Conservative Party, which used mobile vans and trains to spread this message nontheatrically across the country.[27] Indeed the genesis of documentary film and public relations within Britain was born out of this broader desire to promote imperial economic interests. Within this context, Grierson highlighted the potential of film beyond the classroom, "providing congregations that run into the millions" and finding a "bigger audience" than any book, lecture, or poem. Grierson was focusing, as the 1926 Imperial Conference had, on the "particular economy of cinema," by which "the ends of the earth are brought to a cutting bench in Wardour Street" and "the unconverted spiritual and temporal are brought within the range of a director's megaphone."[28]

Much of the work in this period focused on the broader educational value of cinema—a desire to spread British ideologies and products across the empire. This was a feature of the 1926 Imperial Conference, which had addressed the paucity of British films shown both in Britain and the empire and, most notably, led to the introduction of the Cinematograph Act (a quota on British films). To this end, the General Economic Sub-Committee on Empire Films, formed at the 1926 conference, argued that "the Cinema is not merely a form of entertainment, but, in addition, a powerful instrument for education in the widest sense of that term."[29]

British producers complained throughout this period when their imperial-themed pictures, such as *Livingstone* (1925), failed to find distribution in America and Commonwealth territories. In partial response to this perceived American cultural imperialism, the British Empire Film Institute was established in 1926 to promote British film (initiating awards for imperial-themed pictures). It also sought to organize film libraries throughout the world and to support films that portray "the history, geography, ethnology, economics, and character of the British Commonwealth and its peoples."[30] The 1927 Imperial Education Conference also discussed the "use of the cinema as an aid to increasing knowledge of the Empire," both of the empire in Britain and, equally significantly, of Britain across the empire. In the same year, the Colonial Office Conference considered the use of film within the colonies, in both formal schooling and general education, particularly with respect to "health and economic development."[31] By the second half of the 1920s, film was imagined as a part of imperial "public relations," but there are two more specific ways in which film would function within colonial education: as a form of classroom pedagogy and in instructing "native races" within the colonies.

James Marchant, who had led the Cinema Commission for the National Council of Public Morals between 1917 and 1925, directly cited the empire when writing in *The Times* in 1926 about the "almost unsupplied field" of educational film. Marchant noted how leading American producers had collaborated with Yale professors to produce exemplary films on American history, and he explained that he had tried without success to generate support for a similar series on the British Empire. "Is it not possible," he asked, "for the British and Dominion Governments to do for the children of the Empire what is being done for American children? Why are we behind in using these wonderful means of maintaining and consolidating our Empire, which our children, if we rightly educate them, will make mightier still?"[32]

These questions were also raised by eminent geographers, most notably James Fairgrieve, who first published his hugely influential book *Geography in School* in the same year. Fairgrieve subsequently chaired a British Film Institute (BFI) committee responsible for the production of geography films in the 1930s, and he repeatedly bemoaned the lack of development within this area. "How many schools even now really use films regularly in teaching?" he asked in 1932. "Movies flooded the land and teachers did mighty little. Then came the talkies, and we have done not much more." Fairgrieve again compared the situation unfavorably with France, Italy, Japan, the United States, Germany, Holland, Belgium, Canada, and Russia, and his conclusions that a "good deal of investigation has taken place" likely did little to assuage Grierson's fears. Most significant, Fairgrieve connected the discussion on film in British classrooms to the "larger educational problem" regarding the teaching of "the native races of the Empire." Complaining about the existing films shown within the empire—"For good or ill, they are being educated by films. Many films that they see are positively bad; most of the others are unintelligible or uninteresting"—Fairgrieve outlined the broader political value of film in "the education of the masses." He suggested that the educational film "might help to save political trouble" within the colonies, supporting his oft-quoted earlier assertion that "the function of geography in school is to train future citizens to imagine accurately the conditions of the great world stage."[33]

The emergence of documentary cinema was motivated, in part, by this desire to create productive British and imperial citizens. In a study of a series of Gaumont-British Instructional (GBI) films on Indian towns from 1937, Priya Jaikumar emphasized the intersection between the "visual practices of geopolitics and curricular geography." Jaikumar's work brilliantly dissects the building blocks and vocabulary of these geographical films, situating them within the discourses of disciplinary geography, foregrounding geography, and, specifically, imperial geography as a particularly receptive discipline for film.[34]

Before delivering his paper in 1932, Fairgrieve screened *A Punjab Village*, a film originally produced by BIF as part of its Empire Series. *A Punjab Village* was now "supervised" by Fairgrieve and viewed and approved by the Geographical Association and the Commission on Educational and Cultural Films. This reworked film and the Empire Series more broadly elucidate the discussions about film's pedagogical function, whether in the British classroom or in the education of imperial citizens across the empire. A close examination of another film produced in the series, *Black Cotton*, better illustrates how the practices, processes, and institutions of educational film were developed and organized within Britain and its empire during this interwar period.

Black Cotton: The Case of British Instructional Films

The journey of *Black Cotton* throughout the 1920s uncovers the attempts, by state and commerce, to locate, adapt, and utilize educational film within Britain and its colonies.[35] *Black Cotton* traveled from Africa to exhibition halls in London, cinemas, schools, and, at the end of the decade, back to Africa. The film, including footage taken in West Africa in February 1923 by the London-based Greville Brothers, was first exhibited publicly at the British Empire Exhibition of 1924–25, a "stock taking of the whole resources of the empire." Across its two seasons, the exhibition welcomed twenty-seven million visitors to its Wembley site and included 100,000 feet of film, much of which played in cinema halls within the specially constructed pavilions that represented each colony and dominion.[36]

The initial screening venue for this cotton footage helped determine how and where colonial nonfiction film would play. Such films were largely pedagogical and nontheatrical. They often followed *Black Cotton* in promoting and endorsing a newly configured imperial economy, depicting an industrial process, and defining not only individual colonies by products and industries but also its inhabitants by vocation or ethnic type. The exhibition also illustrated a growing recognition, on the part of the Colonial Office and colonial governments, of the educational possibilities of film. The London-based journal *West Africa* claimed that "it is beyond doubt" that the films shown at the exhibition would "give to 99 people out of every 100 at Wembley who know nothing of West Africa their master impression of the country." The journal recognized the broader influence that film could exercise over popular perceptions of the empire.[37] It is perhaps unsurprising, then, that before the exhibition even opened its doors, there were discussions about what to do with the films after the exhibition.

As early as October 1923, Sir Edward Davson, a leading light on numerous imperial trade committees, publicly suggested that the exhibition films "represent the greatest collection of geographical films that has ever been made" and could thus serve to "educate our people . . . in an appreciation and knowledge of our Dominions and Colonies, of their scenery and the life of their people, of their industries and products." Davson wanted to see these films accompanied by "competent lecturers in continuous exhibition throughout the Kingdom." These ideas were taken forward by Graham Ball, a film expert attached to the Department of Overseas Trade, who proposed a series of fifty-two short films under the title "Scenes in the British Empire," which he hoped would play in four hundred theaters before eventually moving to schools and even overseas.[38]

The plans for the series reveal a desire to use film, initially within a cinema setting, to educate and teach British audiences about the colonies, to promote imperial trade and emigration, and to exploit commercially the widely viewed films of the Empire Exhibition. In his attempts to bridge the commercial and the educational, Ball chose to work with BIF. BIF produced films for nonspecialist audiences and had, by this time, accrued a reputation for its coverage of overseas imperial tours, historical military films, and its Secrets of Nature series, which spawned more than one hundred films by the end of the decade. The films within the Secrets of Nature series represent arguably the most numerous and widely seen nonfiction films of the interwar period, a form of nonfiction cinema as influential today (for example in natural history television) as any other from the period.[39] These films pioneered specialist techniques—such as time lapse, underwater photography, animation, and microscopic cinematography—and recognized cinema as "*the* ideal medium for the study of life."[40]

During its fourteen-year existence, BIF produced films for trade and state, within different generic frameworks that projected an image of the empire back to British audiences. These films largely endorsed dominant government attitudes by highlighting British primacy, the social and industrial development of the colonies, and the critical import of imperial loyalty. By 1927, the Imperial Institute acknowledged that the "productions of British Instructional Films are in every way superior to those obtained from other sources," adding that the company had "succeeded most happily in introducing little scenes of native life, recreations, native types and customs into nearly all of their films."[41]

The completed series was released theatrically in three sets, each between six and twelve films, in November 1925, February 1927, and August 1928. BIF sought to bring *Black Cotton* and other films of the Empire Exhibition to a commercial audience. This was a somewhat complicated process, as the series incorporated material

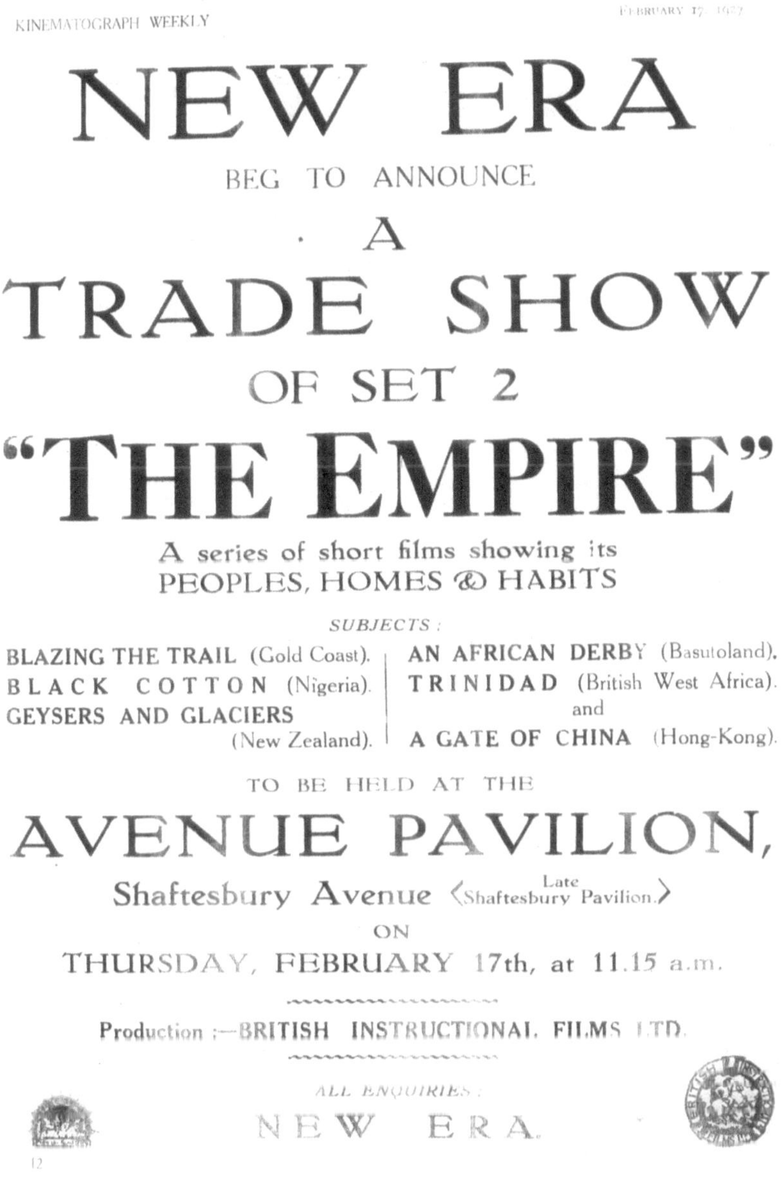

KINEMATOGRAPH WEEKLY FEBRUARY 17, 1927

NEW ERA

BEG TO ANNOUNCE

A

TRADE SHOW

OF SET 2

"THE EMPIRE"

A series of short films showing its
PEOPLES, HOMES & HABITS

SUBJECTS:

BLAZING THE TRAIL (Gold Coast).
BLACK COTTON (Nigeria).
GEYSERS AND GLACIERS (New Zealand).
AN AFRICAN DERBY (Basutoland).
TRINIDAD (British West Africa).
and
A GATE OF CHINA (Hong-Kong).

TO BE HELD AT THE

AVENUE PAVILION,

Shaftesbury Avenue (Late Shaftesbury Pavilion.)

ON

THURSDAY, FEBRUARY 17th, at 11.15 a.m.

Production:—BRITISH INSTRUCTIONAL FILMS LTD.

ALL ENQUIRIES:

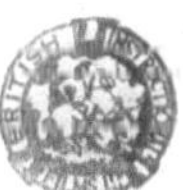

NEW ERA.

12

Fig. 3.2. An advertisement for the "The Empire" series in *Kinematograph Weekly*, February 17, 1927, 12.

from at least three different sources which was produced by a variety of companies with different ideological aims. One of the ways of standardizing these disparate pictures and of adapting them for a paying audience was through the intertitles. Lighthearted intertitles sought to relate the events on screen to British viewers, emphasized British technological and social developments, and highlighted British primacy (often contrasting modern British methods with the traditional, local "primitive" methods). The reorganization of these images—introducing titles, maps, and using eminent academics like Arthur Percival Newton, Rhodes professor of Imperial History at King's College, London, to advise on the films—sought to bridge the commercial and the educational, not always successfully. While stating that the pictures are "very interesting and instructive," *West Africa* lamented the "usual idiotic" intertitles in *Black Cotton*. Complaining about the use of the word *black* in the film title, *West Africa* concluded that "film educationists cannot educate unless they are educated themselves."[42]

Commercially, the films fared no better, and after their poor showing in the cinema, the Crown agents, administering across the British Empire, concluded "that purely propaganda or educational films are not the type to succeed commercially." They instead suggested that *Palaver* (1926), which "combined fiction with a background of local customs . . . would appear to be the type of film which is most likely to appeal to cinema audiences in this country."[43] *Palaver* shared much in common with the Empire Series, and it also reflected an increasing move to recontextualize these imperial studies within a fictional framework. This attempt at recontextualization was seen in later BIF productions like *Stark Nature* (1930) but, as the example of *One Family* pointedly revealed, was only partially successful.

So where next for *Black Cotton*? By 1927, BIF had explained, with reference to the Empire Series, that it was "now concentrating on making the films available for educational purposes." *Black Cotton* featured in a BIF demonstration in London on the future of the educational film, introduced by imperial historian Sir Charles Lucas, while an account in the *Christian Science Monitor* ("Geography Enlivened by Film") discussed the value of *Black Cotton* as an aid to classroom teaching. The report suggested that students would already have some knowledge of Nigeria—its place on a map, its climate, and main export trade—but by showing the industries and daily life, "Nigeria will become to them a definite conception, a 'real life place' as the child describes it."[44]

The attempts to reposition this film—from public exhibition to commercial cinema, and then to the classroom—illustrate the uncertain place of educational film within Britain during the 1920s. As a further example from 1927, London County Council used BIF for a season of "displays of films suitable for schools" on Saturday mornings. The council sought to navigate the educational and commercial market here. Students would be charged an admission to ensure that "no charge shall be borne by the rate payer" but would also now be accompanied by their teachers.[45]

At this moment when *Black Cotton* was made available for schools, a more permanent center for these short imperial films emerged. The Imperial Institute's cinema, which opened in July 1927 and was described by its director as a "permanent Wembley," showed children imperial films four times a day and regularly screened films from the Empire Series.[46] Yet the BIF also discussed with the institute "the need for a central bureau for distributing Empire films."[47] By 1928, *Black Cotton* (now titled *Cotton Growing in Nigeria*) was advertised for nontheatrical hire through British Instructional's Education Department.[48] The EMB also published an empire films catalog, listing 130 titles in 1931 that could be shown, it claimed, in up to five hundred schools. "Projectors are being steadily hired by all types of schools," a report in *The Times* explained, "and opinion among teachers is almost unanimous in favour of the film both for making a reality of history and geography and for interesting and amusing the children."[49] However, Colonel Levey, who wanted to place the Empire Series back in cinemas, argued that showing the films in schools was "valueless propaganda" and that if you didn't pay an admission, "it was regarded more in the nature of an advertisement and people took much less interest in it." Gervas Huxley, then of the EMB, seemingly acknowledged this footage's value as advertising for products, places, and, in particular, ideologies, when he asked to rework "extracts for inclusion in new films," which might be exhibited in shop windows and other public spaces.[50]

In 1929 *Black Cotton* undertook another journey as one of three films supplied by the EMB and taken to East Africa by noted biologist Dr. Julian Huxley. Huxley was sent on behalf of the Colonial Advisory Committee on Native Education as part of an educational experiment to test levels of comprehension among African audiences.[51] Despite traveling for several weeks, Huxley screened the films in only two "native" schools, in Kenya and Uganda (partly because of a paucity of projecting facilities). Yet from these two screenings, he drew a set of conclusions that helped shape the uses of film within African education. He explained that the three films "had been deliberately chosen to represent three levels of difficulty," with *Cotton Growing in Nigeria* (as *Black Cotton* was listed) the simplest.

Huxley estimated that for the second screening in a cinema hall in Uganda, more than three-quarters of the several hundred boys and girls in attendance were seeing film for the first time. His findings highlighted film's value in the biopolitical shaping of colonial labor. He explained that once the audience saw "natives" working on the screen, they grew "wildly excited," with the noise "particularly deafening when anyone was seen on the film doing a hard job of work." After the screenings, the children from the government schools wrote essays about the films. "We found that the people of Nigeria are now civilized," one wrote. Schoolchildren in Uganda noted, in contrast to their own situation, how the cotton was used in the local trade, not only shipped overseas. Huxley suggested that the film appealed because it "represented people like themselves, engaged in familiar occupations," highlighting the importance of making films that directly represented and responded to African audiences.[52]

Based on these two screenings, Huxley determined that "films can be profitably used both as an adjunct to school education, and for adult education and propaganda." His screenings highlighted some of the challenges faced in using film within African education—whether with equipment or in using local commentators or translators to relay the intended message—but his was a significant initiative in propelling colonial audiences into educational film discourse. Most strikingly, Huxley "was very enthusiastic regarding the potential of African audiences to comprehend sophisticated film techniques" and concluded that "African audiences should be treated no differently from any other group." Questions over the cognitive capabilities of African audiences dominated discussions about the development of educational film, particularly within Africa, for the remainder of the colonial era. Huxley voiced a minority opinion in his conclusions from his Africa travels.[53]

While in East Africa, Huxley also visited Dr. Alec Paterson, the deputy director of medical services in Kenya, who had made and exhibited health films to support the department's campaigns. Huxley determined that "this will become a very important use of the cinema—the recording of special activities of Government Departments for demonstration and propaganda purposes."[54] At this same moment, William Sellers, a government health inspector in Nigeria, began making films on subjects such as plague prevention, tropical disease, and child welfare, which he later played through traveling mobile cinema vans. In contrast to Huxley, Sellers subsequently argued that films for African audiences required a specialized filmmaking technique—one without excessive movement in the frame and with minimal editing. He pioneered many developments in the mobile exhibition of film and in the use of educational and instructional film as an adjunct to government campaigns.[55]

The appearance of *Black Cotton* within Africa marks a significant moment in the development of film within colonial education. It also illustrates an increasing move, on the part of BIF, to extend its pedagogy overseas. In 1928, BIF signed a deal to ensure that its existing productions could be exhibited in Australia and New Zealand and arranged a similar deal through its distributor in South Africa. In 1930, when a Colonial Films Committee was established to "promote the better distribution of British films in the colonies" and to supply films of an "educational value to the native races," reports noted that BIF already was sending "instructional and interest films to places so far distant as the West Indies, Nigeria and the Gold Coast, the Malay States, India and New Zealand for exhibition in places other than those of entertainment."[56] The committee further proposed producing a series of films—sixteen health, twelve agricultural, eight educational, and four general interest—for the West Indies, with a similar program for Africa and another for the Far East.[57] Away from these short instructional films, BIF also looked to the colonies for coproductions. In 1928, Bruce Woolfe traveled to India to oversee the production of *Shiraz*, a BIF coproduction with the celebrated German company UFA (Universum Film-Aktien Gesellschaft), which was followed a year later by

A Throw of Dice. These feature coproductions also hint at a shift within BIF. By the early 1930s, with BIF's finances crumbling, the company was absorbed by British International Pictures and its educational remit was subsumed by a more "brusque and commercial" approach.[58]

The Legacies of Talk in the 1930s

Even in 1933, the place and function of educational film within Britain might still appear somewhat unclear. In this year, both the leading producer of educational shorts, BIF, and the central state organization for the production and promotion of film pedagogy, the EMB, were disbanded. Further proposals to follow up Huxley's initiatives in Africa failed to secure funding, while isolated experiments into film's use within the classroom (as seen in Glasgow in 1933, when edited EMB shorts were used as part of a quantitative experiment into classroom film) appeared to indicate the lack of a central, coherent policy on educational film.[59]

However, earlier initiatives and discussions helped shape the ways in which film was used and imagined within education as these processes become more institutionalized in the 1930s. Three brief but related examples provide context. First, after Huxley's report, there was an increase in the number of attempts to use film as a tool for government education within the colonies. There were proposals from filmmakers (such as Geoffrey Barkas, who had previously filmed in Nigeria for BIF), educationalists (J. Russell Orr), and health officials (such as Dr. Alec Paterson, who proposed in 1934 to use film in the "production of the prosperous peasant" in Africa). Yet the perilous state of the nation's finances—exacerbated by the need to prop up and monetize the sprawling empire—ensured that none of these proposals achieved funding.[60] Indeed the one major initiative in this area during the 1930s—the Bantu Education Kinema Experiment (BEKE), which cited and owed a debt to Huxley's earlier experiments—was largely funded by American philanthropy (Carnegie Corporation) and African mining interests.[61]

It took the outbreak of war in 1939 for the British government to intervene directly in educating (and mobilizing and "shaping") colonial citizens through film, as imperial funds were assigned to meet the full cost of the new Colonial Film Unit (CFU). Over the next fifteen years, until its formal disbandment in 1955, the CFU produced more than two hundred films, which it showed through its network of mobile cinema vans across the British Empire. The producer and driving force of this unit, which promoted health, welfare, and development initiatives, particularly within Africa, was William Sellers, who had begun making instructional films in Nigeria in the 1920s as a health official. The unit's director, working closely with Sellers, was George Pearson, a former headmaster and hugely influential figure in silent British cinema. Pearson described his role with the CFU as coming "full circle," back to his roots in education.[62]

Second, the institutionalization of instructional cinema within the colonies was connected to concurrent educational initiatives within Britain. *The Film in*

National Life (1932) advocated the establishment of the BFI, which was formed in 1933. One of the founding aims of the BFI was to vet and promote the circulation of educational films. It sought to set up a national film library, while its publications, *Sight and Sound* and *Monthly Film Bulletin*, provided a forum and repository for reviews and discussion on educational film (for example, with reviews from a geography committee and information about teaching notes). The BFI was also at the heart of moves to develop educational film within the colonies, through its Dominions, India, and Colonies Panel, which had been set up "to consider means for improving the machinery for the distribution and display of educational films in educational and similar institutions within the British Empire."[63]

However, at the closure of the EMB, the Empire Film Library was transferred not to the BFI but to the General Post Office (GPO) and then, in 1935, to the Imperial Institute. In the opening address, Lieutenant Colonel J. Colville, MP, president of the institute's board of governors, claimed that three-quarters of a million schoolchildren had visited the Imperial Institute during the previous year and seen "films of the day to day life of the Empire." He argued that "it is not enough to merely show the Empire under one roof," foregrounding the institute not only as a fixed site within the imperial center but also as a central bureau for the distribution of nontheatrical classroom films.[64] Over the next four years, the number of registered borrowers increased from two thousand to thirty-five hundred, and by 1938 it was claimed, somewhat generously, that "last year the films in the library were shown to audiences estimated altogether at 5,000,000."[65]

The third example, which highlights the prominent place of empire within the institutionalization of educational cinema in Britain, involves Bruce Woolfe, a founding member of the BFI's governing board, and a leading figure on the Dominions, India, and Colonies Panel. On leaving BIF, Woolfe set up GBI, working closely with educationalists to "foster the growing interest in educational films." The company's commitment to imperial subjects was apparent in 1936, when it sent Frank Bundy and two cameramen on a six-month tour of the West Indies as the first part of an intended film series that would show "the whole Empire as it is for the benefit of school children in various parts of the British possessions."[66] Bundy's completed films, which included *Jamaican Harvest* (1938), came with additional teaching notes that provided information about the local industries, included suggested questions, and were approved by the Royal Empire Society. Alistair Weigall, the chairman of council for the society, in discussing its work with GBI, noted the "urgent need" to present the story of the empire to children, so that "as they grow older they have a reasoned foundation for their political faith."[67] The company's output marks a sustained attempt to embed the importance of the empire within the educational curriculum. In a decade when political and ideological divisions intensified to a crushing nadir, this educational cinema held a strong political function, shaping and homogenizing the "political faith" of schoolchildren in an attempt to maintain the empire for a next generation.

GBI worked closely with educationalists, producing other film series from the colonies—most notably a set of four Indian geography shorts in 1937—but they faced familiar challenges in making these films available and useful within the classroom. Darrel Catling, who was at GBI from 1935, noted that the market for these educational pictures was "necessarily limited by the number of schools equipped with projectors (and at the time this was infinitesimal)." Catling suggested that the GBI came into existence to create a market for the projectors, "but at best it would be a long term game, as not many schools could afford projectors." The *Daily Gleaner* noted that attempts by the educational department to introduce the GBI educational films in Jamaica were also restricted by the shortage of places equipped to show film.[68]

This did not deter Woolfe; in 1939 he spoke once more "of his desire to make a series of films of the Empire," although, tellingly, he referred to "a discouraging lack of support from those who should be most interested in such a policy."[69] The proposed series was to be directed by Mary Field and based on a "new teaching method," while thematically the films were focused not on individual colonies or products but on the oceans.[70] Field went on to head Children's Entertainment Films, producing and presenting entertainment films as part of Saturday morning cinema clubs. Her work had a strong imperial focus and, in many respects, bridged the works of these early educational films in trying to both instruct schoolchildren about the peoples and places of the empire and, moreover, create—through these cinema clubs, with their membership cards, group songs and themed activities—productive citizens of the British Empire.

To return once more to the classroom sequence within *One Family*, described within the opening of this chapter, one can see an attempt to both imagine a more inspiring form of geography instruction and create a next generation of imperial citizens. The fortunes of *One Family* might attest to the broader institutional failings to support and prioritize educational film. What does appear in this period, however, is the origins of an educational cinema, and an attempt to think through the form, function, and place of film as a pedagogical tool. Whether imagined in the British classroom, the British cinema, or the African colonies, the maintenance, control, and economic productivity of the empire remained at the center of British film discourse. The history of educational film in Britain remains a massively neglected area of study—subsumed within histories of the celebrated British documentary movement—yet the discussions and early examples of this cinema form an integral part of British documentary history and, what's more, helped determine the place of film in representing, teaching, and shaping British citizens.

Acknowledgments

I would like to thank Karl Magee at the John Grierson Archive, University of Stirling; Julia Bohlmann for very generously sharing some materials with me; and Lee Grieveson for his suggestions on an earlier draft.

Earlier versions of portions of this essay appear in Tom Rice, *Films for the Colonies: Cinema and the Preservation of the British Empire* (Berkeley: University of California Press, 2019). ©2019 University of California Press. Used by permission of the publisher.

Notes

1. *One Family*, and many of the films described within this chapter, are available to view at Colonial Film: Moving Images of the British Empire (www.colonialfilm.org.uk).

2. Scott Anthony, *Public Relations and the Making of Modern Britain: Stephen Tallents and the Birth of a Progressive Media Profession* (Manchester: Manchester University Press, 2012).

3. House of Commons Debates (henceforth HC Deb), 30 March 1950, vol. 473, cc. 572–96.

4. *Sight and Sound* 41, no. 3 (1972): 149; Paul Swann, *The British Documentary Film Movement, 1926–1946* (Cambridge: Cambridge University Press, 1989), 35.

5. *Sight and Sound* 41, no. 3 (1972): 149; John Grierson, "Annual Report on the Activities of the Empire Marketing Board Film Unit, 1931," G2:8:4, John Grierson Archive, Special Collections, University of Stirling.

6. These films played nontheatrically, available for hire through the Empire Film Library. See Tom Rice, "Castles and Fisherfolk," Colonial Film: Moving Images of the British Empire, Arts and Humanities Research Council, accessed June 19, 2019, http://www.colonialfilm.org.uk/node/63.

7. Paul Rotha, *Documentary Film* (London: Faber and Faber, 1936), 18. See also Terry Bolas, *Screen Education: From Film Appreciation to Media Studies* (Bristol: Intellect Books, 2009), 11–36.

8. See Basil Wright, "Filming in Ceylon," *Cinema Quarterly* 2, no. 4 (Summer 1934), 231–32.

9. Article beginning "The cinema can play a wonderful part in stimulating the demand for British goods in the world's markets," File G2:17:10, John Grierson Archive, University of Stirling.

10. John Grierson, "New Worlds for Cinema," 1931, unpublished manuscript, File G2:21, John Grierson Archive, University of Stirling.

11. Ibid.

12. Rachael Low, *The History of British Film, 1929–1939: Documentary and Educational Films of the 1930s* (London: George Allen and Unwin, 1979).

13. National Council of Public Morals, *The Cinema: Its Present Position and Future Possibilities* (London: Williams and Norgate, 1917), 207.

14. "England Wakes Up," *Cinema News and Property Gazette*, March 26, 1913, 2; "The Cinematograph and Education," *The Times*, March 29, 1913, 10.

15. *St. Andrews Citizen*, November 30, 1913, 6. See Eve McVey, "A Pilgrim Town: The Mix of Old and New on North Street," Cinema St. Andrews, accessed June 19, 2019, http://cinemastandrews.org.uk/exhibition/a-pilgrim-town-the-mix-of-old-and-new-on-north-street/. The first show at the cinema presumably did little to alleviate the provost's concerns as it included the comedy *The Amateur Plumber*.

16. "The Use of the Cinematograph as an Aid to Teaching in Elementary Secondary and Technical Schools," ED46/6, The National Archives of the UK (hereafter cited as TNA).

17. "Cinema in Schools," *The Times*, January 26, 1917, 5; "Films of the Dominions," *The Times*, May 26, 1914, 9. When the Victoria League discussed the potential use of the

cinematograph in the colonies and dominions in 1914, it imagined film bringing before the children "scenes which have been described to them by the teachers."

18. Cinema Commission of Enquiry (Cinematographs) 1916–1923, GD281/82/51, National Archives of Scotland.

19. "Education by Kinema Films," *Manchester Guardian*, May 9, 1927, 11.

20. See for example Low, *History of British Film*, 7–12.

21. W. H. George, *The Cinema in School* (London: Sir Isaac Pitman & Sons, 1935), 40, 49–50; ibid., 8.

22. Commission on Educational and Cultural Films, *The Film in National Life* (London: George Allen and Unwin, 1932), 6.

23. "Memorandum on Educational Films," 1929, ED 121/134, TNA.

24. *Film in National Life*, 129–30.

25. ED 11/239, TNA; ED121/34, TNA; *The Times*, August 8, 1924, 10; HC Deb, 2 March 1925, vol. 181, cc. 46–7W. The report noted the use of film in isolated schools from Natal to New Zealand and from Manitoba to Hong Kong.

26. Colonel Sir Arthur R. Holbrook, "British Films," *Royal Society of Arts Journal*, June 3, 1927, 684–709; Anthony, *Public Relations*, 37.

27. See Lee Grieveson, "The Cinema and the (Common)Wealth of Nations," in *Empire and Film*, ed. Lee Grieveson and Colin MacCabe (London: Palgrave Macmillan, 2011), 73–114.

28. Grierson, "New Worlds for Cinema"; John Grierson, "Teach the World What We Have to Sell," 1931, File G2:17:12, John Grierson Archive, University of Stirling.

29. *Imperial Conference, 1926, Appendices to the Summary of Proceedings*, cmd. 2769, 1926, 403.

30. See Tom Rice, "Livingstone," Colonial Film: Moving Images of the British Empire, Arts and Humanities Research Council, accessed June 19, 2019, http://www.colonialfilm.org.uk/node/1844; *Manchester Guardian*, February 27, 1926, 13.

31. Imperial Education Conference, "Memorandum Concerning the Use of the Cinema as an Aid to Increasing a Knowledge of the Empire," 1927, ED121/134, TNA; "The Educational Uses of Cinematograph Films," Colonial Office Conference, May 1927, ED121/134, TNA.

32. *The Times*, January 6, 1926, 10.

33. James Fairgrieve, "The Use of Films in Teaching," *Geography* 17, no. 2 (1932): 129–40; James Fairgrieve, *Geography in School* (London: University of London Press, 1926). Subsequent editions included a chapter entitled "Films in the Classroom." See also James Fairgrieve, "The Educational Film in England," *International Review of Educational Cinematography* 4, no. 3 (1932): 224–26.

34. Priya Jaikumar, "An 'Accurate Imagination': Place, Map and Archive as Spatial Objects of Film History," in *Film and the End of Empire*, ed. Lee Grieveson and Colin McCabe (London: Palgrave Macmillan, 2011), 167–88.

35. *Kinematograph Weekly*, November 19, 1925. I have written more extensively on this series in "Exhibiting Africa: British Instructional Films and the Empire Series (1925–1928)," in Grieveson and MacCabe, *Empire and Film*, 115–33.

36. Marjorie Grant Cook, in collaboration with Frank Fox, *The British Empire Exhibition 1924: Official Guide* (London: Fleetway Press, 1924). See also John Mackenzie, *Propaganda and Empire: The Manipulation of British Public Opinion, 1880–1960* (Manchester: Manchester University Press, 1986), 96–120; Daniel Stephen, *The Empire of Progress: West Africans, Indians and Britons at the British Empire Exhibition, 1924–25* (New York: Palgrave Macmillan, 2013).

37. Stephen, *Empire of Progress*, 93; *West Africa*, April 26, 1924, 393.

38. Edward Davson, "Empire Films," *The Times*, October 10, 1923, 11; "Memorandum by Graham Ball," CO 323/919/11, TNA.

39. In 1931 Grierson described *Secrets of Nature* as "the most solid achievement in the whole course of production in this country" (John Grierson, "New Worlds for Cinema").

40. Mary Field, J. Valentine Durden, and F. Percy Smith, *See How They Grow: Botany through the Camera* (Middlesex, UK: Pelican Books, 1952), viii.

41. "Encouragement in Production of British Films," 1927, CO 323/985/23, TNA.

42. *West Africa*, February 19, 1927, 175.

43. Letter from Crown agents to the undersecretary of state, Colonial Office, July 11, 1927, CO 323/985/23, TNA.

44. Ibid.; *The (Melbourne) Age*, February 27, 1926, 6; *Educational Screen*, June 1926, 321–22.

45. "British Educational Films," *The Times*, May 5, 1927, 14.

46. *Daily Mirror*, August 20, 1927, 9; *Daily Mirror*, October 15, 1927, 9; "The Cinema in Education: Popularizing the Imperial Institute," *The Times*, October 31, 1927, 8.

47. CO 323/985/23, TNA.

48. British Instructional Films Education Department, *Catalogue of Films for Non-Theatrical Exhibition* (London: British Instructional Films, 1928). The BIF catalog contained sixty geography films, the largest section by far, which were divided by country. The catalog entry for *Cotton Growing in Nigeria* emphasized the economic value of the colonies to Britain, as in showing an industrial process up to export, "the interdependence of one nation upon another is realised."

49. "Empire Films for Schools," *The Times*, October 31, 1931, 8.

50. Meeting at Crown agents, 22 January 1931; Imperial Institute to Crown agents, 28 May 1935, Colonial Films—Inclusion of, in, the Empire Series of Films, CSO 15/8/20, Ghana Public Records and Archives Administration Department, Accra (PRAAD). The royalties for *Black Cotton* up to September 30, 1931, were listed as £21 18s 7d.

51. James Burns, *Flickering Shadows: Cinema and Identity in Colonial Zimbabwe* (Athens: Ohio University Research in International Studies, 2002), 27; Low, *History of British Film*, 43; Rosaleen Smyth, "The Development of British Colonial Film Policy, 1927–1939, with Special Reference to East and Central Africa," *Journal of African History* 20, no. 3 (1979): 437–50.

52. Julian Huxley, *African View* (London: Chatto and Windus, 1931), 57–60, 291–96; Julian S. Huxley, "Report on the Use of Films for Educational Purposes in East Africa," 1930, CO323/1252/15.

53. Ibid.; see also Rosaleen Smyth, "Grierson, the British Documentary Movement, and Colonial Cinema in British Colonial Africa," *Film History* 25, no. 4 (2013): 82–113.

54. Huxley, *Africa View*, 158–63.

55. "Educational Film: Encouragement for Use in the Colonies," CO323/1130/12, TNA. See William Sellers, "Mobile Cinema Shows in Africa," *Colonial Cinema* 9, no. 4 (1951): 77–82. Other countries were carrying out similar initiatives. The Trinidad Medical Department was working with the Trinidad Cinema Company to produce films on subjects such as cleanliness, dental care, and mosquitoes.

56. *The Times*, January 26, 1928, 10; *The Times*, January 23, 1929, 14; *The Times*, April 9, 1930, 14.

57. *Times of India*, August 15, 1930, 12.

58. Low, *History of British Film*, 122.

59. See George, *Cinema in School*, 76–77.

60. Smyth, "Development of British Colonial Film Policy, 1927–1939," 437–450; Rob Skinner, "'Natives Are Not Critical of Photographic Quality': Censorship, Education and Films in African Colonies between the Wars," *University of Sussex Journal of Contemporary History* 2 (2001): 1–9; Burns, *Flickering Shadows*, 37–59; British Film Institute: Sub-Committee on Local Cinematography Scheme in Africa, 1934, CO323/1252/16, TNA.

61. Low, *History of British Film*, 44; Glenn Reynolds, "The Bantu Educational Kinema Experiment and the Struggle for Hegemony in British East and Central Africa, 1935–1937," *Historical Journal of Film, Radio and Television* 29, no. 1 (2009): 57–78.

62. George Pearson, *Flashback: The Autobiography of a British Filmmaker* (London: George Allen and Unwin, 1957), 215.

63. Geoffrey Nowell-Smith, "Foundation and Early Years" in *The British Film Institute, the Government and Film Culture, 1933–2000*, ed. Geoffrey Nowell-Smith and Christophe Dupin (Manchester: Manchester University Press, 2012), 14–29; British Film Institute, "Proposal for Colonial Film Unit to Circulate Educational Films within the Empire," CO 323/1356/3, TNA.

64. *Sight and Sound* 4, no. 14 (1935): 52.

65. *Documentary Newsletter*, February 1940, 11; *The Times*, March 16, 1938, 19.

66. "British Educational Films," *Sight and Sound* 3, no. 12 (1934): 131; "Filming the Caribbean for the Classroom," *Daily Gleaner*, August 15, 1936, 23.

67. *The Times*, June 9, 1938, 10.

68. *Today's Cinema*, May 27, 1937, 7; *Cine Technician*, February 1955, 21; *Daily Gleaner*, August 15, 1936, 23.

69. *The Times*, July 15, 1939, 10; *Today's Cinema*, July 15, 1939, 1.

70. One of these films, *Atlantic* (1941), uses animated diagrams to tell a history of exploration and trade. It is available at British Council Film Collector, http://film.britishcouncil.org/atlantic.

Filmography

Atlantic (Mary Field, Gaumont British Instructional, 1940). Available online via British Council: http://film.britishcouncil.org/atlantic.

Black Cotton (British Instructional Films, 1927). Available online via the Colonial Film Website: http://www.colonialfilm.org.uk/node/1322.

Drifters (John Grierson, Empire Marketing Board, 1929).

Jamaican Harvest (Frank Bundy, Gaumont British Instructional, 1938). Available online via the Colonial Film Website: http://www.colonialfilm.org.uk/node/33.

Livingstone (M. A. Wetherell, Hero Films, 1925).

One Family (Walter Creighton, British Instructional Films, 1930). Available online via the Colonial Film Website: http://www.colonialfilm.org.uk/node/40.

Palaver: A Romance of Northern Nigeria (Geoffrey Barkas, British Instructional Films, 1926). Available online via the Colonial Film Website. http://www.colonialfilm.org.uk/node/1342.

A Punjab Village (British Instructional Films, 1925). Available online via YouTube: https://www.youtube.com/watch?v=LREl5rBVCqs.

Song of Ceylon (Basil Wright, GPO Film Unit, 1934). Available online via the Colonial Film Website: http://www.colonialfilm.org.uk/node/486.

A Throw of Dice (Franz Osten, 1929).

Bibliography

Anthony, Scott. *Public Relations and the Making of Modern Britain: Stephen Tallents and the Birth of a Progressive Media Profession*. Manchester: Manchester University Press, 2012.

Bolas, Terry. *Screen Education: From Film Appreciation to Media Studies.* Bristol: Intellect Books, 2009.

"British Educational Films." *Sight and Sound* 3, no. 12 (1934): 131.

British Instructional Films Education Department. *Catalogue of Films for Non-Theatrical Exhibition.* London: British Instructional Films, 1928.

Burns, James. *Flickering Shadows: Cinema and Identity in Colonial Zimbabwe.* Athens: Ohio University Research in International Studies, 2002.

Commission on Educational and Cultural Films. *The Film in National Life.* London: George Allen and Unwin, 1932.

Cook, Marjorie Grant, in collaboration with Frank Fox. *The British Empire Exhibition 1924: Official Guide.* London: Fleetway Press, 1924.

Educational Screen (June 1926): 321–22.

Fairgrieve, James. "The Educational Film in England." *International Review of Educational Cinematography* 4, no. 3 (1932): 224–26.

———. *Geography in School.* London: University of London Press, 1926.

———. "The Use of Films in Teaching." *Geography* 17, no. 2 (1932): 129–40.

Field, Mary, J. Valentine Durden, and F. Percy Smith. *See How They Grow: Botany through the Camera.* Middlesex, UK: Pelican Books, 1952.

George, W. H. *The Cinema in School.* London: Sir Isaac Pitman & Sons, 1935.

Grierson, John. "Annual Report on the Activities of the Empire Marketing Board Film Unit, 1931." G2:8:4, John Grierson Archive, Special Collections, University of Stirling.

Grieveson, Lee. "The Cinema and the (Common)Wealth of Nations." In *Empire and Film*, edited by Lee Grieveson and Colin MacCabe, 73–114. London: Palgrave MacMillan, 2011.

Holbrook, Colonel Sir Arthur R. "British Films." *Royal Society of Arts Journal* (June 3, 1927): 684–709.

Huxley, Julian. *African View.* London: Chatto and Windus, 1931.

Jaikumar, Priya. "An 'Accurate Imagination': Place, Map and Archive as Spatial Objects of Film History." In *Film and the End of Empire*, edited by Lee Grieveson and Colin McCabe, 167–88. London: Palgrave Macmillan, 2011.

Low, Rachael. *The History of British Film, 1929–1939: Documentary and Educational Films of the 1930s.* London: George Allen and Unwin, 1979.

Mackenzie, John. *Propaganda and Empire: The Manipulation of British Public Opinion, 1880–1960.* Manchester: Manchester University Press, 1986.

McVey, Eve. "A Pilgrim Town: The Mix of Old and New on North Street." Cinema St. Andrews. Accessed June 19, 2019. http://cinemastandrews.org.uk/exhibition/a-pilgrim-town-the-mix-of-old-and-new-on-north-street/.

National Council of Public Morals. *The Cinema: Its Present Position and Future Possibilities.* London: Williams and Norgate, 1917.

Nowell-Smith, Geoffrey. "Foundation and Early Years." In *The British Film Institute, the Government and Film Culture, 1933–2000*, edited by Geoffrey Nowell-Smith and Christophe Dupin, 14–29. Manchester: Manchester University Press, 2012.

Pearson, George. *Flashback: The Autobiography of a British Filmmaker.* London: George Allen and Unwin, 1957.

Reynolds, Glenn. "The Bantu Educational Kinema Experiment and the Struggle for Hegemony in British East and Central Africa, 1935–1937." *Historical Journal of Film, Radio and Television* 29, no. 1 (March 2009): 57–78.

Rice, Tom. "Castles and Fisherfolk." http://www.colonialfilm.org.uk/node/63.

———. "Exhibiting Africa: British Instructional Films and the Empire Series (1925–1928)." In *Empire and Film*, edited by Lee Grieveson and Colin MacCabe, 115–33. London: Palgrave Macmillan, 2011.
———. "Livingstone." http://www.colonialfilm.org.uk/node/1844.
Rotha, Paul. *Documentary Film*. London: Faber and Faber, 1936.
Sellers, William. "Mobile Cinema Shows in Africa." *Colonial Cinema* 9, no. 4 (1951): 77–82.
Sight and Sound 4, no. 14 (1935): 52.
Sight and Sound 41, no. 3 (1972): 149.
Skinner, Rob. "'Natives Are Not Critical of Photographic Quality': Censorship, Education and Films in African Colonies between the Wars." *University of Sussex Journal of Contemporary History* 2 (2001): 1–9.
Smyth, Rosaleen. "The Development of British Colonial Film Policy, 1927–1939, with Special Reference to East and Central Africa." *Journal of African History* 20, no. 3 (1979): 437–50.
———. "Grierson, the British Documentary Movement, and Colonial Cinema in British Colonial Africa." *Film History* 25, no. 4 (2013): 82–113.
Stephen, Daniel. *The Empire of Progress: West Africans, Indians, and Britons at the British Empire Exhibition, 1924–25*. New York: Palgrave Macmillan, 2013.
Swann, Paul. *The British Documentary Film Movement, 1926–1946*. Cambridge: Cambridge University Press, 1989.
Windel, Aaron. "The Bantu Educational Kinema Experiment and the Political Economy of Community Development." In *Empire and Film*, edited by Lee Grieveson and Colin McCabe, 207–26. London: Palgrave Macmillan, 2011.
Wright, Basil. "Filming in Ceylon." *Cinema Quarterly* 2, no. 4 (Summer 1934): 231–32.

TOM RICE is Senior Lecturer in Film Studies at the University of St. Andrews. He is the author of *Films for the Colonies: Cinema and the Preservation of the British Empire* (University of California Press, 2019) and *White Robes, Silver Screens: Movies and the Making of the Ku Klux Klan* (Indiana University Press, 2016).

4 Far and Close

The Gemeentelijke Schoolbioscoop in Rotterdam

Floris Paalman

Introduction

Educational cinema embodies a paradox. On the one hand, it has a history that spans over a century. It has continuously been an important social force supported by various agents, due to a persistent belief in its educational potential. On the other hand, it has a discontinuous history that has been characterized by institutional jolts and struggles. Educational cinema has repeatedly needed defending.[1] The problem has not been a lack of institutional recognition, however, but rather one of institutional adaptation. Institutions need to adapt to the conditions of the learners and their world, including what they already know and what makes sense to them. This creates a tension between a general development and adaptation to specific, local conditions. The main question is therefore how educational cinema became appropriated and locally embedded in a way that would make sense to local viewers while also participating in a general development of institutionalization across different places.

While the "paradox of continuity" concerns the long term, the question of how films make sense within the context of a particular environment is most clearly noticeable in what we will call the first stage of the institutionalization of educational film. This chapter will outline different stages of institutionalization but will focus mainly on a second, later stage. During the first stage of institutionalization, when a social-cultural phenomenon emerges, things are still uncertain. During the second stage, when it is about to assume a function within a social-cultural system that will have to support it, it must become embedded in the environment. Therefore modifications must be made in order to connect with existing functions and routines. This is a critical stage in the process of institutionalization. A case study of the Gemeentelijke Schoolbioscoop (GSB) (Municipal School Cinema) in Rotterdam, which existed from 1920 until 1933, will be instructive to understand the dynamics at work. This chapter will analyze the school cinema's early film programs and how they were linked to its emergence as a municipal institution in the larger context of the institutionalization of educational cinema in the Netherlands.

Prominent in the literature on early educational cinema in the Netherlands is the discourse from the 1910s regarding the social dangers of cinema, to which educational cinema was a reaction.[2] The idea of offering an alternative spurred the emergence of the *schoolbioscoop* (school cinema) across the country.[3] Pivotal was the addition of a lecture tailored specifically to address a young audience; the need for a lecture was also emphasized in discussions on sound film later on.[4] The schoolbioscoop was actively promoted by the socialists, but as an institution it was politically neutral, although the Catholics soon established their own school cinemas.[5] However, substantial differences existed between the individual school cinemas.[6] Although ideological issues raised some discussion, the main problem was the lack of films suitable for educational purposes, as several scholars have explained. At the same time, this lack created opportunities for commercial film companies to produce such films, which also contributed to the institutionalization process.[7] Alternatively, the schoolbioscoop in Rotterdam started to produce films itself, showing local conditions, which followed a progressive agenda similar to other governmental initiatives, especially social housing.[8] While the films as such make sense within the local context, another layer of meaning can be revealed by considering the programs of which these films were a part, which also included other films. Unique records have been preserved by the city archive, including detailed program schedules, that make such a focus an option and that allow for research to illuminate how educational cinema became locally appropriated and institutionalized.

This chapter builds on Julian Steward's classical anthropological theory of cultural ecology.[9] He defines "culture change" as a change that concerns a culture at large—and the emergence and institutionalization of educational film could be seen as part of such a change, of the process of modernization. Culture change is driven by *environmental* and *historical factors*. Environmental factors pertain to certain possibilities for making a living, which are explored and appropriated through particular ideas and values. This creates a "culture core": a set of preoccupations, practices, and understandings and a knowledge base that directly relates to a culture's subsistence. In the case of Rotterdam, the city's subsistence is based on the port, and the culture core can be identified accordingly.[10]

Expanding from this core, but still informed by it, there will be a proliferation of practices and associated ideas and values. This development is characterized by increasing complexity through the division of tasks.[11] The way these tasks are related is a matter of "integration," as Steward calls it, which happens at a higher level of organization.[12] For example, the task of a parent teaching a child makes sense in relation to other activities within a household, and so the household constitutes the higher level of organization that integrates the different activities. Teaching at a school is integrated at the neighborhood level, while a phenomenon such as the schoolbioscoop is integrated at the city level. Different practices become interrelated and meaningful within a specific environment, which creates a "cultural ecology." However, the "culture core" that lies at its basis is not fixed. As conditions may change, the culture core may change accordingly.

In addition to environmental factors there are historical factors (or "influences") coming from the outside.[13] Such factors could be ideas, practices, or interests that have developed elsewhere, as part of other histories or a general development, national or international. They may have no intrinsic relationship to the culture core of the place they affect, but the culture core provides the conditions for the application and appropriation of such influences. The introduction of the phenomenon of the schoolbioscoop in Rotterdam could be considered as such an external, historical factor, since it started in The Hague. However, Steward is not entirely clear how environmental and historical factors relate. For The Hague, one could argue that its schoolbioscoop is "environmental," but people there were probably inspired by initiatives elsewhere too. Still higher levels of integration must thus be taken into account to see how different "locales" connect. I will attempt to render the relationship clear by using anthropologist Ulf Hannerz's concept of the city as a "switchboard of culture."[14] A city is not the source of all inventions; rather, it is a place where things come in, where connections are made and transmissions take place. Through the "switchboard," ideas are simultaneously locally appropriated and sent into "the world," feeding a general trend.

Before turning to the GSB in Rotterdam—its emergence, programming, and production—this chapter will sketch out general trends in the Netherlands during the first stage of institutionalization of educational cinema in the 1910s by examining the existing literature and additional archival material regarding early initiatives, including those by the Koloniaal Instituut, a museum and research organization promoting all sorts of knowledge about the Dutch colonies. Considering colonial interests and the position of Rotterdam as a major port city connected to the world, the chapter will pay special attention to the relation with the Dutch East Indies.[15] Most important for this case study are newspaper reports and documents preserved by the city archive of Rotterdam, particularly the program schedules of the schoolbioscoop, which will be analyzed in order to find patterns regarding the subjects of the films.[16] Some of the films have been preserved, and those will be consulted too.[17] In this way the chapter will show how educational cinema not only became locally embedded but also institutionalized as part of an "extended cultural ecology."

Educational Film in the Netherlands

A broad and long-term historical development like the institutionalization of educational cinema is the result of dispersed events and processes across different places. However, at a certain moment, events and processes may combine to serve as a reference for other events and initiatives elsewhere. When such a moment occurs in the case of educational cinema, what are the programming models and exhibition dispositifs, and how are they institutionally appropriated? There has been some discussion about the beginning of educational cinema in the Netherlands, and different dates and places have been mentioned.[18] According to the data available, the first educational screening announced as such took place on June 12 and 13, 1911, at the Friso Bioscoop (theater) in Leeuwarden.[19] That Leeuwarden is in the north of the country lends perspective to the discourse that has thus far mainly focused on the big cities in the west.

Reports in the press make clear that this first screening was an experiment—to find out if film was a suitable medium to serve educational purposes. This screening was supported by the municipality, and the films were shown to schoolchildren and education authorities. The program consisted of thirteen films (see table 4.1). All but one (about the cheese market in Alkmaar) were foreign productions. The experiment was successful according to both organizers and critics, who deemed film a suitable medium indeed, and more screenings followed.[20] A discussion arose among educators about how this successful experiment could be improved on and implemented in educational curricula. Some teachers advocated for tailor-made films that would correspond to the subjects taught in class.[21] However, this idea was refuted by a critic, Johan Pot, who had asked his children which films they liked most and learned that they had most enjoyed precisely those films that were the least didactic in nature (see table 4.1, "rating" column; —most appreciated [indicated by 1] is *Kinderen met vacantie*). He made an argument in favor of the pleasure of watching a film, positing that that was the best way to learn something. The most boring of the films, he reported, were also the most didactic in nature—the films about the Danube and about flourishing flowers.[22]

On October 6, 1912, the Friso Bioscoop had another scoop, presenting the first Dutch educational film made as such.[23] It was about the reclamation of wasteland in the south, which enabled northern children to see what was happening at the opposite end of the country. More screenings would follow.[24]

Besides having screenings at regular theaters, an important force in the development of educational film in the Netherlands was the Koloniaal Instituut in Amsterdam. Due to the importance of the colonies, various attempts were made to inform the Dutch about them.[25] In 1912, the institute commissioned Johann Lamster, captain in the Dutch East Indies army, to make films for its collection.[26] During that year, several newspapers reported on his proceedings.[27] Although these films were not made as educational films to be shown at schools, education was their main purpose.

On April 21, 1915, at the Nederlandsch Lyceum in The Hague, the institute presented a selection of the fifty films made by Lamster. This secondary school had already been at the forefront of using film for educational purposes.[28] The program, which was attended by the queen, government ministers, former ministers, and other representatives and officials, included films about the lives of natives of the colonies and European colonists, rice cultivation, medical aid, crafts, street life, and so on. A journalist reporting on the program recounted that the films were narrated by a lecturer, L. A. Bakhuis, who, once in a while, froze the frame to explain something important.[29] This novel ability to freeze the frame was possible because of an invention by Dr. E. Reinders, teacher at the Nederlandsch Lyceum,

Table 4.1. First educational film program in the Netherlands, June 12, 1911, Friso Bioscoop, Leeuwarden, including the rating by the children of reviewer Pot. The original/foreign release titles and the producers have been traced through among others "The German Early Cinema Database," Universität zu Köln, Institut für Medienkultur und Theater, accessed January 2, 2016, http://www.earlycinema.uni-koeln.de. Uncertainty about identification is marked by "(?)". Numbers in the first column refer to the order in which the films were presented.

Dutch (translated) title as listed	Original (or foreign release) title	Producer	Rating
1. *De vogels in hunne nesten*	*Die Vögel im Nest*	Eclipse (F), 1909	
2. *Langs de oevers der Donau van Passau tot Weenen.*	*Les bords de Danube, de Passau à Vienne*	Pathé, 1910	
3. *Door de Noordelijke IJszee*	*A Dash to the North Pole* (?)	Urban, 1909	5
4. *Afrikaansche vogels en hunne vijanden*	*Les oiseaux d'Afrique et leurs enemis*	Pathé, 1911	
5. *Kinderen met vacantie*	*En vacances*	Pathé, 1906	1
6. *Bloeien der bloemen*	*Comment naissent les fleurs*	Pathé, 1911	
7. *Hoog water te Parijs*	*Paris unter Wasser* (?)	Raleigh & Robert (F), 1910	
8. *De manoeuvres der Duitsche oorlogsvloot*	*Manöver der Hochseeflotte*	Deutsche Mutoskop und Biograph, 1910	
9. *De panter als erfstuk*	*Babylas vient d'hériter d'une panthère*	Comica (I), 1911	2
10. *De kaasmarkt te Alkmaar*	*Een kijkje op de kaasmarkt te Alkmaar*	Welte's Cinematograph, 1911	
11. *Gondelvaart in Venetië*	*Gondelfahrt in Venedig*	Karl Werner (D), 1908	4
12. *Nijlpaardenjacht*	*Hunting the Hippopotamus*	Pathé, 1909	6
13. *Een autotocht van Fontolini*	*A Car Trip by Fontolini* (?)		3

who was serving as the film operator on this occasion. Although mention of freezing the frame was a casual remark in the newspaper report, the device that enabled it would later be emphasized as a crucial feature for teaching purposes. Different people would claim to have invented it when the use of film for educational purposes was discussed during a meeting in—again—Leeuwarden, in 1918, as a part of the efforts to organize the establishment of school cinemas across the country.[30] The invention, which would be adopted in every schoolbioscoop, helped refute the pedagogical criticism alleging that film went too fast for educational purposes.[31] At that meeting, attended by representatives of different municipalities and educational institutions, there was great enthusiasm for organizing screenings not only for elementary schools in large cities but also for children in the countryside and for secondary schools and universities. An important player in the discussion was the

Museum ten bate van het Onderwijs (educational museum) in The Hague, which started educational screenings before 1915.[32] Supported by the socialists, it would become an independent institution in 1918. Directed by David van Staveren, this school cinema served as a model for similar institutions elsewhere in the country.[33]

It is not entirely clear how the initiatives in Amsterdam, The Hague, and Leeuwarden were related. It is clear, however, that contacts between representatives of educational bodies existed at a national level; the initiatives in Amsterdam and The Hague were enabled by national institutions. However, the organization of each schoolbioscoop took place locally, which also suggests that its integration took place at the local level, within the cultural ecology of the city. This might become clear through a closer look at how the schoolbioscoop developed in Rotterdam, which was the first to follow the initiative in The Hague.

Gemeentelijke Schoolbioscoop in Rotterdam

After the socialists won the municipal elections in Rotterdam in 1919, two socialist aldermen were appointed: Arie Heijkoop for social interests, and Arie de Zeeuw for education. As a result, a plan for public housing was developed, and as part of the educational plan, a schoolbioscoop was envisioned.[34] The so-called Gemeentelijke Schoolbioscoop was established as a municipal organization to serve all public elementary schools in the city, while private schools could make use of it too. Its director was Abraham Melis van der Wel, who had been a teacher of drawing. He was assisted by an operator, an employee of the Shipping Institute and Museum, which hosted the schoolbioscoop.[35] The GSB's opening took place on July 12, 1920, with a screening for invited guests. On the program were films about silk cultivation in France and the port of Rotterdam.[36] The latter is no coincidence, given that the schoolbioscoop was hosted by the shipping institute and museum. Moreover, on the program schedules that were sent to the schools, a visit to the museum was also recommended. In this way, the two organizations supported each other. Most importantly, a direct cultural-ecological connection can be observed. With the shipping institute and museum representing the city's "culture core," the new phenomenon of the schoolbioscoop literally developed out of it.

The schoolbioscoop programs, of about seventy-five minutes each, were shown to children from the last two grades of elementary school (ages ten through twelve), and explained by Van der Wel, who presented four shows every school day. In this way, more than 20,000 children visited the schoolbioscoop three times per year until 1926, when the schoolbioscoop got its own facilities and operator; in each of the subsequent years, between 40,000 and 60,000 pupils from two hundred to three hundred schools in Rotterdam visited.[37] In 1928, the GSB opened a second location, in south Rotterdam.[38] Out of a population of about 600,000 citizens, at least 200,000 children visited the GSB—each child six times—over a period of twelve years.

While the school cinema served primarily public schools, private schools made use of it too.[39] Among them were religious schools, although the Catholics had withdrawn from participating by 1922, as they started their own screenings.[40] This bifuraction underscores the institutionalization of educational film in its second stage, as a process of institutional modification, adapting to existing social differences. While this complicated the general development of the schoolbioscoop, it did not threaten the existence of the municipal schoolbioscoop in the short term. Director Van der Wel received many requests from secondary schools hoping to attend screenings, but these were rejected due to the limited capacity of the cinema. Only the evenings allowed for additional screenings. In fact, the schoolbioscoop attracted so much attention that there were often additional screenings for all kinds of organizations and guests, including press, education authorities, state and municipal inspectors, and various other representatives. Teachers had the opportunity to attend lectures before bringing their classes, and many of them made use of this possibility. Schools received the screening schedule and detailed descriptions of the film to be used in class before the visit. Van der Wel said about this: "The influence of such preparations was very noticeable, with many teachers asking pupils to write an essay afterward about a part of the program, sometimes by choice. The results, as far as I know, were very satisfying."[41]

The schoolbioscoop in Rotterdam became successful, but it was nevertheless dissolved in 1933, due to two factors. First, there was an ongoing discussion about the question of whether educational film should be shown in cinemas or in the classroom, which had become more of an option due to less expensive equipment.[42] Second, and most prominent, its end was the result of budget cuts. During the Great Depression, the city of Rotterdam was in serious trouble, to the extent that the municipal finances had become a ward of the national government, and many public services were terminated.

The First Programs

Not unlike the very first educational film screenings in Leeuwarden, the first series of programs in Rotterdam focused on geography and biology and to some extent industry. These had been marked by David van Staveren, director of the schoolbioscoop in The Hague, as the preferred subjects; he had also suggested finishing with a short entertaining film, but this recommendation was not followed in Rotterdam.[43] The first three programs all contained a film that had been shown in the educational film screenings at the Friso theater in Leeuwarden, alongside films that had been shown by the schoolbioscoop in The Hague. The earlier initiatives provided a starting point and a template.

The first show in Rotterdam consisted exclusively of foreign educational films (table 4.2). The second program consisted of foreign films and a Dutch production about bees and the production of honey made by Willy Mullens in 1917, which had been part of the first program of the school cinema in The Hague.[44] This film established a connection with Mullens's company Haghe Film, and more of its films were rented by educational cinemas afterward.[45] The third program contained two

Dutch films. The first, about the reclamation of a wasteland in the province of Brabant, had been part of the film screenings in Leeuwarden.[46] Next, there was a new film, *Trawlervisscherij* (Trawler fishing, Isidor Ochse, 1921), about trawler fishing in the North Sea. It had been an initiative from a fishing school in Vlaardingen, near Rotterdam; and Van der Wel, whose GSB was located in the shipping institute and museum, established the contact with film company Polygoon.[47] Polygoon went to IJmuiden, the port nearest its hometown Haarlem, to make the recordings. While the images were shot elsewhere, the film still established a connection to the environment of the schoolchildren, as it showed precisely the way fish were caught and traded in their city too.

The maritime connections and accompanying knowledge of Rotterdam, ingrained in its culture core, now serving the city's function of a "switchboard of culture," facilitated the production of an educational film. It shows not only how Rotterdam's culture core radiated into educational cinema but also how the city's cultural ecology relates to different places. Moreover, *Trawlervisscherij*, as an educational film, would be distributed across the country, and so the film even contributed to the national development of educational cinema. In fact, the film was the first in a series of four about fishing at sea that, combined, constituted the film *De Nederlandsche Noordzeevisscherij* (Dutch North Sea fishing, Cor Aafjes, 1921–23). For Polygoon, this collaboration was valuable because its productions became directly embedded in a network of educational institutions, which Polygoon actively tried to extend.[48] To that end, in 1921, the company also started a traveling educational film service, which would soon develop into a traveling schoolbioscoop, serving eighty-four districts across the country by 1926.[49]

While the first program of the schoolbioscoop in Rotterdam consisted of only foreign films, the third consisted of only Dutch films. However, the fourth program established more of a balance. It started with a film about rubber production in the Dutch East Indies from the collection of the Koloniaal Instituut.[50] It was followed by films about the life of a butterfly, coil mat production in the Netherlands, and Niagara Falls. Such a mix is also reflected by the films that Van der Wel bought (instead of renting) that year: besides *Trawlervisscherij*, he purchased the film about coil mats from Hollandia (precursor of Polygoon) and three films about the Dutch East Indies from the Koloniaal Instituut.[51] Combining films about subjects both far away and nearby established a pattern, but, surprisingly, only one film from the Koloniaal Instituut would be programmed the next year.

The programming in the second year (see table 4.3) became gradually more attuned to the needs of the schoolchildren, in the sense that the programs included references from the children's own surroundings that helped them to establish connections. The first program of 1922 contained three films. The first film was a long one about the cultivation of tea in the Dutch East Indies, its transport to Rotterdam, and its processing at the (old) factory of Van Nelle in Rotterdam.[52] This film was the onset of Van Nelle's extensive program of film production, and served the purpose of public relations for the city with which it was closely connected. For

Table 4.2. The film programs of the Gemeentelijke Schoolbioscoop Rotterdam in 1921. Uncertainty about identification is marked by "(?)". Numbers refer to the order in which the films were presented.

Program	Dutch title, as mentioned by the GSB	(Translated) English or original title	Producer	Year
1	1. *Deensche porcelein industrie*	*Danish Porcelain Industry*	Nordisk Films Kompagni	1920
	2. *Yellowstone Park*	*Yellowstone National Park*		
	3. *Boschexploitatie Canada*	*Forestry in Canada (Holzfällen in Kanada–?)*	Dentler (?)	1910
	4. *Uitbarsting van een vulkaan*	*Eruption of a Volcano*		
	5. *Water*	*Eau*	Pathé	1912
2	1. *De Alpen*	*The Alps*		
	2. *Het leven der bijen*	*The Life of Bees*	Haghe	1917
	3. *Kleine veld- en waterdieren*	*Small Water and Field Animals*		
	4. *De koekoek*	*The Cuckoo*	Pathé	1912?
3	1. *Ontginning van woesten grond door de Nederlandsche Heidemaatschappij*	*Reclamation of Wasteland by the Nederlandsche Heidemaatschappij*	Pathé	1912
	2. *Trawlervisscherij*	*Trawler Fishing*	Polygoon	1921
4	1. *Rubbercultuur in Indië*	*Rubber Cultivation in the Dutch East Indies*	Pathé	1916
	2. *De wortelrups*	*The Caterpillar*		
	3. *Rolmattenindustrie te Genemuiden*	*Coil Mat Industry of Genemuiden*	Hollandia	1914
	4. *Niagara waterval*	*Les Chutes du Niagara* (?)	American Standard Film?	1913

youths in Rotterdam, all familiar with the brand, the film rendered visible the relationship between the colonies and their hometown. As such, the film concretizes the network of what I propose to call the "extended cultural ecology."

The two other films were rather different. One short film was about the life of the otter, finishing with remarks about its being threatened with extinction due to its being hunted for its pelt. The last film was about an expedition to the North Pole (*De Noordelijke IJszee*). It relates to Dutch history, owing to its images of Spitsbergen—which was discovered by Willem Barentsz in 1596 as he attempted to find a northern sea route to the east—and of the area of Franz Josef

Land, which was discovered by whaler Cornelis Roule in 1675. One could thus understand this program as a combination of the subjects of geography, biology, and history.

In a similar way, the next program, which started in March 1922, included a long film about the production of margarine (*De fabricatie van plantenboter*). It shows the harvest and preparation of coconuts in the Philippines and margarine production at the Jurgens factory in Zwijndrecht, close to Rotterdam. Two observations could be made here, pertaining to different levels of integration. Whereas Van Nelle's film shows the city's connection to the Dutch colonies, the film about Jurgens shows that the city's network was even larger. Both films show the city's "extended cultural ecology," of which the films are parts themselves, for promoting the system of the industrial production of goods. The way Rotterdam, the colonies, and other countries are part of a larger system shows an integration of activities at a global level. At the same time it should be noted that Jurgens's main competitor, Van den Bergh, was located in Rotterdam. In the GSB year-end report, Van der Wel explicitly mentioned that Jurgens had made this film available for free. While Van den Bergh used film to show its international connections, it also showed its local engagement. One can only speculate about the company's publicity strategy, but five years later, in 1927, the two competitors merged into a company that became Unilever. Integration took place at the local level too.

The second program of 1922 also contained a film about Wilton's Shipyard (*Wiltons Groote Droogdok*). As in the film about Jurgens, it made sense to tell the children a story about the connections among the different economic sectors in the city to emphasize that there would be no trade without ships. However, the program also contained a short about Giethoorn, a picturesque Dutch village known for its canals and bridges, and a short about winter sports in Switzerland. These shorts were not yet included in the announcement in March, but they were mentioned in the year-end report. They must have been added to the program at the last minute, possibly for a geographical lesson about land use, how this had shaped the countryside in the Netherlands, and, by comparison, in Switzerland. However, the Giethoorn film had just been released by Mullens's Haghe Film, which also made the Jurgens film. Mullens was the other film company, besides Polygoon, that was involved with educational cinema. Strategic issues, and keeping good contacts with both companies, may have played a role here.

The third program of 1922 contained two films, the one about trawler fishing in the North Sea and one about rice cultivation by the Karo Batak people in Sumatra (*Rijstbouw op droge velden bij de Karo-Bataks*). The program thus combined topics of subsistence in the Far East and close to home. The final program of the year was slightly different. It contained Mullens's film about bees and films made by Van der Wel himself—about the Dutch rescue work at sea and the mounted police in Rotterdam, both of which enabled a direct engagement for pupils, since the setting was recognizable. From then on, almost all programs included films by Van der Wel.

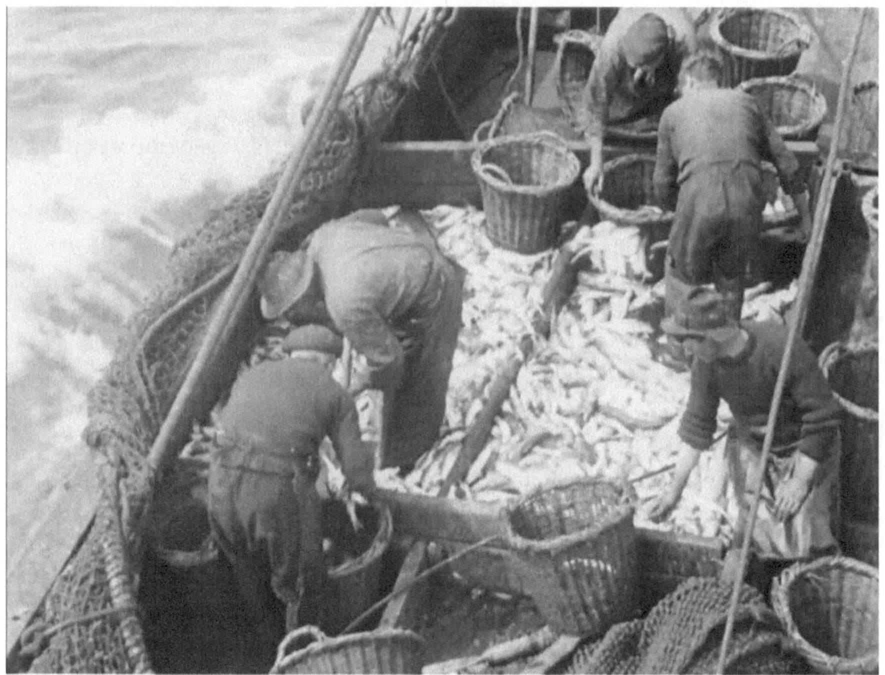

Fig. 4.1. Trawler fishing at the North Sea; film still from *Trawlervisscherij* (I.A. Ochse/Polygoon, 1921), shown by the GSB in the third program of 1922. The film is in the public domain and available online via Eye Film Museum Amsterdam: https://www.eyefilm.nl/collectie/filmgeschiedenis/film/de-rijstbouw-op-droge-velden-bij-de-karo-bataks.

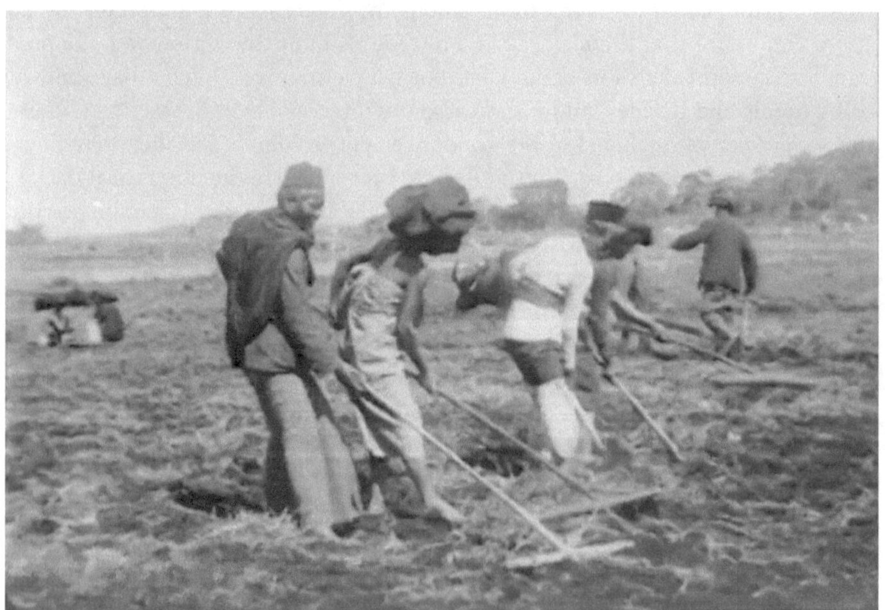

Fig. 4.2. Rice cultivation in Sumatra; film still from *Rijstbouw op de droge velden bij de Karo-Bataks* (J. P. de Bussy/KI, 1917), shown by the GSB in the third program of 1922. The film is in the public domain and available online via Nederlands Instituut voor Beeld en Geluid: http://in.beeldengeluid.nl/collectie/details/expressie/430600/false/true.

Table 4.3. The film programs of the Gemeentelijke Schoolbioscoop Rotterdam in 1922. Numbers refer to the order in which the films were presented.

Program	Dutch title, as mentioned by the GSB	(Translated) English title	Producer	Year
1	1. *De thee van de plantage naar het pakje*	*The Tea from the Plantation to the Packet*	Van Nelle	1919
	2. *De Otter*	*The Otter*	Pathé	1922
	3. *De Noordelijke IJszee*	*The Northern Ice Sea*		1911
2	*De fabricatie van plantenboter*	*The Production of Margarine*	Haghe	1918
	1. Oogst en bereiding der cocosnoten op de Philippijnen	1. Harvest and preparation of coconuts from the Philippines		
	2. Een bezoek aan de plantenboterfabriek van Jurgens	2. A Visit to the Margarine Factory of Jurgens		
	3. *Wiltons Groote Droogdok*	*Wilton's Large Dry Dock*		
	4. *Giethoorn*	*Giethoorn*	Haghe	1922
	5. *Wintersport in Zwitserland*	*Winter Sports in Switzerland*	Bufa	1918
3	1. *Trawlervisscherij*	*Trawler Fishing*	Polygoon	1921
	2. *Rijstbouw op de droge velden bij de Karo-Bataks*	*Rice Cultivation at the Dry Fields of the Karo-Bataks*	De Bussy, Koloniaal Instituut	1917
4	1. *Het leven der bijen*	*The Life of Bees*	Haghe	1917
	2. *Het Nederlandsche reddingswezen*	*The Dutch Rescue Work at Sea*	GSB	1922
	3. *Het ruiterfeest der bereden-politie te Rotterdam*	*Celebration of the Mounted Police in Rotterdam*	GSB	1922

Film Production

While the phenomenon of the schoolbioscoop was common in the Netherlands in the 1920s, the one in Rotterdam was exceptional because it not only showed but also produced and distributed films. The fact that a schoolbioscoop started to produce films shows the institutional modification of a general trend which propelled its success as well. This section will demonstrate how two different forces—one informed by local interest, the other by a national development—were at work in the films produced, which requirements had to be met to be part of the schoolbioscoop program, and how the films and the programs reflected these different interests and orientations. According to Steward, cultural change and evolution is fueled by the culture core that is to be found in subsistence, which in the case of Rotterdam encompasses the practices and values connected to the port and the crucial role it plays in the city's economy. Therefore, this section will consider whether the local production of educational films, which helped children learn about their world, radiated indeed from this culture core while both rendering it visible and reflecting on it. This manifestation of the culture core would imply that educational film practice's being at the forefront of educational innovation, both in production and programming, was inherently related to subsistence—hence principle economic possibilities and interests—causing an ontological intertwining of content and conditions. Historical factors external to the culture core, however, might still be connected to this ontology. Educational film productions, both national and local, should therefore be considered in their competing functions at different levels of integration, local and national or even international.

After Van der Wel had established the contact between the fishing school and Polygoon for the production of *De Nederlandsche Noordzeevisscherij* (dir. Cor Aafjes, 1921–23),[53] he collaborated on another production, a feature-length educational film about the Rhine River (*De Rijn van Lobith tot aan zee* [The Rhine from Lobith till the sea], Isidor Ochse, 1922), which was heralded as the first Dutch educational film made on a grand scale. Following the course of the mighty river through the Netherlands, the film shows how important the Rhine has been for the development and economy of the country, in both its agricultural and trade centers. The film reaches its apotheosis as it approaches Rotterdam, with its gigantic industry and harbors where the river meets the sea. It is no coincidence that these two major educational films by Polygoon, showing how the Dutch depend on the sea and the river, deal with the subsistence on which Rotterdam's development has been based. It suggests that the city's culture core directed not only the practice of the GSB but also its content.

Considering the fact that Van der Wel had screened some of the same films as those shown at Friso in Leeuwarden, a similarity between *De Rijn van Lobith tot aan zee* and *Les Bords de Danube, de Passau à Vienne*, which was also shown at Friso (table 4.1), should be noted. However, it was exactly this didactical film about the Danube that had been singled out for criticism by Johan Pot in the *Leeuwarder Courant*. Why, then, would precisely this film serve as a model? Was its didacticism irresistible to the educators, or was it because of its premise? Was the film not fully appreciated in the Netherlands because it lacked the aspect of recognition? The latter would then call for a "remake" to make sense in a different context, in particular to children from Rotterdam, since the city's existence depended on the Rhine.

In the Rhine film, which premiered in Rotterdam on December 14, 1922, Van der Wel plays the guide traveling down the river by boat, from the border with Germany to the sea. His presence in the film can be understood as a "social cue,"[54] particularly for the children in Rotterdam who also listened to his explication *in the theater* while watching the film. At the premiere, Polygoon's director stressed the importance of the collaboration between his company and educational institutions for creating films tailor-made for education.[55] Considering the Rhine film's national distribution, and Polygoon's ambitions, one can question this rhetoric once the film would be shown outside Rotterdam and without a lecture by Van der Wel; like the Danube film, its impact would be different according to the context in which it was shown. It was precisely the ontological density of the Rhine film that was effective. Polygoon continued to produce educational films, but without Van der Wel. Instead, the municipality permitted Van der Wel to buy a camera, and, in February 1922, he made his own recordings (*In en om Rotterdam*). He was satisfied with the results, and to the alderman he enthusiastically wrote that the lens of the camera was of "superior quality." That year he spent his vacations making films.[56] Due to weather conditions, however, he was not able to finish them all; he planned to do so over the course of 1923.

The GSB's programming for the year of 1923 was based on the Rhine film, which contained six acts; each program presented two of them, combined with shorts made by Van der Wel (about sailing, birds, and dunes, respectively). In the year-end report, Van der Wel remarked that at each screening, the pupils were well prepared and that they had remembered a lot from the previous lesson, three months earlier.[57]

The Rhine film was critically acclaimed in the national press, and as a result, Van der Wel was approached by H. van den Bussche, of a secondary school in Yogyakarta (Java), who had read about the film in the *Nieuwe Rotterdamsche Courant* (*NRC*), which was also distributed overseas.[58] Van den Bussche was a teacher of drawing, just like Van der Wel had been before (although they probably didn't know that about each other).[59] He made educational films about the East Indies himself, and he proposed that they collaborate and exchange films. Van der Wel was interested, but in order to send prints of his films, he needed equipment. Being able to make film prints to facilitate the production and distribution of his films had already been his idea. Immediately after receiving the letter, he wrote a request for funding to the alderman of education, in which he used the letter by Van den Bussche as a supporting argument.[60] The colonies thus played a discursive role in the micropolitics of the schoolbioscoop and became part of Rotterdam's "extended cultural ecology."

There was more interest from the East. Among the guests visiting the GSB in 1923, was H. Stuy, head of a secondary school in Medan, Sumatra, who was interested in showing educational films at his school, and he kept in touch afterward. This interest was fueled by the discussion about need for educational films that was also taking place in the Dutch East Indies. The *Sumatra Post* (on January 26, 1924), for example, published a lyrical report about the latest films by Van der Wel, which all dealt with Dutch nature and rural life.[61] The article cites these films rhetorically to stress the importance of educational cinema, concluding that there had been plans for educational films and school cinemas in the Dutch East Indies before, which had been canceled due to budget cuts. Therefore, the journalist calls his readers in patria, especially investors profiting from the Dutch East Indies investment funds, to open up their hearts and wallets in order to provide the Dutch East Indies with modern pedagogical means. Although the Dutch government was reluctant to provide financial resources, the Dutch East Indies Society of Teachers made concrete plans itself to begin using educational films.[62] In the fall of 1923, the society bought a projector and started a campaign, with demonstrations across Java, to promote its usefulness for education. Besides its "usual advantages," society members emphasized the possibility of showing pupils the "pure Dutch environment to which the subject material transports the children all the time." In this way, Van der Wel once more played a discursive role in the "extended cultural ecology," now seen from the perspective of the Dutch East Indies.

Such attention strengthened Van der Wel's position. The alderman started to discuss his request for equipment. After more than a year, an agreement was reached, and the alderman sent a letter back to Van der Wel, saying that he was allowed to buy films from Van den Bussche, and that his request for a production facility was supported. The alderman of public works started to look for a suitable location and eventually found the attic of a kindergarten.[63] While preparations for the new accommodation were made, Van der Wel became ill. For two months, there were no programs and Van der Wel could not discuss the plans, but the facility was finally opened on August 23, 1925. It was called the Gemeentelijke Filmfabriek (municipal film factory), although Van der Wel and his assistant were the only staff members.

On the occasion of its opening, an *NRC* journalist visited the film factory and reported that the school cinemas of Arnhem and The Hague had already made use of films made by Van der Wel, that this had resulted in some revenues, and that the factory enabled further distribution.[64] Moreover, the factory offered new possibilities: for example, to make microscopic recordings for films on biological subjects and for the municipality to produce relatively cheap films about its own departments to be shown at the school cinema and for promotional activities. In this way, Van der Wel collaborated with engineer D. Boomsma of the port authorities on the film *Haven van Rotterdam* (Port of Rotterdam, A.M. van der Wel, 1925).[65] According to the journalist, this film was distributed around the world, in countries as different as Finland, El Salvador, and the Dutch East Indies. The establishment of the "factory" thus exemplifies the double movement, simultaneously inward and outward, contributing to both local engagement and the general development of educational cinema.

Hauschild's Film of Java

While the GSB was in touch with Van den Bussche in Java, another film had appeared, whose exhibition could potentially affect the functioning of the schoolbioscoop. In 1924, the now forgotten German anthropologist and specialist of anatomy, Dr. Wolfgang Hauschild from Berlin, in collaboration with the Universum

Film-Aktien Gesellschaft, led an anthropological film expedition to Java. On his way back, on a ship between Batavia and Colombo, he died from a tropical disease.[66] His film recordings, however, were edited, and in 1925 the resulting film was released. A promotional booklet, *Het Paradijs Java*, with twelve stills and a text by the Javanese journalist and poet Noto Soeroto was issued.[67] The film itself seems to be lost today.

On September 23, 1925, the premiere for *Het Paradijs Java* took place at the Rembrandt Theatre in Amsterdam. The film was introduced by Javanese dances, and a reading by Dr. Willem Royaards of the story of "Saidjah and Adinda" (from the well-known socially critical book *Max Havelaar* by Multatuli published in 1860).[68] The film, with live music, including Krontjong songs, presents the town and villages on the island, its peoples and their way of life, and its rice fields and tropical flora. The film was well received by the audience, and a critic called the film "exceptionally successful, so that it commands our respect": "The Java film is a triumph of cinematography; it comes to help us Dutch to get to know our beautiful, rich possessions over there in the Far East. We still know so little about our Colonies, and we have no idea what splendid country or great natural beauty is to be found there. The film gives us an image of Java today and in the past. Natural tableaux, scenes from folk life; the enterprise of great cultivations, remainders of early architecture, dances at the royal courts, et cetera, et cetera."[69]

The critic finishes by saying that it is an excellent chance for everyone interested in the cultural value of film, who might have previously criticized the cinema business, to support the theaters showing such films, and that this film "will undoubtedly be received with great enthusiasm by the educational authorities." In Rotterdam it was shown by Luxor, whose director, Carel van Zwanenburg, inspired by the critic, contacted the alderman of education to offer schoolchildren screenings at a reduced price.[70]

However, the alderman had objections to children going to the movies; moreover, he made clear that the municipality had its own educational cinema that enabled children to see such films. Van Zwanenburg then proposed to the alderman that a committee could view the film, with the possibility of buying it for a reasonable price to be shown at the GSB if the committee approved. As a result, Van der Wel himself came to see the film, and he wrote a report to the alderman about the film on November 10, 1925:

> The film contains very nice natural scenes, which, unfortunately, pass the eye too quickly. I subsequently noticed that too little attention was paid to the cultures, so that the picture is not sufficient. A superficial image is provided of batik, while copper works and fishing are completely missing. It extensively shows how a serum against snake bites is acquired from the blood of a horse. Measuring the prisoners at Noesa Kambangan [prison island] could reasonably have been left out. The film shows nice images of the Borobudur [temple] and the Bromo crater. Classical dances are performed. However characteristic and often impressive these movements may be, for children such images have little value. To me the

film appears to be a rather inconsistent whole, and therefore it is not suitable as an acquisition for the GSB.[71]

Van der Wel's criticism diverges from the enthusiastic review quoted above, which Van Zwanenburg sent to the alderman. However, there also had been critical reviews in the press. The *NRC* called the film "a series of successful snapshots"—nice images, but too short to create a profound understanding of the country and the topics, so that eventually only vague impressions would be left.[72] According to the *NRC*, the film would be most suitable for an audience outside the Netherlands, since many of the images were already familiar to the Dutch, who knew them from photographs and earlier films. This must have affected Van der Wel's impression. His criticism regarding the inconsistency of the film corresponds with the main argument of the *NRC* critic. However, this critic was writing about an audience of adults. For children, the film could have been a valuable introduction at the least. Moreover, Van der Wel did not always show films in their full length, so he could have selected useful acts. Besides that, children visiting the GSB always prepared for their visit in class, for which the GSB provided documentation to prevent "vague impressions." Finally, instead of providing musical accompaniment, Van der Wel narrated the films, which would have compensated for possible omissions.

There seems to have been another agenda in play here. Van der Wel had used the proposal by Van den Bussche as an argument for establishing his own "film factory." Its production was threatened by allowing the market to gain a strong position. Moreover, allowing commercial cinema to gain a foothold in the educational film market could threaten the institution of the schoolbioscoop itself. Rather than supporting diversification of the cinema business to provide opportunities for educational films and socially and culturally responsible programs, the municipal schoolbioscoop needed to be secured first of all. Once educational cinema had become institutionalized, it became subject to market forces.

In response to Van den Bussche's proposal to exchange films, Van der Wel finally obtained two of Van den Bussche's films, *Indische Visscherij* (Dutch East Indian fishing, 1923) and *Djokja's Koperwerk* (Yogya copper work, 1923), and it is likely that Van der Wel eventually made prints of his own films and sent them in return.[73] It is not clear, however, what happened next, as Van den Bussche changed positions, to become a teacher in Surabaya (Java), so conditions changed.[74] But a new request came from the East, this time from Stuy, the head of a secondary school from Medan in Sumatra, who had paid a visit to the GSB in 1923. In his letter, written on Christmas Eve 1926, he explained that his school planned to buy projection equipment, but that they lacked films to show. He therefore asked to borrow films from the GSB. Moreover, he proposed to distribute them throughout the Dutch East Indies. He politely asked for a quick answer, as correspondence overseas could be delayed quite easily. The letter arrived in Rotterdam about three weeks later. Van der Wel immediately wrote to the municipal administration, explaining that there were too many complications to lend the films, but he proposed, understandably, that new film prints be offered at cost, or used prints at half price. The alderman immediately wrote back to Stuy to communicate this proposal.[75] The outcome of this correspondence is difficult to trace, but it seems quite possible that Stuy would indeed have ordered the distribution of copies.[76]

Local Inclination

The films made by Van der Wel, responding to local needs and often showing local conditions, would gradually become more prominent in the programs of the GSB. This "local inclination," as the development could be called, is especially noticeable in the programs of 1924 and 1925, which mainly consisted of his films. The year 1926 was a bit different. Its first program consisted of Mullens's film about the life of bees; the second and third consisted of parts of a film about Switzerland. Although Van der Wel had the film factory at his disposal, he simply had had no time to make films: after many discussions, investigations and preparations, the GSB had opened its own theater.[77] With a capacity of 160 seats, it was the right size for Van der Wel to give his lectures. At the opening, attended by many representatives, Van der Wel showed his film *De Haven van Rotterdam*, even though it was not included in the regular school programs.

The fourth and last program of 1926 consisted of three films, according to the template that Van der Wel had followed before. The first film was *Haringvisscherij* (Herring Fishing, Polygoon, 1923), a part of *De Nederlandsche Noordzeevisscherij* that he had helped to realize. It was about herring fishing in the North Sea including the preparations of the ships and the fishing equipment before leaving, as well as processing and selling the fish after the ships returned, all in a traditional fashion. Next was *Indische Visscherij*, about fishing in the Dutch East Indies and, hence, directly connected to the first film. The third was Van der Wel's own film, *Lichtschip Maas*, about a lightship at sea, twelve miles away from the Nieuwe Waterweg (port of Rotterdam), which helped ships to navigate.

Although there are no records left for the last years of the schoolbioscoop, the "local inclination" is suggested by the steadily increasing number of films made by Van der Wel, with a total of more than forty films by 1933, each of a duration between ten minutes and one hour. In the records that are left, a trend is distinguishable that also points to the predominance of the films by Van der Wel himself. Some of them are more didactic and instructive than informational, like previously, and some were only shown to specific classes or to a limited number of children from secondary schools, since Van der Wel collaborated more often with municipal departments.

Van der Wel's film about the port had opened the way for collaborations with other municipal departments, including films about the municipal waterworks, the phenomenon of electricity, and traffic. The traffic film was made in collaboration with B. G. Meyer, head of the municipal traffic department. It became the first Dutch educational film about traffic safety (*Veilig Verkeer*, Safe traffic, 1930), showing children how to behave in traffic while demonstrating the principles of modern urban planning that were being much discussed in Rotterdam. This film attracted substantial attention; it received press coverage, even in the Dutch East Indies, before it was released.[78] The film continued a trend of children acting in the films, a format that Van der Wel had had previously applied and that he also would apply in the future.[79] Van der Wel let the children demonstrate both what not to do in traffic and how to navigate traffic successfully. It enabled children to identify with the film while providing concrete examples and instructions about how to act. As a result, Van der Wel was ahead of the curve for finding an effective way to use film for education.[80]

Over the course of the next few years there was increasing collaboration between the schoolbioscoop and the municipal inspector of education, H. Kreiken. He began to select films offered to the GSB, assisted with productions, and wrote explanatory texts.[81] Besides showing films set in Rotterdam, the company maintained its already established focus on films concerning biology, geography, history, or some aspect of industry. Whereas the geography films chosen had previously encompassed the world, they gradually became focused on provinces and regions in the Netherlands, often specifically on Rotterdam. The programs became more attuned to the experiential world and needs of the youth of Rotterdam, even as many of the films were being distributed across the country.

Conclusion

The point of departure of this study has been the paradox of continuity, in which cinema's educational strength is accompanied by institutional weakness. It stresses the complex connection between content and its purposes and institutional organization. It has investigated how educational cinema became appropriated and locally embedded to make sense to local viewers while participating in a general development of its own institutionalization and ability to connect different places. By reviewing the film programs of the school cinema in Rotterdam and the conditions under which they were developed, this chapter has elaborated on theories of cultural ecology by adopting a local and an intralocal perspective. This parallax view of locality sees local appropriation operating both within and contributing to a broader development, a development that happens through and between localities instead of through an organization at, for example, the national level.

In the first stage of institutionalization in the 1910s, the historical development was necessarily "environmental" too; it was not a top-down implementation of a particular policy but an exploration of possibilities that took place in particular environments. Important were the events in Leeuwarden, the initiatives by the Koloniaal Instituut in Amsterdam, and the establishment of the schoolbioscoop in The Hague. After these first institutional attempts, there was a second stage of institutionalization, the one that has been the focus of this study. It encompassed the establishment of school cinemas that were locally organized and adapted to local circumstances. Supported by the socialists, Rotterdam's was the first to follow The Hague's. During its existence, between 1920 and 1933, the schoolbioscoop in Rotterdam showed films to more than 200,000 children—out of a total population of about 600,000 inhabitants—and each of them saw six different programs. During its first years, the schoolbioscoop focused on biology and geography, mainly films that had been shown in Leeuwarden and The Hague. Soon, films from far away were shown with local films, reflecting the extended cultural ecology.

In accordance with the concept of the culture core, which in Rotterdam refers to the port, the GSB was hosted by the shipping institute and museum. GSB director Abraham Melis van der Wel established contact with production company Polygoon, and a film about fishing in the North Sea was made, followed by a film about the Rhine. The sea and the river and the port that results from them were major environmental factors in the life of Rotterdam, so this programming reflected and participated in Rotterdam's cultural ecology, in which the culture core enables the adaptation of historical factors.

The local effort to improve on the schoolbioscoop in Rotterdam gained strength when it started to produce its own educational films. After a successful film about the port was created, various films were made in collaboration with municipal departments. This too matches the model of the culture core radiating into different realms. However, such films did not only make sense locally. In accordance with the idea of the city as a "switchboard of culture," several films by the GSB were distributed elsewhere, including in the Dutch East Indies. The GSB in Rotterdam thus simultaneously appropriated and propelled a general trend. It exemplifies the parallax view of local and intralocal development, in which films that are programmed differently, become integrated into the cultural ecology differently and make sense at different levels.

In short, within the emerging general development of educational cinema in the Netherlands, with programs consisting mainly of foreign films, the Gemeentelijke Schoolbioscoop in Rotterdam gradually developed its own course by showing combinations of films from far away and close to home, which enabled recognition and identification on the part of the viewer. Identifying with images from home provided access to what was happening elsewhere, and those from far away—including the colonies—helped put one's own world into perspective. This chapter has termed the development of local productions gaining prominence and embedding films from elsewhere "local inclination." Local appropriation and differentiation continued but eventually may have obstructed a broader perspective, as fewer films from elsewhere were shown in the end.

A difficulty in this case study has been determining whether actions, events, or the development of the schoolbioscoop are incidental, idiosyncratic, or part of a structural pattern. The efforts of the GSB in Rotterdam took place at a relatively large scale and over a significant duration and reached almost all children from the city over a period of thirteen years. Moreover, Van der Wel (and his assistant) worked in close collaboration with the alderman of education and the inspector of education. They were in touch with about three hundred schools and many representatives who attended the schoolbioscoop. Moreover, journalists frequently wrote about the GSB. This institution was therefore truly engaged in public service, representing the public interest and, to a reasonable extent, was publicly controlled. Another consideration is how the course of institutionalization spurred by environmental factors, may have been affected in a nonlinear way by various historical factors, such as the introduction of new pedagogical and learning theories. This would require additional research.[82] Ideally, this new research would also encompass a study of the lectures and the preparatory lessons at school or related excursions, since they embody the local connection. However, no notes from the lectures have been preserved, which is a particularly difficult historiographical issue to overcome. Even more challenging would be finding documentation of the lectures' reception.[83]

To conclude, this case study suggests that local appropriation of general phenomena is inherent to the cultural ecology that is informed by the culture core. Moreover, local inclination might be a feature of the second stage of the institutionalization of educational cinema. This, however, complicates the parallax view—how a city is a "switchboard of culture" and how local development fuels general development. A better understanding could be gained by researching how the films made in Rotterdam were integrated into programming elsewhere or even how the GSB and its films served as references in a discourse (e.g., on educational film in the Dutch East Indies). This would highlight the problems of the extended cultural ecology and its exchanges (or intentions) and how the same films made sense in different environments and at different levels of integration. Alternatively, comparative studies could be conducted, but to do so may raise another methodological problem, as the GSB in Rotterdam was not only a relatively large and successful institution but also unique for the fact that it produced films itself.

One remaining question is whether the logic of the culture core affects the educational film *practice* (its dispositif, organization, and programming) in the same way as its *films*. Put differently, did the GSB itself emanate *from* the culture core or was film inherently *part of* the culture core itself, regulating the city's collective cognition, including the transmission of values to children? This question remains unanswered, especially with respect to the closing of the GSB in 1933. If the GSB was indeed important in terms of collective cognition, what happened afterward? Did the local inclination toward educational film programming eventually result in fragmentation due to equipment now being available to schools? Was organization at a higher level lacking? The educational films by the GSB might have been among the more effective learning instruments, but the dissolution of the GSB underscores once more the paradox of continuity. At a larger scale (but inherently connected to the cultural ecology), one could understand the crisis of the 1930s as a "historical factor" that would be appropriated in the long run. This study has laid bare some of the dynamics of appropriating and supporting the use of educational films that may also have been at work when educational cinema made its comeback after World War II.[84] In the post-war period the institutionalization of educational cinema took shape nationally. At the same time, schools were enabled to organize their own film screenings, and educational cinema became more attuned to the specific needs of its audiences to learn about their worlds, though still subject to the "paradox of continuity."

Notes

1. This is exemplified by the exhibition "Een eeuw onderwijsfilms" (Nationaal Onderwijsmuseum, Rotterdam, 2009–2010). See Ed van Berkel. "Onderwijsfilm: Domein van pioniers en doordouwers." *Lessen, Periodiek van het Onderwijsmuseum* 4, no. 1 (2009): 13–18.
2. Ansje Beusekom, "Film als kunst: Reacties op een nieuw medium in Nederland, 1895–1940" (PhD diss., Vrije Universiteit Amsterdam, 1998), 104–6.
3. Bert Hogenkamp, "De Schoolbioscoop," *Skrien* 140 (1985): 42–45.
4. Edith van der Heijde, "Dissonante geluiden en sprekende filmvertoningen" (MA thesis, Universiteit Utrecht, 2011), 25.
5. Samuel Zwaan, "Achter de schermen van de schoolbioscoop: De politiek-ideologische inbedding van de Nederlandse schoolbioscopen" (BA thesis, Universiteit Utrecht, 2013).
6. Saffira Buré, "Filmvoorstellingen in schoolbioscopen: Een historisch onderzoek naar de schoolbioscopen in Nederland van circa 1912 tot en met 1925" (BA thesis, Universiteit Utrecht, 2013), 8.
7. Bert Hogenkamp, *De Nederlandse documentaire film 1920–1940* (Amsterdam: St. Film en Wetenschap/Van Gennep, 1988); Jitze de Haan, *Polygoon spant de kroon: De geschiedenis van filmfabriek Polygoon, 1919–1945* (Amsterdam: Cramwinckel, 1995).
8. This was part of my larger research project, *Cinematic Rotterdam: The Times and Tides of a Modern City* (Rotterdam: 010 Publishers, 2011).
9. Julian Steward, *Theory of Culture Change: The Methodology of Multilinear Evolution* (Urbana: University of Illinois Press, 1976; originally published 1955).
10. Paalman, *Cinematic Rotterdam*, 40.
11. Steward, *Theory of Culture Change*, 40.
12. Ibid., 49–50.
13. Ibid., 41–42.
14. Ulf Hannerz, *Transnational Connections: Culture, People, Places* (London: Routledge, 1996), 149.
15. This is enabled by Delpher's newspaper database, which contains extensive collections of digitized historical newspapers from the Netherlands and its former colonies. "Delpher," Koninklijke Bibliotheek, 2010, www.delpher.nl.
16. Among the records preserved by the Rotterdam city archive are policy notes, letters, and annual reports pertaining to the GSB. While some of the program schedules from the last few years are missing, this chapter will analyze closely those of the early years.
17. Most of the films made by the GSB Rotterdam have been preserved by Stadsarchief Rotterdam, sometimes accompanied by the original briefings for teachers, and EYE (Amsterdam); the latter also has custody of several of the other films mentioned in this study.
18. Beusekom, "Film als kunst," 68; Buré, "Filmvoorstellingen in schoolbioscopen," 6.
19. Johan Pot, "Bioscoopvertoningen voor kinderen," *Leeuwarder Courant*, June 24, 1911, 7.
20. For example, on November 8, 1912, also at the Friso Bioscoop in Leeuwarden (Buré, "Filmvoorstellingen in schoolbioscopen," 6).

21. B. bij de Leij, D. Schaaf, and A. C. van der Nube, "De bioscoop in dienst van 't onderwijs," *Leeuwarder Courant*, June 14, 1911, 7. Cf. "De bioscoop en de school," *Nieuwsblad van het Noorden*, June 14, 1911, 2.

22. Pot, "Bioscoopvertoningen voor kinderen," 7.

23. "Kinematografisch onderwijs," *Het Nieuws van de dag*, October 5, 1912. Friso showed *Ontginning van woesten grond door de Nederlandsche Heidemaatschappij* (Reclamation of Wasteland by the Dutch Heath Company, Pathé, 1912).

24. It was shown again (on November 8, 1912, and later), together with five foreign shorts, about water, a cuckoo, a diver, monkeys, and the tale of Little Red Riding Hood. Note that only the screening of November 8, 1912, is mentioned by EYE. See "Filmfabriek Hollandia en de Schoolfilm," EYE, Film Institute Netherlands, accessed September 15, 2017, https://www.eyefilm.nl/collectie/filmgeschiedenis/artikel/filmfabriek-hollandia-en-de-schoolfilm.

25. "De Koloniale Landbouwtentoonstelling te Deventer," *Sumatra Post*, August 5, 1912, 1; "Aan het verslag over 1917 van het Comité voor Indische lezingen en leergangen is het volgende ontleend," *NRC*, June 4, 1918, evening edition.

26. Janneke van Dijk, Jaap de Jong, and Nico de Klerk, *J. C. Lamster: Een vroege filmer in Nederlands-Indië* (Amsterdam: KIT Publishers, 2010).

27. "Gemengd indisch nieuws: Indische films," *Bataviaasch Nieuwsblad*, May 22, 1912; "De Koloniale Landbouwtentoonstelling te Deventer," *Sumatra Post*, August 5, 1912, 1.

28. "Films over Oost-Indië," *NRC*, April 22, 1915, morning edition, 2. The reference to the Nederlandsch Lyceum is also found in E. Bonebakker, "Onderwijs: Het bewegende lichtbeeld voor het onderwijs," *NRC*, April 9, 1918, evening edition.

29. "Films over Oost-Indië." *NRC*, April 22, 1915, morning edition, 2.

30. Bonebakker, "Onderwijs." Bonebakker attributes this invention to the son of Van Cappelle, the director of the educational museum in The Hague, who applied it. Hogenkamp mentions that Van Cappelle Jr. patented his invention, but that others claimed this invention as well, for example Jules Stoop, which resulted in a dispute (Hogenkamp, *De Nederlandse documentaire film, 1920–1940*, 152n45).

31. For the adoption of the invention, see Buré, "Filmvoorstellingen in schoolbioscopen," 9. For the criticism, see Beusekom, "Film als kunst," 106–8. Beusekom pays attention to the discourse about educational cinema, in which this view was expressed by different critics, among others J. W. van Smeelen and Philipp Kohnstamm, still in the early 1920s.

32. The screenings were organized by Herman van Cappelle, director of the Museum ten bate van het Onderwijs in The Hague (today's Museon); Hogenkamp, *De Nederlandse documentaire film, 1920–1940*, 12. Hogenkamp explains that plans for a school cinema in The Hague were already presented in 1913. The existence of a school cinema as part of the museum, prior to 1916, is mentioned in "Schoolbioscoop," *Algemeen Handelsblad*, October 5, 1916, evening edition (third leaf), 10.

33. Bonebakker, "Onderwijs"; Beusekom, "Film als kunst," 105; Hogenkamp, "De Schoolbioscoop"; Bert Hogenkamp, "Staveren, David van," BWSA 6 (1995): 208–11.

34. The latter was accepted by the city council on February 14, 1920. Floris Paalman, "Een kwestie van betrokkenheid: De films van de Gemeentelijke Schoolbioscoop Rotterdam, 1920–1933," *Lessen, Periodiek van het Onderwijsmuseum* 4, no. 1 (2009): 19–22.

35. During the first years it was the operator of the Scheepvaartkundig Instituut en Museum; when the Schoolbioscoop got its own accommodation, in 1926, it got its own operator, Arnold Willem Methöfer (born August 31, 1891), a trained mechanic. Abraham van der Wel, document to the alderman about the application for the job of operator, March 2, 1926, Collection: Stadsarchief Rotterdam; archive, depository number, folder (year) and record number: Archief

van de Gemeentesecretarie Rotterdam afd. Onderwijs: 351.01/110 (1926), Schoolbioscoop, volgnr. 1a.

36. "Schoolbioscoop te Rotterdam," *De Telegraaf*, February 17, 1920, evening edition (second leaf), 6; "Schoolbioscoop te Rotterdam," *Algemeen Handelsblad*, July 12, 1920, evening edition (third leaf), 10.

37. These figures are mentioned in the annual reports of the schoolbioscoop, provided by Van der Wel. In 1925, for example, a total number of 23,731 pupils attended the screenings. After moving to its own location, with a double capacity, the figures increased accordingly. In 1927, for example, a total number of 47,800 pupils attended the screenings. Abraham van der Wel, "Verslag Gemeentelijke Schoolbioscoop in Rotterdam over het jaar 1927," March 30, 1928, Stadsarchief Rotterdam: Archief van de Gemeentesecretarie Rotterdam afd. Onderwijs: 351.01/64 (1928), Schoolbioscoop, volgnr. 2.

38. On Afrikaanderplein, as decided by the city council on July 19, 1928; "Gemeenteraad," *Rotterdamsch Nieuwsblad*, July 16, 1928, 13.

39. Cf. Zwaan, "Achter de schermen van de schoolbioscoop," 22.

40. Abraham van der Wel, letter to the alderman, July 3, 1922, Stadsarchief Rotterdam: Archief van de Gemeentesecretarie Rotterdam afd. Onderwijs: 351.01/1061–76 (1922), Schoolbioscoop, volgnr. 1.7.

41. Abraham van der Wel (translated by the author), "Verslag van den Gem. Schoolbioscoop, dienstjr. 1921," June 19, 1922, Stadsarchief Rotterdam: Archief van de Gemeentesecretarie Rotterdam afd. Onderwijs: 351.01/1061–76 (1922), Schoolbioscoop, volgnr. 8.

42. Cf. Buré, "Filmvoorstellingen in schoolbioscopen," 11.

43. Ibid., 16.

44. Hogenkamp, *De Nederlandse documentaire film, 1920–1940*, 16.

45. Abraham van der Wel, letter to the alderman, June 6, 1922, 1061–76 (1922), Schoolbioscoop, volgnr. 6. Van der Wel reports on his visit to Haghe Film. He established contacts with other distributors too, such as HAP en BenS Film Company that had similarly collaborated with the school cinema in The Hague; cf. Beusekom, "Film als kunst," 105.

46. "Kinematografisch onderwijs," *Het Nieuws van de dag*, October 5, 1912.

47. Hogenkamp, *De Nederlandse documentaire film, 1920–1940*, 30. It is unclear when this contact took place. Hogenkamp dates the film 1923; however, part 1 (*Trawlervisscherij*) was already released in 1921.

48. De Haan, *Polygoon spant de kroon: De geschiedenis van filmfabriek Polygoon, 1919–1945*, 29.

49. Ibid., 47.

50. "Rubbercultuur in Indië (AV0142)," Regionaal Historisch Centrum, Groninger Archieven, accessed June 29, 2019, www.groningerarchieven.nl. "Maatschappij van Nijverheid," *Algemeen Handelsblad*, March 31, 1916, morning edition (second leaf)

51. These three films are: *Rijstbouw bij de Karo-Bataks*, *Rijstbouw op West Java*, *Sapirennen*. Van der Wel, "Verslag van den Gem. Schoolbioscoop, dienstjr. 1921."

52. It was made in 1919 by Dick van der Leeuw, the youngest brother of the family who owned Van Nelle. Matthijs Dicke, *Hoe komt wie vliegt ooit tot bedaren: M.A.G. van der Leeuw, ondernemer in het interbellum* (Rotterdam: De Hef Publishers, 2007), 43.

53. Ibid, 30.

54. Tamara van Gog, "Voorbeeldig Leren" (Oration, Erasmus Universiteit Rotterdam, 2013), 10. She gives the example of the film *Rolmattenindustrie te Genemenuiden* (1914), for its explicit way of articulating important aspects (i.e., a hand indicating Genemuiden on the map), as an efficient educational strategy.

55. Brand Ochse in "De Rijn van Lobith tot aan zee," *Voorwaarts*, December 16, 1922, third leaf.

56. The films he then made were *Langs duin en strand*, *Het Nederlandsch Reddingswezen*, *Het ruiterfeest der bereden politie*, *Het vlas*, *De suikerbiet*, *Een touwslagerij*. Abraham van der Wel, "Verslag Gemeentelijke Schoolbioscoop te Rotterdam over het jaar 1922," January 23, 1923, 1079–82 (1923), Schoolbioscoop, volgnr. 5.

57. Abraham van der Wel, "Verslag Gemeentelijke Schoolbioscoop te Rotterdam over het jaar 1923," February 26, 1924, 1093–114 (1924), Schoolbioscoop, volgnr. 3.

58. H. K. J. van den Bussche, letter to mayor and aldermen, January 21, 1923, 1079–82 (1923), Schoolbioscoop, volgnr. 10.

59. Van den Bussche came from The Hague; he received grades in teaching drawing in The Hague in 1914 and in Rotterdam in 1915: "Schoolnieuws," *Het Nieuws van de Dag*, July 25, 1914, fifth leaf, 18; "Onderwijs," *De Tijd*, August 24, 1915, 6.

60. Abraham van der Wel, letter to the alderman, February 26, 1923, 1079–82 (1923), Schoolbioscoop, volgnr. 10.

61. *Veluwe*, *Melk en Melkproducten*, and *Langs duin en strand*, in "Onderwijsfilms," *Sumatra Post*, January 1, 1924, 13.

62. "Het kind en de bioscoop," *De Indische Courant*, April 30, 1924, 5. Dutch East Indies Society of Teachers = *Nederlandsch-Indisch Onderwijzers Genootschap*.

63. Alderman of education, letter to Van der Wel, May 6, 1924, 1093–114 (1924), Schoolbioscoop, volgnr. 2c; M. de Roode (Directeur Gemeentewerken) et al., "Policy note concerning film production facility," 1924, 1093–114 (1924), Schoolbioscoop. The council accepted the proposal on September 2, 1924. The production facility (6 x 12m) was located in the Tielestraat 12.

64. "Rotterdam: Gemeentelijke Filmfabriek," *NRC*, August 23, 1925, morning edition C, 1.

65. At that time, another film was in production too, about the municipal waterworks (*Watervoorziening van een grote stad*).

66. "Twee Duitsche Anthropologen †," *Algemeen Handelsblad*, October 22, 1924, 7.

67. Reden Mas Noto Soeroto, *Het Paradijs Java: Souvenir aan de Java-film* (Amsterdam: Electrische Drukkerij 't Kasteel van Aemstel, 1925).

68. "Java-Film," *Het Vaderland*, September 24, 1925, 6.

69. Translated by the author: "Een belangwekkende film: Een triomf der cinematografie—Java op de film" (signed by T. L.), unknown source, sent as an appendix to a letter by Carel van Zwanenburg, to mayor and aldermen, September 11, 1925, 111–15 (1925), Schoolbioscoop, volgnr. 8.

70. Letter by Carel van Zwanenburg, to mayor and aldermen, September 11, 1925, 111–15 (1925), Schoolbioscoop, volgnr. 8.

71. Translated by the author, Abraham van der Wel, letter to the alderman, November 10, 1925, 111–15 (1925), Schoolbioscoop, volgnr. 8a.

72. "Java op de film," *NRC*, October 15, 1925, 1; "De film van Java," *NRC*, November 5, 1925, 1. See also "De Java Film," *Het Vaderland*, October 15, 1925, 2; "Filmkritiek: Java-Film," *Het Vaderland*, October 17, 1925, 6.

73. As the exchange had already been approved, further activities did not need additional approval, and hence there are no records left to clarify this.

74. "Officieele mutaties," *De Indische Courant*, October 20, 1925, East Java edition, 3. Van den Bussche had become a teacher at the HBS, and later on at the Technische School in Bandung: "Technische School," *De Indische Courant*, March 17, 1927, second leaf, 7.

75. H. Stuy, letter to mayor and alderman, December 24, 1926, 1138–64 (1927), Schoolbioscoop, volgnr. 1; Abraham van der Wel, letter to Mr. Pera, administrator of education, January 20, 1927, 1138–64, Schoolbioscoop, volgnr. 1a; alderman of education, letter to Stuy, February 1, 1927 (written on January 27), 1138–64 (1927), Schoolbioscoop, volgnr. 1b.

76. Only letters to and from the municipal administration have been preserved, and only those letters that needed an official agreement. Eventual requests for prints were directly addressed to and handled by Van der Wel. In his annual reports, only the total revenues from rentals and acquisitions are mentioned.

77. The address being Goudschestraat 26; opening on April 8, 1926.

78. "De film van het verkeer in Rotterdam," *Bataviaasch Nieuwsblad*, June 7, 1930, 22.

79. For example, in *Langs duin en strand*, and *Boomplantdag*, and later on in, for example, *School voor vrouwenarbeid.*

80. For such affective ways, see Van Gog, "Voorbeeldig Leren," 8.

81. Examples are the booklets accompanying the feature length films about birds and the province of Zeeland: H. G. C. Kreiken, *Toelichting Onderwijsfilm "Vogelleven in en om Rotterdam"* (Rotterdam: Gemeente Drukkerij, 1930) and *Toelichting Onderwijsfilm "Zeeland"* (Rotterdam: Gemeente Drukkerij, 1932).

82. Beusekom, in her treatment regarding the discourse on the (school) cinema, pays attention to several pedagogical ideas and visions ("Film als kunst," 107). This might be a starting point for such research.

83. An option could be to consider the frequent presentation of different provinces in the GSB films, which is relevant regarding the "extended cultural ecology." Children who watched these films were probably inspired, once they had become parents in the 1950s, to visit the regions as holiday destinations, a phenomenon that could be traced.

84. This could be connected to research done on later periods: Eef Masson, *Watch and Learn: Rhetorical Devices in Classroom Films after 1940* (Amsterdam: Amsterdam University Press, 2012).

Bibliography

Berkel, Ed van. "Onderwijsfilm: Domein van pioniers en doordouwers." *Lessen, Periodiek van het Onderwijsmuseum* 4, no. 1 (2009): 13–18.

Beusekom, Ansje. "Film als kunst: Reacties op een nieuw medium in Nederland, 1895–1940." PhD diss., Vrije Universiteit Amsterdam, 1998.

Buré, Saffira. "Filmvoorstellingen in schoolbioscopen: Een historisch onderzioek naar de schoolbioscopen in Nederland van circa 1912 tot en met 1925." BA thesis, Universiteit Utrecht (Theater, Film en Televisiewetenschap), 2013.

Dicke, Matthijs. *Hoe komt wie vliegt ooit tot bedaren: M.A.G. van der Leeuw, ondernemer in het interbellum*. Rotterdam: De Hef Publishers, 2007.

Dijk, Janneke van, Jaap de Jong, and Nico de Klerk. *J. C. Lamster: Een vroege filmer in Nederlands-Indie*. Amsterdam: KIT Publishers, 2010.

"Filmfabriek Hollandia en de Schoolfilm." Eye, Film Institute Netherlands. Accessed June 29, 2019. https://www.eyefilm.nl/collectie/filmgeschiedenis/artikel/filmfabriek-hollandia-en-de-schoolfilm.

Gog, Tamara van. "Voorbeeldig Leren." Oration, Erasmus University Rotterdam, 2013. Accessed June 29, 2019. https://repub.eur.nl/pub/51024/.

Haan, Jitze de. *Polygoon spant de kroon: De geschiedenis van filmfabriek Polygoon, 1919–1945*. Amsterdam: Cramwinckel, 1995.

Hannerz, Ulf. *Transnational Connections: Culture, People, Places.* London: Routledge, 1996.

Heijde, Edith van der. "Dissonante geluiden en sprekende filmvertoningen." MA thesis, Universiteit Utrecht, 2011.

Hogenkamp, Bert. *De Nederlandse documentaire film 1920–1940*. Amsterdam: St. Film en Wetenschap / Van Gennep, 1988.
———. "De Schoolbioscoop." *Skrien* 140 (1985): 42–45.
———. "Staveren, David van." BWSA 6 (1995): 208–11.
Kreiken, H. G. C. *Toelichting Onderwijsfilm "Vogelleven in en om Rotterdam."* Rotterdam: Gemeente Drukkerij, 1930.
———. *Toelichting Onderwijsfilm "Zeeland."* Rotterdam: Gemeente Drukkerij, 1932.
Masson, Eef. *Watch and Learn: Rhetorical Devices in Classroom Films after 1940*. Amsterdam: Amsterdam University Press, 2012.
Noto Soeroto, Reden Mas. *Het Paradijs Java: Souvenir aan de Java-film*. Amsterdam: Electrische Drukkerij 't Kasteel van Aemstel, 1925.
Paalman, Floris. *Cinematic Rotterdam: The Times and Tides of a Modern City*. Rotterdam: 010 Publishers.
———. "Een kwestie van betrokkenheid: De films van de Gemeentelijke Schoolbioscoop in Rotterdam, 1920–1933." *Lessen, Periodiek van het Onderwijsmuseum* 4, no. 1 (2009): 19–22.
Steward, Julian. *Theory of Culture Change: The Methodology of Multilinear Evolution*. Urbana: University of Illinois Press, 1976; originally published 1955.
Zwaan, Samuel. "Achter de schermen van de schoolbioscoop: De politiek-ideologische inbedding van de Nederlandse schoolbioscopen." BA thesis, Universiteit Utrecht, 2011.

FLORIS PAALMAN is Senior Lecturer of Media Studies at the University of Amsterdam and a staff member of the Master's Programs in Film Studies and in the Preservation and Presentation of the Moving Image. He is author of *Cinematic Rotterdam: The Times and Tides of a Modern City*.

5 Partners in Screen Education

Philanthropic Organizations and the Film Industry

Marina Dahlquist

During the 1910s and 1920s, the momentous and far-reaching social work done by philanthropic organizations can be illustrated by the health slogans used by the Rockefeller Foundation in Lee County, North Carolina, where exclamations such as "Ill health retards social progress," "Better milk, better babies, better citizens," "Every home a healthy home," and "Join in the fight against tuberculosis" were used in campaigns intertwining health and societal concerns.[1] Social uplift and improved health were pivotal aspects of the Progressive project peaking in the United States during the first decades of the twentieth century. The objective for numerous nonprofit organizations emerging at this time was to raise awareness about modern society and its social and sanitary shortcomings—or "evils" in contemporary vernacular—among the working class, immigrants, and children. Philanthropic foundations led the way in resolving health-related issues that affected large parts of the world, promoting and expanding the development of Western medicine and public health globally.[2] By way of clean-up campaigns, both literally and metaphorically, human bodies as well as their daily lives were regulated to promise happier, healthier, and financially more lucrative citizens, more in accordance with the idea of a modern lifestyle. Preeminent nonprofit organizations such as the Rockefeller Foundation, Russell Sage Foundation, and American Red Cross were all pioneers when it came to social and medical activism together with, for example, the YMCA, women's clubs, and health departments. This didactic was particularly prominent in the United States during the Progressive era, when such commitments recurrently provided a rationale for the film medium as its usefulness for civic education contrasted to what by many reformers thought to be undesirable representations offering problematic and immoral entertainment.

A topic vividly debated among reformers was which campaign method would most effectively catch the attention of the target audience. In exhibition and campaign work, visual material was often used to more vividly illustrate the object lesson. However, early on, moving pictures were singled out as the perhaps most useful visual tool, owing to the medium's putative pedagogical might, its instructive quality, and its appeal to a mass audience.[3] This chapter will serve as an illustration of the change of medium for campaign methods during the early twentieth century, graduating from visual aids such as posters, photographs, and illustrated pamphlets toward a regular use of moving pictures designed to appeal to a mass audience.

Moving Pictures and Burgeoning Progressive Efforts

From 1910 on, moving pictures were regularly harnessed as a pedagogical tool for health campaigns in a multitude of contexts across the United States. These educational films were generally the result of collective efforts by networks of politicians, reformers, and others united by similar commitments to social and health issues. The film production itself was often a close collaboration between organizations such as municipal, medical, and philanthropic institutions and the film industry. Rarely commercially released, the films had a circulation and exhibition practice outside the traditional movie theater; screenings took place in classrooms, community houses, or outdoors. There were of course exceptions. In the 1910s, the Edison Company regularly produced social-interest films in cooperation with various welfare organizations and institutions, such as the American Red Cross and the National Association for the Study and Prevention of Tuberculosis. In spite of the fact that these films were part of the agencies' campaign work, the majority of them were commercially released. Just to mention a few examples from 1912: *Hope, a Red Cross Seal Story* was made in collaboration with the Society for the Study and Prevention of Tuberculosis. The social reform title *The Public and Private Care of Infants*, was produced in cooperation with the Department of Child-Helping at the Russell Sage Foundation, and *Charlie's Reform* was likewise produced by Edison but devised by Clarence A. Perry, who was in charge of the Division of Recreation at the Russell Sage Foundation.[4]

Uplift campaigns, usually initiated in a top-down fashion, zoomed in on sanitation, working conditions, childcare, education, and recreation. But the direction of institutionalization is not evident; it was often enabled by already existing institutional infrastructure and built up by a multitude of local initiatives and practices. Striving for better health conditions brought together a cross-section of civic movements and organizations, which in turn inspired the implementation of governmental infrastructures at federal, state, or municipal levels. Within this context, the primary focus of this chapter is on one organization and one production within the larger context of educational cinema, a context and industry that was in fact examined and mapped by the Rockefeller Foundation in preparation for its own planned film project. This film, which would be named *Unhooking the Hookworm*, was in planning for years as a part of a larger health campaign regarding the hookworm disease, a plague widespread not only in the southern United States but also countries across the tropical and equatorial belt. Victims affected by the worm became slow and apathetic and were thus often considered lazy; hence, the popular moniker for the condition was "the laziness disease." The production process for this film and its context will be used as a vector directing us into the wider circle of educational cinema in its earliest phase, prior to its having a well-defined organization or system.

In 1913, the staff of the newly founded International Health Commission (what in 1916 would become the International Health Board and in 1927 the International Health Division) at the Rockefeller Foundation devised a script for an educational film about the dangers of hookworms. The filming began that very summer. Even though the production was headed by Ernest C. Meyers, director of Surveys and Exhibits, it became a collective effort, with a production phase of almost seven years. The idea to make a film for the commission's hookworm campaign seems to have emerged after Wickliffe Rose—the first director of the International Health Commission—along with health officers from the foundation, returned from a meeting with representatives of Great Britain's Colonial Office in London. The meeting was presumably about setting up a British colonial branch of the International Health Commission, enabling the use of Britain's infrastructure for the commission's international campaign work.[5]

From the very start, the purpose of the film was to serve as a visual tool for health campaigns in rural communities in the American South. Already in 1909, John D. Rockefeller had founded the Rockefeller Sanitary Commission for the Eradication of Hookworm Disease, donating $1 million. A five-year campaign was to create awareness and perhaps even eradicate hookworms in the southern United States, where more than two million people were estimated to be suffering from them.[6] The campaign work to educate the public was massive. From the start, a slew of visual media was used in accordance with the exhibition practices of the time: leaflets, charts, billboards, and the like. Initially, district inspectors went from house to house to explain to households the cause and effect of the worm. Whether or not the field agents reached a considerable number of people in this way, actually demonstrating what they were talking about was considered crucial. To mention one example, Dr. J. S. Lock, one of three sanitary district inspectors in the mountain area of Kentucky, expressed how he anxiously awaited his stereopticon outfit, as the great mass of people at the mining camps knew nothing on the subject and "would pay very little attention to me often thinking that I was trying some trick on them."[7] Photographs, but above all lantern slides, were sought to considerably improve the pedagogical prerequisites, making the lectures much more effective and enabling the field agents to accomplish as much on one occasion as was now possible only after many visits.

The correspondence between field agents and the main office during the first years of the 1910s discloses a strong belief in visual aids as a major tool for capturing the targeted audience's attention and informing them about the potentially devastating outcomes of hookworms. Leaflets and charts were circulated from the commission headquarters in Washington, DC, and state directors exchanged photographs, mainly of hookworm victims. Gradually, these gave way to local figures

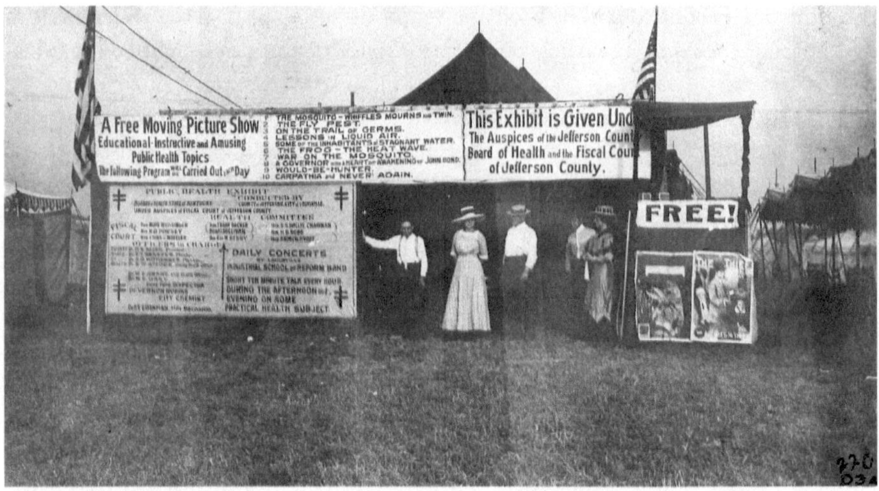

Fig. 5.1. Moving-picture show at the Kentucky State Fair in 1913 arranged by the Jefferson County Board of Health and the Fiscal Court of Jefferson County. Image used with the permission of the Rockefeller Archive Center.

and photographs, as they supposedly created more urgency and gave the presentation a personal touch.

But even if visual aids in general were considered vital to the success of a campaign, the impact of the moving picture medium escaped no one. At the Kentucky State Fair in 1913, where the Sanitary Commission's hookworm campaign was presented, there was not yet a hookworm film, but there was nevertheless a free moving-picture show in many ways typical of this time arranged by the Jefferson County Board of Health as part of the statewide campaign for better health conditions. The guiding principle was that people who would not readily attend a public health lecture would throng to see a film.[8]

The film titles on public health topics at the Kentucky show were accordingly educational, instructive with amusing diversions mixed in—a form that was common practice for educational films shown at moving picture theaters. With the mixed-bill principle, titles within the same program thus ranged from popular-science films and educational dramas to comedies. Almost all of them were produced in 1912. The films on offer in this specific example related to tuberculosis, with Selig's film *On the Trail of the Germs* and Edison's *The Awakening of John Bond* (1911), including mosquitoes via Edison's *The War on the Mosquito*, flies with Urban's *The Fly Pest*, and germs with Pathé's *Some Inhabitants of Stagnant Water.* These types of educational or instruction films were, together with the exhibition practices they were presented within, decisive for the upcoming film productions by the Rockefeller Foundation, and this specific example was documented by the foundation as part of its demonstration and exhibition work.

Mapping Health Work and Educational Methods

With the preparatory work for the International Health Commission's exhibit at the Panama-Pacific International Exposition, promoting its hookworm work in the American South, and with Ernest C. Meyers in charge,[9] exhibition techniques and practices were exchanged with other national associations concerned with social uplift and health issues.[10] A circular with a description of films available, suggested titles for rural and urban audiences, and technical information was distributed widely among boards of health, educational authorities, and private organizations interested in health. This circular not only promoted educational work through the medium of film but also documented the illustrated matter used along with the film titles.[11] Agencies involved in health work were also put forward in Rockefeller Foundation's own survey concerning methods and results in teaching the public in matters of health from 1915.[12]

The process of documenting educational methods was as thorough as the production and use of visual media. The agencies most relevant to this text are found under the heading "Private agencies whose primary functions are of a health nature." The Rockefeller Foundation and the Russell Sage Foundation are explicitly mentioned together, along with the General Education Board, Harris Trust Fund, and the American Museum of Natural History.

In the report, the activities in the field were grouped into three categories. The first two where performed by governmental agencies: "1. Education of the public (exclusive of that part of the public in attendance at educational institutions) by governmental agencies. 2. Education of those who are in attendance at educational institutions by governmental agencies." The third group, however, pointed toward education by private agencies: "Education of the public (including both that in and out of school) by private agencies."[13] Both governmental and private agencies were to be studied in order to explore their breadth of experience and the campaign strategies they used. The survey suggested that methods used by agencies in all states should be collected, along with samples of the educational materials they used—printed and visual—to inspire all those engaged in the work.

Health education was growing rapidly during the 1910s and 1920s, as was the use of moving pictures in this context, which is evident in publications such as *Motion Pictures for Community Needs* published in 1922 (written by Gladys and Henry Bollman), Ernest A. Dench's *Motion Picture Education* of 1917, and Don Carlos Ellis and Laura Thornborough's *Motion Pictures in Education* from 1923.[14] Health campaign work, with moving pictures as a main visual tool, was becoming more and more common on local as well as national levels, in manifestations such as the 1910 anti-fly campaign conducted at the initiative of Edward Hatch—the chair of the Fly-Fighting Committee of the American Civic Association—using the Urban 1909 film *The Fly Pest*. The film was one of the titles advertised at the Kentucky State Fair described above. Municipal agencies such as the New York Health Department provided another early example of extensive, even local, initiatives for having arranged

TENTATIVE PLAN OF SURVEY OF METHODS AND RESULTS IN TEACHING THE PUBLIC IN MATTERS OF HEALTH.

by Ernst C. Meyer

General Considerations.

1. The agencies concerned in this work may be classified as:

1) Governmental agencies
2) Private agencies

2. Governmental agencies may be classified as:

1) Federal agencies--U. S. Public Health Service, Bureau of Education, health activities of other departments.
2) State agencies--state boards of health, educational authorities, state universities, other divisions of state government doing health work
3) County agencies
4) Town agencies
5) Municipal agencies

3. Private agencies may be classified as:

1) Agencies whose primary functions are of a health nature.
2) Agencies whose primary functions are industrial.

4. Private agencies whose primary functions are of a health nature include such as the following:

1) The American Medical Association
2) The American Public Health Association
3) The American Academy of Medicine
4) Other private organizations numbering no less than 24, with numerous minor agencies not included.
5) Special foundations such as Rockefeller Foundation, Russell Sage Foundation, General Education Board, Harris Trust Fund, American Museum of Natural History, etc. etc.

5. Private organizations whose primary function is industrial include the following:

1) Life insurance companies
2) International Harvester Company
3) National Cash Register Company
4) United States Steel Corporation
5) Numerous other industrial establishments carrying on extensive health campaigns.

Fig. 5.2. A 1915 survey of methods and results in teaching the public in matters of health by Rockefeller Foundation. Image used with the permission of the Rockefeller Archive Center.

free outdoor health-related moving pictures that gathered large audiences in the city parks from the early 1910s on.[15]

The extent of organizations' involvement in the production process of educational moving pictures differed greatly between productions and agencies. Private philanthropic organizations, municipal and burgeoning governmental agencies engaged in different levels of involvement. It is often difficult to discern from remaining documentation, including the films' credits, how the collaborations were actually undertaken: On whose initiative was it produced? Who wrote the script? For what purpose was a film made, et cetera? For example, the New York Health Department produced numerous lantern slides in order to promote their campaigns in moving picture theaters—one of their most important venues for advertisement—but when it comes to moving pictures, they seem to have exclusively screened titles that were already on the market, such as *The Long vs. the Short Haul* (screened in 1916, at minimum). According to the credits on this promotional print, it was produced by National Motion Pictures in collaboration with the Indiana State Board of Health, the American Association for the Study and Prevention of Infant Mortality, and the Children's Aid Association in Indianapolis.[16] In Chicago, on the other hand, the health department was evidently collaborating more directly with production companies. *Summer Babies*, for example, was produced by Essanay in 1911 and depicts the Chicago Health Department's work to safeguard babies during the hot summer months. As was usual for educational films at this time, *Summer Babies* was released as a split reel with the Essanay comedy *Gossiping Yapville.*

Collaborations between agencies and production companies took different forms. The Russell Sage Foundation's involvement in the moving picture industry was multifarious. This is especially true for the Department of Child Hygiene and the Division of Recreation, where Lee F. Hanmer and Clarence A. Perry were in charge. The efforts of the Division of Recreation were focused on playgrounds both in terms of entertainment—which included social aspects and sports—and physical training. Moving pictures were used across the board: as means of recreation, for education, and to raise the opinion of the foundation's campaigns. In addition, the Russell Sage Foundation conducted several studies that examined the medium. The best-known and often quoted study is *The Exploitation of Pleasure. A Study of Commercial Recreations in New York City*, published by the Department of Child Hygiene in 1911. In this work, Michael M. Davis mapped commercial recreations in New York City, including a survey of moving-picture shows.

In his survey, Davis formulates a kind of blueprint for the Russell Sage Foundation's use of the medium of film in its campaigns, in line with the progressive discourse's fundamental trust in authorities. In this case, experts from different fields would collaborate during the production process to achieve the best possible impact on the viewer. According to Davis: "We ought to have motion-pictures specially produced as instruments of education—physical, intellectual, spiritual—for the adult as well as the child, and for America's child, the immigrant of many races. The film can handle topics historical, dramatic, scientific, local and international.

People of human insight and democratic instinct must sketch the subjects for these motion-pictures and turn them over to the technicians to work out."[17] At least four films were produced or coproduced under the auspices of the Russell Sage Foundation during 1911 and 1912. All were shot in the Edison Studios, all were one-reelers, and all were distributed by the General Film Company. Similarly to other collaborative Edison films, the educational object lesson was inserted into a dramatic framework. For example, the film *A Sane Fourth of July*—used in the work of making Independence Day celebration safer by exchanging fireworks for substitutes such as concerts, stereopticon lectures, and moving pictures—was advertised and marketed by the Russell Sage Foundation themselves. The foundation sent out press material, suggested marketing strategies for the film, and included suggestions for safe celebrations.[18] Hanmer even composed an article that could be sent to newspapers in the area targeted for the campaign. In 1920, Russell Sage's Department of Survey and Exhibit Series continued their educational work by publishing a book about exhibition tours and traveling motion pictures shows, offering valuable insights about health campaigning in rural areas.[19]

Preproduction Process of *Unhooking the Hookworm*

At the Rockefeller Foundation, the planning of a tailor-made moving picture started on a wide front in 1913. The production process was largely an internal affair, and extensive material including memorandums, correspondence, and manuscripts as well as reports from the planning, production, and distribution stages of the film have survived at the Rockefeller Archive Center, making them an extraordinarily rich example to study. Ernst C. Meyer, director of Surveys and Exhibits at the International Health Commission, was the key player behind the production as well as the survey of the film industry.

Even though the film production would take considerable time to complete, scenes were filmed early in the process. In 1914, moving images were taken from several southern states—Georgia, Virginia, North Carolina—depicting the health work done.[20] In April 1914, an eventful film expedition was carried out in a Kentucky mountain region, during which both film crew and horses almost drowned in flooded rivers and quicksand. Some scenes were arranged by Dr. A. T. McCormack, from the State Board of Health of Kentucky. He was also the chief sanitary inspector in charge of the Rockefeller Sanitary Commission's local hookworm campaign and was greatly involved in the moving picture.[21] Similarly to sets of photographs used in campaign work, the topics selected portrayed the progressing campaign in the American South: the tearing down of old privies and erection of new ones and the microscopists at work. There were pictures of improved conditions as well as areas where nothing had been done to make the contrast between the sanitary and unsanitary conditions evident.

The making of a scenario was a lengthy and collaborative process within the foundation, and the suggestions of possible scenes and images were multiple. State and field directors across the American South, as well as those located internationally, were asked to comment on the draft scenarios. One of the suggestions that would never be realized was to create an educational cartoon—humorous presentations were thought to be more instructive than purely scientific ones. In this case, the main character would be an upright worm-boy wearing a hat and carrying a cane—no other clothing to distract the attention—who, together with other self-important worms, was traveling on the back of a bird and had the goal of conquering the world. The scenario was prepared by Phyllis A. Russell in order to target illiterate victims of the hookworm disease.[22] As Dr. S. T. Darling argues, by promoting Russell's scenario, even if the idea with animated hookworms might be grotesque, the form "might appeal to native people and excite their interest in hookworms."[23] Dr. Paul F. Russell, presumably Phyllis Russell's husband, who worked as a health officer in Brazil, also sent out a proposal for a film scenario that would open and close with the same animation but would be followed by a live-action sequence from Java, Brazil, or Panama as, according to Russell, diverse races were to be found in these areas, and this approach might show that examples used in one locality could be universally applicable.[24]

Undertaking the production work with the targeted audience in mind was a major and recurrent concern. Within the foundation, there were extensive discussions concerning whether the emphasis should be on scientific images, which could be seen as dull, or a drama constructed around a particular case.[25] But using magnified images was also questioned, as magnified worms might "instill more terror than sense in the audience." This perception of the illiteracy of the audience when it came to the medium of film, cultural differences, and educational gaps would become even more of an issue when *Unhooking the Hookworm* was considered for international campaigns.

A recurrent apprehension was that the film scenario, when it was finally worked out, would be ideal for the rural south but inappropriate for "backward" communities in foreign countries. A letter to John Ferrell of the International Health Board concludes with a commentary on the difficulty such audiences would have understanding the film, particularly the microscopic amplification: "Everything is foreign to him, from the homes, people, dress, and the customs down to the great snakes they see depicted writhing in the human bowel."[26] According to the historian James Burnes, this letter appears to be an early suggestion that audiences in tropical colonies would struggle to understand the complexities of "sophisticated" film techniques. This idea of an untrained film audience with difficulties understanding the narrative became an article of faith for filmmakers in British, French, and Belgian colonies in Africa during the 1930s and 1940s, who often refused to use slow-motion, cartoons, or microscopic magnification in films for fear of confusing their audience.[27]

Parallel to the work with the manuscript production, companies such as Éclair and Kinemacolor were contacted for their expertise with moving pictures using experimental scientific techniques.[28] And once they became a player in the field, the

Rockefeller Foundation was in turn approached by major producers of educational films such as Pathé Frères and Universal, who encouraged the organization to use moving pictures in their work.[29] The correspondence with Pathé Frères specifically concerned macro-photographic images of the worms and their life cycle, which few production companies were able to produce. Pathé, however, was unable to produce any scientific images during World War I, as this work was entirely done in France. The idea of producing a public health film for the hookworm campaigns gathered steam only after the end of World War I.

Proposals of scripts/concepts/scenarios also came from production and distribution companies specializing in moving pictures geared toward more pointed or private audiences outside of cinema exhibition, such as the Colonial Film Company in Washington, DC, which promoted pictures made for the theater, home, school, store, and factory; Katherine F. Carter Inc. Educational and Motion Picture Service Bureau, which produced "motion picture entertainments arranged and managed for clubs, hotels and private residences"; and Katharine Russell Bleecker's Motion Picture Records, which specialized in depictions of children, weddings, anniversaries, lawn parties, and amateur photo plays.[30] The correspondence from these companies supports the foundation's memos reporting that the idea was to produce a moving picture with the International Health Commission's proposal as guiding principle. In the end, the film would be produced using educational footage and Pathé's microscopic images, with a narrative that told of a boy with hookworm disease.

The film production was not only an internal affair. During the Rockefeller Foundation's preparatory process, the film industry in the United States in regard to educational films was documented. Overall, the documentation at Rockefeller Archive Center provides invaluable insight into the strategies used to conduct and troubleshoot the health campaigns. And, in addition, we see the range of possibilities the film industry and exhibition circuit had to offer viewers at this time.

In the 1910s, the demand for educational titles in schools and from private organizations was great, a circumstance that many studies, including Floris Paalman's in this volume, underlines. Requests for available titles that would be useful for educational screenings were commonly addressed to production companies but also went to institutions such as the Rockefeller Foundation.[31] Even with the available educational catalogs by Kleine and others, which could be useful only to varying degrees since the necessary material infrastructures were not always in place. The Rockefeller Foundation was not only documenting all production companies but also the overall availability of titles on health subjects and indicating subject areas, length, and rental charge.[32] In February 1916, Meyer contacted producers and distributers of health films hoping to view existent titles for possible use in health campaigns as well as to inspire their own productions, for example: *The Awakening of John Bond* (Edison, 1911), *A Man Who Learned* (Edison, 1910), *Summer Babies* (Essanay, 1911), and *Charlie's Reform* (Edison, 1912) at General Film Company.[33]

The National Motion Picture Company was also contacted as the distributer of the Motion Picture Health Series in 1916, with titles such as Edison's *The War on the Mosquito* (1912). Several of these films had been produced for and screened at the Panama-Pacific Exposition in 1915; for example, *Oral Health* shown at the Oral Hygiene exhibit.[34] Each of the films viewed was commented on and its educational importance, narrative clarity, and logic evaluated in internal memorandums about the health films. *The Fly*, seen at Russell Sage Foundation in February 1916, was described as a rather poor educational film: "There is practically nothing constructive in the film,—no suggested fly traps, no suggestions of how manure may be protected against becoming a breeding place for flies, nothing of when the fly campaign can be most effectively carried on." *The Long and the Short Haul*, seen at the same occasion, sparked critique for other reasons: "The acting in the play is poor. . . . The young girl, who is the only individual prominently in the picture, is obviously a novice who probably never before appeared in a film. Every movement is self-conscious. She hesitates as to where to step next." *The Mishaps of Musty Suffer*, which was seen a few days later, was criticized for its narrative obscurity and problematic portrayal of medical authorities: "Tramp enters house. No reason for his doing this is apparent. He is immediately seized by a much be-whiskered doctor (who has a notable mysterious and unpleasant appearance) and his attendant who looks like an amateur prize-fighter. . . . The picture has no point whatsoever unless the purpose be to ridicule doctors, their appliances, methods and results."[35] The commentaries from the screenings put on display the public health officers' reactions to the film medium and health films in particular. Narrative logic and clarity were considered fundamental, together with pedagogical instruction about how to evade sanitary evils or infection. Total belief in modern medicine and its representatives, such as medical doctors, was required. Any deviation to these "qualities" was harshly criticized.

Even if the Rockefeller Foundation's staff unanimously agreed about a formula of narrative logic and pedagogical instruction, when the hookworm campaign went international the script was rewritten numerous times by educators, scientists, and health officials in search of a formula with international appeal so that it would work in transcultural contexts for a global audience. The key problem was, again, the importance of "local color" or its connection to "local conditions."

The interest in using moving pictures in health campaign work gradually increased because the medium was thought to represent an efficient and economical method of instruction. The International Health Commission calculated in 1915 that for every $500 invested, it would be possible to give seventy-five thousand people one and a half hours of instructive enjoyment and at the same time steer their minds toward the urgent health problems of the day.[36] When in 1915 the Rockefeller Foundation's International Health Commission produced a memorandum titled "Health Films as a New Field of Activity for the Commission" the possibilities the medium carried when it came to preventing diseases, building an infrastructure for public health, and increasing support to agencies interested in the improvement of public health, seemed immense.[37] But to reach this goal of supplying boards of health and other authorities in health and education with suitable health films proved more difficult than anticipated. The production process for *Unhooking the Hookworm* illustrates how an institution during the 1910s got into film production at a time when the educational film production and distribution were not yet institutionalized. The lengthy production process included the mapping of a possible infrastructure for educational methods as well as finding appropriate production companies and ascertaining the availability of existing titles on health subjects. There was also the need to consider distribution methods, the writing of a scenario, and the production and distribution process at a time when there were a number of players and initiatives but no set standards. *Unhooking the Hookworm* was finally ready to be used in 1921, after seven years of preparation.

Philanthropic organizations had an important role to play in social and health reform as moving picture customers that not only documented the educational field but developed collaborations with existing film producers, all outside the area of school-film proper. The efforts of the International Health Commission/Board to produce a film that would work for global audiences with varied screen experiences offered almost insurmountable obstacles that would never be solved. The film *Unhooking the Hookworm* is perhaps most important as an expression of the vision for the future of educational films that could eliminate health hazards worldwide and help to organize a public health structure in numerous countries. With the narrative clarity of universal standards, together with the attraction the medium seemed to have for almost every possible audience and the almost limitless pedagogical impact, it is an important example of a top-down experiment that never really fulfilled expectations. During the decades to come, cinema was nevertheless put on the educational agenda, becoming a regular part of theatrical shows and appearing in nontheatrical contexts: in schools, universities, museums, and libraries, as well as in many other locations. As such, it was an important visual tool for the many reform and information campaigns to come.

Notes

1. Health slogans Lee County, North Carolina, Rockefeller Foundation records (henceforth RF), RF Pamphlets RG Public Health Education, North Carolina 1914–1932, box 6, folder 86.

2. Benjamin B. Page and David A. Valone, eds., *Philanthropic Foundations and the Globalization of Scientific Medicine and Public Health* (Lanham, MD: University Press of America, 2007).

3. See, for example: Mary Swain Routzahn, *Traveling Publicity Campaigns: Educational Tours of Railroad Trains and Motor Vehicles* (New York: Russell Sage Foundation, 1920); Don Carlos Ellis and Laura Thornborough, *Motion Pictures in Education: A Practical Handbook for Users of Visual Aids* (New York: Thomas Y. Crowell Company, 1923); Gladys Bollman and Henry Bollman, *Motion Pictures for Community Needs* (New York: Henry Holt and Company, 1922).

4. For a discussion on Edison's social interest films, see Kevin Brownlow, *Behind the Mask of Innocence* (London: Cape, 1990), and Eileen Bowser, *The Transformation of Cinema, 1907–1915* (Berkeley: University of California Press, 1990), 37–52.

5. James Burns, "Unhooking the Hookworm: The Making and Uses of a Public Health Film," Rockefeller Archive Center Research Report, 2009, 2–3; John Farley, *To Cast Out Disease: A History of the International Health Division of the Rockefeller Foundation (1913–1951)* (New York: Oxford University Press, 2004), 61–62. For a description of the visit see "International Health Commission," 902.2. RF, RG 5, series 1:2, box 18, folder 289.

6. Rockefeller Sanitary Commission for the Eradication of Hookworm Disease, Annual Report 1910 (Washington, DC: Offices of the Commission, 1910).

7. Letter to Dr. A. T. McCormack, dated December 18, 1911, from Dr. J. S. Lock, Rockefeller Sanitary Commission Records, series 1, administration, box 6, folder 113.

8. "Kentucky Hookworm 1913," 220 D3a, Photographs, RF, box 49, folder 1186.

9. For a discussion on the International Health Commission's exhibit see Marina Dahlquist, "Health on Display: The Panama-Pacific International Exposition as Sanitary Venue," in *Performing New Media, 1890–1915*, edited by Kaveh Askari, Scott Curtis, Frank Gray, Louis Pelletier, Tami Williams, and Joshua Yumibe (New Barnet: John Libbey Publishing, 2014), 174–85.

10. See, for example, correspondence between Ernest C. Meyers and E. G. Routsalm, associate director of surveys and exhibits at Russell Sage Foundation 1914–15, especially letter to Ernest C. Meyers, dated April 9, 1914, from E. G. Routsalm, and the reply dated April 10, 1914, RF, RG5, series 1:1, box 9, folder 146.

11. "Details of Plan for Making Health Films Available to the Public," dated November 24, 1915, RF, RG 5, series 1:2, box 20, folder 303.

12. "Tentative Plan of Survey of Methods and Results in Teaching the Public in Matters of Health," RF, International Health Board/Division records, RG 5, reports—United States, 1911–1931, series 2:200: Special Reports—United States, box 1, folder 3.

13. Ibid.

14. Bollman and Bollman, *Motion Pictures for Community Needs*; Ernest A. Dench, *Motion Picture Education* (Cincinnati: Standard, 1917); Ellis and Thornborough, *Motion Pictures in Education*.

15. Marina Dahlquist, "'Swat the Fly': Educational Films and Health Campaigns 1909–1914," in *Kinoöffentlichkeit: Cinema's Public Sphere (1895–1920)*, edited by Corinna Müller (Marburg: Schüren Verlag, 2008); Marina Dahlquist "Health Instruction on Screen: The Department of Health in New York City, 1909–1917," in *Beyond the Screen: Institutions, Networks and Publics of Early Cinema*, edited by Marta Braun, Charles Keil, Rob King, Paul Moore, and Louis Pelletier (New Barnet, UK: John Libbey Publishing, 2012).

16. For an account of New York State Department of Health and their use of moving images in their campaign work, as well as titles used; see letter to Ernst C. Meyer, signed by Charles J. Storey, dated June 28, 1915, RF, RG5, series 1:2, box 20, folder 303.

17. Michael M. Davis, *The Exploitation of Pleasure: A Study of Commercial Recreations in New York City* (New York: Department of Child Hygiene of the Russell Sage Foundation, 1911), 56.

18. Letter signed by Lee F. Hanmer, associate director, May 15, 1911, Edison Archive.

19. Routzalm, *Travelling Publicity Campaigns*.

20. Letter to Dr. Wycliffe Rose, from Roger Eddy Treat, dated August 21, 1914, RF, RG5, series 1:2, box 20, folder 302.

21. Letter to Ferrell dated April 27, 1914.

22. "Suggested Sketch for Hookworm Film" by P. A. Russell, RF, RG 1, series 100, box 5, folder 41.

23. Letter to Dr. P. F. Russell, General Director at the International Health Board, dated May 15, 1924, from Dr. S. T. Darling, RF, RG 1, series 100, box 5, folder 41.

24. Memo RF, RG 1, series 100, box 5, folder 41.

25. See, for example, VGH's report of interview with Professor Fulleborn of the Hamburg School of Tropical Medicine, dated December 8, 1923, RF, RG 1, series 100, box 5, folder 41.

26. RF, RG 1,1, series 100, Box 5, Folder 40-44 Films—Reports, 1917–1927, December 17, 1923, letter to John Ferrell, IHB, in regard to proposed change in hookworm film.

27. For a discussion of colonial theories of African film literacy see James Burns, "Watching Africans Watch Movies: Theorizing Film Literacy in Colonial Africa," *Historical Journal of Film, Radio and Television*, June 2000: 197–211; for a discussion on the educational film movement in making films for colonized people during the period 1913–1940, see James Burns, *Cinema and Society in the British Empire, 1895–1940* (Basingstoke; Palgrave Macmillan, 2013), 93–132.

28. RF, RG 5, series 1:2, box 19, folder 300.

29. Letter to Rockefeller Foundation dated April 7, 1919, RF, RG 4, series 1:2, box 86, folder 1226.

30. Letter to International Health Commission dated December 29, 1915, from Nelson M. McKernan at the Colonial Film Company, RF, RG 5, series 1:2, box 20, folder 305; letter to Ernst C. Meyer dated September 24, 1915, from Katherine F. Carter, RF, RG5, series 1:2, box 20, folder 305; letter to Dr. Ernst C. Meyer dated October 19, 1915, from Katharine Russell Bleecker, RF, RG 5, series 1:2, box 20, folder 305, and February 6, 1916, RF, RG 5, series 1:2, box 38, folder 90; *Pittsburgh Press*, August 14, 1916, 5; *Pittsburgh Press*, October 1,1916, 7.

31. See, for example, letter to Rockefeller Foundation dated February 21, 1916, from William E. Grady, Public School No. 64, Manhattan, RF, RG 5, series 1:2, box 38, folder 590.

32. See, for example "List of Films on Health Subjects," dated October 13, 1915, RF, RG5, series 1:2, box 20, folder 303.

33. Letter to General Film Company dated February 8, 1916, from ECM RF, RG 5, series 1:2, box 38, folder 590.

34. Letter to Dr. E. C. Meyer, at the International Health Commission, from Dr. Herbert L. Wheeler dated February 11, 1916, RF, RG 5, series 1:2, box 38, folder 590; correspondence between Ernst C. Meyer and Samuel E. Ramseyer, 1917, RF, RG5, series 1:2, box 56, folder 823; and in 1918, RF, 5, series 1:2, box 72, folder 1030.

35. "Memorandum of Health Films," dated February 19, 1916, RF, RG5, series 1:2, box 38, folder 589. As Joel Frykholm has pointed out to me, the title seen was probably *Cruel and Unusual*, which was the first installment of the *Mishaps of Musty Suffer* series from 1916 in which Musty enters a medical clinic where hookworm treatment is offered.

36. Memorandum of Health Films as a New Field of Activity for the Commission, November 23, 1915, RF, RG 3, series 1:2, box 20, folder 303.

37. Ibid.

Filmography

The Mishaps of Musty Suffer (George Kleine Productions, 1915–16).
A Man Who Learned (Edison Company, 1910).
A Sane Fourth of July (Edison Company, 1910).
The Awakening of John Bond (Edison Company, 1911).

Charlie's Reform (Edison Company devised by Clarence A. Perry, Division of Recreation, Russell Sage Foundation, 1912).
The Fly (Edison Company, 1913).
The Fly Pest (Charles Urban Trading Company, 1910).
Gossiping Yapville (The Essanay Film Manufacturing Company, 1911).
Hope, a Red Cross Seal Story (dir. Charles Brabin, Edison Company in collaboration with the Society for the Study and Prevention of Tuberculosis, 1912).
The Long vs. the Short Haul (produced by National Motion Pictures in collaboration with the Indiana State Board of Health, the American Association for the Study and Prevention of Infant Mortality, and the Children's Aid Association in Indianapolis).
On the Trail of the Germs (dir. William V. Mong, Selig Polyscope Company, 1912).
Oral Health (Oral Hygiene Committee of the Dental Society of the State of New York, c. 1915).
The Public and Private Care of Infants (dir. Charles M. Seay, Edison Company in cooperation with the Department of Child-Helping at the Russell Sage Foundation, 1912).
Some Inhabitants of Stagnant Water (*Quelques petits habitants de l'eau stagnante*, Pathé Frères, 1911).
Summer Babies (The Essanay Film Manufacturing Company, 1911).
Unhooking the Hookworm (International Health Division, Rockefeller Foundation, 1920). Published at YouTube by the Rockefeller Foundation Records. Finding Aid: FA752.
The War on the Mosquito (Edison Company, 1912).

Bibliography

Bollman, Gladys, and Henry Bollman. *Motion Pictures for Community Needs*. New York: Henry Holt and Co., 1922.
Bowser, Eileen. *The Transformation of Cinema, 1907–1915*. Berkeley: University of California Press, 1990.
Brownlow, Kevin. *Behind the Mask of Innocence*. London: Cape, 1990.
Burns, James. *Cinema and Society in the British Empire, 1895–1940*. Basingstoke; Palgrave Macmillan, 2013.
———. "Unhooking the Hookworm: The Making and Uses of a Public Health Film." Rockefeller Archive Center Research Report, 2009.
———. "Watching Africans Watch Movies: Theorizing Film Literacy in Colonial Africa." *Historical Journal of Film, Radio and Television*, June 2000, 197–211.
Dahlquist, Marina. "Health Instruction on Screen: The Department of Health in New York City, 1909–1917." In *Beyond the Screen: Institutions, Networks and Publics of Early Cinema*, edited by Marta Braun, Charles Keil, Rob King, Paul Moore, and Louis Pelletier, 107–116. New Barnet, UK: John Libbey Publishing, 2012.
———. "Health on Display: The Panama-Pacific International Exposition as Sanitary Venue." In *Performing New Media, 1890–1915*, edited by Kaveh Askari, Scott Curtis, Frank Gray, Louis Pelletier, Tami Williams, and Joshua Yumibe, 174–85. New Barnet: John Libbey Publishing, 2014.
———. "'Swat the Fly': Educational Films and Health Campaigns 1909–1914." In *Kinoöffentlichkeit: Cinema's Public Sphere (1895–1920)*, edited by Corinna Müller, 211–25. Marburg: Schüren, 2008.
Davis, Michael M. *The Exploitation of Pleasure. A Study of Commercial Recreations in New York City*. New York: Department of Child Hygiene of the Russell Sage Foundation, 1911.

Dench, Ernest A. *Motion Picture Education*. Cincinnati: Standard, 1917.

Ellis, Don Carlos, and Laura Thornborough. *Motion Pictures in Education*. New York: Thomas Y. Crowell Company, 1923.

Farley, John. *To Cast Out Disease: A History of the International Health Division of the Rockefeller Foundation (1913–1951)*. New York: Oxford University Press, 2004.

Page, Benjamin B., and David A. Valone, eds. *Philanthropic Foundations and the Globalization of Scientific Medicine and Public Health*. Lanham, MD: University Press of America, 2007.

Rockefeller Sanitary Commission for the Eradication of Hookworm Disease. Annual Report 1910. Washington, DC: Offices of the Commission, 1910.

Routzahn, Mary Swain. *Traveling Publicity Campaigns: Educational Tours of Railroad Trains and Motor Vehicles*. New York: Russell Sage Foundation, 1920.

MARINA DAHLQUIST is Associate Professor of Cinema Studies at Stockholm University. She is editor of *Exporting Perilous Pauline: Pearl White and the Serial Film Craze* and coeditor (with Doron Galili, Jan Olsson, and Valentine Robert) of *Corporeality in Early Cinema: Viscera, Skin, and Physical Form* (Indiana University Press, 2018).

6 The Best Teachers and the Best Preachers

Film, University Extension, and the Project of Assimilation in Alberta, 1917–36

Zoë Druick

IMAGINE TURNING UP to a nontheatrical film screening in a schoolhouse or community hall in 1920s rural Alberta expecting to be entertained by a baseball movie and instead having to endure a biblical epic. Precisely just such a misunderstanding happened through a coincidence of names. The film, called *A Prince of the House of David*, was publicized as *House of David*, which happened to be the name of a local touring novelty baseball act. Edward Annand (Ned) Corbett, who screened the film, remembers it this way: "As the shepherds with their sheep appeared on the hills of Judea there were gasps of dismay and low mutterings among the crowd. As soon as it became apparent that the film had nothing to do with baseball, but with a section of Old Testament history, the audience began to dwindle away, and after a half hour of the film had been shown there were only the children and disgruntled members of the Women's Institute left in the hall."[1]

This humorous story, recounted three decades after the fact, gives us some insight into the rural film circuits run by the University of Alberta from 1917 until the function was taken over by the National Film Board in 1942. Films were combined with a particular Protestant zeal for conversion and assimilation as a way of connecting with immigrants, most of whom hailed from eastern Europe and Ukraine. However, it is not at all clear how interested the spectators were in the fare provided. As with other contrived viewing situations where working-class audiences were compelled to watch films provided by their bosses, resistance manifested in a variety of ways, including exiting the screening, making loud comments, or interfering with the projection.[2] We know very little about the audiences for such screenings, beyond their description in newspapers and remarks such as Corbett's, but the views of the organizers are much more likely to be recorded: "The writings of teachers and social scientists reveal a great deal about how *they* conceived of spectatorship, and the cinema's effect upon audience members" (italics added).[3]

Although we don't know where this particular screening took place, we do know that Alberta's population was then rural and immigrant by a large margin.

We also see from Corbett's bemused description the nonalignment between his interests and those of the films he was sent to show. In order to understand the complexities of this scene, we must reconsider what we know about early Canadian film history, especially as it relates to its educational mandate. The rural film circuits of Alberta and their religious origins force us to rethink in significant ways the prevailing narratives about the nationalist impulse of Canadian media institutions of the 1930s. In particular we may need to recognize that, among other factors, the inception of the National Film Board of Canada (NFB) in 1939 has its roots in this early religious work with film.

On the fringes of the Canadian state, the University of Alberta's Department of Extension in the northern frontier town of Edmonton, population fifty-three thousand, took an early lead in the use of visual education. Established in 1912, the department was notable in several ways, not least in its independence from any other department of the university and its broad ambitions to reach the rural population of the province by a variety of means. The agency became a national leader in establishing film and slide libraries and in extending the reach of both educational and nontheatrical cinema into the population at large.[4]

Alberta has many historical connections to the United States, so perhaps it is not surprising that American educational initiatives with film, which took another two decades to catch on in most other parts of Canada, found an early reception there. Where American public libraries and YMCAs made use of film to connect with immigrants in the teens and twenties, similar initiatives didn't take place in Canadian libraries and YMCAs until the 1930s and 1940s.[5] Yet in the newly formed province of Alberta, the idea took off at virtually the same time as in the United States. In addition, Alberta was in sync with American land-grant universities, which were experimenting with film and educational broadcasting in the teens and twenties. Later, when the ideas of nontheatrical film work were more widely adopted and had gained momentum at a national level in the 1930s, Alberta became a model and a network adopted by national media organizations such as the Film Board and the Canadian Broadcasting Corporation (CBC). In addition, employees of the University of Alberta Department of Extension went on to found and nurture national organizations such as the Canadian Association of Adult Education (CAAE), the Canadian Radio League, and the National Film Society (NFS), all important groups supporting the work of educational media. One of the goals of this chapter, then, is to make visible the networks of institutions and individuals that crystalized at the University of Alberta and then went on to make their mark on the national film and media scene.[6]

However, merely mapping out the foundations laid by Alberta might risk this being a provincial story of rather limited interest. Instead, this chapter aims to focus more generally on the ambivalences of film education in this transitional period before the concepts of educational film, nontheatrical distribution, citizenship training, and even national culture had been fully cemented. A range of actors mobilized an array of discourses, technologies, justifications, and legitimations around film and education that make visible certain ways of thinking through the problems of identity and citizenship that would not otherwise be quite so apparent in the historical record. Not least, we must consider the strong role that religion played in the justifications and mobilizations of educational media. Whether because of its novelty, its synecdochic relationship to modernity, its international cachet, its capacity to gather audiences, its presumed abilities to connect with non-readers, or its perceived facility to convey practical knowledge, cinema was above all else an engine for the production of discourse. In this, the study follows Haidee Wasson's film-historical directive that "whether the criterion is film type, exhibition context, technological system, or audience composition, we must develop more nuanced and productive terms to understand the fullness of film's social, cultural, and political life."[7]

Mainly by necessity, this chapter relies on a kind of decentered media studies that "looks past the screen," refusing to overemphasize representations above the other aspects by which the circulation of film attempted to organize modern life.[8] It also considers the discourse surrounding the role of film in constituting modern, educated citizens in the very early history of Alberta as part of a genealogy of governmentalized media relations in the warp and woof of modern life.[9] Mobility is an important vector in this story as well, since mobile technologies were invented and framed in part to contend with mobile populations and bodies, all of which were formed into provisional assemblages as projects of state control were brought to bear and then dismantled and reimagined in a regular pattern of creative destruction.[10]

Distribution, the focus in this analysis, has long been the Cinderella of film studies, with its glamorous sisters, production and exhibition, receiving all the attention. Its relationship to infrastructure and networks, the material forces and forms that are the actual intermediaries or relays between production and exhibition, clearly makes it central to the cinema circuit. Yet in periods of relative technological and institutional stability, such as the one cinema enjoyed during the long middle of the twentieth century, it tends to become almost entirely invisible. In any period of technological and social change distribution again becomes visible, and the story of nontheatrical educational film is one that might benefit from precisely such a foregrounding of considerations of distribution, especially because the depots, machines, and transportation that facilitated such networks enlisted telling discourses about the articulation of technology to state projects. In this case potential audience members were immigrants who, when brought into contact with technologies such as railways, roads, projectors, generators, celluloid and screens—as well as actors such as extension workers—had the potential to more fully adopt proper middle-class Anglo-Protestant sensibilities. At least attention to distribution promises to delineate more clearly the mobile assemblage being formulated between the immigrant audience, university extension, and film apparatus. Building on film historian Frank Kessler's suggestion that researchers pay close attention to how "distribution networks function locally, regionally, nationally, and

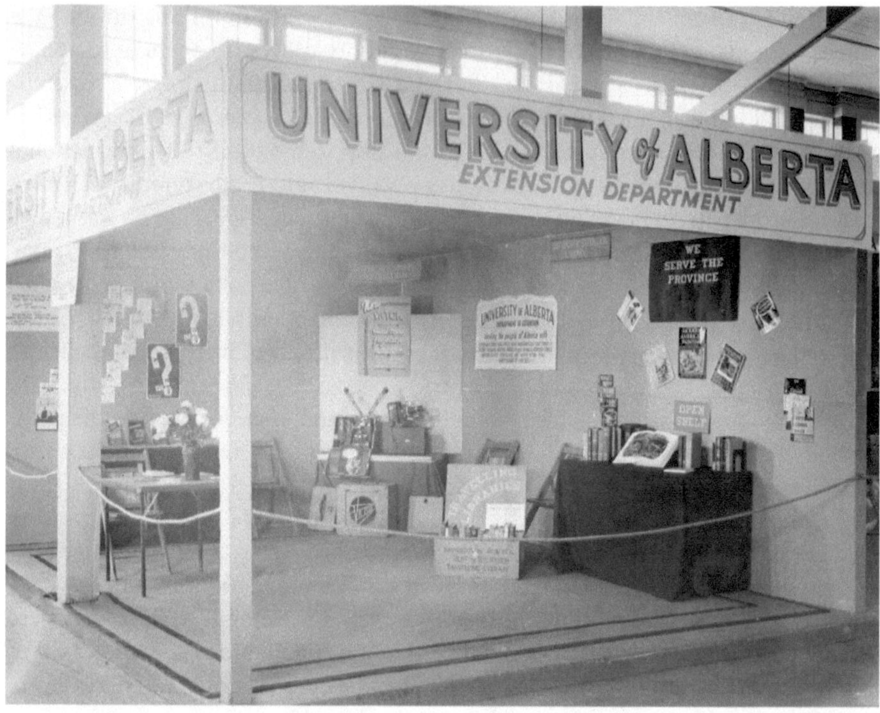

Fig. 6.1. A display of the Department of Extension's services. Although undated, its promotion of the Banff School of Fine Arts shows it must be from after 1933, as does the promotion of the new Victor Animatograph sound projector. Image used with the permission of the University of Alberta Archives.

internationally," this study adds a subsidiary research problematic: With which technologies, bodies, and economies are such networks integrated?[11]

In the phase dubbed "the transitional period" (1908–17) by silent-film scholars, cinema was still, as Kessler points out, "an emerging medium which [had] to fit into a variety of cultural, political or social contexts."[12] One might expand and reframe this observation by thinking about the context of the medium in terms of how it articulates to a material network of human and nonhuman actors. Libraries of films, labs, projectors, railways, roads, cars, generators, auditoria, and so on, are all necessary corequisites for the circulation of film as part of the extension department's moral and educational mission. To make this argument, this chapter provides some context on race, religion, and nation-building in Alberta in this period and delineates the network of technological and human actors put into play at the University of Alberta. It then situates this history alongside the extension movement and considers its national features in Canada. Finally, the study concludes with a consideration of the debt owed to the University of Alberta's extension program by the NFB, the CBC, and other national organizations.

Nation-Building on the Frontier

When established in 1905, the new prairie province of Alberta inherited the troubled legacy of the Northwest frontier, a history that encompassed the complex social relations of the fur trade, including the rapacious violence of colonization imposed on aboriginal inhabitants of the land under administration by various churches, the Northwest Mounted Police, the Canadian Pacific Railway (CPR), the Hudson's Bay Company, and other fur-trading entities. Prior to obtaining the status of a province, the land was already the site of "technological nationalism," owing to an infrastructure of railway lines that had been built across its expanse in the 1880s and 1890s.[13] The preference for British settlers after Confederation (1867) was supported by policies of free land offered by the railroad. However, the prospects of homesteading in Alberta presented many challenges, and the territory seemed dangerously unsettled to a Canadian government intent on displacing the Indigenous peoples with British settlers who would help make the CPR profitable. So, starting in 1896, the Liberals began an aggressive policy of immigration and settlement (the Sifton Policy) to bring immigrants from other parts of Europe. These inducements, along with the violence and chaos of late nineteenth-century Europe, brought about an immediate effect: Canada's population increased by one-third between 1901 and 1911. In this decade, Alberta's growth was even more marked: the population increased by five and a half times, reaching 375,000 by 1911, 57 percent of whom had been born abroad.[14]

Immigrants arrived from the former Austro-Hungarian Empire, particularly the provinces of Galicia and Bukovina. Many of them came in groups and formed what were known as "rural bloc settlements," in which they attempted to create utopian communities that would remain somewhat—or very—separate from the Canadian state. Alberta had large groups of Ukrainians and Mennonites, as well as smaller numbers of Doukhobors, Chinese, and Japanese.[15] The province also lay claim to the only Canadian settlement of Mormons and had the largest concentration of Hutterites in the country.[16] This settlement pattern distinguished Alberta from other parts of Canada where, prior to the railroad, large tracts of land had not been opened up to group settlement and British and French settlement had dominated.

World War I served as a tipping point in the province. While many of the British- and Canadian-born Albertans signed up to serve in the military and ended up dead on the battlefields of Europe, prejudices against the European immigrants, many of whom had fled to Canada in response to the dissolution of the Austro-Hungarian Empire in the first place, rose to the surface. After the Winnipeg general strike of 1919, the Canadian government imposed sanctions on these "enemy alien" groups, removing their right to vote, closing their newspapers, outlawing their political organizations, and, in some extreme cases, placing them en masse into internment camps.[17] Wartime measures were also directed at pacifist groups, Mennonites, Doukhobors, and Hutterites, even though they had come to Canada under specific guarantees from the government that they would not be subject to conscription.[18]

Despite this anti-immigrant sentiment, after the war, immigration picked up again. During the 1920s, almost one hundred thousand immigrants came to Alberta. Despite provisions of the Empire Settlement Act (1922) to subsidize the costs of British emigration to Canada, only one-quarter of the total number of immigrants during this decade were British. Between 1925 and 1930, the government entered into the Railways Agreement with the CPR and CNR, opening the doors to more people from the "non-preferred" countries of central and eastern Europe to settle as "agriculturalists, agricultural workers, and domestic servants." However, when R. B. Bennett's Conservative government was elected in 1930, the Railways Agreement was canceled and immigration was once again more or less suspended. Moreover, between 1930 and 1933, thousands of immigrants on relief were deported.[19]

One result of this immigration pattern in an otherwise predominantly British and French Canada was that Alberta became a hotbed of nativism, with Anglo-Protestants of all stripes opposing the racial, religious, and political threats to the Canadian nation seen to reside in the immigrant population. Although Christian, Slavs tended to be members of Orthodox or Catholic churches regarded as "backward and authoritarian" by Protestant clergymen.[20] The goal of the Anglo-Protestant elite was assimilation as a means to both improve the lives of the immigrants and to shore up British Canadian institutions.[21] Nonwhites, on the other hand, were thought to be unassimilable and subject to restrictive immigration dictates.[22]

Reverend W. H. Pike of the Edmonton's United Church mission put the fear of being overcome by foreigners explicitly in an address he gave in the early 1920s:

> We have extensive foreign colonies or settlements eith [*sic*] a population numbering from 1,000 to 60,000 where a foreign life has been transplanted to our fertile soil, taken root and thrives, and to-day we have colonization from these colonies—offshoots—and the buying out of the Anglo Saxon farmers and it is safe to predict that within fifty years there are parts of this west where the A.S. farmer will be a stranger. . . . Surely this is sufficient to indicate that here is a great problem, a problem agitating the mind of our legislators, a problem worthy of intelligent attention by our great dailies, a problem challenging the churches and organizations of Canada. They are here from the ends of the earth and we must lead them into the rights, privileges and responsibilities of Canadian citizenship.[23]

The solution of assimilation proposed by Pike was a common refrain among religious reformers.

Although children were an obvious target, adult education was also considered an essential tool. In a 1929 report for the World Association of Adult Education edited by C. M. MacInnes, a Canadian-born history lecturer at Bristol University, the race issue in Canada is foregrounded. MacInnes points out that in Canada the population is 75 percent rural and that it is more diffuse in Alberta than anywhere else in the dominions.[24] According to him, the prairies involve special challenges: "The illiterate voter in Canada, whatever his native tongue, is a menace, for experience, both in Canada and in the USA, has conclusively shown that the uneducated foreigner in new and strange surroundings tends to be exceedingly suspicious and proves to be the very best material possible for the political agitator and the social revolutionary. In no part of Canada is this problem of the foreigner more obvious than Winnipeg, and, looked at in this light, adult education is not a luxury, but a compelling necessity."[25] MacInnes spares no detail that might aggravate the British Canadian educator: "Frequently these 'new Canadians,' as they are sometimes called, have seen nothing of Canada at all . . . strangers in a great new country, they cling tenaciously to their own tongue. . . . They remain little islands of eastern and southern Europe in the ocean of the Canadian prairie."[26] MacInnes's connection of education and assimilation, not to mention his candid identification of the problems and issues facing the mainstream British-identified Canadian educator, clearly demonstrates the imbrication of race, religion, politics, and nation on the prairies in the interwar period. Conservatives such as MacInnes would turn to media education as a distasteful but necessary strategy to reach the rural populations of foreign "illiterates" with their backward ways.

Adult Education and the University of Alberta Department of Extension

As previously sketched, Alberta was on the western frontier of Canadian nation-building, and its immigration history combined a number of unique factors. The unequal relationship of aboriginal groups with fur traders and governments, the significance of the development of the railway, the patterns of ethnic bloc settlement—especially for religious dissidents—the role of the churches, and the rise of a populist farmer's movement all mapped the land and gave contour to local politics in distinctive ways that called on involvement from the newly formed state university. Like the other new prairie province of Saskatchewan, the University of Alberta formed a public state university with a vision quite different from the religiously affiliated universities of the more established eastern provinces.

The founding president of the university, Henry Marshall Tory, declared that 10 percent of the university budget would be put toward extension, an overblown promise that never quite materialized on a budget line. But he did make good by establishing the first independent extension department in the country (as opposed to one affiliated with a department of agriculture, for instance). Tory took this initiative in a province marked by its rural population of non-English-speaking and non-Protestant immigrants. At this same time, American progressives were turning toward university extension services and modifying their meaning. Whereas, in Britain the extension movement of the nineteenth century had been characterized by bringing credit classes to workers and others for whom university education was out of reach (including middle-class women, who took up the opportunity in droves), American extension programs as developed by the land-grant universities had a more populist bent.[27]

In many ways, the American model of extension education represents a shift from an Arnoldian vision, where culture is used to obtain popular consent to bourgeois norms of national culture. The North American model grappled with race and cultural difference as well as that of class; its primary objective was assimilation and its methods varied enormously. In the nineteenth-century United States, for example, mesmerists, phrenologists, and laughing-gas experimenters were included on the educational circuits.[28] A less ambitious vision of higher education was customized for the working class—yielding entertainment and vocational training cleansed of any trace of radical politics. Joseph Kett well describes the patronizing attitude that prevailed: "Advocates of the pursuit of culture reached out to the multitude by inventing ways to reconcile higher knowledge with mediocre interests and aptitudes."[29]

Charles Van Hise, president of the University of Wisconsin, was a leading advocate of the idea that the publicly supported university had a special obligation to the ordinary people, and he initiated his new approach in 1907.[30] Going beyond the traditional classroom delivery and the usual academic content, Wisconsin experimented with correspondence courses, audiovisual technologies, short courses and workshops, and information pamphlets, utilizing traveling field men to connect people to the university.[31] According to one dean at the University of Wisconsin at the time, "Right or wrong, you find here a type of University Extension that does not disdain the simplest forms of service. Literally carrying the University to the homes of the people, it attempts to give them what they need—be it the last word in expert advice; courses of study carrying university credit; or easy lessons in cooking and sewing. University Extension in Wisconsin endeavours to interpret the phraseology of the expert and offers the benefits of research to the household and the workshop, as well as to the municipalities and state."[32] Saskatchewan, which, in 1910, started the first extension service in western Canada as part of its Agriculture Department, was inspired by the Wisconsin model. By the early teens, all the western provinces had established publicly funded universities, each one with an extension unit.[33] The cost was justified by the perceived need to reach and educate those beyond the usual university population. However, whatever the rationale, the content of the extension programs is worthy of note, as much of it was connected to new forms of popular culture: patriotic songs, entertaining lectures, and movies.[34] Alongside an entertaining lecturer, audiovisual aids were considered essential. As Ned Corbett, director of the University of Alberta Extension Department, put it in 1929 after more than a decade of experimenting with visual aids: "In our experience nothing has been found yet to equal lantern slides and moving pictures as an aid to the extension lecturer. . . . When lecture material and pictures are successfully synchronized, the effectiveness is greatly increased, particularly for the mixed audiences which the Extension lecturer must face."[35] In rural communities without regular film exhibition, media enhanced extension programs thus both redefined the category of "student" and created new networks of contact and distribution.

Ronald Greene's work on the use of film by the YMCA organization in the United States in the 1920s provides a useful counterpoint to the work at University of Alberta. In that context, he argues, following Foucault, film was used for "pastoral exhibition"; its power to "assemble an audience . . . provided its use value."[36] In a parallel way, we might consider educational film through the extension programs not in terms of how *Canadian* the content of their screenings were, but rather as the use of set of pastoral apparatuses—indeed, as a "technology of attraction"—for projects of immigrant assimilation.[37] In this regard, the development of the technique of group discussion, which emerges alongside the use of radio by the University of Alberta Department of Extension, provides an excellent example of the use of media as a relay between educational authorities and local communities in a state moving somewhat reluctantly toward governmentalization.[38]

In Alberta, as in much of the rest of Canada, education was seen to be the best way to create allegiances to Anglo-Protestant traditions and the fostering of a British Imperial orientation in "New Canadians."[39] Yet, the Department of Extension would combine elements of Anglo-Protestant cultural bias with a promiscuous reliance on French nontheatrical cinema technologies and American theories of university extension to craft a unique cultural amalgam. In retrospect, it can also be seen to have provided a key stepping stone to the involvement of the Canadian state in educational media.

Audiovisual Instruction and the Department of Extension

The Department of Extension used many media forms to reach Albertans, including packages of books; support for dramatic societies; debating packages for high schools; films; lantern slides; traveling lecturers; and, after 1925, radio broadcasting.[40] Albert Ottewell, a student preacher who had worked as a miner, lumberjack, and farmer before attending the University of Alberta at the age of twenty-seven, was recruited by H. M. Tory to lead the newly formed Department of Extension in 1912. Corbett described him as "garguantuan . . . a kind of educational Paul Bunyan" and said that his lectures demonstrated his interest in assimilating the "strangers within our gates."[41] In a lecture given to University of Alberta's Faculty Club on October 20, 1923, most likely by Ottewell, titled the "Assimilation of Aliens in Canada," the presenter speaks openly about what he considers to be the problematic legacy of the Sifton Policy of settlement. Far from the usual public line about helping immigrants acclimatize to Canadian ways, with this audience he explicitly expresses the establishment's anxiety about being politically overcome by these new voters. Pointing to the large number of foreign-language newspapers circulating in Alberta, he foments anxiety about immigrants' revolutionary and nationalist organizations and condemns their churches. He explicitly emphasizes the role of schools as "machinery for spreading information" and highlights "what we are doing from this institution in solving the problem of unification of the widely divergent elements of our polyglot and racially heterogeneous population."[42] The speaker makes clear that the extension program was in no small part a project of assimilation.

A Presbyterian preacher from Nova Scotia who had worked in a mission in northern Alberta in 1908, Corbett was recruited to be Ottewell's assistant in 1920. He later became director of extension in 1928 and then went on to be the inaugural director of the Canadian Association of Adult Education from 1936 to 1951. Corbett would become a pivotal figure in Canadian adult education and audiovisual media, becoming a founding member of the executive of the Canadian Radio League, doing some of the preliminary research on the potential for school broadcasting on CBC in the late 1930s and helping to coordinate contributions to the Royal Commission on National Development in the Arts, Letters and Sciences in the late 1940s.[43] The fact that before John Grierson, Corbett was offered the post as Canada's first film commissioner indicates the degree to which he was respected as a media educator.[44]

Corbett's memoirs give a good sense of the rough-and-tumble conditions in which film projection took place, and the self-deprecating and ironic tone he uses throughout highlights the absurdity he and others felt about using film for the work of immigrant education. He later remembered how he had always carried a "28 mm moving picture machine, with a twelve-volt battery, and a large collection of films; a slide projector, with several boxes of slides; a box of books and pamphlets; and in addition to my own suitcase and [*sic*] a shotgun in case I encountered an invasion of prairie chicken, mallards or wild geese (a consummation devoutly to be wished)."[45] As late as 1929, Corbett, while lecturing on the topic of adult education, acknowledged the different standards for extension work: "Perhaps the most important part of the work is the contact established with country people by means of travelling lectures. . . . We do not pretend that this had any great educational value. It may be that the day for that particular kind of work will disappear with pioneer conditions. Meanwhile it would appear worthwhile in this way to strengthen the morale of the people, and lighten the burden of loneliness and discouragement that is the inevitable accompaniment of frontier life."[46] There was, of course, other cinematic entertainment to be had in Alberta, mainly in the cities and larger towns.[47] However, given the largely rural population and the suspicion about new media felt by some religious groups, the University of Alberta still had a large part to play in the early twentieth-century cinema culture of the province. In the United States, in this same period, the movie house was becoming the "central working-class institution," surpassing church and pub.[48] However, in Alberta, with 75 percent of its population situated in rural areas, and its religious and sometimes abstemious communities, the distribution and framing of film experiences could be more effectively undertaken by university workers bringing film to rural communities than in the usual forms of cinema exhibition.

In the case of the Department of Extension, the cultural arbiters all had their formation in mainstream Protestant religious missions (Corbett, Ottewell, Tory, and others were ministers by training). Rather than make them less likely to adopt new technologies, it appears as though the Department of Extension's decision to use films stemmed precisely from its links to Methodist and Presbyterian churches, which were using new media to proselytize.[49] Although at the time all Canadian universities had links to religious organizations, few had the kind of zealous commitment to bringing enlightenment to the rural population that was found in Alberta. The Annual Report of the Department of Extension from 1915 to 1916 notes that the most constant borrowers of lantern slides were ministers in rural districts "who usually make the round of their circuits which may include anything from two to one-half dozen points."[50]

H. P. Brown, the supervisor of the Extension Department's Visual Instruction Unit from 1917 to 1952 and a founding member of the National Film Society, remembers being at the 1909 inaugural meeting of the Alberta Methodist Lantern and Slide Association, an Edmonton group that imported methods from England for using slides in missionary work.[51] In 1915 the holdings of the association were merged with the University of Alberta's extension service, forming the nucleus of its audiovisual library.[52] Thus, in Alberta, as in the United States and United Kingdom, religious reformers seized on new media as the ideal machinery for spreading their message into the community, as "the best teachers and the best preachers in the history of the world."[53]

Nevertheless, despite its root in religious missions, some immigrant communities were resistant. In Alberta, certain religious perspectives threatened to keep citizens from being addressed by film:

> Some interesting letters have come in to the Department from teachers, ministers and community leaders using the lantern slide loaning service, particularly from the "New Canadian" districts. In many cases religious beliefs prevent attendance at moving picture shows, but the slides are welcomed. One teacher says: "Two aims were kept in mind. First to arouse a consciousness in the grown ups of the beauty and greatness of Canada, and secondly to supplement the textbook in the classroom." The result was attendances of 95–99 percent of the adults of the district during extremely cold weather, and an added interest in such subjects as geography on the part of the schoolchildren. In another case the teacher reports that he is required to lead in social activities of the community. In this particular district the people are divided by racial and religious difficulties, and the one common form of entertainment, namely, dances, is very offensive to one group. He states that in trying to provide his share and still satisfy both parties, he used lantern slides most effectively.[54]

What did the Extension Department's film work look like? There is no indication that there was any attempt at production. The emphasis was on rental distribution through their film and slide library, and exhibition by way of traveling lectures and sales of equipment to organizations around the province as well as to neighboring western provinces British Columbia, the Northwest Territories, Saskatchewan, and Manitoba. In 1917, the department purchased 15 Pathéscope 28 mm projectors and 115 films. Pathé produced a portable projector and noninflammable stock that was characterized as "safe and simple," although a staff member's description of the projector is daunting: "a sewing machine with a fly wheel about the same size and a huge crank which had to be turned vigorously by hand to generate power for a 6 volt lamp."[55]

As Mebold and Tepperman observe, Pathéscope's 28 mm format appeared at the end of the transitional period, precisely the moment in which university extension and other early adopters of educational film were making inroads.[56] Pathéscope attempted to corner the emerging educational market by modeling itself on the great civic institution of the library.[57] Jennifer Horne characterizes their approach as a "vernacular public library," an attempt to frame popular film texts with "legitimate spaces for reception."[58] The pastoral use of films that Ronald Greene associates with 16 mm networks—using films to shape conduct—can thus be seen to begin even earlier, with 28 mm. Like "the Y," adult education of the University of Alberta Extension Department imagined itself in "direct competition with radical labor unions."[59] And like the Y's reformers, for the University of Alberta extension department film was a cultural technology useful for the project of creating the assimilated publics.[60]

In sync with Pathéscope's international education work, Alberta's extensive film library was one of the earliest nontheatrical film exchanges in Canada.[61] By 1920 the department was so successful that it had begun to have difficulty meeting popular demand. According to Ottewell's report from that year, "The demands upon the Division of Visual Instruction tax its resources to the utmost limit."[62] More money was added to the budget for staff and supplies, and by the next year, the department was trafficking in feature films: "The departure has been made this year of securing some of the high class film productions for special circulation in churches and schools. For example, the super-production entitled 'The Manger to the Cross' was purchased and put into circulation among the churches in such cities as Edmonton, Calgary and Saskatoon, with the result that large audiences have seen the pictures, which are of a very high character, and the resultant film rental has almost paid for the film, which is still enjoying a large circulation."[63] By 1924, the list of organizations making use of the extension's service had expanded to include "city and country churches of all denominations, schools of all sorts, various departments of the government service, mental hospital at Oliver, boys' clubs, YMCA, farmers' organizations, Community Leagues, Imperial Order of the Daughters of the Empire, United Grain Growers, Dominion Chautauqua, public meetings of various sorts, summer camps and communities." Investigations were being made into acquiring a daylight screen for use in summer. At its peak, in 1925, the department reports reaching aggregate film audiences of 400,000, a full two-thirds of the province's entire population, despite being subject to funding cuts.[64] If accurate, this figure indicates a distribution network that was, in less than a decade, almost ubiquitous throughout the province.

University of Alberta's extension service film library was likely its most impressive accomplishment. It is mentioned in every survey of film distribution in

Canada in the first half of the twentieth century. For instance, Donald Buchanan singles it out in his report *Educational and Cultural Films in Canada* (1936), characterizing it as the only regional film work of "any consequence."[65] In a report put out by the Dominion Bureau of Statistics in conjunction with the National Film Society the following year, it is noted that, of anywhere in Canada, "rural schools in Alberta are most likely to use films regularly" and that Alberta's Department of Extension has the largest educational film library in Canada, even including those of Associated Screen News, General Films (formerly Pathéscope), Bell Telephone, CNR and CPR, and the Canadian Government Motion Picture Bureau.[66] In his 1938 report to the Imperial Relations Trust, "Canadian Film Activities," Grierson singles out the "good work" being done in Alberta by educational groups in building up a local film library, even while he identifies a lack of national distribution for nontheatrical film.[67] Even after World War II, the well-known report of the Royal Commission on National Development in the Arts, Letters and Sciences (1952), makes note of it.[68]

Thus, despite the extension workers' religious reformer credentials and their affinities to nativism and normalization of Anglo-Protestant dominance in a period marked by massive social change, we may productively consider their role in bringing about a surprising articulation of tradition and modernity with their film work. Although they may have despaired of their constituents and belittled the films they brought to show, the fact remains that film distribution and exhibition was central to their work of enmeshing racialized immigrant communities with a governmentalizing state. A byproduct of this work was the establishment of a large and complex film distribution network that melded new technologies and educational ideas with the institutionalization of nontheatrical exhibition sites.

The experiments with film for education at the University of Alberta illustrate historian of education Paul Saettler's observation that prior to the early 1920s, "a distinct line of demarcation between the entertainment and the educational, or instructional, motion picture" had not yet been drawn.[69] Entertainment films, such as comedies, dramas, and cartoons, were shown alongside industrial and government films. Screenings were combined with lectures, community meetings, and even dances, where local sensibilities allowed. For that reason, the content of the films seems less important than the way the assemblage of cinematic technologies operated to draw people together in the presence of state university agents.

As the dominance of 28 mm Pathéscope waned, the Department of Extension gradually transitioned to 16 mm—although, notably, they didn't jettison their collection of silent films immediately.[70] By 1935, 28 mm was almost entirely eliminated from the collection, and avowedly educational films were starting to play a more prominent role:

> With the disposal of most of our old 28 mm, a system which became obsolete, we have continued to build up the collection of 16 mm reels, the newer system which is being generally adopted for educational purposes. An arrangement was made with the Canadian Government Motion Picture Bureau for 40 reels of Canadian life, industries and resources and several reels of Eastman Classroom Teaching

> Films obtained for experimental work in schools. We now have a total of 175 reels of silent films and 40 reels of sound films. In the latter field there are four machines in use in Alberta using the sound-track on film system, and the results so far point to great possibilities with the so-called "talkies" in educational work. Three feature subjects have been in good demand for school and community work—*The Lady of the Lake*, *South Sea Adventures*, and *Black Beauty*—and we are hoping before long to obtain good dramatizations of the classics, as well as films depicting advances in exploration and other fields.[71]

Indeed, once sound film on 16 mm became the industry norm in 1933, University of Alberta's extension program went from being an outlier to becoming a part of what Wasson has called the "16 mm network," an integrated discursive and operational apparatus based on sedimented knowledge about how film could be utilized in nontheatrical contexts.[72] And it is precisely in the context of the formation of such a network in Canada in the 1930s that so many of the prairie-based educators began to connect up with the formation of national educational and media organizations, such as the Canadian Radio League, the CBC, NFS, CAAE, and, finally, the NFB.[73] These national organizations, though genealogically connected to Alberta's film experiments, utilized justifications far removed from the missionary and assimilationist rationales expressed in the teens and twenties. Along with sound 16 mm film, the national story became more dominant, and Canadian-made educational forms began to be more clearly delimited from fare merely shown by Canadian educators.

Conclusion

As the story of University of Alberta's Extension Department makes clear, there is ample evidence that, due to a confluence of unique social and political factors, Alberta led the way in the realm of media education in Canada, innovating novel forms of film distribution. When Grierson helped to form a national Canadian institution dedicated to film and education in 1939, it was met by local networks, which themselves were imbricated with international currents in education, international technologies such as 28 mm, and discourses circulating through adult education and extension conferences. Transportation networks were central to early film distribution in Canada as well, with roads, railways, and even postal services as important as projectors and images on non-inflammable film stock. Wary immigrants attempting to forge utopian settlements might be approached using this set of technologies and, once assembled, could be reached by church-trained university lecturers spreading Anglo-Canadian Protestant values.

These early experiments in education and citizenship-formation at the very edges of the state's reach confirm the Derridean hypothesis, explored in different ways by Gauri Viswanathan (1989) and Amin Alhassan (2007), that the colonial margins are central for the constitution of knowledge and practices of modern life.[74] When looked at in terms of biopower, or the material formation of Canada's workforce, Canada's immigration history comes to play a much more important role in the development of state media apparatuses than is usually acknowledged. Rather than the usual interpretation of these agencies as emerging either from Canada's cultural elites or from the state itself as an extension of technological projects such as the railroad, the "film-immigrant couple" that Greene identifies and other instances of racialization ought to move to the forefront when considering rationales of media governmentality. Beyond the creation of Canadian content, the need to reach "non-readers" with what James Carey has called the "media of illiteracy" was therefore central to the formation of the national media network.[75] As Richard Abel points out, this occurs not through a vanguard project led from the top-down but rather through the agglomeration of a multitude of local practices out of which institutions are built up.[76]

In short, in trying to create modern subjects, Canadian educators modernized themselves, forcing themselves—sometimes even against their own inclinations—to utilize the new medium of film. In this regard, it is arguable that university extension programs, as pioneered in Alberta, became the model for institutional media practice in Canada, in which traces of reticence are often perceptible even as instrumental logics are clearly present. As universities expanded their reach, in some ways absorbing the idea of extension into their continuing studies and lifelong learning initiatives, they became somewhat more receptive to the economic efficiencies of mass distribution that might be offered by the media. Given the ongoing project of the technological extensions of the university, the ambitious and nationally unprecedented experiment in educational film distribution undertaken at the University of Alberta between 1917 and 1936 has a great deal to impart about the imbrication of local initiatives with regional, national, and international educational discourses, economic shifts, technological innovations, and mobile populations.

Notes

1. E. A. Corbett, *We Have with Us Tonight* (Toronto: Ryerson Press, 1957), 86.
2. A telling example is recounted in J. M. Burns, *Flickering Shadows: Cinema and Identity in Colonial Zimbabwe* (Athens: Ohio University Press, 2002), where African cinema viewers making fun of the simple-minded, patronizing British colonial cinema they were made to endure were interpreted by the British as not understanding the films (123–33). See also Judith Mayne, "Immigrants and Spectators," *Wide Angle* 5, no. 2 (1982): 32–41.
3. Lea Jacobs, "Reformers and Spectators: The Film Education Movement in the Thirties," *Camera Obscura* 8, no. 1 (22) (1990): 30.
4. To be sure, parallels exist between the University of Alberta Extension film program and Canada's early governmental film agencies, the Ontario Motion Picture Bureau (1917–34) and the Canadian Government Motion Picture Bureau (1918–41). It is beyond the scope of this essay to compare these agencies, but see Charles Tepperman, "Digging the Finest Potatoes from Their Acre: Government Film Exhibition in Rural Ontario, 1917–1934," in Kathryn H. Fuller-Seeley, ed. *Hollywood in the Neighborhood: Historical Case Studies of Local Moviegoing*, 130–48 (Berkeley: University of California Press, 2008).

5. The YMCA Motion Picture Bureau, established in 1914, was the earliest instructional film distribution network in North America (see Paul Saettler, *A History of Instructional Technology* [New York: McGraw-Hill Book Company, 1968], 113). Schools and universities tended to develop their film libraries after World War I with films from the US Bureau of Educational Motion Pictures (Saettler, *History of Instructional Technology*, 114). See also Ronald Greene, "Y Movies: Film and the Modernization of Pastoral Power," *Communication and Critical/Cultural Studies* 2, no. 1 (March 2005): 20–36; Ronald Greene, "Pastoral Exhibition: The YMCA Motion Picture Bureau and the Transition to 16 mm, 1928–39," in *Useful Cinema*, ed. Charles Acland and Haidee Wasson (Durham, NC: Duke University Press, 2011), 205–29; Jennifer Horne, "A History Long Overdue: The Public Library and Motion Pictures," in Acland and Wasson, *Useful Cinema*, 149–77.

6. A list of some of the figures who made their way from prairie organizations to the national stage gives some sense that what was being pioneered on the prairies was eventually scaled up to the national level: E. A. (Ned) Corbett, director of the Department of Extension at University of Alberta (1928–36) went on to head the Canadian Association of Adult Education, which played a major role in bringing Alberta's radio experiments to the CBC; J. S. Thomson, president of the University of Saskatchewan, was named general manager of CBC in 1942; Ross McLean, a Rhodes scholar from Yorkton, Saskatchewan, worked with Vincent Massey at the Canadian mission in London and later became chairman of NFB, worked at UNESCO and then returned to Yorkton in 1950 to help run its film festival, which, begun in 1948, was reportedly the first in Canada. Donald Buchanan, founder of the National Film Society was born in Lethbridge, Alberta, and worked at CBC and the NFB, where he established the stills division, and later at the National Gallery.

7. Haidee Wasson, *Museum Movies: The Museum of Modern Art and the Birth of Art Cinema* (Berkeley: University of California Press, 2005), 36.

8. Jon Lewis and Eric Smoodin, eds. *Looking Past the Screen: Case Studies in American Film History and Method* (Durham: Duke University Press, 2007).

9. See D. Orgeron, M. Orgeron, and D. Streible, eds., *Learning with the Lights Off* (New York: Oxford University Press, 2012); Charles Acland and Haidee Wasson, eds., *Useful Cinema* (Durham: Duke University Press, 2011); Kirsten Ostherr, *Cinematic Prophylaxis: Globalization and Contagion in the Discourse of World Health* (Durham: Duke University Press, 2005); Tepperman, "Digging the Finest Potatoes from Their Acre," 130–48.

10. Leo Carney and Vanessa R. Schwartz, eds., *Cinema and the Invention of Modern Life* (Berkeley: University of California Press, 1995); Raymond Williams, *Television: Technology and Cultural Form* (Glasgow: Fontana, 1974); Jeffrey Ruoff, ed., *Virtual Voyages: Cinema and Travel* (Durham: Duke University Press, 2006); Nick Couldry and Anna McCarthy, eds., *MediaSpace: Place, Scale and Culture in a Media Age* (New York: Routledge, 2004); Zoë Druick, "Mobile Cinema in Canada in Relation to British Mobile Film Practices," in *Screening Canadians: Cross-Cultural Perspectives on Canadian Film*, ed. Wolfram R. Keller and Gene Walz (Marburg, Germany: Universitatsbibliothek, 2008), 13–33.

11. Frank Kessler, "Distribution—Preliminary Notes," in *Networks of Entertainment: Early Film Distribution 1895–1915*, ed. Frank Kessler and Nanna Verhoeff (Eastleigh, UK: John Libbey Publishing, 2007), 1.

12. Kessler, "Distribution," 2.

13. Maurice Charland, "Technological Nationalism," *Canadian Journal of Political and Social Theory* 10, no. 1 (1986), 196–220.

14. Canadian government, *Census of Prairie Provinces 1926: Population and Agriculture* (Ottawa: King's Printer, 1929).

15. Howard Palmer, *Patterns of Prejudice: A History of Nativism in Alberta* (Toronto: McClelland and Stewart, 1982), 10.

16. Ibid., 11.

17. Enemy aliens were defined as those born in an enemy country, whose mother tongue was the language of an enemy country, and who had been naturalized after March 31, 1902. See Palmer, *Patterns of Prejudice*, 49.

18. Ibid., 50.

19. Ibid., 132.

20. Ibid., 40.

21. Ibid., 41, 45. Although assimilation was first seen as a means of facilitating conversion, it eventually came to be seen as an end in itself.

22. After a small influx of African American bloc settlements just after the turn of the century, Alberta became a major force behind the federal government's restrictions, introduced in 1911, on black immigration to Canada. Similarly, Asian immigration was maintained at very low levels through astronomical head taxes and other restrictive measures.

23. Rev. W. H. Pike, "Our New Canadians and Citizenship," n.d., University of Alberta Archives RG 74-23-44, 1–2.

24. C. M. MacInnes, *Adult Education in the British Dominions* (London: World Association for Adult Education, 1929), 6.

25. Ibid., 31–32.

26. Ibid., 12.

27. In England, the earliest sustained extension movements were begun in the 1870s by its most prestigious universities, Cambridge and Oxford, thereby both democratizing access and maintaining status of the universities themselves (Scott McLean, "University Extension and Social Change: Positioning a University of the People in Saskatchewan," *Adult Education Quarterly* 58, no. 1 [November 2007], 4–5). This model was brought to Canada in the 1880s and 1890s. The Canadian Association for the Extension of University Teaching was established in 1891, one year after its American counterpart. In the 1890s, the Universities of Chicago, Wisconsin, and Kansas came to the forefront of the field. By the early 1900s the English model had declined and one more suited to the North American context was being developed at land-grant universities, most notably Wisconsin.

28. Joseph Kett, *The Pursuit of Knowledge under Difficulties: From Self-Improvement to Adult Education in America, 1750–1990* (Stanford: Stanford University Press, 1994), 147.

29. Ibid., 143. Like the YMCA, the WEA (Workers' Educational Association) was established in Britain (the former in London in 1844 and 1853 in Toronto, the latter in 1903). WEA founder Albert Mansbridge coauthored a report (1919) for the British Special Commission of Ministry of Reconstruction that envisioned "adult education [as] a permanent national necessity, an inseparable aspect of citizenship, and therefore should be universal and lifelong" (cited in J. R. Kidd, *Adult Education in the Canadian University* [Toronto: Canadian Association for Adult Education, 1956], 1). The WEA was established in Toronto in 1918 with close ties to the Anglo-Imperial establishment, including the extension department of the University of Toronto (Ron Faris, *The Passionate Educators* [Toronto: Peter Martin Assoc., 1975], 4). In *Adult Education in the British Dominions*, MacInnes observes that "one of the reasons why the Workers' Educational Association has not caught on better in Canada than it has is probably the fact that it too obviously has the blessing of officialdom and plutocracy" (150). Nevertheless, Drummond Wren, a "militant socialist" in Corbett's estimation, affiliated WEA to CAAE (Corbett, *We Have with Us Tonight*, 121–22). The WEA cosponsored the NFB's wartime trade union circuits (C. W. Gray, *Movies for the People: The Story of the National Film Board's Unique*

Distribution System [Ottawa: NFB, 1977], 52). After the Second World War, like the NFB, the WEA was smeared as being a red organization, but unlike the NFB, it was not able to shake the allegations and its significance dwindled (Ed Philip, "A Few Perspectives on the Workers' Educational Association 1917 to ____," in *History of the Workers' Educational Association*, ed. Albert Field [Toronto: Workers' Educational Association of Canada, 1977], 28). However, the story of the WEA does raise the question of the difference in emphasis between "worker" education and "adult" education (see W. J. Morgan, "Antonio Gramsci and Raymond Williams: Workers, Intellectuals, and Adult Education," in *Gramsci and Education*, ed. C. Borg, J. Buttigieg, and P. Mayo [Lanham, MD: Rowman & Littlefield, 2002], 255). Adult education continued to be a radical activity in England and founding figures in British cultural studies Raymond Williams and Stuart Hall, among others, taught in adult education programs as a form of politics. Williams later became disillusioned with university extension, saying: "In the end you cannot be financed and academically controlled by those kinds of universities and carry out a program of education of the working class" (Morgan, "Antonio Gramsci and Raymond Williams," 255).

30. Kidd, *Adult Education in the Canadian University*, 36.

31. Gordon Selman et al., *The Foundations of Adult Education in Canada*, 2nd ed. (Toronto: Thompson Educational Publishing, 1998), 39.

32. Cited in Kidd, *Adult Education in the Canadian University*, 35–36.

33. McLean, "University Extension and Social Change," 6.

34. Indeed extension was not seen to be the exclusive purview of the university and was carried out by a variety of actors, from governments and public agencies to voluntary associations and the private sector, such as fertilizer companies and financial institutions (Selman et al., *Foundations of Adult Education in Canada*, 38).

35. Edward Corbett, "Adult Education," n.d. (1929?), University of Alberta Archives RG 74-23-45, 4.

36. Greene, "Pastoral Exhibition," 211.

37. Greene, "Y Movies," 21.

38. Foucault discusses "governmentality" in terms of the "governmentalization of the state" ("Governmentality," in *The Foucault Effect: Studies in Governmentality*, ed. Graham Burchell et al. [Chicago: University of Chicago Press, 1991], 102–3). In this prewelfare state era, the Canadian state was often reluctant to take on governmental responsibilities, mostly leaving those to religious groups, charitable organizations, and other nongovernment actors. Although education is constitutionally a provincial responsibility in Canada, the federal government has had special responsibility for certain areas of education, such as that relating to indigenous people as well as populations in the armed forces and federal penal institutions. Language and citizenship training for immigrants has always been a federal responsibility. However, in recognition of the work being done by western provinces in 1913, the federal government passed the Agricultural Instruction Act, making federal funds available for use by provinces for agricultural extension work (Selman et al., *Foundations of Adult Education in Canada*, 63). This funding helps explain in part the vigor of the Alberta program.

The dispersed population meant that radio broadcasting was another tactic in the objective to reach the newly arrived and barely assimilated, something that space prevents me from fully exploring here. In 1925, the Extension Department began experimenting with radio, supplying programs to a station run by the *Edmonton Journal* on Monday evenings. Two years later it set up its own transmitter on the Edmonton campus (CKUA), broadcasting lectures by faculty from the university on topics such as animal husbandry, horticulture, agricultural engineering, poultry, dairying, soils, and entomology, as well as mostly live music, including the first broadcasts from the Metropolitan Opera. After a grant from the Carnegie foundation for record player and music library of nine hundred recordings in 1932, CKUA began to play classical music for an hour each night. This was the beginning of the Foothills Network, the first regional radio network in Canada.

39. This is certainly true of the National Council of Education, which, as Charles Acland has traced, was a strong supporter of British documentary film movement in the 1930s but not because of any left-leaning orientation. A turn toward fascist politics led to the resignations of numerous high-profile members. Charles Acland, "Mapping the Serious and the Dangerous: Film and the National Council of Education, 1920–1939," *Cinémas: Revue d'Études Cinematographiques* 6, no. 1 (1995): 114. See also Faris, *Passionate Educators*, 11.

40. The department used glass lantern slides, many of which were made in-house until 1937, when they adopted a new system called "Picturols," at which point their collection of fifty thousand slides became obsolete.

41. Corbett, *We Have with Us Tonight*, 27. The second phrase is a reference to a 1909 publication by J. S. Woodsworth's, *Strangers within Our Gates* (Toronto: F. C. Stephenson). Woodsworth would go on to found the Cooperative Commonwealth Federation, a socialist political party, in 1932. For the links between socialism and eugenics, see Angus McLaren, *Our Own Master Race: Eugenics in Canada, 1885–1945* (Toronto: McClelland & Stewart, 1990).

42. N. A. (Ottewell?), "Assimilation of Aliens in Canada," paper for Faculty Club, October 20, 1923, University of Alberta Archives RG 16, 74-23-37, 3.

43. Faris, *Passionate Educators*, 91, 120; Frank Peers, *The Politics of Public Broadcasting* (Toronto: University of Toronto Press, 1969), 65.

44. Corbett, *We Have with Us Tonight*, 150–51.

45. Ibid., 29.

46. Cited in Kidd, *Adult Education in the Canadian University*, 13.

47. Vaudeville theater and itinerant cinema exhibitors arrived in Calgary and Edmonton around 1897; from 1898 exhibitors set up in "churches, town halls, theatres, and opera houses," as well as tents on fairgrounds. By 1909, a family of Calgary-based exhibitors, the Allens, had opened the first Canadian film exchange. Robert M. Seiler and Tamara P. Seiler, *Reel Time: Movie Exhibitors and Movie Audiences in Prairie Canada, 1886–1986* (Edmonton: Athabasca University Press, 2013), 85.

48. Roy Rosenzweig, "From Rum Shot to Rialto: Workers and Movies," in *Moviegoing in America: A Sourcebook in the History of Film Exhibition*, ed. Gregory A. Waller (Oxford: Blackwell, 2002), 30.

49. Lee Grieveson and Peter Krämer point out that anxiety about immigrants was central to discussions of cinema's potentially deleterious effects, and religious programming was one way to combat other cinematic influences. For instance, numerous film versions of the Passion Play were made after 1897 and "religious groups, particularly Protestant ones, increasingly sponsored film programmes in the late 1890s" ("Film Production and Variety Shows: Introduction," in *The Silent Cinema Reader*, ed. L. Grieveson and P. Krämer [New York: Routledge, 2004], 35).

50. Annual Report, 1915–16, Department of Extension, University of Alberta Archives RG 16, 74–118, 6. An account book available in the University of Alberta Extension Department archives shows that a large percentage of clients were churches. An excerpt from a letter sent by Rev. John Pate is included in the 1915–16 annual report: "I have been devoting three nights each week to this kind of work in the country schools within a radius of 20 miles from Alix, and the delight on the faces of young and old has been reward for the long and sometimes extremely cold drives. I appreciate very much your kindness in letting me have the use of such interesting sets" (April 1, 1916, appendix, 4).

51. Gray, *Movies for the People*, 27. This is particularly early when one considers that Victor Animatograph Co. only perfected the first portable lantern slide projector and accompanying smaller, lighter slides in 1910 (Saettler, *History of Instructional Technology*, 100).

52. Methodist ministry was an early adopter, among the first to obtain the new nontheatrical film projectors. The first films it obtained were from the Pathé Film Library in Paris with English titles and subtitles and were in the vein of popular science, cartoons, and short comedies, which, according to Brown, "(being French) had to be selected with great care" (H. P. Brown, "Recollections of An Audio-Visual Instructionist Part 1: Early Days in the West, 1917–1937," n.d., University of Alberta Archives, RG 69–94).

53. Evangelist colonel Henry Hadley quoted in Terry Lindvall, "Silent Cinema and Religion: An Overview (1895–1930)," in *The Routledge Companion to Religion and Film*, ed. J. Lyden (New York: Routledge, 2009), 15.

54. Annual Report, 1934–1935, Department of Extension, University of Alberta Archives.

55. H. P. Brown "Alberta Pioneers Again," Radio Broadcast, November 7, 1949, University of Alberta Archives RG 69–94, 7. Pathé, the leading supplier of 35 mm films during the nickelodeon era (1905–9), had developed a 28 mm nonflammable diacetate film stock and projector suitable for the nontheatrical market by 1911. Around that time, a clutch of companies entered the home projection field en masse, including DeVry, Bell and Howell, Edison, Atlas, and Kleine (Saettler, *History of Educational Technology*, 99–100). Of these, Pathé's 28 mm format allowed for larger and less grainy images. However, at $150 for a hand-cranked model and $250 for a motor-driven cabinet model "Pathéscope was by far the most expensive home projector on the market" (Ben Singer, "Early Home Cinema and the Edison Home Projecting Kinetoscope," *Film History* 2 [1988], 42). The format arrived in Canada by 1916 and was adopted as the industry's safety standard in 1918 (Peter Lester, "The Perilous Gauge: Canadian Independent Film Exhibition and the 16 mm Mobile Menace," in *Cinema and Technology: Cultures, Theories, Practices*, ed. Marc Furstenau, Adrian Mackenzie, and Bruce Bennett [New York: Palgrave, 2009], 26; Anke Mebold and Charles Tepperman, "Resurrecting the Lost History of 28 mm Film in North America," *Film History* 15, no. 2 [2003], 137). Pathé held a monopoly on its software as well, maintaining a strong control over the complete cinema circuit by being the only provider of films for the projector (Singer, "Early Home Cinema," 42). The film was safer to use than nitrate 35 mm and both the University of Alberta and the Ontario Motion Picture Bureau adopted the format in 1917 (Mebold and Tepperman, "Resurrecting the Lost History," 146).

56. Mebold and Tepperman, "Resurrecting the Lost History," 138. According to Mebold, one of the earliest Pathéscope catalogues (1914–15) included the following subsections: Humor, Education, Travel, Pathos. Later this was expanded to include Travel, Sports, Manners, and Customs; Industries, Forestry, and Agriculture; Popular Science, Natural History; Comedies and Juvenile; Dramas, Serials; Religious; Reconstructed and Modern History; and Animated Cartoon Comedies (Anke Mebold, "'Just Like a Public Library Maintained for Public Welfare': 28mm as a Comprehensive Service Strategy for Non-Theatrical Clientele, 1912–23," in *Networks of Entertainment: Early Film Distribution 1895–1915*, ed. Frank Kessler and Nanna Verhoeff [Eastleigh, UK: John Libbey Publishing, 2007], 270).

57. Horne, "History Long Overdue," 154.

58. Ibid., 158.

59. Greene, "Y Movies," 23.

60. Ibid., 25–26.

61. Mebold and Tepperman, "Resurrecting the Lost History," 143.

62. Albert Ottewell, Annual Report, 1920–21, Department of Extension, University of Alberta Archives, 5.

63. Ottewell, Annual Report, 1921–22, 1. Lindvall observes that Sidney Olcott's version of Jesus's life, *From the Manger to the Cross* (made for Kalem in 1912), was considered particularly impressive for being shot on location in Palestine and Egypt ("Silent Cinema and Religion," 15).

64. According to the census of prairie provinces, the population of Alberta in 1926 was 607,599 (Canadian government, *Census of Prairie Provinces*, iv).

65. Donald Buchanan, *Educational and Cultural Films in Canada* (Ottawa: National Film Society, 1936), 9–10.

66. Canadian government, *The Use of Films and Slides in Canadian Schools*, Dominion Bureau of Statistics, Education Bulletin No. 3 (1937), 2, 7–11.

67. John Grierson, "Canadian Film Activities," 1939, Grierson Archive G3:5.4, 3.

68. Yvette Hackett continues in this vein in her 1986 history of the National Film Society of Canada, in which she writes, "the largest circulating library of educational films, *oddly enough*, was located as [*sic*] the University of Alberta in Edmonton" ("The National Film Society of Canada, 1935–1951: Its Origins and Development," in *Flashback: People and Institutions in Canadian Film History*, ed. Gene Walz [Montreal: Mediatexte, 1986], 136; italics added).

69. Saettler, *History of Educational Technology*, 96.

70. In the Annual Report of 1930–31, Corbett wrote: "Despite the advent of the 'talkies,' the educational silent film continues to attract, and audiences of up to 600 people have been recorded during the year. We are accomplishing the transition from the obsolete 28 mm film to the new 16 mm without serious difficulty" (Annual Report, 1930–31, Department of Extension, University of Alberta Archives, 11).

71. Annual Report, 1934–35, Department of Extension, University of Alberta Archives, 22.

72. Wasson, *Museum Movies*, 58.

73. Even so, the 16 mm network was slow to get started in Canada. A 1937 survey of nontheatrical film use in Canada undertaken by the Dominion Bureau of Statistics found only 260 projectors in Canadian schools, of which only fifteen (approximately 6 percent) were sound-enabled, with another one hundred silent projectors privately owned by teachers. By contrast, at the time there were ten thousand projectors in city schools across the United States, a disparity that can't be explained away solely as a ratio of population (Canadian government, *Use of Films and Slides*, 1).

74. Gauri Viswanathan, *Masks of Conquest: Literary Study and British Rule in India* (New York: Columbia University Press, 1989); Amin Alhassan, "The Canonic Economy of Communication and Culture: The Centrality of the Postcolonial Margins," *Canadian Journal of Communication* 32, no. 1 (2007): 103–18.

75. James Carey, *Communication as Culture* (New York: Routledge, 1989), 9.

76. Richard Abel, "The Perils of Pathé, or the Americanization of Early American Cinema," in Charney and Schwartz, *Cinema and the Invention of Modern Life*, 183

Bibliography

Abel, Richard. "The Perils of Pathé, or the Americanization of Early American Cinema." In *Cinema and the Invention of Modern Life*, edited by Leo Charney and Vanessa Schwartz, 183–223. Berkeley: University of California Press, 1995.

Acland, Charles. "Mapping the Serious and the Dangerous: Film and the National Council of Education, 1920–1939." *Cinémas: Revue d'Études Cinematographiques* 6, no. 1 (1995): 101–18.

Acland, Charles, and Haidee Wasson, eds. *Useful Cinema*. Durham: Duke University Press, 2011.

Alhassan, Amin. "The Canonic Economy of Communication and Culture: The Centrality of the Postcolonial Margins." *Canadian Journal of Communication* 32, no. 1 (2007): 103–18.

Buchanan, Donald. *Educational and Cultural Films in Canada.* Ottawa: National Film Society, 1936.

Burns, James M. *Flickering Shadows: Cinema and Identity in Colonial Zimbabwe.* Athens: Ohio University Press, 2002.

Canadian Government. *Census of Prairie Provinces 1926: Population and Agriculture.* Ottawa: King's Printer, 1929.

Canadian Government. *The Use of Films and Slides in Canadian Schools.* Dominion Bureau of Statistics. Education Bulletin No. 3 (1937).

Carey, James. *Communication as Culture.* New York: Routledge, 1989.

Carney, Leo, and Vanessa R. Schwartz, eds. *Cinema and the Invention of Modern Life.* Berkeley: University of California Press, 1995.

Charland, Maurice. "Technological Nationalism." *Canadian Journal of Political and Social Theory* 10, no. 1 (1986): 196–220.

Corbett, E. A. *We Have with Us Tonight.* Toronto: Ryerson Press, 1957.

Couldry, Nick, and Anna McCarthy, eds. *MediaSpace: Place, Scale and Culture in a Media Age.* New York: Routledge, 2004.

Druick, Zoë. "Mobile Cinema in Canada in Relation to British Mobile Film Practices." In *Screening Canadians: Cross-Cultural Perspectives on Canadian Film*, edited by Wolfram R. Keller and Gene Walz, 13–33. Marburg, Germany: Universitatsbibliothek, 2008.

Faris, Ron. *The Passionate Educators.* Toronto: Peter Martin Associates, 1975.

Foucault, Michel. "Governmentality." In *The Foucault Effect: Studies in Governmentality*, edited by Graham Burchell et al., 87–104. Chicago: University of Chicago Press, 1991.

Gray, C. W. *Movies for the People: The Story of the National Film Board's Unique Distribution System.* Ottawa: NFB, 1977.

Greene, Ronald. "Pastoral Exhibition: The YMCA Motion Picture Bureau and the Transition to 16mm, 1928–39." In *Useful Cinema*, edited by Charles Acland and Haidee Wasson, 205–29. Durham: Duke University Press, 2011.

———. "Y Movies: Film and the Modernization of Pastoral Power." *Communication and Critical/Cultural Studies* 2, no. 1 (March 2005): 20–36.

Grierson, John. "Canadian Film Activities." 1939. Grierson Archive G3:5.4.

Grieveson, Lee, and Peter Krämer. "Film Production and Variety Shows: Introduction." In *The Silent Cinema Reader*, edited by Lee Grieveson and Peter Krämer. New York: Routledge, 2004.

Hackett, Yvette. "The National Film Society of Canada, 1935–1951: Its Origins and Development." In *Flashback: People and Institutions in Canadian Film History*, edited by Gene Walz, 135–68. Montreal: Mediatexte, 1986.

Horne, Jennifer. "A History Long Overdue: The Public Library and Motion Pictures." In *Useful Cinema*, edited by Charles Acland and Haidee Wasson, 149–77. Durham: Duke University Press, 2011.

Jacobs, Lea. "Reformers and Spectators: The Film Education Movement in the Thirties." *Camera Obscura* 8, no. 1 (22) (1990): 29–49.

Kessler, Frank. "Distribution—Preliminary Notes." In *Networks of Entertainment: Early Film Distribution 1895–1915*, edited by Frank Kessler and Nanna Verhoeff, 1–3. Eastleigh, UK: John Libbey Publishing, 2007.

Kett, Joseph. *The Pursuit of Knowledge under Difficulties: From Self-Improvement to Adult Education in America, 1750–1990.* Stanford: Stanford University Press, 1994.

Kidd, J. R. *Adult Education in the Canadian University.* Toronto: Canadian Association for Adult Education, 1956.

Lester, Peter. "The Perilous Gauge: Canadian Independent Film Exhibition and the 16mm Mobile Menace." In *Cinema and Technology: Cultures, Theories, Practices*, edited by Marc Furstenau, Adrian Mackenzie, and Bruce Bennett, 23–36. New York: Palgrave, 2009.

Lewis, Jon, and Eric Smoodin, eds. *Looking Past the Screen: Case Studies in American Film History and Method.* Durham: Duke University Press, 2007.

Lindvall, Terry. "Silent Cinema and Religion: An Overview (1895–1930)." In *The Routledge Companion to Religion and Film*, edited by J. Lyden, 14–30. New York: Routledge, 2009.

MacInnes, C. M., ed. *Adult Education in the British Dominions.* London: World Association for Adult Education, 1929.

Mayne, Judith. "Immigrants and Spectators." *Wide Angle* 5, no. 2 (1982): 32–41.

McLaren, Angus. *Our Own Master Race: Eugenics in Canada, 1885–1945.* Toronto: McClelland & Stewart, 1990.

McLean, Scott. "University Extension and Social Change: Positioning a University of the People in Saskatchewan." *Adult Education Quarterly* 58, no. 1 (November 2007): 3–21.

Mebold, Anke. "'Just Like a Public Library Maintained for Public Welfare': 28mm as a Comprehensive Service Strategy for Non-Theatrical Clientele, 1912–23." In *Networks of Entertainment: Early Film Distribution, 1895–1915*, edited by Frank Kessler and Nanna Verhoeff, 260–74. Eastleigh, UK: John Libbey Publishing, 2007.

Mebold, Anke, and Charles Tepperman, "Resurrecting the Lost History of 28mm Film in North America." *Film History* 15 (2003): 137–51.

Morgan, W. J. "Antonio Gramsci and Raymond Williams: Workers, Intellectuals, and Adult Education." In *Gramsci and Education*, edited by Carmel Borg, Joseph Buttigieg, and Peter Mayo, 241–62. Lanham, MD: Rowman & Littlefield, 2002.

Orgeron, Devin, Marsha Orgeron, and Dan Streible, eds. *Learning with the Lights Off.* New York: Oxford University Press, 2012.

Ostherr, Kirsten. *Cinematic Prophylaxis: Globalization and Contagion in the Discourse of World Health.* Durham: Duke University Press, 2005.

Palmer, Howard. *Patterns of Prejudice: A History of Nativism in Alberta.* Toronto: McClelland and Stewart, 1982.

Peers, Frank. *The Politics of Public Broadcasting.* Toronto: University of Toronto Press, 1969.

Philip, Ed. "A Few Perspectives on the Workers' Educational Association 1917 to ____." In *History of the Workers' Educational Association: Diamond Anniversary, 1917–1977*, edited by Albert Field, 25–28. Toronto: Workers' Educational Association of Canada, 1977.

Rosenzweig, Roy. "From Rum Shot to Rialto: Workers and Movies." In *Moviegoing in America: A Sourcebook in the History of Film Exhibition*, edited by Gregory A. Waller, 27–46. Oxford: Blackwell, 2002.

Ruoff, Jeffrey, ed. *Virtual Voyages: Cinema and Travel.* Durham: Duke University Press, 2006.

Saettler, Paul. *A History of Instructional Technology.* New York: McGraw-Hill Book Company, 1968.

Seiler, Robert M., and Tamara P. Seiler. *Reel Time: Movie Exhibitors and Movie Audiences in Prairie Canada, 1886–1986.* Edmonton: Athabasca University Press, 2013.

Selman, Gordon, Mark Selman, Michael Cooke, and Paul Dampier. *The Foundations of Adult Education in Canada.* 2nd ed. Toronto: Thompson Educational Publishing, 1998.

Singer, Ben. "Early Home Cinema and the Edison Home Projecting Kinetoscope." *Film History* 2, no. 1 (1988): 37–69.

Tepperman, Charles. "Digging the Finest Potatoes from Their Acre: Government Film Exhibition in Rural Ontario, 1917–1934." In *Hollywood in the Neighborhood: Historical Case Studies of Local Moviegoing*, edited by Kathryn H. Fuller-Seeley, 130–48. Berkeley: University of California Press, 2008.

Viswanathan, Gauri. *Masks of Conquest: Literary Study and British Rule in India*. New York: Columbia University Press, 1989.

Wasson, Haidee. *Museum Movies: The Museum of Modern Art and the Birth of Art Cinema*. Berkeley: University of California Press, 2005.

Williams, Raymond. *Television: Technology and Cultural Form*. Glasgow: Fontana, 1974.

Woodsworth, J. S. *Strangers within Our Gates*. Toronto: F. C. Stephenson, 1909.

ZOË DRUICK is Professor of Communication and Associate Dean of Graduate Studies at Simon Fraser University. She is author of *Projecting Canada: Government Policy and Documentary Film at the National Film Board* and *The Grierson Effect: Tracing Documentary's International Movement.*

7 "A Casual Glance Reveals a Perfect Mine of Treasures"

George Kleine's Catalogue of Educational Motion Pictures *(1910)*

Oliver Gaycken

George Kleine's *Catalogue of Educational Motion Pictures* (1910) appeared at a pivotal moment in the history of nonfiction cinema in the United States, coming just after cinema's consolidation as a cultural institution—its so-called second birth but well before the establishment of a viable nontheatrical market in the 1920s.[1]

This ambitious catalog, which ran to 336 pages and comprised over a thousand titles, contained a curious assortment of films compiled by Kleine on the basis of his experience as a distributor.[2] The opening pages included a series of texts that argued for the use of cinema as an educational medium. The first, entitled "Plan and Scope," supplied an initial rationale for the use of motion pictures in education:

> The plan and scope of a work of this kind is not sharply defined. In a sense, all subjects are educational, but in classifying a mass of motion picture films for educational purposes the line must be drawn about a reasonable area. A dramatic or comic tale in motion pictures, laid in some foreign country, is educational in so far as it shows the manners, customs and environment of the people; an Indian tale, the habits of the aborigines. But there must be a halt before we reach fanciful ground, where there is danger of accuracy being sacrificed to dramatic effect. Here and there a subject has been included in this list which lies on the border, and perhaps outside of it. But there is an educational application in every instance. The word "Educational" is here used in a wide sense, and does not indicate that these films are intended for school or college use exclusively. They are intended rather for the education of the adult as well as the youth, for exhibition before miscellaneous audiences, as well as for more restricted use.[3]

One way to understand the strategic imprecision that characterizes this passage is to see it as a justification for the large number of films included in the catalog; although some, such as surgical films, were indeed appropriate for more specialized audiences, most of them were made for general audiences.[4] Alternatively, however, while this wavering definition of the educational field might seem a weakness born out of either imprecise thinking or an economic strategy that sought to include as

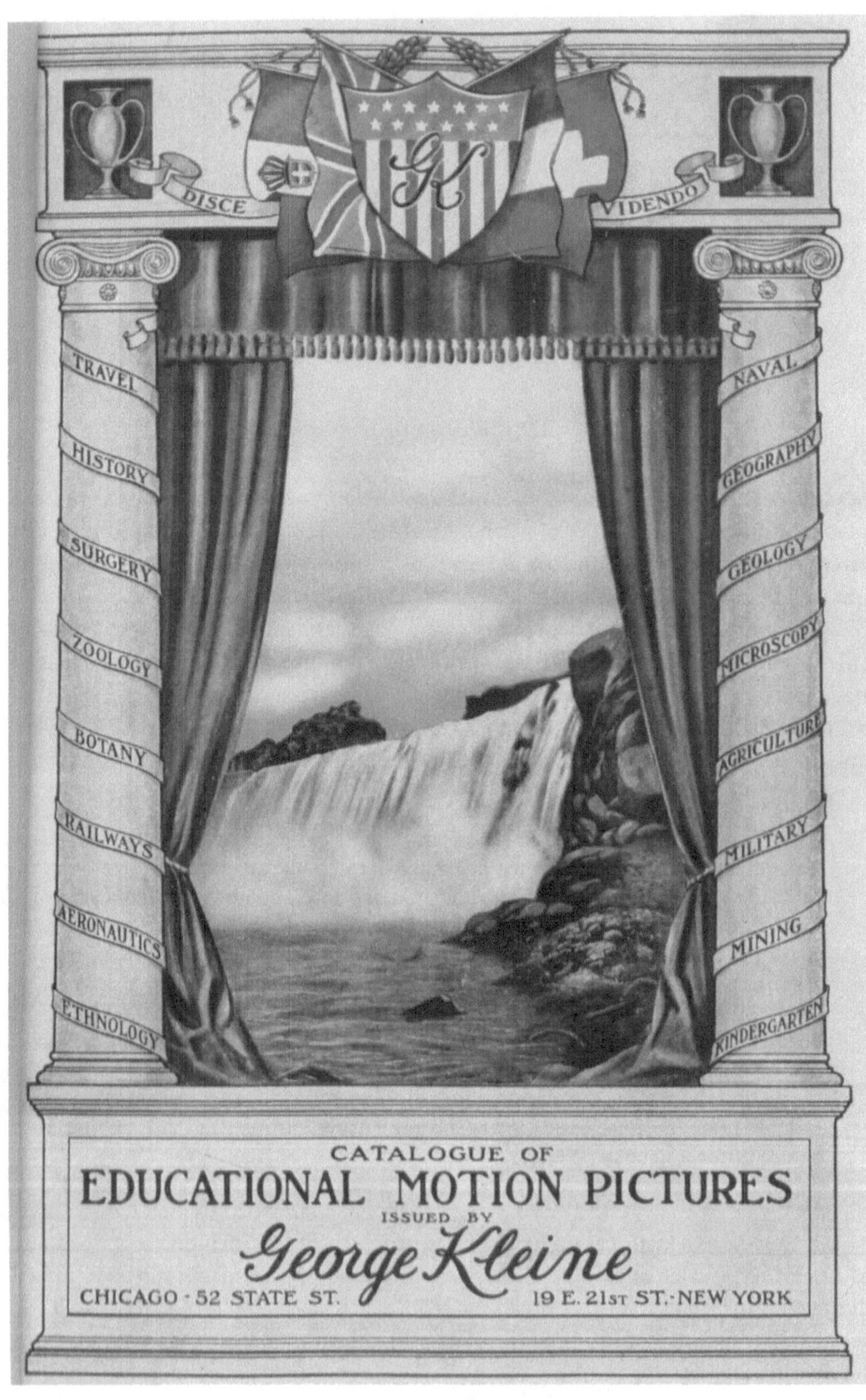

Fig. 7.1. Cover of Kleine's 1910 educational film catalog. Billy Rose Theater collection, New York Public Library.

many films as possible in the creation of a new market segment, it also can be seen as a precise description of a protean object. In other words, Kleine's uncertainty about how to define an educational film attests to unsettled definitions, which would only begin to be formulated in a systematic way in the early 1920s.

This chapter focuses on the wide range of responses that the catalog generated. They constitute a trove of reception history for the nonfiction film during the early 1910s, and Kleine's broad definition of his undertaking finds a corollary in them. Taken together, these responses describe a wide field, limning nontheatrical cinema's nascent institutional form as it emerged alongside cinema's entertainment edifice. The responses to the catalog indicate enthusiasm for the idea of educational cinema as well as frustration that the material infrastructure was not yet capable of providing the actual experiences that the catalog promised. A metaphor for the catalog, then, is that it functioned as a hinge, a collection of fragments in the service of a vision of cinema as an educational resource, a vision that did not yet exist but that it would help create. The catalog functioned both retrospectively, marshaling an impressive inventory of films that sought to validate the view of cinema's educative capabilities, as well as prophetically, joining a chorus of voices that sought to provide a rhetorical blueprint for a cinema of the future.[5]

Before Kleine published the catalog, he corresponded with and sent proofs to Thomas A. Edison, to whom he also dedicated the catalog as its ideal and idealized recipient, emblematic of its goals and values. The dedication read:

> to the most democratic of men \ the most unassuming \ whose energy is compassed only by the number of hours in the day \ whose measureless intellect finds kinship in every branch of knowledge \ whose inventions have bettered the condition and added to the pleasures of uncountable millions \ to the man who is most honored and revered by those who know him best \ To Thomas A. Edison this compilation is most respectfully dedicated."[6]

The values enumerated in this dedication—democracy, humility, limitless energy, and intellectual breadth, all in the service of the practical betterment of humanity—are what Kleine sought to promote with his "compilation." Pleased with Edison's appreciative response, Kleine reproduced it in the catalog's opening pages: "I have examined the proofs of your catalogue of Educational Motion Pictures with great interest and congratulate you on your careful work in gathering and editing the lists. Motion Pictures are and will be a great factor in education of the public and your catalogue shows the possibilities of motion pictures in teaching the public science, history and geography, as well as a knowledge of how other peoples live, work and play."[7]

Edison's approving letter was part of a flurry of congratulatory correspondence that greeted the catalog's release, with the motion picture trade press taking the lead. The *Moving Picture World* sent Kleine a telegram stating, "Educational film catalogue a surprise accept congratulations on the completeness and excellency of the stupendous work." The editorial department at *The Billboard* complimented him "upon this volume which we believe to be as neat and comprehensive as any that has been brought to our notice." And *Variety* sent a telegram thanking Kleine for the "very handsome catalogue of educational subjects."[8]

Other members of the film industry paid Kleine similar compliments. Fellow Chicagoan Sidney Smith, the booking manager of Thielen's circuit for the George K. Spoor Company, wrote, "I desire to offer you my sincere thanks for your beautiful, educational, catalogue which I received on Saturday. It is of incalculable value to an up-to-date moving picture manager and is well worthy of the efforts of the pioneer of the film industry of which you are the recognized head."[9] The copy sent to the educational publishers Scott, Foresman and Company thanked Kleine for the "very handsome educational catalogue. I think your binder has achieved a triumph; the book certainly presents a very attractive appearance. What labor of compilation has amounted to of course, I can form a fair idea. It must have taken a long time to get this data together and put it out in the shape which you have done."[10] Theater managers expressed their enthusiasm as well. C. E. van Duzee, manager of the Twin City Calcium and Stereopticon Company, a licensed film exchange in Minneapolis, Minnesota, expressed his "appreciation of the serviceable and very attractive catalog you have just sent me of the educational films"; the president of the Montana Film Exchange in Butte wrote, "You evidently have gone to great trouble"; and a letter from the Clune Film Exchange in Los Angeles noted, "You certainly have spared no expense."[11]

As positive as these responses were, the focus on the catalog's appearance hints at a shortcoming. The word *handsome* is telling in this regard; although likely meant to connote the secondary meanings of "substantial" or "impressive," the adjective is more suited to a description of furniture or a fancy encyclopedia set. The suspicion that these responses raise is that the catalog would gather dust alongside the expensive encyclopedia sets, fated to function primarily as learned furniture.

Some responses went beyond appreciating the catalog's production values and held out the possibility of increased business, however. S. M. Walkinshaw, general manager for Lyman H. Howe's "Festivals of Travel," wrote, "We frequently receive requests from traveling exhibitors, lecturers, etc. asking us for information regarding educational subjects, and we shall be pleased indeed to refer the writers of all such requests to you in future."[12] The resident manager of the Bijou Theatre in Fitchburg, Massachusetts, mentioned that the local Normal School would soon install "a cinematograph for educational purposes," and he urged Kleine to send another copy of the catalog to the school's principal.[13] Both of these responses, however, offered little in the way of immediate gains, although both certainly gestured in directions that must have pleased Kleine—the "high-class" lecture circuit of Lyman Howe and the as-yet-untapped educational market.

Kleine sent copies of the catalog to boards of health, state medical associations, and other civic groups, presumably as part of a strategy to expand the field of cinema exhibition. But this foray into uncharted territory encountered the significant problem that these organizations, almost without exception, lacked both the material infrastructure—motion picture projection equipment, projection booths, appropriate screening spaces—and sources of funding that would allow for the adoption of cinema. The secretary of the State Board of Health of Indiana commented, "We expect next year to use a projecting lantern with our traveling tuberculosis show. We will buy some motion pictures if we possibly can and will not forget you in this matter."[14] The chief clerk at the California Board of Health wrote, "All health officers in this State are contemplating taking up this line of work for educational purposes. At present, this Department has no money to spend for material of this sort, but after the meeting of the next Legislature, which will be in January, it may be able to see its way clear to purchasing some of your goods."[15] And the president of Louisiana's Board of Commissioners for the Protection of Birds, Game, and Fish wrote to request a catalog, mentioning, "We shortly intend to go into educational work using films and a motion picture machine."[16] Whether the word was *expecting*, *contemplating*, or *intending*, the common thread in these responses is that no one was in a position to order any films.

Even seemingly good news had often contained negative nuggets. M. A. Robison, the secretary of the Nevada State Medical Association, wrote, "We have been and are fortunate here in having a Moving Picture House that gives us good service along the line of educational films. We've had the Fly film, Sleeping sickness, the Man Who Learned, in fact most of those in that list. And they tell me they will get any or all along those lines we wish. I am going to arrange with them to furnish a regular weekly or monthly service for our Society."[17] As encouraging as this letter may have been, the exhibitions nonetheless took place as occasional special events in a commercial cinema. In other words, instead of a vibrant or even developing sector, Kleine addressed his catalog to an embryonic market that would take years to develop.

Other responses indicated that even people who had a specific interest in films listed in the catalog would often meet with considerable difficulties. Norman P. Heffley, president of the Heffley Institute in Brooklyn, New York, wrote, "Your catalogue of educational motion picture films at hand and find there are quite a number of films which I could use from time to time; but as we would not have occasion to use them very often we would hardly be justified in their purchase. I am unable to find anywhere in New York any one whom I can obtain the same on rental. Should you be unable to give me the address of any New York firm from whom I could secure them will you kindly let me know whether or not you could make duplicates of any films of the enclosed list."[18] The catalog contained two indexes—one "classified" (i.e., subject) index and another alphabetical index. Heffley requested three programs, one about Russia, another about Japan, and a third about Hawaii; the programs contained ten, nine, and twenty-nine films, respectively.

A closer look at one of Heffley's programs provides a sense of the challenges underlying the catalog's façade of plenty. Heffley asked for all the films listed under the "Russia" entry in the subject index: *Caucasian Customs* (387ft.), *Cold Plunge in Moscow* (246ft.), *Moscow Clad in Snow* (459ft.), *Moscow under Water* (274ft.), *Nobles*

Leaving Kremlin, Moscow, after Reception by the Czar (100ft.), *Riot in St. Petersburg* (246ft.), *Streets of St. Petersburg before the Revolution* (175ft.), *Traveling through Russia* (690ft.), *A Trip through Russia* (262ft.), *Winter and Summer Panoramas on the Trans-Siberian Railway* (175ft.). The total amount of footage for the program was 2,987 feet, which would have run approximately fifty minutes at 16 feet per second. Kleine's response to Heffley pointed out that the films in the catalog were only for purchase, not for rent, and Kleine's standard per-foot charge was $0.13, so the total price for the program would have been $391.82, which meant a cost of almost $8 per minute of screen time. The total is the equivalent of roughly $10,400 in 2019.[19]

Kleine's response also included a sentence whose basic point became a common refrain: "It is to be regretted that the overwhelming demand for films that are of an amusing nature has not permitted exchanges to develop assortments which are purely educational, but this matter is receiving attention from film manufacturers."[20] Kleine blames public taste ("overwhelming demand") for not permitting exchanges to develop a stock of educational titles, but he was not willing to develop an educational exchange himself. And his insistence on the purchase model was an anachronism in 1910. The rental system had begun, after all, in 1904 in the United States and became the primary mode of film distribution during the nickelodeon era, as exchanges proliferated and launched the careers of several later moguls.[21] Kleine's reliance on an obsolete distribution strategy contributed to the catalog's lack of commercial viability, and it underlines the gap between his rhetorical and financial support of the educational cinema.

Another example of the catalog's shortcomings becomes apparent from Kleine's correspondence with Reverend A. M. Gardener, general secretary of the World in Boston: America's First Great Missionary Exposition, which took place from April 24 to May 20, 1911, in the Grand Hall of the Mechanics Building, which had been built to host exhibitions. A promotional pamphlet described the exhibition as "organized on the lines of the successful Missionary Expositions recently held in England" and noted that it would display "in novel and striking ways the people and their lives, the work the Missionaries are doing, and the difference the Gospel makes in all non-Christian countries." Some of the "striking scenes" the exhibition promised to provide were "Japanese Street, Congo Village, Indian Zenana, Lumber Camp, Bengali Bazaar, Alaskan Totem Poles, Chinese Opium Den, Buddhist Temple, American Indian Tepee, Mission Hospital, Native Churches, Arab Compound." In addition to the built environments, the spectacle included "young men and women (called *stewards*) from the churches of Boston and vicinity, dressed in native costumes and giving character and life to each scene."[22]

The exhibition's alternate title, "World in Boston: A Living Exposition of World-Wide Christian Missions," indicates how crucial the creation of verisimilar spectacle was to the event. An article in the *New York Times* further underscored the prominence of "spectacular reality" by mentioning how the great exhibition would give "vivid reproductions" of church work in foreign lands.[23] Indeed, the World in Boston built on an established culture of exhibitions that flourished in western Europe and the United States in the latter half of the nineteenth century. As multiple historians have noted, cinema was integrated into exhibition culture immediately after its appearance, and so it comes as no surprise that the World in Boston also envisioned a role for the motion picture: "In another hall an almost continuous moving-picture show will be going on, the films for which are being obtained in all the great cities of the world. They are to be actual scenes, not fake pictures. It will show the teeming life of a great city in China or a missionary preaching in India; pupils studying in the native and the mission schools in another foreign country, and other things that pertain to the various phases of foreign life which mission work touches."[24]

In order to make these envisioned scenes a reality, Reverend Gardener wrote to the producer Charles Urban requesting "a list of films you have for sale, representing life in China, Japan, India, Africa, or other foreign countries, together with any that you have of life among American Indians or Eskimos in North America."[25] Urban forwarded the letter to Kleine, who was the US representative for Urban's films, and Kleine sent Gardner a catalog along with information about terms and conditions: the films were supplied on an "indefinite lease basis," American films not in stock could be provided in ten to fourteen days, imported films not in stock could be made up in five to six weeks, and the catalog contained various indices that would help him find the films in which he had expressed an interest. Gardner then sent Kleine a list of eighteen films that he wanted.[26]

Gardner inquired specifically about films made in Burma and India by Dr. Gregory Mantle, a missionary friend of his. Gardener mentioned that "he [Mantle] had, however, several other pictures which I should be glad to obtain, one, especially, representing the patients entering the mission hospital at Medak, another representing natives crossing a river, a third representing a boy preaching in the open air."[27] Despite the seeming plenitude of his archive, Kleine was not able to supply all the Mantle films, and he pointed out, "It is probable that the subjects you mentioned were never published by Dr. Mantle as he retained a number of subjects for his exclusive use."[28] In what must have represented another kind of disappointment, instead of granting a volume discount, Kleine quoted Gardner the standard price of 13 cents per foot for the almost four thousand feet of film, for a total cost of around $520. The film program for the "World in Boston" did seem to have been part of the exhibition, however, with the *Boston Daily Globe*'s account of the opening day of the exhibition reporting: "Moving Picture Hall, 2.20 to 9.20 pm—Missionary travelogues on India and Burmah, tours in several lands, and Hawaiian and Nome scenes."[29] Here, then, the catalog proved useful in aiding with the supply of films to a major event.

Kleine's correspondence with Gardner provided an initial indication of a problem that appeared in several other instances—namely, the expectations of expert audiences, whose specialized knowledge led to criticism of the films' content. Mr. Matthew Dudgeon, the secretary of the Wisconsin Free Library Commission, wrote to Kleine asking about "films on literary topics." Dudgeon went on to qualify his request, noting, "While there are many educational films, we have found very few that meet our exact situation. Most of those which are educational in nature are admirable films and well fitted for use in schools, etc., but still do not meet our needs."[30] Kleine did not address Dudgeon's specific interest, instructing him instead about how to "keep posted on what is being placed on the market in the line you are especially interested in."[31] A professor at the University of Illinois wrote to ask whether Kleine would allow him to preview films, providing the following rationale, "I ask this because in your films of the steel industry the technical features are not made quite clear in your description. Also I should wish to see that the processes depicted were modern processes; at one of the Chicago theatres I once saw a film of the steel making industry which showed the blast furnaces being charged with ore by <u>women</u>. This may be done in some small furnaces in foreign countries, but we should not wish to show such film to our students."[32] In addition to finding fault with the films on offer, expert users often were interested in only a handful of titles. P. A. Maignen, a Philadelphia developer of a water filtration system, was interested in titles 27120 (*Little Drops of Water*) and 27121 (*Pond Life*) "or other films giving representations of bacterial life."[33] These responses indicated the problems that arose when Kleine's grand edifice of education confronted the reality of capillary forms of knowledge.

J. H. Kellogg's letter to Kleine provided an extended example of a specialist's engagement with the catalog. Kellogg wrote asking about a particular kind of film, "I enclose a newspaper clipping giving an account of moving pictures. Can you send me a film which will produce these effects?"[34] The newspaper article, entitled "Bacteria War Shown," covered a November 18, 1910, screening at the Royal Institute of Public Health in London by Dr. Constantin Levaditi of the Pasteur Institute.[35] The article, subtitled "Cinematograph Gives Battle between Phagocytes and Spirochaeta: Human Life Is at Stake; Defenders of Body Are Worsted until Medical Aid Comes to the Rescue," provided an account of "one of the most interesting and instructive cinematography shows ever witnessed, in the shape of a fierce battle between an army of phagocytes and several million spirochaeta." The journalist described how Levaditi supplied a running commentary for the screening: "In the first few pictures the phagocytes had rather a bad time of it in their battle with the invaders, and, like a general commanding his forces, Dr. Levaditi cried: 'See! They weaken!' Following with his pointer the combatants appear[ed] on the screen like weird creatures conjured up in a nightmare." The following sentence must have been especially interesting to Kellogg, "From a cold in the head upward the various human ailments entail a fight by the phagocytes in defense of their home, and the problem of the doctor is to discover the best food for the health of the soldier, according to the nature of the battle it has to wage."[36]

Kleine's skeptical answer indicates a familiarity both with these types of films and the enthusiasm to which they gave rise, "Films of this nature are extremely interesting, but I doubt whether the present state of the art of cinematography will permit the making of a film that will indicate as clearly as the article suggests the

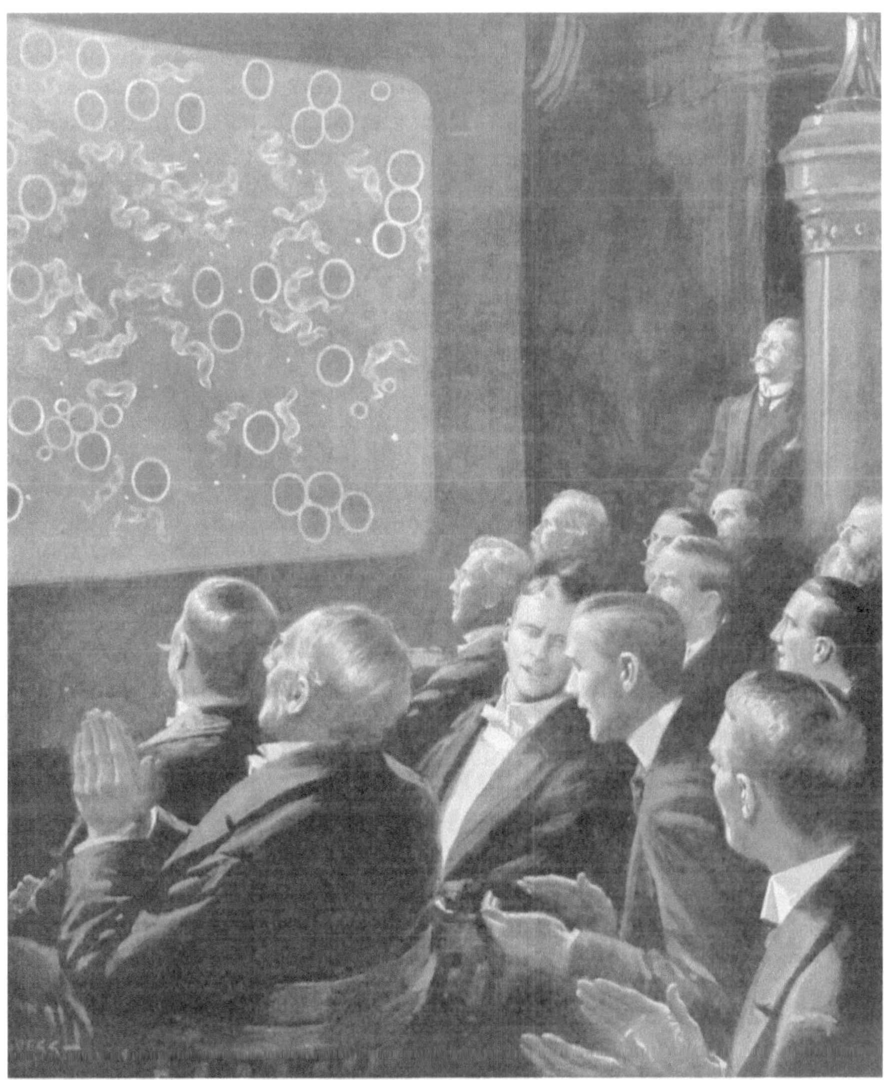

Fig. 7.2. *Illustrated London News* image of a screening at the King's College Hospital Medical Society of Jean Comandon films in November 1910; Levaditi is the man standing at the right. *Illustrated London News* 137, no. 3733 (November 5, 1910). The caption for the image notes: "Amongst the films was a series illustrating the experimental production of sleeping-sickness in a rat. The movement of the trypanosomes among the blood corpuscles and their gradual development until the death of the rat were shown with great clearness on the screen. Many interesting films followed. All the films were exhibited by Messrs. Pathé Freres."

action of the germs." The rest of his response is typical of the deflationary tactics that he employed after the release of the catalog: "We are watching the developments in the application of cinematography to scientific subjects very closely, but few films are available that have practical value upon such topics as these. You may have read of a film showing the operations of the stomach. I have seen this subject which has little value either for scientific demonstration or institutions."[37] Here, too, a gulf stretches between the rhetoric surrounding the catalog's release and Kleine's defensive responses to eager inquirers.

Kleine's inability to follow through on the catalog's promise led to a spectrum of frustration, ranging from slightly nonplussed to downright irritated. James P. Heaton of *The Survey*, a journal published by Charity Organization Society of the City of New York, complained about the catalog's inclusiveness, noting that Kleine had "given an altogether too wide interpretation to the term Educational Pictures in your catalogue. . . . I feel that you have included very many which are really very trivial in subject. . . . I would think you would do better by issuing a smaller catalogue of pictures, including in it only those of a higher grade."[38] From the Civics Committee of the Iowa Federation of Women's Clubs, Mrs. B. R. Johnston of Cedar Rapids expressed her annoyance with using the catalog by noting, "You see, if the majority of your catalogued films are unobtainable for ordinary use, it limits the usefulness of your catalogue considerably." Her group had selected fifteen films for a special screening at a local cinema, but when their local manager tried to book them, none were available. A second attempt to book the films, this time from the General Film Company (the MPPC's distribution company, in which Kleine was a prominent shareholder), was not satisfactory either. "After interesting the public generally in the better class of films and getting up public expectations to a high point our manager here was able to obtain for this very especial meeting only enough educational films to last thirty minutes." Mrs. Brown concluded, "We were so thoroughly disgusted that we have done nothing since and unless I find just how to overcome these difficulties shall discontinue . . . work along this line. I cannot imagine any local manager so stupid in a business sense as to disappoint so large an audience of the better citizens."[39]

Kleine was not insensitive to the various shortcomings of his efforts, writing to John Shoop, a Chicago educator: "Ample as the list may appear to be at first glance it is wholly insufficient to one who may search for a comprehensive list of films to illustrate a particular subject in geography, history, etc; but with the encouragement and assistance of educational institutions as well as the better class of exhibitors film manufacturers will develop the list in many directions."[40] Kleine's response acknowledged a number of shortcomings, such as how many of the films in the catalog were not in stock, had to be shipped from Europe, or had to be printed on order. Looking back on the catalog's publication from the vantage point of the early 1920s, Kleine provided a frank assessment and an excellent summation of the reasons it was not more successful.

> Many of the early subjects were in a sense instructional or educational. Our catalogue issued in 1910 will show that even at that time there were many films of this character in existence. The list included the product of Edison, Charles Urban, Gaumont, Eclipse, Pathé, Selig, Biograph and others. The chief weakness of the assembled list of films lay in the fact that there was a lack of coherence as to topics, the assortment forming a miscellaneous and unrelated group. Also, the films were not easily available. The negatives were held by various producers in different countries of Europe, principally England, France and Italy, and in the United States. The traffic was so limited that it was not practical to carry prints in stock and films were made up on receipt of orders. A single order for a few short subjects might have to be placed in England, France, Italy and the U.S. It was not possible for the buyer to see the film before purchase, and there was a usual delay of six to eight weeks before delivery.[41]

Of course, the frustration ran both ways. As Jennifer Peterson has noted, "Educators regularly approached Kleine attempting to obtain films at low prices, but Kleine was a businessman, not a reformer or an educator. He wanted to commercialize the nonfiction film, and he complained about those educational and religious institutions who "tried to get something for nothing," even calling the nontheatrical users "parasites."[42] The solution that Kleine repeatedly mentioned—the establishment of rental depots devoted to educational films—presaged the establishment of the nontheatrical industry a decade hence. To Malcolm McKay, at the Iris Theatre in Kansas City, Missouri, Kleine wrote, "While inquiries are coming from all parts of the United States to take proper care of them would require a number of depots, each of them heavily stocked with films at enormous expense which would not be recovered in a number of years. In compiling our Educational film catalogue it was our intention to offer these subjects for sale and not for rental, excepting such as were taken by rental exchanges in the regular course of their business."[43] Kleine wrote to another correspondent:

> We hope in the course of time to establish a series of rental depots which will make a specialty of Educational subjects with the purpose of renting them to Educational institutions and exhibitors other than theatrical. This, however, is a laborious and expensive matter, and our plans have not yet been definitely formulated. We regret that a more definite and satisfactory letter cannot be written at the present time. There is a great deal of missionary work to be done by way of preparation for the Educational field which is opening up, and we will do our share to place this subject upon a practical basis.[44]

Indeed, these letters recall the cautionary note sounded in the original catalog, when Kleine wrote, "We are far, very far, from offering a motographic library which is complete as to every subject that can be profitably treated in this manner. It will require years of further effort and great sums of money to even scratch the surface of the rich mine which lies at our feet. No single commercial, scientific or educational organization can hope to accomplish more than a small fraction of the work to be done."[45] Here Kleine both acknowledged the incompleteness of his undertaking and made a sober estimation of the difficulties involved in advancing the cause of educational cinema.

These external and internal criticisms had an effect on the catalog's second edition, published in 1915. First, the new edition was severely abridged—at only 162 pages, it represented a decrease of over 50 percent just in terms of pages, and instead of over a thousand titles, it contained only 162 reels. Second, Kleine's business model had also changed. Instead of selling prints, Kleine based his second catalog on a rental system, and he made a point of mentioning, "The list includes only such subjects as we actually have in stock."[46] Rhetorically, too, there was a shift from the claims of plenitude in the prefatory material to the first catalog to this more nuanced and conservative estimation of what the second catalog provided:

> We do not claim that this collection is anything like a complete motographic library containing every subject that could be profitably treated in this manner. It could not thus be characterized even if it included every educational moving picture ever made. There is no branch of human endeavor which could not be treated advantageously by cinematography, and the possibilities of this art as an educational factor have never even been scratched. To do this, years of further effort and the expenditure of vast sums of money will be required. Manufacturers must receive a great deal more encouragement from educators than has been given them in the past. The manufacture and exploitation of educational film has never been commercially profitable, and the progressive manufacturers who have devoted brains, energy and money to this work have been unrewarded save for the satisfaction they have received from the knowledge of a valuable work well done. The public mind, however, and especially that part of it which is concerned with the problems of modern pedagogic methods, is awakening to the value of animated photography as an educational force.[47]

The second catalog also made allowances for the variety programming format: "Many audiences demand a few purely entertaining subjects in connection with an educational program—a bit of dessert following a feast of solid food—and for the benefit of those exhibitors who wish to include clean, harmless comedies or wholesome dramatic subjects in their programs, we have added a carefully selected list of such pictures."[48]

While the initial catalog fell short of its goals in a number of notable ways, it also constituted a significant achievement, particularly in terms of its archival zeal and rhetorical force, which serve as emblems of arguments for cinema's particular suitability as a medium of visual education. The catalog served, in Joel Frykholm's words, "as a book-length ad vouching for the dignity of Kleine, the MPPC and the motion pictures," functioning thus as a harbinger for the development of nontheatrical cinema in the decade to come.[49] One remark from the first wave of responses to the 1910 catalog encapsulated the promise and the peril of Kleine's undertaking; E. J. Rhoad wrote to Kleine, "a casual glance reveals a perfect mine of treasures."[50] That a more careful look reveals a haphazard and fragmentary collection does not detract, however, from how Kleine's catalog stands as a monument to a vision of what cinema could be. Ultimately, the catalog offered a mirage: the promise of something, like the thirsty traveler's vision of water in the desert, greatly desired that in the end could not be delivered.

Notes

1. The notion of cinema's "second birth" is articulated in André Gaudreault and Philippe Marion, "A Medium Is Always Born Twice . . ." *Early Popular Visual Culture* 3, no. 1 (May 2005), 3–15.

2. I analyze the catalog's composition by comparing it to the tradition of the cabinet of curiosities in my *Devices of Curiosity: Early Cinema and Popular Science* (New York: Oxford University Press, 2015), ch. 4, "A Modern Cabinet of Curiosities: George Kleine's Collection of Popular-Science Films," 129–57.

3. George Kleine, *Catalogue of Educational Motion Picture Films* (Chicago: Bentley, Murray & Co., 1910), 1; hereafter abbreviated *Catalogue* (1910). I consulted the copy that is part of the Kleine Records at the Billy Rose Theater Collection, New York Public Library. A more easily accessed copy of the catalog is reproduced on reel three of *Early Rare British Filmmakers' Catalogues* (London: World Microfilm Publications, 1982).

4. The surgical films in the catalog, by Dr. Eugène-Louis Doyen, were taken from the Eclipse catalog. See *Catalogue* (1910), 36–39.

5. For a survey of the early rhetoric surrounding educational cinema, see Jennifer Peterson, *Education in the School of Dreams: Travelogues and Early Nonfiction Film* (Durham, NC: Duke University Press, 2013), 101–36, and my "The Cinema of the Future: Visions of the Medium as Modern Educator, 1895–1910," in *Learning with the Lights Off: Educational Film in the United States*, ed. Devin Orgeron, Marsha Orgeron, and Dan Streible (New York: Oxford University Press, 2011), 67–89. For a concise account of the 1910 catalog, see Joel Frykholm, *George Kleine and American Cinema: The Movie Business and Film Culture in the Silent Era* (London: BFI/Palgrave, 2015), 133–37.

6. *Catalogue* (1910), 1.

7. Thomas A. Edison to George Kleine, December 29, 1909; reproduced in *Catalogue* (1910), 4. Edison's classroom films were being produced in the early 1910s as well; see my, "The School of the Future or Ganot's *Physics*? Edison's Foray into Educational Cinema," in *Beyond the Screen: Institutions, Networks, and Publics of Early Cinema*, ed. Charlie Keil, Rob King, Marta Braun, and Paul Moore (Bloomington, IN: John Libbey, 2012), 143–52.

8. *Moving Picture World* to George Kleine, March 29, 1910; Editorial Department of *The Billboard* to George Kleine, April 5, 1910; *Variety* to George Kleine, April 22, 1910; box 39, file "Nontheatrical, General, 1909–1910," George Kleine Papers, Manuscripts Division, Library of Congress (henceforth GKP).

9. Sidney M. Smith to George Kleine, April 4, 1910; box 39, file "Nontheatrical, General, 1909–1910," GKP.

10. Charles E. S. Fielder to George Kleine, April 25, 1910; box 39, file "Nontheatrical, General, 1909–1910," GKP.

11. C. E. van Duzee to George Kleine, April 18, 1910; Frank T. Bailey to George Kleine, April 5, 1910; Theo M. Newman to George Kleine, April 18, 1910, box 39, file "Nontheatrical, General, 1909–1910," GKP.

12. S. M. Walkinshaw to George Kleine, April 4, 1910, box 39, file "Nontheatrical, General, 1909–1910," GKP. For more on Howe, see Charles Musser, with Carol Nelson, *High-Class Moving Pictures: Lyman H. Howe and the Forgotten Era of Traveling Exhibition, 1880–1920* (Princeton, NJ: Princeton University Press, 1991), and Peterson, *Education in the School of Dreams*, 108–12.

13. H. F. Jackson to George Kleine, April 14, 1910, box 39, file "Nontheatrical, General, 1909–1910," GKP.

14. J. N. Hurty to George Kleine, December 23, 1910, box 39, file "Nontheatrical, General, 1909–1910," GKP.

15. John Leinen to George Kleine, December 21, 1910, box 39, file "Nontheatrical, General, 1909–1910," GKP.

16. Frank M. Miller to George Kleine, December 8, 1910, box 39, file "Nontheatrical, General, 1909–1910," GKP. Other responses in this vein included a letter from the secretary of the State Medical Association of Texas, who wrote, "I am pleased to have this information, as I have received a number of inquiries concerning this same subject. At the present time the Association is not in a position to purchase or lease any films on its own account" (Holman Taylor to George Kleine, December 23, 1910, box 39, file "Nontheatrical, General, 1909–1910," GKP). And the secretary of the Maine State Board of Health simply mentioned that the catalogue "will be preserved for future reference" (A. [illegible] to George Kleine, December 27, 1910, box 39, file "Nontheatrical, General, 1909–1910," GKP).

17. M. A. Robison to George Kleine, December 27, 1910, box 39, file "Nontheatrical, General, 1909–1910," GKP. "The Fly film" likely refers to *The Fly Pest* (Charles Urban/Percy Smith, 1910); "sleeping sickness" likely refers to either *Trypanosoma brucei* (Pathé/Jean Comandon, 1910) or *La Cinématographie des microbes* (Pathé/Jean Comandon, 1909); *The Man Who Learned* (Edison 1910) is a hygiene film about milk safety.

18. Norman P. Heffley to George Kleine, November 15, 1910, box 39, file "Nontheatrical, General, 1909–1910," GKP. Heffley was the director of Pratt Institute's Department of Commerce, which became the Heffley Institute in 1895. Both institutions are prominent examples of Progressive-era education reform, which often envisioned a significant role for cinema and other visual media.

19. I arrived at this figure by using the Consumer Price Index calculator, which is a feature of the website of the Bureau of Labor Statistics (http://www.bls.gov/data/home.htm). According to the calculator $1 from 1913 has the same buying power as $26.13 in 2019. Since the calculator does not go back beyond 1913, I rounded up to $26.50 for my conversions.

20. George Kleine to N. P. Heffley, November 19, 1910, box 39, file "Nontheatrical, General, 1909–1910," GKP.

21. See Charles Musser, *The Emergence of Cinema: The American Screen to 1907* (New York: Charles Scribner's Sons, 1990), 366–68, 433–39, and Max Alvarez, "The Origins of the Film Exchange," *Film History* 17, no. 4 (2005): 431–65.

22. Flyer attached to A. M. Gardner to George Kleine, November 26, 1910, box 39, file "Nontheatrical, General, 1909–1910," GKP.

23. See Vanessa Schwartz, *Spectacular Realities: Early Mass Culture in Fin-de-Siècle Paris* (Los Angeles: University of California Press, 1998).

24. "Ten Thousand People to Portray Missionary Life," *New York Times*, January 22, 1911. For descriptions of how turn-of-the-century exhibitions incorporated cinema, see Emmanuelle Toulet, "Cinema and the Universal Exposition, Paris 1900," *Persistence of Vision* 9 (1991): 10–36; Tom Gunning, "The World as Object Lesson: Cinema Audiences, Visual Culture and the St. Louis World's Fair, 1904," *Film History* 6, no. 4 (1994): 422–44; Alison Griffiths,

Wondrous Difference: Cinema, Anthropology, and Turn-of-the-Century Visual Culture (New York: Columbia University Press, 2002), 46–85; Brian R. Jacobson, "Film, Technology, and Imperialism at the Pan-American Exposition, 1901," in *Meet Me at the Fair: A World's Fair Reader*, ed. Laura Hollengreen, Celia Pearce, Rebecca Rouse, and Bobby Schweizer (Pittsburgh: ETC Press, 2014), 349–61; Marina Dahlquist, "Health on Display: The Panama-Pacific International Exposition as Sanitary Venue," in *Performing New Media, 1890–1915*, ed. Kaveh Askari, Scott Curtis, Frank Gray, Louis Pelletier, Tami Williams, and Joshua Yumibe (New Barnet, UK: John Libbey, 2015), 174–85.

25. A. M. Gardner to Charles Urban Trading Company, November 8, 1910; box 39, file "Nontheatrical, General, 1909–1910," GKP.

26. A. M. Gardner to George Kleine, November 26, 1910; box 39, file "Nontheatrical, General, 1909–1910," GKP. Fifteen of the films are Urban titles, with two by Pathé and one by Edison.

27. Ibid. The Mantle titles that Gardner recognized were *Open-Air Bible Classes in India* (cat. no. 17017, 90ft.), *Hindu Burning Ghats (Natives' Cremation)* (cat. no. 27317, 107ft.), and *Elephants at Work in the Timber Yards, Rangoon* (cat. no. 17033, 170ft.).

28. George Kleine to A. M. Gardner; January 11, 1911, box 39, file "Nontheatrical, General, 1909–1910," GKP. Gardener also asked whether Kleine could provide safety film copies of the films and whether Kleine was in a position to provide "jumping letters." Gardener explained that "jumping letters" were "sentences formed by letters which moved upon the sheet," which is likely a reference to animated intertitles.

29. "7000 March in Mission Cause," *Boston Daily Globe*, April 24, 1911, 1–2.

30. Matthew S. Dudgeon to George Kleine, November 22, 1910, box 39, file "Nontheatrical, General, 1909–1910," GKP.

31. George Kleine to Matthew S. Dudgeon, November 28, 1910, box 39, file "Nontheatrical, General, 1909–1910," GKP.

32. H. F. Moore to George Kleine, August 10, 1910, box 39, file "Nontheatrical, General, 1909–1910," GKP, emphasis in original.

33. P. A. Maignen to George Kleine, March 21, 1912, box 39, file "Nontheatrical, General, 1909–1910," GKP. Both titles he mentions are Urban films. He also wanted Kleine's help in another area, "I have some cultures here which I would like reproduced very much, but I do not know where to go to have them done, or how much it would cost." Kleine's response is not preserved, but it is unlikely that he was able to provide microcinematographic services.

34. J. H. Kellogg to George Kleine, November 21, 1910, box 39, file "Nontheatrical, General, 1909–1910," GKP.

35. Levaditi was a Romanian-born microbiologist whose specialty was the polio virus.

36. "Bacteria War Shown," *Chicago Record Herald*, November 1910,; newspaper clipping accompanying J. H. Kellogg to George Kleine, November 21, 1910, box 39, file "Nontheatrical, General, 1909–1910," GKP.

37. George Kleine to J. H. Kellogg, November 23, 1910, box 39, file "Nontheatrical, General, 1909–1910," GKP. The X-ray film to which Kleine refers is probably *Examen de l'estomac par les rayons X* (Pathé, October 1910), the third film released under the rubric "scenes de vulgarisation scientifique."

38. James P. Heaton to George Kleine, March 20, 1912, box 39, file "Nontheatrical, General, 1909–1910," GKP.

39. Mrs. B. R. Johnston to George Kleine, March 21, 1912, box 39, file "Nontheatrical, General, 1909–1910," GKP.

40. George Kleine to John D. Shoop, November 25, 1910, box 39, file "Nontheatrical, General, 1909–1910," GKP.

41. Kleine, draft of article, box 40, file "Nontheatrical; Lectures, 1910–1912 and undated," GKP; published as "Co-operation in Visual Instruction," in *Proceedings of the National University Extension Association at Lexington, Kentucky, April 20, 21, 22, 1922* (Boston: Wright & Potter, 1923), 27–43.

42. Peterson, *Education in the School of Dreams*, 121. Peterson cites R. D. Williams to George Kleine, March 31, 1921, and George Kleine to R. D. Williams, March 25, 1921, box 39, GKP.

43. George Kleine to Mr. Malcolm McKay, August 19, 1910, box 39, file "Nontheatrical, General, 1909–1910," GKP.

44. George Kleine to H. F. Moore, August 11, 1910, box 39, file "Nontheatrical, General, 1909–1910," GKP.

45. *Catalogue* (1910).

46. George Kleine, *Catalogue of Educational Moving Pictures* (Chicago: G. Kleine, 1915), 4.

47. Ibid., 3–4.

48. Ibid., 4. For an elaboration and other examples of Kleine's metaphor (of film as food or medicine) that links it to the industry practice of issuing educational films on split reels with dramas or comedies, see Frykholm, *George Kleine*, 134–35.

49. Frykholm, *George Kleine*, 134.

50. E. J. Rhoad to George Kleine, March 1, 1911, box 39, file "Nontheatrical, General, 1909–1910," GKP.

Filmography

La Cinématographie des microbes (Pathé/Jean Comandon, 1909).
Examen de l'estomac par les rayons X (Pathé, October 1910).
The Fly Pest (Charles Urban/Percy Smith, 1910).
The Man Who Learned (Edison 1910).
Trypanosoma brucei (Pathé/Jean Comandon, 1910).
Titles 27120 [*Little Drops of Water*] and 27121 [*Pond Life*] (Urban).
"Russian Program": *Caucasian Customs* (387ft.), *Cold Plunge in Moscow* (246ft.), *Moscow Clad in Snow* (459ft.), *Moscow under Water* (274ft.), *Nobles Leaving Kremlin, Moscow, after Reception by the Czar* (100ft.), *Riot in St. Petersburg* (246ft.), *Streets of St. Petersburg before the Revolution* (175ft.), *Traveling through Russia* (690ft.), *A Trip through Russia* (262ft.), *Winter and Summer Panoramas on the Trans-Siberian Railway* (175ft.).
Gregory Mantle missionary films: *Open-Air Bible Classes in India* (cat. no. 17017, 90ft.), *Hindu Burning Ghats (Natives' Cremation)* (cat. no. 27317, 107ft.); and *Elephants at Work in the Timber Yards, Rangoon* (cat. no. 17033, 170ft.).

Bibliography

Alvarez, Max. "The Origins of the Film Exchange." *Film History* 17, no. 4 (2005): 431–65.
Dahlquist, Marina. "Health on Display: The Panama-Pacific International Exposition as Sanitary Venue." In *Performing New Media, 1890–1915*, edited by Kaveh Askari, Scott Curtis, Frank Gray, Louis Pelletier, Tami Williams, and Joshua Yumibe, 174–85. New Barnet, UK: John Libbey, 2015.
Frykholm, Joel. *George Kleine and American Cinema: The Movie Business and Film Culture in the Silent Era*. London: BFI/Palgrave, 2015.

Gaudreault, André, and Philippe Marion. "A Medium Is Always Born Twice . . ." *Early Popular Visual Culture* 3, no. 1 (May 2005): 3–15.

Gaycken, Oliver. "The Cinema of the Future: Visions of the Medium as Modern Educator, 1895–1910." In *Learning with the Lights Off: Educational Film in the United States*, edited by Devin Orgeron, Marsha Orgeron, and Dan Streible, 67–89. New York: Oxford University Press, 2011.

———. *Devices of Curiosity: Early Cinema and Popular Science*. New York: Oxford University Press, 2015.

———. "The School of the Future or Ganot's *Physics*? Edison's Foray into Educational Cinema." In *Beyond the Screen: Institutions, Networks, and Publics of Early Cinema*, edited by Charlie Keil, Rob King, Marta Braun, and Paul Moore, 143–52. Bloomington, IN: John Libbey, 2012.

Griffiths, Alison. *Wondrous Difference: Cinema, Anthropology, and Turn-of-the-Century Visual Culture*. New York: Columbia University Press, 2002.

Gunning, Tom. "The World as Object Lesson: Cinema Audiences, Visual Culture and the St. Louis World's Fair, 1904." *Film History* 6, no. 4 (1994): 422–44.

Jacobson, Brian R. "Film, Technology, and Imperialism at the Pan-American Exposition, 1901." In *Meet Me at the Fair: A World's Fair Reader*, edited by Laura Hollengreen, Celia Pearce, Rebecca Rouse, and Bobby Schweizer, 349–61. Pittsburgh: ETC Press, 2014.

Kleine, George. *Catalogue of Educational Motion Picture Films*. Chicago: Bentley, Murray & Co., 1910. Available at MoMA (New York City), the New York Public Library, the Margaret Herrick Library (Beverly Hills), and the UCLA Library, and on microfilm on reel three of *Early Rare British Filmmakers' Catalogues* (London: World Microfilm Publications, 1982).

———. *Catalogue of Educational Moving Pictures*. Chicago: G. Kleine, 1915.

———. "Co-operation in Visual Instruction." In *Proceedings of the National University Extension Association at Lexington, Kentucky, April 20, 21, 22, 1922*, 27–43. Boston: Wright & Potter, 1923.

Musser, Charles. *The Emergence of Cinema: The American Screen to 1907*. New York: Charles Scribner's Sons, 1990.

Musser, Charles, with Carol Nelson. *High-Class Moving Pictures: Lyman H. Howe and the Forgotten Era of Traveling Exhibition, 1880–1920*. Princeton, NJ: Princeton University Press, 1991.

Peterson, Jennifer. *Education in the School of Dreams: Travelogues and Early Nonfiction Film*. Durham, NC: Duke University Press, 2013.

Schwartz, Vanessa. *Spectacular Realities: Early Mass Culture in Fin de Siècle Paris*. Los Angeles. University of California Press, 1998.

Toulet, Emmanuelle. "Cinema and the Universal Exposition, Paris 1900." *Persistence of Vision* 9 (1991): 10–36.

OLIVER GAYCKEN is Associate Professor of English and a core faculty member of the Film Studies and Comparative Literature Programs at the University of Maryland, College Park. He is author of *Devices of Curiosity: Early Cinema and Popular Science*.

8 George Kleine and the Institutional Film Exchange

An Experiment in Nontheatrical Film Distribution, 1921–29

Joel Frykholm

Of all optimists, he who has looked for the commercial success of the so-called "Educational" film has had optimism strained beyond all competition.

—George Kleine, *Morning Telegraph*, September 24, 1922

Introduction

George Kleine (b. 1863) was an optician by trade who began selling motion picture equipment and films out of his Chicago optical store in 1896. This marked the start of a career in the motion picture business that would last for thirty-five years.[1] He was a central figure in American cinema for much of this time, with many claims to fame. These include his reputation as an adamant champion of educational film, noted as early as 1910 by his contemporary Robert Grau and emphasized by present-day film historians too.[2] Kleine's influential *Catalogue of Educational Motion Picture Films*, issued in 1910, is habitually referenced in histories of educational cinema in the United States, and Kleine himself is held to have belonged to a troika of pioneering promoters of educational film that also included Charles Urban and Thomas Edison.[3]

What has gone mostly unnoticed, however, is that Kleine's efforts to cultivate educational cinema in the United States continued in the late 1910s and throughout the 1920s, all the way to his death in 1931. The most significant project from this latter phase of Kleine's career was an attempt to forge a self-sufficient nationwide, nontheatrical motion picture distribution network consisting of rental exchanges operated by extension divisions at state universities across the United States. This work was experimental in character and set out to explore the commercial potential of nontheatrical cinema; specifically, whether this field could successfully develop into a financially viable, autonomous cultural institution. The term *nontheatrical* indicates a wide realm, but the experiment was closely tied to "educational cinema."

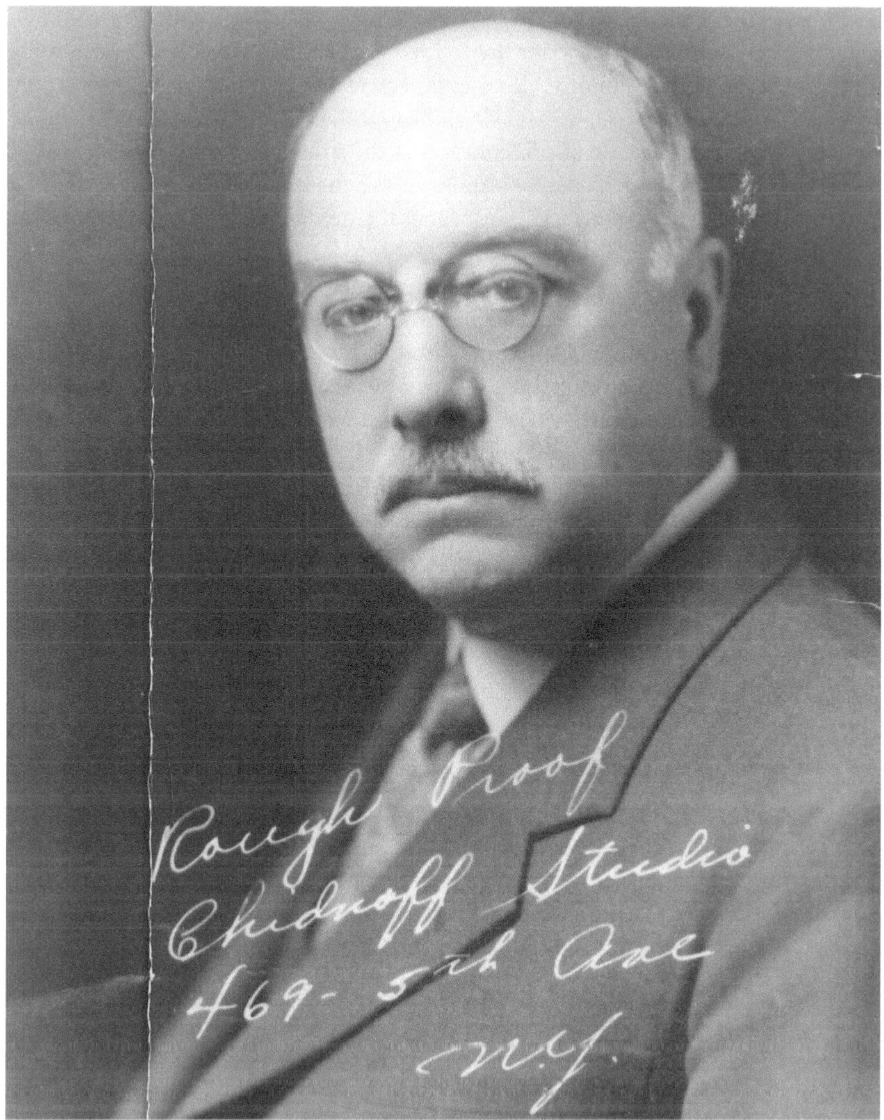

Fig. 8.1. George Kleine, ca. 1927, rough proof, Chidnoff Studio, NYC. Photographic print in the Visual materials from the *George Kleine Papers*, Library of Congress, Washington, DC.

A commitment to explore and advance the educational uses of motion pictures informed the project deeply and in all facets. Furthermore, at the time, terminological distinctions between nontheatrical and educational were not always clear-cut, and the terms were sometimes defined in contradictory ways. For example, in the early 1920s Kleine repeatedly suggested that the label "educational film" was obsolete and had been replaced with the word *nontheatrical*; in one letter from 1921 he talked about his two-decade-long effort to promote "what was formerly called 'educational film'," and in another letter from the following year he referred to "'educational film,' which we are now fondly calling nontheatrical."[4] At other times, however, he argued that "in current use, the term 'nontheatrical' is employed with regard to the customary place and mode of presentation of the film rather than its character."[5] As we will find out, both the exhibition sites *and* the types of film usually figured into the equation, and the terms "nontheatrical cinema" and "educational cinema" often implied each other.

Elsewhere I've analyzed how Kleine's experiment in nontheatrical distribution panned out as a business venture and as an attempt to reform film culture, often in explicit opposition to the Hollywood commercial mainstream. I've connected the somewhat disappointing results of the project to the overall trajectory of Kleine's career and to the transformation of American cinema in the 1910s.[6] Parts of what follows overlap with this previous work, but here I will analyze in greater depth the key assumption that underpinned the project: Kleine's notion that a viable nontheatrical cinema must be built on a "sound commercial basis." This idea connects Kleine's experiment to the "institutionalization" of educational cinema in several respects. First, the notion of a "sound commercial basis" was not merely a proposition to be experimentally tested; it was presented as a solution for the problem of how nontheatrical cinema could be fashioned into an endurable, autonomous institution. According to Kleine's analysis, the nontheatrical field's best hope for prosperity, stability, and independence lay in establishing standard commercial procedures and protocols (roughly the same business practices that he had grown accustomed to after having spent many years supplying regular movie theaters with motion pictures) as the norm for coordinating the nontheatrical use of film. In the long run, through the continuous accumulation of an economic surplus, the field would become self-sustaining when it came to film production, distribution, and exhibition. Second, if Kleine's goal was to establish nontheatrical cinema as an institution in its own right, the process involved a (partial) incorporation of nontheatrical cinema into *other* institutions.[7] The phrase that Kleine and his associates chose to describe the nodal points in the distribution network is indicative. They were known as "institutional exchanges." At the time, for the people involved, the connotation may have been primarily material, invoking the physical placement of cans of films in the physical institution of university extension divisions, but it does not seem unreasonable to suggest that the term also implied a more abstract sense of institutionalization. Aside from linking cinema to the educational sector—materially and figuratively—Kleine's ambition to secure a "sound commercial basis" for nontheatrical cinema also points to efforts to attach the nontheatrical field to the institution we refer to as the "market."

The last observation suggests that if we are to understand Kleine's attempt to institutionalize nontheatrical cinema, "the market" is something to explain rather than assume as a natural order. For this purpose, we may pick up some cues from disciplines such as economic sociology, where the market has been extensively theorized and analyzed as an institution and as a concept. One such basic cue (originating in essence from the work of Max Weber) is that markets should be studied as social and cultural institutions in themselves, as "embedded" in larger social institutional arrangements. Another cue is that the notion of the market has a material as well as a metaphorical dimension. When Kleine worked out a design for what he hoped would become a well-oiled nontheatrical market—a nontheatrical cinema resting on a "sound commercial basis"—he was not merely imagining a regularized form of economic exchange between a specific set of buyers and sellers trading a specific commodity within a specific spatiotemporal organization (i.e., an empirically observable institution); he was also mobilizing certain values, beliefs, and protocols of evaluation. As we will learn, the values, beliefs, and protocols of evaluation associated with the market did not always match their equivalents within the other institution that featured prominently in Kleine's experiment—the university (or, more broadly, "education"). This resulted in many institutional and personal conflicts, and even though there were many reasons for the ultimate failure of Kleine's experiment, unresolved tensions within the institutional matrix certainly did not help.

Extending this last line of argument, I also want to make the more general historical point that a widely shared belief in the allegedly awesome power of motion pictures became the subject of a variety of institutional claims in the 1920s and that the so-called "nontheatrical field" was an important arena for the struggles that ensued. From this viewpoint, Kleine's experiment perfectly illustrates the multifaceted, sometimes contradictory institutionalization of nontheatrical cinema in the 1920s, characterized equally by a shared desire to forge a new and different kind of film culture and by the diversity of institutional and personal interpretations and initiatives that this collective desire spawned.

Preambles to the Experiment

By mid-1919, George Kleine had not left the commercial motion picture business completely, but he had given up any ambitions of playing a pivotal role in a reconfigured movie economy increasingly dominated by the large corporations that would eventually make up the core of the Hollywood studio system. He had dismantled his distribution organization and ceased almost all production efforts, but he owned an extensive back catalog of motion pictures. Now he was looking to repurpose these films for new markets and to explore the potential of nontheatrical cinema more generally. With regard to the reissuing of his old films, an opportunity presented itself in March 1919 via the Visual Instruction Section of the newly inaugurated Division of Educational Extension, Department of the Interior. This was "a new organization, created by Presidential authority," created for the purpose of "the establishment of a national distributive system which will enable films, slides, still pictures and other exhibits of an educational character to be circulated throughout the schools, colleges, universities and other educational institutions in this country."[8] Kleine offered to outright sell them prints of selected pictures from a group promoted as George Kleine's Cycle of Film Classics, including *Quo Vadis?* (Cines, 1912), *The Last Days of Pompeii* (Ambrosio 1913), *Antony and Cleopatra* (Cines 1913), *Spartacus* (Pasquali, 1913), *Othello* (Ambrosio, 1914), and *Julius Caesar* (Cines 1914), under the condition that they would only be used in nontheatrical venues and in no "public amusement places."[9] Nothing concrete came of this, but it planted the idea with Kleine that extension divisions at state universities might serve as nodal points in a nontheatrical distribution network.

Aside from searching for a new outlet for entertainment films such as his classics, Kleine also tried to assess the nontheatrical demand for more strictly educational or pedagogical film subjects. Much of his back catalog consisted of those kinds of pictures, but the issue was whether potential customers—schools primarily—would have any use for them. He moved ahead on two fronts. On the one hand, he set out to pitch his old educational subjects, which had previously been shown mostly in movie theaters, to nontheatrical customers. On the other hand, seeming to consider initiating production of new pedagogical films tailor-made to fit the curriculum, he made an effort to gauge the size and potential of the market among schools. More specifically, he sent a circular to "all State superintendents of schools of the United States" in September 1919, inquiring whether they believed the schools in their respective states would be interested in a series of motion pictures that covered American geography.[10] The replies were discouraging, but C. P. Cary, school superintendent of the state of Wisconsin, forwarded Kleine's letter to Professor William H. Dudley.[11] Dudley and Kleine had been in touch sporadically since 1894.[12] When they reconnected in 1919, it was immediately clear that they shared an enthusiasm for visual instruction and educational film. Dudley became the primary liaison between Kleine and the state universities.

At this juncture, Dudley was in charge of the Bureau of Visual Instruction (established in 1914) at the University of Wisconsin–Madison, and he had also worked for the aforementioned Visual Instruction Section of the Department of the Interior in Washington, DC. His role within this governmental organization was to assist universities across the United States to organize departments of visual instruction within already existing extension divisions, following the model Dudley himself had designed at the University of Wisconsin.[13] Accordingly, when Kleine made contact with Dudley in 1919, extension divisions at a number of state universities were already hosting film libraries. These film libraries catered to campus needs, but the films were also made available to other nontheatrical venues.

Universities and colleges engaged in extension education could become members of the National University Extension Association (NUEA), established in 1915 with the purpose of advancing new ideas and methods in this area. As visual instruction became an increasingly common component of the university extension, the institutions that were most actively engaged in this line of work founded another, more narrowly focused association in January 1920: the National Academy of Visual Instruction (NAVI).[14] William Dudley was a driving force in both the NUEA and the NAVI, among other things serving as the latter's first president.

Dudley, then, was a key figure in the movement to promote the use of film for a wide range of purposes—within the university and beyond—and Kleine was fortunate to connect with him, thereby gaining entry to the center of the budding nontheatrical film field. What could Kleine offer in return? For one, the dearth of (suitable) motion pictures was a perennial problem for extension divisions, and arguably for the nontheatrical field in general, so any additions to the supply might have been of interest. Secondly, Kleine and Dudley shared a similar outlook concerning the future development of nontheatrical cinema.

The parties agreed that adding a selection of Kleine's films to the extension division film libraries would be mutually beneficial, but it took some time before anything material emerged from this general agreement. One reason was probably the difficulty of agreeing on financial terms, although the sources I've studied reveal little about what kind of negotiations took place in late 1919 to early 1920. Another reason might have been that Dudley and his fellow extension division directors around the country had their hands full with more pressing issues. For instance, the process of inaugurating the aforementioned NAVI began in January 1920 at an informal gathering in Cleveland during the annual meeting of the National Education Association (NEA), which was followed by further meetings in Ann Arbor, Michigan, in April the same year. Finally, the constitution and bylaws of NAVI were ratified at the association's constituting meeting, held at the University of Wisconsin–Madison on July 14–17, 1920.[15] In parallel, some of the same people who were involved in the founding of NAVI had also launched a campaign to strengthen the cooperation between the university extension sector and Henry Ford—a major supplier of motion pictures to the nontheatrical market at this time.[16] A committee chaired by L. E. Reber, dean of the extension division at the University of Wisconsin, also including William Dudley, G. E. Condra (director of State Conservation and Soil Surveys, University of Nebraska–Lincoln), and F. W. Reynolds (director of extension, University of Utah–Salt Lake City), was appointed "to visit Mr. Henry Ford to the end of interesting him in establishing and maintaining, by endowment or otherwise, an educational film negative library."[17] A series of meetings took place in September 1920, but it is unclear what the practical results were—if any.[18] Plans to inaugurate some form of cooperation with Ford were shelved, but, as it turned out, only temporarily.

Meanwhile, the correspondence between Kleine and Dudley resumed in late 1920. On November 6, Kleine wrote to Dudley to inquire whether the various departments of visual instruction that Dudley had helped organize might be interested in acquiring a selection of Kleine's films. This letter is missing from the George Kleine Papers, but the ensuing correspondence makes clear that Kleine was primarily bringing the Conquest Program, plus the special feature *Julius Caesar*, to the table. *Julius Caesar* was one of the Kleine Film Classics previously discussed. The Conquest Program consisted of a mixture of feature films, one-reel comedies,

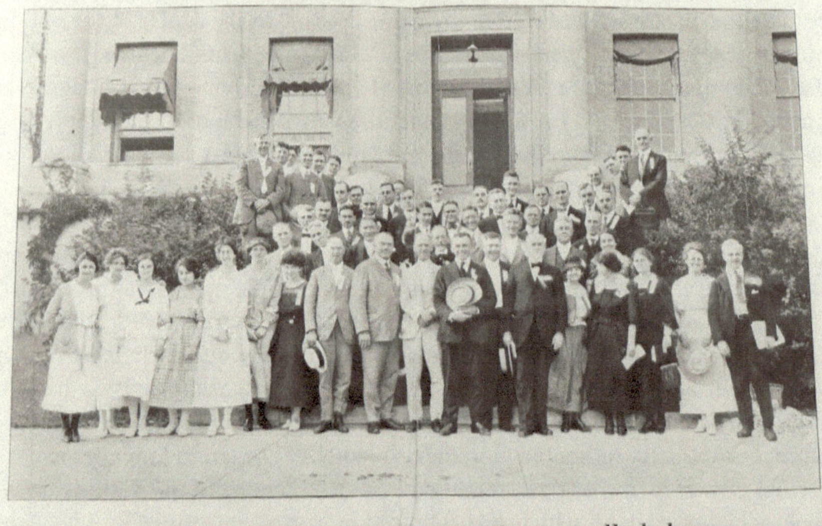

Fig. 8.2. Poster issued by the National Academy of Visual Instruction following its first convention in 1920. Copy in the George Kleine Papers, box 41, file "Nontheatrical; National Academy of Visual Instruction, 1921 and undated," Library of Congress, Washington, DC.

and educational short subjects originally produced by the Edison Company and distributed by Kleine as a series of preconstituted educational film programs in 1917 and 1918. The distribution of these programs to commercial movie theaters had yielded lackluster results, but Kleine was certain that if they were retooled for a nontheatrical market, they would find their proper audience and eventually turn a profit.[19]

Dudley explained to Kleine that there were presently over fifty institutions—predominantly state universities—that had organized visual instruction departments based on the model worked out at the University of Wisconsin. He was convinced that Kleine's films would be of great value to many of these but noted that the cost of some of the more elaborate pictures might be prohibitive. A rental agreement, however, might work for this category of films. For less expensive films, outright purchase with no restrictions in regard to nontheatrical use would be preferable—this was the standard policy at most of the visual instruction departments. In any event, Dudley promised to pass Kleine's offer on to "the members of the Association" (i.e., NUEA) as a "formal memorandum," and asked Kleine to send back to him "as definite and concrete a proposition as possible" to forward to the members.[20] Shortly thereafter, Kleine sent Dudley a "list of our Conquest Films [*sic*] out of which subjects will be selected for outright sale."[21]

Exactly what happened in the months that followed is not evident from the sources I've examined, but judging by the events of June and July 1921, Kleine and Dudley must have continued the dialog, trying to hatch a plan that would make Kleine's films accessible to a wider network of extension divisions and departments of visual instruction and would also help accomplish the overarching, long-term goal of making these institutions the foundation of an enduring, nationwide system for nontheatrical film distribution. They must also have decided to use the occasion of NAVI's second annual meeting, which took place in Des Moines in July 1921, as an opportunity to present their idea to a wider circle of people involved in the visual instruction movement.

Aims, Objectives, and Terms of the Experiment

In the weeks running up to the July meeting, Kleine convinced Thomas A. Edison to endorse NAVI and its efforts to promote the educational uses of film.[22] His correspondence with the inventor, in combination with an undated "Plan for Co-ordinating [*sic*] the Operations of University Departments of Visual Education Extension through the United States and to Increase the Volume of Their Operations," reveals the basic elements of the plan that Kleine and the NAVI people had been discussing. The goals were to (a) standardize a system of nontheatrical film distribution via institutional exchanges hosted by extension divisions at state universities; (b) arouse public interest in the uses of film in visual instruction and in nontheatrical contexts; (c) stimulate the use of motion pictures in schools, churches, community organizations, and other nontheatrical venues; and (d) supply these customers with the motion pictures they desired and needed.[23] These would include motion pictures "made purely for entertainment as well as historical, religious and technically educational [films]."[24] The operation would be placed on what Kleine repeatedly came to refer to as a "sound commercial basis" so that the universities involved would not suffer any financial losses. Indeed, the institutional exchanges were supposed to accumulate a surplus to be used "for the benefit of the Community," e.g., for reinvestment in the production of films on special subjects or to equip nontheatrical venues with projectors.[25] Gradually, a huge market would open up and attract private producers, which would solve the supply problem without the institutional exchanges having to make any heavy investments in production. Or, as Kleine argued in one of his letters to Edison, production of suitable films for nontheatrical customers would sort itself out once the "enormous market [had] been organized." In Kleine's assessment, there were thousands and thousands of potential customers who were "at sea as to the sources" of "satisfactory films."[26] Once realized, the network of institutional exchanges would "easily reach every prospective non-theatrical exhibitor" in the United States.[27] Naturally, a host of producers, theatrical as well as educational, would happily offer their products to a distribution organization of such tremendous scope—provided that the whole operation actually rested on a sound commercial basis. As Kleine put it: "Commercialism must enter in connection with the production of films and to maintain these bureaus [i.e., the institutional exchanges] on a self-supporting basis."[28]

We will learn that a commercial approach to nontheatrical cinema followed logically from the kind of market ideology that Kleine adhered to, but it was also a means to a specific end: the creation of an autonomous nontheatrical field, no longer reliant on theatrical movie companies, government agencies, industrial corporations, and philanthropists. In Kleine's words: "non-theatrical exchanges in the hands of private parties have lived a hand-to-mouth existence. Institutional exchanges have depended upon state or municipal appropriations; film prints from Washington either free or at the cost of positives, without allowance for production costs; prints issued by business firms for advertising purposes; and entertainment films bought secondhand. These conditions have seriously hampered the growth of the exchanges and impaired their efficiency in public service."[29]

In a survey of the national conditions for nontheatrical cinema that Kleine sent to Dudley in late June 1921, Kleine cautioned against the delusion that an endurable system for nontheatrical distribution could operate on a "philanthropic" basis.[30] Instead, he argued that "ultimately this work can be placed on a sound commercial basis with great benefit to the public, and profit to the commercial interests."[31] Thanks to the "enormous volume of the business that will eventuate," moderate rental prices would suffice to sustain the exchanges *and* make film production tailored for nontheatrical audiences economically viable.[32] In sum, then, the whole idea was to give a mass market of nontheatrical customers access to suitable motion pictures at affordable prices, which, as Kleine emphasized, ultimately hinged on their success in "converting these users to the idea that film service is a material thing that must be paid for, just as schools, colleges, libraries, etc. pay for other things of value."[33]

According to the plan, the institutional exchanges would build their motion picture libraries by purchasing suitable films—old and new—outright. But acquiring a fully adequate stock of films would be too costly in the short run. In the meantime, and while gradually acquiring more and more films outright, they could expand their supply through percentage deals with individual suppliers. These suppliers would maintain ownership of their pictures and let the institutional exchanges distribute them in exchange for a slice of the rental revenues. The profits reaped by the exchanges could be used to purchase new films or otherwise expand the operation. This leads us to the actual experiment and Kleine's role in it: he would happily deposit some of his films at a selection of institutional exchanges in order for them to test the practice of percentage deals in the nontheatrical market, and he would assess whether this would contribute to the more general long-term goal of establishing a self-sufficient system of nontheatrical distribution and production along the lines that Kleine and Dudley had worked out. Or, as Kleine summarized the idea later that summer: "This is an experiment to determine whether it is practical for these institutions to cover their respective states and to earn enough income to cover distribution, value of prints and production cost. If successful, the field of operations will be enlarged."[34]

The Experiment Begins

On the last day of June 1921, Kleine wrote to Dudley, listing the films he was offering and spelling out the terms.[35] The institutional exchanges would have nonexclusive distribution rights that were limited to the state in which they were operating.[36] The institutional exchanges were to retain 35 percent as a distribution fee, with the exceptions of classics such as *Julius Caesar.* In those cases, the exchanges would keep 25 percent of the income.

In early July, Kleine met with Dudley and the group who had gathered in Des Moines for NAVI's second-annual meeting, which provided an opportunity to anchor the plan to a wider network of people working in extension education. Shortly thereafter, on July 15, 1921, W. H. Dudley sent a letter to a selection of NAVI members, outlining Kleine's proposition and the rationale behind the experiment. The most immediate purpose was to determine which six institutions would be the most suitable for the "pilot" exchanges, preferably the ones "most active . . . in the work of extending the use of films in their respective states."[37] Based on the replies, Dudley chose the following six: University of Wisconsin, University of California–Berkeley, University of Florida, University of Utah, Washington State University, and University of Kansas.[38] Prints were shipped to these institutions in July and August 1921.[39]

Dudley's own institution, the Bureau of Visual Instruction at the University of Wisconsin, signed up for virtually all of the nearly 110 titles that Kleine was offering. The majority of these came from the Conquest Program, including four-reel entertainment features of the "wholesome" kind (e.g., *Knights of the Square Table, Little Chevalier, The Customary Two Weeks, Kidnapped*, and *Putting the Bee in Herbert* [all Edison productions from 1917]) and some one- and two-reel dramas and comedies (e.g., *He Couldn't Get Up in the Morning* [Edison, 1917], *Two Kentucky Boys* [Edison, 1917], and *The Midnight Ride of Paul Revere* [one-reel version, first released as part of Conquest Program no. 12 in 1917, original two-reel version produced by Edison in 1914]), as well as a third type of conquest film that was more strictly "educational" (as indicated by titles such as *Crystals in Formation* [revised version of *Crystals: Their Making, Habits and Beauty*, Edison, 1914], *Gold and Diamond Mines in South Africa* [Edison, 1914], *Quaint Provincetown on Cape Cod* [Edison, 1917], *Microscopic Pond Life* [Edison, 1915], *Caring for Birds in Winter* [Edison, 1917], and *Curious Scenes in Far Off India* [Edison, 1913]). Aside from the Conquest films, Kleine also shipped a number of special features to Wisconsin, including selected titles from his Cycle of Film Classics (including *Julius Caesar, Antony and Cleopatra,*

Spartacus, The Last Days of Pompeii, For Napoleon and France [Cines, 1914]; *Pilgrim's Progress* [Ambrosio, 1912]; *The Unbeliever* [Edison, 1918]; *Vanity Fair* [Edison, 1915]; and *Othello* and *The Merchant of Venice* [Eclipse, 1913]) as well as a selection of five-reel features produced by the Edison Company in 1916 and 1917 (including *A Message to Garcia, The Royal Pauper, One Touch of Nature, The Awakening of Ruth, The Apple Tree Girl, Cy Whittaker's Ward, The Courage of the Commonplace,* and *Salt of the Earth*).[40] Wisconsin also secured twelve Montgomery Flagg one-reel comedies.[41] Finally, a print of *Deliverance*—a biopic about Helen Keller starring Keller herself, distributed commercially by Kleine in 1919 (with depressing results), and produced by the Helen Keller Film Corporation (in which Kleine had a financial interest)—was also shipped to Wisconsin, and to three of the other pilot institutions (Utah, Washington, and Kansas). Similar to the Wisconsin exchange, the University of Utah's also placed orders for most of what Kleine had to offer, whereas the University of California at Berkeley and the University of Florida exchanges opted for somewhat fewer features, but all or most of the Conquest pictures.[42] The institutional exchanges in Kansas and Washington State were more selective, partly because they only had access to roughly forty of the Conquest films due to previous distribution deals for selected Conquest titles with the Educational Film Bureau in Spokane, Washington, and with the Film Service Bureau in Kansas City.[43]

Around the same time that prints were shipped to the six pilot institutions, W. H. Dudley embarked on a tour around the country to promote the experiment among NAVI members and to get additional institutions to sign up. By the end of August, he reported to Kleine that he had had satisfactory meetings with members in Indiana, Kentucky, Tennessee, and Ohio.[44] By late November 1921, Dudley had made four or five trips to universities as well as boards of education across the United States, and reported to Kleine on meetings in Illinois, Pennsylvania, New York, Massachusetts, New Jersey, Maryland, Virginia, West Virginia, Iowa, Nebraska, Arkansas, Oklahoma, and Texas.[45] Reactions were generally favorable, but Dudley emphasized that it was a gradual process to convert the institutions to the ideas and practices of visual instruction that Kleine and Dudley were trying to promote with their experiment. Whereas some were "sold" on the proposition, some had to face difficult negotiations with the university administration, and others were somewhat reluctant to use anything other than strictly pedagogical films. Some were also hesitant about the commercial basis of the Kleine experiment, as they were currently offering whatever films they had free of charge. In early 1922, Dudley toured the South, visiting universities and agricultural colleges in Louisiana, Alabama, Mississippi, Georgia, and South Carolina.[46] Prospects for the experiment looked promising in some of these places, too, but some of the institutions in this part of the country only did extension work in the agricultural area, and Dudley predicted that it would be difficult to get them to expand in other directions.

By November 1921, five institutions beyond the pilot exchanges had joined the experiment: University of Kentucky–Lexington, Indiana University–Bloomington, University of Iowa–Iowa City, State University of Montana–Missoula, and the

State Department of Education, Division of School Extension, Raleigh, North Carolina.[47] Prints were shipped to Kentucky and Indiana as early as September and October 1921 and to the other three somewhat later. The number of pictures varied frominstitution to institution, ranging from a handful to over seventy. In January 1922, Kleine wrote to a business associate at Edison Inc. that fifteen institutions were now involved in the project.[48] The most recent to join were North Dakota Agricultural College–Fargo, University of Oklahoma–Norman, Ohio University–Athens, and University of Oregon–Eugene. Two further additions—Mississippi Agricultural and Mechanical College at Starkville and Michigan State Normal College at Ypsilanti—brought the tally up to seventeen institutional exchanges, sixteen of which were featured in an ad that appeared in the *Classical Weekly* in February 1922.[49] According to one estimate, these institutional exchanges served territories covering twenty-four states and a population of forty million people.[50]

Another Attempt to Bring Henry Ford Onboard

Already in January 1921, Kleine had noted to Dudley, “We have gone far beyond our first plan of placing films in six of these exchanges.”[51] The rapid expansion of the experiment may have inspired their hatching increasingly grandiose plans. More specifically, someone rekindled the idea to court Henry Ford, with the aim of securing not only the auto tycoon’s endorsement but also the kind of financial backing that would make possible (or speed up) the realization of an expanded, firmly established and durable network of institutional exchanges. Presumably, this would amount to a quick fix, or a once-and-for-all solution, to the problem of nontheatrical distribution. In the months running up to the Seventh Annual Meeting of the National University Extension Association to take place in Lexington, Kentucky, on April 20–22, 1922—an event that featured a joint session with the Third Annual Meeting of the National Academy of Visual Instruction (April 18–20)—Kleine and an inner circle around Dudley launched a campaign to get Ford’s endorsement in time for the convention.

According to Kleine’s later recollections, the first step was to try to get “our friend in Orange” to help them set up a meeting with “our friend in Detroit.”[52] Kleine wrote to Edison on March 1, 1922,[53] outlining the idea of consolidating the network of institutional film exchanges and suggesting that Edison forward the letter to Ford as a voucher, endorsement, and door-opener. On the same day, March 1, Kleine sent a similar letter to George Eastman (Kleine explained to Dudley that Eastman “might be interested in case Mr. Ford is not”).[54] The letter to Eastman makes clear that their primary goal was to obtain financial support. This was stated frankly to Eastman, but in dealing with Ford, Kleine acted on the instinct that the true purpose was better explained in person, on-site.[55]

The plan initially seemed to play out in the manner Kleine and his associates had wished for. By March 9, Kleine had received replies from Edison as well as Eastman, and Edison’s assistant, William Meadowcroft, had forwarded Kleine’s letter to Henry Ford.[56] On March 13, Ford's private secretary E. G. Liebold wrote to Kleine, confirming the arrival of the Edison letter and extending an invitation to discuss the matter further. Kleine replied on March 20, suggesting that they meet as soon as March 25, making clear that he hoped to get Ford onboard before the joint NUEA and NAVI meeting in Lexington on April 20: "The cause of Institutional Film Distribution could be greatly assisted if those directly concerned could announce to their colleagues that Mr. Ford is ready to give his support to a definite proposition such as that briefly outlined in my letter to Mr. Edison."[57] Telegrams were exchanged, and a date was set to Tuesday March 28, 1922.[58] Dudley arrived in Chicago on Monday evening together with L. E. Reber, set to continue to Detroit in Kleine's company the morning after.

We do not know exactly what transpired at the meeting, but it is certain that Kleine and the two Wisconsin men returned without the funding they had sought, and without even having met with Ford in person. The way Kleine recalled the experience a few years later, "We believed we were to meet #2 [Ford] personally, and Dudley and Reber of Wisconsin went with me, or I with them, to Michigan to ask for 8 millions."[59] According to this version of events, the trio went out to the Ford plant, met with Liebold, had lunch, and then discussed the matter. "Either [Ford] was away, or didn't care to see us. We did not meet him."[60] The meeting with Liebold did not go as hoped for. "He was frank, surprisingly so," Kleine claimed. "[Liebold] said plainly [Ford] was not interested in philanthropy. His film operations were purely business. [He] would not be interested in anything that did not advertise the [Ford] corporation. . . . Pleasant interview, but hard as nails."[61]

The magnitude of the ask—$8 million—indicates that key people within the university extension movement had ambitions regarding nontheatrical cinema that went far beyond quotidian uses of film on their own campuses or within the closest communities. These ambitions persisted, at least for some time, in spite of the Michigan setback. Furthermore, the episode hints at nontheatrical cinema's position within an institutional matrix, and its force of attraction for different institutional stakeholders—in this case including the commercial movie business (Kleine), the educational sphere (Dudley and Reber), and the industry (Ford). Arguably, the situation also involved the industrialist posing as (or being perceived as) philanthropist, and the commercial businessman posing as (or being perceived as) champion of the loftier, nonmonetary values of motion pictures.

If the respective interests of the different stakeholders were partly at odds with each other—indicative of the state of the nontheatrical field at large—in this particular case there was at least one shared viewpoint that had the potential to override possible tensions between the parties involved: antisemitism. Kleine was an avowed, albeit closeted, antisemite—he never expressed antisemitic views in public, but private correspondence leaves no doubt regarding his attitude.[62] For example, when Kleine moved his New York offices to 145 West Forty-Fifth Street in the spring of 1921, he wrote to one of his employees that this building "in former years was known as the Hebrew Roost of the film business" and that he hoped the place had "been purified, if not sanctified."[63] Or consider this barrage of ethnic and racial slurs, culled from a letter Kleine sent to his nephew J. J. Thompson in November 1920: "The philologist of the future will no doubt make an interesting topic out of the influence of the Hebrew upon American language and literature. He will probably differentiate between the Polish Jew, the Russian Kike and the Oriental semite. Their influence upon the language and pronunciation of New York English is already apparent. The element of moisture in their speech without going to the extreme of being slobbery is quite marked, although a careful analysis will show that a percentage of them actually slobbers when talking about money, going or coming."[64]

There is evidence to suggest that antisemitism actually provided a basic rationale for the experiment in nontheatrical film distribution via institutional exchanges. In June 1921, just as the experiment was about to start, Kleine wrote to Thomas Edison and explained, "An advantage, by no means the least, will be the possibility of divorcing this field of operations from objectionable individuals and concerns that are operating at present in the theatrical end of the motion picture business."[65] A letter to George Blair at Eastman-Kodak the following year gives us reason to believe that an element of racism informed Kleine's misgivings about "objectionable individuals and concerns": "You will understand that after maintaining a policy of silence during the past three years I am now about to break into publicity in competition with Hebrews."[66] Time and again, Kleine's letters from 1921 and 1922 explicitly juxtaposed his work with the institutional exchanges to what he perceived to be a pervasive and destructive Jewish influence on the theatrical motion picture business.[67]

We also have reason to believe that at least some of Kleine's associates in the university extension sector held similar views. The courting of Henry Ford, then, possibly the most high-profile antisemite in America, was surely not accidental or explicable as owing only to his extraordinary wealth. In fact, against the background of shared antisemitic sentiment, the notion that Ford would be inclined to sponsor Kleine's efforts to develop nontheatrical cinema as a self-supporting market and autonomous film culture appears somewhat less absurd or naïve than at first glance. For the March 1922 meeting, however, neither Ford the antisemite, nor Ford the philanthropist, nor Ford the physical person turned up, only Ford the industrial tycoon—and only by proxy.

Results of the First Season (1921–22)

A few weeks after the Michigan expedition, on April 18, 1922, NAVI's annual meeting in Lexington commenced. It ended on Thursday, April 20, with a joint session with NUEA, whose convention took place in the same city on April 20–22.[68] During this joint session, Kleine gave a speech titled "Co-operation [*sic*] in Visual Instruction,"[69] in which he reminisced about his background in the motion picture business, offered a brief history of educational cinema in the United States, and presented the ongoing experiment in nontheatrical film distribution via institutional exchanges. He emphasized the importance of cooperation on multiple fronts (e.g., among universities, schools, community associations, and local movie theaters), of a sound commercial basis, and of establishing a centralized system for the production and distribution of "pedagogical" films. The latter hinged on the appointment of a group of "experts" who would "lay out film courses that would accompany standardized text books or courses of instruction in schools, colleges, and universities."[70] These experts would also consider production or purchase of suitable films, and the purchase of distribution rights of motion pictures (including pedagogical as well as recreational subjects). Much remained to be done, but Kleine's main message was optimistic: "The non-theatrical business will develop separately and autonomously, and will cease to be a tail to the theatrical kite, an undignified position, which frankness compels us to admit it has held in the past."[71]

With regard to his own experiment, he noted that it was too early to draw any definite conclusions, although the relatively wide circulation of *Julius Caesar* (nineteen prints in total, circulated via seventeen institutional exchanges), a film that served as a test case of sorts due to "its entertainment and instructional values," indicated that the deployed methods of distribution could be both practical and profitable. A few days after the Lexington convention, Kleine wrote to a business associate at the Edison Company that, "While there are no profits as yet it looks as if we had found a dependable and continuous system distribution which is the one crying need in this mercurial film business."[72] Moreover, the number institutions participating in the experiment kept growing.[73]

In a circular sent to the institutional exchanges dated July 10, 1922, Kleine summarized the results of the first season.[74] According to his statistics, the allotment of films had varied from one print of one title in one state to 109 subjects in another state, depending on the capacity of the respective exchanges. A total of 699 films (including duplicate prints of some subjects) had been deposited with the institutional exchanges—a total of 1,405 reels of film. The most widely distributed single picture was *Julius Caesar*, which had been booked for 244 engagements, up until June 17, 1922. Fifty-seven of these engagements had been secured by the exchange in California, reflecting the fact that the Department of Visual Instruction at Berkeley was by far the most active participant in the experiment, accounting for about 23 percent of Kleine's share of the rental revenues during the first season of the experiment.[75] The second and third most active were the University of Wisconsin and the University of Utah. North Carolina and Washington State were also fairly active, whereas business in Mississippi, Montana, North Dakota, and Oklahoma was miniscule.

In spite of the enthusiastic work carried out in many of the exchanges, the total volume of business was far from reaching the point where investment in production would be economically justifiable. Kleine's total share of revenue from all the institutional exchanges over the first season amounted to $13,120. This would not go a long way toward covering even modest costs of production and overhead, but Kleine maintained that production tailored to the nontheatrical field would indeed become viable when potential customers had been converted into actual customers.[76] His general conclusion was that the first season had been a success—not from a commercial perspective, but as an experiment that not only had boosted the level of activity but also modeled a distribution system that eliminated "the danger of immoral, obscene, indecent or otherwise objectionable films entering into circulation."[77]

Nontheatrical Cinema as Autonomous Film Culture—and Gentile Haven: Kleine's Antisemitism

Kleine's summary of the experiment's first season hints at the ways in which he conceived of the nontheatrical field as an arena for reforming film culture.[78] His high-flying ambitions about a better and more refined film culture may appear to conflict with the primarily pragmatic approach to nontheatrical cinema that characterized work in extension divisions. For these institutions, the main reason of cooperating with Kleine was that they were eager to get their hands on whatever films that might be available to them. But even if this applies to the majority of the institutional exchanges, William H. Dudley's outlook on the nontheatrical field actually aligned with Kleine's in significant ways. For example, he too (along with publications such as *The Educational Screen* as well as many of his fellow educators in NAVI) was convinced that the nontheatrical field was instrumental in the promotion of "better" entertainment films, an idea he had expressed as early as 1914 and continued to adhere to in 1921.[79] He also believed that this was a means to elevate film culture in general, and to pressure the theatrical field to aim for higher standards. As he wrote in 1921, the demand for better films would be encouraged via the "systematic cultivation through the schools and civic centers of a taste for that which is clean and wholesome, and that will stimulate and satisfy one's nobler thoughts and feelings. The need for laws and boards of censorship to 'regulate' would largely disappear."[80] This was closely reminiscent of Kleine's views on the same matters.

Dudley also shared Kleine's conviction that nontheatrical cinema should be cultivated as an autonomous, self-reliant field. In September 1922, as the experiment's second season was about to begin, he wrote to Kleine and emphasized the need of "welding our own forces together and building up a productive organization and service entirely independent of the theatrical crowd." He concluded that, "What we need is our own production, our own organization, and an awakening to the realization on the part of the higher authorities in each university that visual instruction should be put on a more solid foundation."[81]

As we have already seen, for Kleine, antisemitism played an important part in his desire to keep the nontheatrical field separate from the theatrical. Imagining the nontheatrical field as a gentile haven, as yet untouched by Jewish influence, Kleine reacted with distress when the National Non-Theatrical Motion Pictures—headed by Harry Levey, a Jew—emerged in the summer of 1922 as a major competitor in the field of nontheatrical distribution.[82] Fearing a hostile takeover of the field, Kleine did his best to undermine Levey and intensified his own efforts to establish nontheatrical cinema as an alternative for what he and some of his associates liked to refer to as "plain Americans."[83] Meanwhile, there were rumors that Levey was establishing some form of collaboration with the *Christian Herald* magazine, a religious publication that was considering branching into nontheatrical distribution of motion pictures for church use. Kleine wrote to Dudley that if these rumors were true, "I wonder at the *Christian Herald* making such an arrangement with a man of his race. If it means anything it is that the large influence of this paper will be used to further the interests of an alien organization that cannot by any possibility have any real sympathy with the movement."[84]

I've found little direct evidence that Kleine's partners at the state universities were antisemites, or that their work in visual instruction was motivated by antisemitic sentiment—with some notable exceptions.[85] Either way, Kleine was clearly under the impression that many of them were of his ilk. In an August 1922 letter he made the following remark: "Note the dignified list of these institutions which seem delighted to talk their own language with a film man, and, between us be it said, I suspect that to most of them the word 'Jew' is anathema."[86]

Discussions between Kleine and Dudley about the possibility of consolidating some form of national organization for the purpose of nontheatrical film distribution continued in the fall of 1922. Dudley floated the idea of forming a national corporation, possibly financing it by soliciting subscriptions for stock, but Kleine was generally skeptic about such schemes, and made no exception in this case.[87]

Seasons Two (1922–23) and Three (1923–24): Dwindling Returns and Parallel Projects in Nontheatrical Cinema

Meanwhile, the 1922–23 season continued. Three new participants joined in: University of Texas–Austin, Louisiana State Normal College–Natchitoches, and University of Michigan–Ann Arbor. There were no major additions of subjects or replacements of prints, but there was a special campaign to promote the Helen Keller biopic *Deliverance* in California, Utah, and Washington. By the end of the season, Kleine's share of revenues from the institutional exchanges was about $12,800—a few hundred less than the previous season.[88] It is safe to assume that Kleine had hoped for increased business, but at least the results were good enough to prolong the experiment for another year.

As the third season commenced, Kleine set out to analyze the situation further, focusing his attention on the effects of commercial competition in the nontheatrical market. In October 1923, a questionnaire was sent to seventeen of the institutional exchanges. The replies indicated that theatrical film exchanges such as Famous Players–Lasky, Fox, Pathé, United Artists, Vitagraph, and the Film Booking Office for the most part did, indeed, supply nontheatrical customers with entertainment films.[89] This spelled trouble for Kleine. One of his cornerstone assumptions about the nontheatrical field was that films could have a perennial life there, instead of being removed from circulation as soon as their commercial earning power began to decrease below the point where a new release would potentially yield more profits. As he had written to Thomas Edison in April 1921: "The non-theatrical business has a great advantage in that a system of suitable negatives has continuing value and does not make it necessary to indulge in continuous production, as such subjects live over an indefinite period."[90] But this did not necessarily hold for the entertainment films that he had deposited with the institutional exchanges. If there was an ample and continuous flow of motion pictures into the nontheatrical field from the leading commercial sources, the chances that these customers would resort to repeat bookings of Kleine's subjects year after year diminished. Indeed, we see that the number of bookings of his films secured by institutional exchanges peaked in the experiment's first season, dropped off slightly during the second season, and declined quite rapidly thereafter. In March 1924, as the end of season three was drawing near, a representative at the exchange in Minnesota wrote to Kleine that he was sad to hear that "your experiment has not been exactly a success financially. It is a shame that good pictures like yours should be pushed aside for the more popular ones that are being produced through the theatrical concerns."[91] Whether this was the main cause or not, Kleine's total income from the institutional changes had dropped to $7,100 in the third season.

Earlier that same season, in December 1923, Kleine had written to an NUEA representative that he had reached a point in the experiment at which he was "in a position to draw conclusions." The main one was that the "volume of business obtainable by this method of distribution is not nearly sufficient to justify investments in new productions."[92] But this did not prompt Kleine to discontinue the project, and neither did he abandon all hope of a prosperous future for nontheatrical cinema in general. Rather, he began exploring alternative ventures. One of these ventures was aimed at coordinating the activities of theatrical rental exchanges that were already serving nontheatrical customers in a manner that benefited Kleine's interests.[93] Other initiatives were focused on the development and commercial exploitation of various projectors—first a 35 mm paper film projector called the Kinereflex[94] and then a new line of machines of the Proctor brand, which included models for both theatrical and nontheatrical exhibitors.[95] The histories of these enterprises, some of which ran their course over several years in the mid- and late 1920s, are intricate and fall outside of the scope of this chapter, but I mention them briefly here in order to emphasize the experimental character of Kleine's work in educational and nontheatrical cinema throughout the 1920s, and also to note that there was a common denominator in all of Kleine's different schemes: the ultimate goal of establishing a solid infrastructure of nontheatrical production, distribution, and exhibition. Moreover, assuming that this was a widely shared goal, Kleine's initiatives gave the field a sense of direction even as it developed through experiment, trial, and error.

The Experiment Begins to Unravel

Parallel to Kleine's (ultimately unsuccessful) enterprises in the equipment sector, the experiment involving institutional exchanges continued. By January 1925, in the midst of the fourth season, seventeen institutions were still in possession of 1,500 reels of Kleine films.[96] Kleine's share of the revenues by the end of the season had increased slightly compared to the previous year, from $7,100 to $7,200, in spite of the defection of exchanges in Kentucky, Montana, North Carolina, Michigan, and Minnesota. Perhaps an ad campaign for *Julius Caesar* and some of the other Film Classics in *Classical Journal* and *Educational Screen* helped boost the number of bookings of these subjects.[97] Nevertheless, at this juncture, Kleine was not only exploring other approaches to the nontheatrical field, he was also considering how to make the use of his backlog of films more financially rewarding. In January 1925, he made an offer to Eastman-Kodak to sell his full catalog of motion pictures for a lump sum of $200,000, promising to withdraw all prints from the institutional exchanges.[98] The deal was never consummated.

Financial considerations aside, another reason why Kleine might have wanted to terminate his collaboration with the institutional exchanges was his mounting dissatisfaction with many exchanges' neglect of what he regarded as routine procedures, such as proper handling of order forms, invoices, reports, cash remittances, and the like. His comment regarding the Agricultural College of Mississippi's mishandling of a shipment sums up his view: "We have had no notice from them, which follows the usual efficiency of the highbrow when he is mixed up with a business transaction."[99] It is troubling that his closest ally on the university side, William H. Dudley of Wisconsin, was one of the worst offenders.[100] In May 1925, the schism had reached a stage at which Kleine wrote to the Extension Division at the University of Wisconsin, declaring that due to the "unsatisfactory manner in which the University of Wisconsin has handled our credits, we have decided to recall all moving picture films."[101] Kleine did not follow through. Instead, Dudley suggested that the films remain in Wisconsin in exchange for a new agreement that included a minimum-guarantee clause.[102]

Dudley also agreed to try to convince the other exchanges to make the same concession. He wrote to the members of NAVI's Film Committee in August 1925, explaining that Kleine was considering pulling out of the experiment due to dwindling economic returns.[103] The first reply came from Russell F. Egner at the University of Utah in Salt Lake City. Egner basically argued that the market for Kleine's entertainment films was already saturated. Nontheatrical venues in his state had either already shown them or could get other comparable pictures for a lower rental price. In conclusion, his message was that "while Mr. Kleine may not receive the revenue that he should have, or wants to have, I sometimes think he is fortunate to get anything out of some of the antiquated productions."[104] Kleine agreed that not all of his films were "active movers," but he also argued that he could not accept the death of a film like *Julius Caesar*—the very notion of a nontheatrical market hinged on the idea that films of such high caliber had lasting value.[105]

The minimum-guarantee discussion petered out without concrete results or any change of policy. With regard to the University of Wisconsin, Kleine notified Dudley in May 1926 that he still had not received the contract regarding a minimum number of engagements.[106] Similar reminders were sent in July and August the same year and again in May and June 1927.[107] Kleine kept badgering Dudley into the fall of 1927, also writing to the dean of the University of Wisconsin, to little avail.[108]

In spite of growing tensions between Kleine and his associates, many of his motion pictures remained with the institutional exchanges, some of them in active circulation. In season five (1925–26), Kleine deposited prints with one new institutional exchange (in Los Angeles), and Minnesota reentered the network, but the exchanges in Mississippi, Alabama, and Louisiana dropped out, bringing the total number of participants down to seventeen. Oregon quit the following season.[109] Kleine's share of receipts collected at the institutional exchanges decreased to $5,100 in 1925–26 but increased slightly to $5,400 in 1926–27. In October 1927, as the seventh season had just begun, Kleine presented the following status update: "We have placed some thousands of reels in the care of Institutional Exchanges at terms that are not commercial. This operation began in 1921 as an experiment that was largely in the interest of public service, in that a test was to be made to demonstrate if possible that a volume of business could be developed along these lines that would induce film manufacturers and distributors to produce special subjects for this field and otherwise to cater to its needs. The result has not been satisfactory from a business angle."[110]

The Experiment Ends

The "experimental" phase was clearly over, but the collaboration continued for two more seasons, and the number of participating exchanges dwindled to nine, following the departure of Florida, Minnesota (again), North Dakota, Ohio, Utah, and Wisconsin at various points in 1926 and 1927. Kleine's returns for the final two seasons (1927–28 and 1928–29) amounted to $2,200 and $2,300, respectively. His total revenues from the institutional exchanges for all eight seasons landed at roughly $55,000. By the late 1920s, as all prints were finally being shipped back to Kleine, a total of twenty-four institutions had been involved since the start in 1921.

As Kleine himself attested to several times, the experiment did not live up to the initial commercial expectations. There are a host of explanations for this, including occasional conflicts with local theatrical interests, lack of equipment, poor storage facilities, and other practical problems.[111] Also, all of Kleine's films were printed on 35 mm nitrate stock—he was very slow to adapt to the emerging 16 mm market—which meant that safety concerns prevented their distribution in certain places.[112]

But a more serious problem had to do with the films. Although a few of them lent themselves well to repeated use school year after school year, the appeal of most of them wore off along with their novelty, similar to the patterns of diminishing returns in the theatrical market. In addition, Kleine's films faced competition from the newer entertainment pictures that most of the exchanges brought in from other sources on a regular basis.[113] Such reliance on other sources was not part of the original plan, which instead was aimed toward the production and acquisition of new subjects. But these components, as well as the solutions to various practical problems, were dependent on either the reinvestment of accumulated profits or institutional support. According to Kleine, the whole experiment was hampered by a lack of institutional support for the extension divisions' efforts to build film libraries and circulate the movies. "None of [the institutional exchanges] receive appropriations that permit the widespread service that they should logically offer, both educational and recreational," Kleine claimed in January 1925.[114] But this observation was an afterthought. At the outset of the experiment, production and acquisition had been seen as a natural outcome of market logics, as inherent to the "sound commercial basis." However, the experiment never reached the expected volume, and the profits never came close to the amounts needed for an investment in production. The main reason for this, as Kleine saw it, was nontheatrical customers' unwillingness to pay. This reluctance was the cause for much frustration at various stages throughout his career, and Kleine came to regard the nontheatrical field as crowded with people who wanted something for nothing.[115]

Kleine's engagement with the nontheatrical field persisted, as did his devotion to commercialism as its founding principle, in spite of the apparent hopelessness of this proposition, and in spite of his own conflicted views on the matter. Arguably, however, his motives were not purely commercial. Later on, Arthur Edwin Krows wrote in the *Educational Screen* that Kleine was driven by "a sufficient number of altruistic reasons in addition to the commercial motives which skeptics who never knew the man will recognize first."[116] It would be more accurate to say that Kleine operated under a generalized ideology of business, according to which profit and progress were not mutually exclusive but logically complementary. Unfortunately for Kleine, this ideological baggage was not transferrable into the sphere of extension education without friction. The solution that Kleine had set forth for the nontheatrical field was in essence a market solution—an attempt to harness nontheatrical cinema to the institution of the market. But when Kleine talked about the "market"—his "sound commercial basis"—he was not merely referring to a sociomaterial arrangement that facilitated repeated transactions between rational buyers and sellers, he was also putting a premium on things such as "competitiveness" and "efficiency."[117] In his dealings with the institutional exchanges, he kept bumping into completely different evaluative protocols, rooted in a completely different institution, i.e., the state university. As we have seen, in Kleine's view, many of the extension division representatives were utterly incompetent when it came to standard business procedures. In the end, however, what was most discombobulating for Kleine was the mystery of how so many people and institutions could simultaneously value something highly yet be unwilling to pay its price. This clearly defied all market logic.

To some extent, Kleine was working in opposition to praxis. It was not uncommon among institutional exchanges to provide at least some of their customers with at least a selection of films and slides free of charge. In some places, this was indeed the general policy. Accordingly, both exchanges and customers had to make an exception for Kleine's films, and Kleine had to struggle to convince them to get used to putting their money where their mouths were. There were also frequent requests from the institutional exchanges that they be allowed to quote a lower rental price than the stipulated minimum. From Kleine's perspective, the consequences were potentially ruinous: "These exchanges cannot realize what it means to throw fortunes into film production and risk having large sections of the country ruined by quotations which make it hopeless to ever earn their prorata [*sic*] share of the investment."[118]

These were concrete, practical conflicts that nonetheless carried an ideological dimension. For example, it would appear that Kleine equated "desire" with "demand." This categorical slippage made sense within the restricted frame of a particular kind of market ideology, but an alternative understanding of "the market" would suggest that the former is a necessary but not sufficient condition for the latter.[119] Kleine was surely right to believe that many (perhaps even most) people saw the great value of educational films, and of the use of motion pictures in visual instruction as well as for a range of community purposes. But he was incorrect to assume that this automatically translated into consumer demand. A potential obstacle might have been that Kleine's target customers did not readily identify themselves as "consumers." For some, this notion might have been a complete mismatch with their own sense of who they were. In other cases, the consumer category might have been subordinated to other, more primary identities, such as "educator." Arguably, these questions of identity can shed some new light on the history of nontheatrical cinema and Kleine's role in it. As Haidee Wasson points out, the nontheatrical field of the 1920s took shape through various experiments with cinematic practices that were predicated not only on an alternative conception of cinema's functions but also on an alternative idea about the audience, no longer conceived of as a monolith, but as varied, with varied needs and tastes.[120] Kleine's views, however, were ambiguous. On the one hand, he clearly made a distinction between the mass audience and more refined segments of the public that he believed could either already be found in, or attracted to, the nontheatrical sphere. On the other hand, the market ideology that informed his vision of nontheatrical cinema existing on a "sound commercial basis" seemed to smuggle in a conception of the audience as a faceless, undifferentiated mass of consumers rather than viewing it as a multitude of specific groups with specific identities, interests, and needs.[121] Perhaps this is an additional reason why his vision turned out to be so difficult to implement.

Kleine's frustration with antimarket behavior among the institutional exchanges and their customers also seems indicative of the tensions that arose when two (or more) institutions ("the market," "the university," "education," etc.) converged in the same location within the field of nontheatrical cinema in the US at this juncture. In addition, we could argue that Kleine emphasized the formal rules of the market, but failed to realize that these rules were only relevant if there were also incentives for participants to play by them. When Dudley and others neglected to file the proper reports to Kleine, or remit his share of the receipts in a timely manner, or circulated one of his films free of charge or below minimum rental price, Kleine seems to have regarded this as a moral deficiency. But these actors might merely have been acting on the insight that they simply had little to gain by playing by Kleine's rules and little to lose by disregarding them.

Concluding Remarks

Extension divisions remained at the heart of nontheatrical film culture, and their work as nontheatrical film distributors continued to expand in spite of the diminishing popularity of Kleine's films. In successful institutions, such as the Bureau of Visual Instruction at the University of Wisconsin, the number of shipments of prints to nontheatrical customers steadily increased throughout the 1920s, reaching an ever-expanding audience, and there were more and more additions to the film library from a growing number of sources.[122] A persistent problem, however, was a lack of films made specifically for the classroom.[123] Clearly, the motion pictures that Kleine had deposited with the institutional exchanges were not the solution, but this was not the point of his experiment. The aim was to explore whether the nontheatrical field could become economically self-sustainable and thereby finance production of whatever films were in demand among nontheatrical customers. In the meantime, throughout the 1920s, the supply of films was somewhat random, although most films came from either the industry or the government (see below). To the extent that there was an influx of films from commercial producers like Kleine, this was because fierce competition resulted in a growing surplus of useless films that were shunned by audiences—if they ever reached the marketplace at all. Some of the subjects that ended up in this "slaughterhouse of cinema" were brought back to life in the nontheatrical field.[124] This was the case with several of Kleine's films. Thanks to the institutional exchanges, these were put to new uses, in new and different contexts, for new and different audiences. With this, they also earned back some of what they had once cost Kleine to produce or purchase. But they failed to fulfill his grander ambition: to prove that nontheatrical cinema could be built on a "sound commercial basis."

In this regard, the experiment was a "failure"—a dead end—but this does not mean that Kleine's cooperation with the institutional exchanges was insignificant within the wider history of nontheatrical cinema. In fact, for several years in the 1920s, he was one of the largest suppliers of films to extension divisions. A survey of visual instruction published by the Department of the Interior's Bureau of Education in 1924 identified twenty state institutions (mainly universities) with institutionalized departments for visual instruction.[125] Eight of these stated that Kleine was one of their main sources of motion pictures, and it is clear that several more were also circulating his films—according to my count, fourteen of the institutions listed were participating in Kleine's experiment. In fact, the survey made a special note about Kleine's pioneering role in the nontheatrical field:

> Kleine was one of the first of the men engaged in theatrical production to sense the future demand of schools and churches, and instead of trying to suppress this demand, as most of the other film men did, he early, in association with Edison, began a search for existing film stories which would have acceptable school and church values. His Julius Caesar, Spartacus, Fall of Pompeii, and Silas Marner were all big productions having such values, and the schools made wide use of them. . . . At the low rental rates asked [Kleine] has not made money on them, but he has paid expenses and blazed a trail that others will follow and reap the larger financial returns.[126]

Among other suppliers that the institutions pointed to as their main sources of films, the most frequently mentioned were Ford, "industrial firms," the US Department of Agriculture, the US Bureau of Commercial Economics (a government-sponsored distributor of educational films), and, simply, the "US" (i.e., the US government). As we have seen, an important goal for Kleine was to "liberate" the nontheatrical field from an unfortunate reliance on precisely these institutions; that is, the government and the industry. In addition, he wanted to separate the nontheatrical field from the regular theatrical movie business, a desire rooted as much in antisemitism as in a kind of cultural conservatism that did not seem to square with the type of entertainment film produced in Hollywood in the 1920s.[127]

Kleine and his main "competitors" in the nontheatrical field all seem to have been trading in slightly different currencies. Nontheatrical cinema was the site of many different types of exchange, not just the market transactions that constituted the building blocks of Kleine's "sound commercial basis." This is indicative of the heterogeneity of the field. Rather than coalescing into an autonomous (albeit market-based) institution along the lines that Kleine had imagined, nontheatrical cinema continued to develop via the intersections of the interests of commercial producers and distributors, philanthropic organizations, the government, and the industry.[128] Kleine was merely one among many prospectors of the field, and his work with the extension divisions—however central these were to nontheatrical film culture—was merely one effort among a plethora of campaigns, events, and initiatives.[129] To give just a few examples, the field attracted general associations like the YMCA, industrial concerns such as the Ford Motor Company, philanthropist initiatives like the Commercial Bureau of Economics, government bodies such as the Department of Agriculture, and raw film or projector manufacturers like Eastman-Kodak and the De Vry Corp.[130] Although each of these may have desired to construct some kind of durable infrastructure for nontheatrical film culture, their respective aims and ambitions varied wildly, ranging from profit-seeking and advertising to tick eradication and the fostering of well-behaved workers-subjects-citizens. Seemingly, then, the thing that joined these different agents was a conviction that motion pictures could somehow be useful—for something.[131] The multiplicity of nontheatrical uses and users could hardly be contained within one vision. Arguably, Kleine's scope was at once too wide and too limited. He imagined nontheatrical cinema as a unified, autonomous formation, but only along the lines of the high-culture aesthetics and market ideology that he subscribed to. In the end, this left him doubly out of step and ultimately disappointed. In 1929, Kleine summed up his experience: "It is regrettable that the non-theatrical field, and more particularly the educational field, is unprofitable to both producers and distributors of motion pictures. Countless attempts have been made by different concerns to develop a volume of business that would at least pay distribution expenses and a fraction of the negative cost. Repeated trials during the past twenty years have led nowhere."[132]

Notes

1. For a book-length history of Kleine's career, see Joel Frykholm, *George Kleine and American Cinema: The Movie Business and Film Culture in the Silent Era* (London: Palgrave Macmillan/BFI, 2015).

2. Robert Grau, *The Business Man in the Amusement World: A Volume of Progress in the Field of the Theatre* (New York: Broadway Publishing Company, 1910). For more recent accounts of Kleine's efforts to promote educational film, see Anthony Slide, *Before Video: A History of Non-Theatrical Film* (New York: Greenwood Press, 1992), and Jennifer Lynn Peterson, *Education in the School of Dreams: Travelogues and Early Nonfiction Film* (Durham: Duke University Press, 2013).

3. On Kleine's 1910 catalog, see Oliver Gaycken in this volume. For an account of Kleine, Urban, and Edison as pioneers in educational cinema, see Amanda R. Keeler, "'Sugar Coat the Educational Pill': The Educational Aspirations of Emergent Film, Radio, and Television" (PhD diss., Indiana University, 2011), but note that Keeler has not consulted the George Kleine Papers at the Library of Congress, the key collection of material relating to Kleine, which makes the sections on Kleine limited in scope and depth.

4. Kleine to Professor R. D. Williams, Pomona College, March 25, 1921, George Kleine Papers (henceforth GKP), Library of Congress, Manuscript Division, box 39, file "Nontheatrical; General, 1911–Aug 1921"; Kleine to Ben Turbett, November 27, 1922, GKP, box 40, file "Nontheatrical; Educational Use of Films, 1919–1922."

5. Kleine, "Co-operation in Visual Instruction," speech at the Seventh Annual Meeting of the National University Extension Association at Lexington, Kentucky, April 22, 1922, published in *Proceedings of the National University Extension Association at Lexington, Kentucky, April 20, 21, 22, 1922* (Boston: Wright & Potter Printing Company, 1923), 38. A copy of the proceedings can be found in GKP, box 41, file "Nontheatrical; University Catalogs, 1920–1927 (2)."

6. Frykholm, *George Kleine and American Cinema*.

7. My approach to "institutionalization" in this essay is informed by Avner Greif's work on the role of institutions in economic history—see Greif, *Institutions and the Path to the Modern Economy: Lessons from Medieval Trade* (Cambridge, NY: Cambridge University Press, 2006). Greif provides a general framework for studying institutions—which he defines as "[systems] of rules, beliefs, norms, and organizations that together generate a regularity of (social) behavior" (30)—from a socioeconomic perspective that brings together issues of economy, social structures, and culture and that draws on the "main traditions of sociological institutionalism" (22) pioneered by figures such as Emile Durkheim and Max Weber. He also notes that organizations are usually components of institutions as well as institutions in themselves, so we may study them as one or the other or both depending on what issue we are interested in exploring (31, 50). This aligns with the dual sense of "institutionalization" I refer to with regard to Kleine's experiment (a similar differentiation of the term appears in Marina Dahlquist and Joel Frykholm's introduction to this volume, as well as in chapter 10, by Gregory Waller).

8. Visual Instruction Section, Department of the Interior to Kleine, March 24, 1919, GKP, box 57, file "U.S. Dept. of Interior (Visual education), 1919–1924."

9. Kleine had imported these Italian multireel epics and circulated them in 1913–14. They were repackaged (together with a few additional films) as George Kleine's Cycle of Film Classics in 1916, which was expanded and reissued again from time to time after 1916 (see Frykholm, *George Kleine and American Cinema*, chapter 5). On Kleine's offer to the Visual Instruction Section, see Kleine to Visual Instruction Section, Department of the Interior, April 17, 1919, GKP, box 57, file "U.S. Dept. of Interior (Visual education), 1919–1924."

10. Kleine to John J. Stevens, High School, Ansonia, Connecticut, September 22, 1919, including enclosed circular "mailed to Superintendents of Schools at Capitals of each State . . . with the exception of Springfield Illinois," GKP, box 40, file "Nontheatrical; Educational Use of Films, 1919–1922."

11. C. P. Cary to Kleine, September 24, 1919; William H. Dudley to Kleine, September 24, 1919, both in GKP, box 40, file "Nontheatrical; Educational Use of Films, 1919–1922." The few superintendents who replied wrote that their states made no appropriations to schools for the purchase of motion pictures. See Kleine to Arthur L. Beeley, Bureau of Visual Instruction, University of Utah, October 8, 1919, GKP, box 40, file "Nontheatrical; Educational Use of Films, 1919–1922."

12. Kleine to L. W. McChesney, Edison Inc., February 27, 1918, GKP, box 16, file "Edison (Thomas A.), Inc., Jan–April, 1918."

13. Broadly speaking, this work was inspired by the "Wisconsin Idea," which stipulated that university research and education should be extended beyond the boundaries of the campus, to the benefit of all citizens of the state. For an analysis of nontheatrical film distribution at the University of Wisconsin as part of the "Wisconsin idea" and a Progressive "service ideal," see Alex Kupfer, "Cinema and the Service Ideal: Nontheatrical Film Distribution and the University of Wisconsin Bureau of Visual Instruction, 1910–1930" (chapter from forthcoming doctoral dissertation).

14. "National Academy of Visual Instruction: History," GKP, box 41, file "Nontheatrical; National Academy of Visual Instruction, 1921 and undated."

15. Ibid.; "Program; First Annual Conference; The National Academy of Visual Instruction," GKP, box 41, file "Nontheatrical; National Academy of Visual Instruction, 1921 and undated."

16. Ford's activities as a film distributor aimed to circulate not just motion pictures but specifically "Fordist" motion pictures that could contribute to the rationalization of work and to the creation of capitalist subjects of the workers (Lee Grieveson, "The Work of Film in the Age of Fordist Mechanization," *Cinema Journal* 51, no, 3 (2012): 25–51).

17. National University Extension Association, "Resolution Adopted at the Annual Meeting in Ann Arbor, April 8, 1920," GKP, box 23, file "Ford, Henry, 1921."

18. It is not clear exactly what the educators who courted Ford wanted to accomplish. Ford's plans to expand his operations in educational cinema by adding the Ford Educational Library to the already long-running film series Ford Educational Weekly had been brewing for some time when Ford representatives first met the four-man NUEA committee in September 1920. The August issue of the *Moving Picture Age* had already reported that Ford was "engaged in the production of a new film library." Ads for the Ford Educational Library from November and December make clear that the involvement of scholars and "experts" in the production of motion pictures for the library was an important selling point and legitimizing strategy. Presumably, the NUEA committee had set out to expand the sphere of scholarly influence to also include the organization and administration of the library and to inject itself into Ford's motion picture activities on a more permanent basis. See L. E. Reber to Messrs. Marquis and Hartman, Ford Motor Company, January 6, 1921, GKP, box 23, file "Ford, Henry, 1921"; "New Educational Film Library," *Moving Picture Age* 3, no. 8 (1920): 22; and advertisements for the Ford Educational Library, *Moving Picture Age* 3, no. 11 (1920): 6; and *Moving Picture Age* 3, no. 12 (1920): 6.

19. Correspondence between Kleine and L. W. McChesney and others at the Edison Company—primarily found in boxes 16 and 17 of the George Kleine Papers—and other sources in the same collection, offer an abundance of information about the conquest pictures. About the initial theatrical release, also see Jennifer Horne, "Nostalgia and Non-Fiction in Edison's 1917 *Conquest Program*," *Historical Journal of Film, Radio and Television* 22, no. 3 (2002): 315–31.

20. Dudley to Kleine, November 11, 1920, GKP, box 42, file "University Propaganda, 1920–1922."

21. Kleine to Dudley, December 4, 1920, GKP, box 42, file "University Propaganda, 1920–1922." The list was sent "pending the completion of our catalogue." A copy of the latter, issued in 1921, is preserved in GKP, box 8, file "Conquest Films, 1917–1928 and undated."

22. Edison could not attend the NAVI meeting, but he wrote to Dudley to express his "gratification" and "pleasure" over the progress made by NAVI. See Dudley to Kleine, June 23, 1921, GKP, box 42, file "Nontheatrical; University of Wisconsin, 1922–1927"; Kleine to Thomas A. Edison, June 24, 1921, GKP, box 17, file "Edison (Thomas A.), Inc., 1921"; Thomas A. Edison to W. H. Dudley, June 29, 1921, GKP, box 18, file "Educational Films, 1916, 1920–1930."

23. "Plan for Co-ordinating [*sic*] the Operations of University Departments of Visual Education Extension through the United States and to Increase the Volume of Their Operations," undated [ca. 1921], GKP, box 42, file "Nontheatrical; University Propaganda, July 1922–1923 and undated."

24. Ibid.

25. Ibid.

26. Kleine to Thomas A. Edison, June 7, 1921, GKP, box 15, file "Edison, Thomas A.; Correspondence, 1921, 1929."

27. Ibid.

28. Ibid.

29. See, for example, Kleine to the State University Film Exchange, State University of Montana, Missoula, November 18, 1921, GKP, box 42, file "Nontheatrical; University Propaganda, 1920–June 1922."

30. Kleine to Dudley, June 27, 1921, GKP, box 39, file "Nontheatrical; General, 1911–Aug 1921."

31. Ibid.

32. Ibid.

33. Ibid.

34. Kleine to C. C. Dill, Educational Film Bureau, Spokane, Washington, August 19, 1921, GKP, box 18, file "Educational Film Bureau, 1921."

35. Kleine to Dudley, June 30, 1921, GKP, box 39, file "Nontheatrical; General, 1911–Aug 1921."

36. Kleine did not demand a minimum guarantee of rental volume or revenues but specified a minimum rental price for the different subjects, e.g., at least $20.00 per day for *Julius Caesar* and $2.50 per reel for the conquest pictures. The $2.50 minimum per reel also applied to two series of films that Kleine had decided to include in the offer in addition to the classics and the conquest films: (a) a selection of Edison-produced five-reel features; and (b) the so-called Flagg Comedies, twelve one-reelers written by and starring celebrity illustrator James Montgomery Flagg, of Uncle Sam's "I Want YOU for U.S. Army" recruitment poster fame.

37. Dudley to F. F. Nalder, State College of Washington at Pullman, General College Extension, July 15, 1921, GKP, box 39, file "Nontheatrical; General, 1911–Aug 1921 (2)." This was also sent to eleven additional institutional members of the National Academy of Visual Instruction.

38. W. H. Dudley to Kleine, August 10, 1921, GKP, box 40, file "Nontheatrical; Dudley, W. H., and Reynolds, F. W., 1921–1923." See also correspondence between Dudley and institutional members of NAVI in GKP, box 39, file "Nontheatrical; General, 1911–Aug 1921."

39. Data on shipments of prints was culled from several files in the George Kleine Papers, primarily box 41, "Nontheatrical; University Engagements, 1922–1924"; box 40, "Nontheatrical; Dudley, W. H., and Reynolds, F. W., 1921–1923"; and various files in box 68 that are labeled "Inventories and Lists; Educational distribution."

40. Kleine had purchased these five-reelers in 1918, when he bought the Edison Company out of the movie business (see Frykholm, *George Kleine and American Cinema*, chapter 3).

41. See note 36 in this chapter.

42. University of Utah received close to a hundred subjects, including the entire roster of conquest pictures (roughly seventy subjects, including a handful of unreleased films that had originally been produced for the Conquest Program), all twelve Flagg comedies, and most of the special features. University of California at Berkeley also ordered the whole series of Conquest pictures, but fewer features than Utah and no Flagg films. Similarly, nearly all of the Conquest pictures were shipped to University of Florida at Gainesville, whereas only a handful of features (three classics, two Edison five-reelers, and the three-reel special release *Star Spangled Banner* [Edison, 1917]), were placed in this institution. University of Kansas was somewhat more selective than Florida with regard to the classics and other features, but did order six of the Flagg comedies. Only one of the classics (*Julius Caesar*), and none of the other feature films, was placed in the sixth pilot institution, the State University of Washington.

43. See miscellaneous documents in GKP, box 18, file "Educational Film Bureau, 1921," and box 20, file "Film Service Bureau (H. T. Collard), 1920–1921."

44. Dudley to Kleine, August 31, 1921, GKP, box 40, file "Nontheatrical; Dudley, W. H., and Reynolds, F. W., 1921–1923."

45. Dudley to Kleine, November 26, 1921, GKP, box 40, file "Nontheatrical; Dudley, W. H., and Reynolds, F. W., 1921–1923."

46. Dudley to Kleine, April 10, 1922, GKP, box 40, file "Nontheatrical; Dudley, W. H., and Reynolds, F. W., 1921–1923."

47. Kleine to Thomas A. Edison, November 4, 1921, GKP, box 18, file "Educational Films, 1916, 1920–1930."

48. Kleine to L. W. McChesney, January 5, 1922, GKP, box 17, file "Edison (Thomas A.), Inc., 1921" [letter misdated January 5, 1921].

49. Ad for *Julius Caesar, Classical Weekly* 15, no. 16 (1922). Copy in GKP, box 39, file "Nontheatrical; General, printed matter."

50. "Territories Covered by Institutional Exchanges," GKP, box 42, file "Nontheatrical; Visual Instruction Association of New York and National Academy of Visual Instruction, 1922 and undated."

51. Kleine to Dudley, January 10, 1922, GKP, box 40, file "Nontheatrical; Dudley, W. H., and Reynolds, F. W., 1921–1923."

52. George K. Spoor to Kleine, October 31, 1927; Kleine to Spoor, November 2, 1927, both in GKP, box 20, file "Essanay Film Manufacturing Co., 1916–1927 and undated."

53. I have been unable to locate this letter in the George Kleine Papers or the Thomas Edison Papers, but other sources in the Kleine Papers reveal its main contents. See, for example, Kleine to Dudley, March 2, 1922, GKP, box 40, file "Nontheatrical; Dudley, W. H., and Reynolds, F. W., 1921–1923"; Kleine to Dudley, March 9, 1922, GKP, box 42, file "Nontheatrical; University of Wisconsin, 1922–1927"; Dudley to Kleine, March 13, 1922, GKP, box 40, file "Nontheatrical; Dudley, W. H., and Reynolds, F. W., 1921–1923"; E. G. Liebold (General Secretary to Henry Ford) to W. H. Meadowcroft (Assistant to Thomas A. Edison), March 13, 1922, GKP, box 18, file "Educational Films, 1916, 1920–1930"; E. G. Liebold to Kleine, March 13, 1922, GKP, box 18, file "Educational Films, 1916, 1920–1930"; Kleine to E. G. Liebold, March 20, 1922, GKP, box 18, file "Educational Films, 1916, 1920–1930"; W. H. Meadowcroft to Kleine, March 20, 1922, GKP, box 18, file "Educational Films, 1916, 1920–1930"; and Kleine to Dudley, March 23, 1922, GKP, box 40, file "Nontheatrical; Dudley, W. H., and Reynolds, F. W., 1921–1923."

54. Kleine to George Eastman, March 1, 1922, GKP, box 13, file "Eastman Kodak Co., General, 1908–1928"; Kleine to Dudley, March 2, 1922.

55. Kleine to Eastman, March 1, 1922.

56. Kleine to Dudley, March 9, 1922.

57. Kleine to E. G. Liebold, March 20, 1922.

58. Telegrams from E. G. Liebold to Kleine, March 23, 1922; from Kleine to Dudley, March 24, 1922; from Dudley to Kleine, March 24, 1922; and from Kleine to Liebold, March 24, 1922, all in GKP, box 18, file "Educational Films, 1916, 1920–1930."

59. Kleine to Spoor, November 2, 1927.

60. Ibid.

61. Ibid.

62. Anthony Slide notes that, with the exception of Siegmund Lubin, none of the members of the Motion Picture Patents Company (MPPC) were Jewish, and he singles out the Vitagraph directors and George Kleine as being especially hostile to Jewish people (Slide, *Early American Cinema*, rev. ed. [Metuchen, NJ: Scarecrow Press, 1994; originally published 1970]), 49. See also Richard Abel, *The Red Rooster Scare: Making Cinema American, 1900–1910* (Berkeley: University of California Press, 1999), 126–27, 256n83. The George Kleine Papers contains ample evidence of Kleine's antisemitism in the post-MPPC period. See, for example, the correspondence between Kleine and L. W. McChesney and Sumner Williams (both of Edison Inc.) in GKP, box 17, file "Edison (Thomas A.), Inc., 1922–1924"; correspondence between Kleine and the author—and fellow antisemite—Peter Kyne in GKP, box 31, file "Kyne, Peter B., 1922–1930"; and Kleine to Arthur F. Warde, July 9, 1920, GKP, box 64, file "World Film Corp.; General, 1920–1925" (in which Kleine expresses his approval of the antisemitic series of articles on "The International Jew," published in Henry Ford's newspaper the *Dearborn Independent* starting in spring 1920).

63. Kleine to Ted Hardcastle, April 29, 1921, GKP, box 25, file "Hardcastle, B. T. (Ted), 1920–1921."

64. Kleine to J. J. Thompson, November 15, 1920, GKP, box 4, file "Branches; inter office, New York and Chicago, July–Dec 1920."

65. Kleine to Thomas A. Edison, June 7, 1921, GKP, box 15, file "Edison, Thomas A.; Correspondence, 1921, 1929."

66. Kleine to George Blair, Eastman-Kodak, September 25, 1922, GKP, box 13, file "Eastman Kodak Co., General, 1908–1928."

67. See, for example, Kleine to L. W. McChesney, January 5, 1922, GKP, box 17, file "Edison (Thomas A.), Inc., 1921" [letter misdated January 5, 1921]; and Kleine to John Roach Straton, February 15, 1922, GKP, box 54, file "Stratoni, John Roach, 1922."

68. "Third Annual Meeting [of the] National Academy of Visual Instruction (Tentative Program)," GKP, box 39, file "Nontheatrical; General, Sept 1921–1924 and undated"; and "Program of the Seventh Annual Conference [of the] National University Extension Association," GKP, box 39, file "Nontheatrical; General, Printed Matter."

69. Kleine, "Co-operation." See note 5.

70. Ibid., 42.

71. Ibid., 40.

72. Kleine to L. W. McChesney (Edison Inc.), April 26, 1922, GKP, box 17, file "Edison (Thomas A.), Inc., 1922–1924."

73. University of Colorado–Boulder, University of Alabama–Tuscaloosa, University of Minnesota–Minneapolis, and University of Nebraska–Lincoln had "placed their applications" on-site in Lexington, shipments of selected prints to follow before the end of the first season of the experiment (ibid.).

74. Kleine, circular to institutional exchanges, July 10, 1922, GKP, box 18, file "Educational Institutions, 1913–1930."

75. Data on rental income from distribution by the institutional exchanges have been derived through comparison of figures appearing in the following sources: "Cash Collected from Universities, Season 1921–1922 and season 1922–1923"; "George Kleine's Share of College Collections, Nov 31 [*sic*], 1922"; "Summary Cash Collection—University Rentals—Fiscal Year Sept 1, 1923 to Aug 31, 1924"; "Non-theatrical Institutional Film Rental Receipts, 1925–1926, 1926–1927"; and "Non Theatrical Institutional Film Rental Receipts (Season 1927–1928)"; all in GKP, box 18, file "Educational Distribution to Universities, 1921–1928"; and "Collections from Institutional Exchanges on 'Julius Caesar' from 9/1/21 to 1/15/23," GKP, box 29, file "*Julius Caesar*, 1914–1930"; Kleine to F. W. Reynolds and W. H. Dudley, January 17, 1923, GKP, box 40, file "Nontheatrical; Dudley, W. H., and Reynolds, F. W., 1921–1923"; "George Kleine Share—College Collections—Oct 1, 1923," GKP, box 41, file "Nontheatrical; Lists of Universities and Schools Using Films"; "George Kleine Share—College Collections—Nov. 1, 1923," GKP, box 39, file "Nontheatrical; General, Sept 1921–1924 and undated"; and "George Kleine Share—Collections—April 1, 1924," GKP, box 68, file "Inventories and Lists; Educational Distribution; University of California, 1922–1930." See also Thomas Simonet, "George Kleine's Effort in Non-Theatrical Film Distribution, 1921–1928," *Educational Broadcasting Review* 7, no. 3 (1973): 177.

76. Kleine, circular, July 10, 1922.

77. Ibid.

78. See Frykholm, *George Kleine and American Cinema*, chapter 5, for a more detailed account of Kleine's agenda for reforming film culture in the 1920s.

79. The idea that the nontheatrical field should embrace entertainment films—of the right kind—was frequently promoted in the editorial pages of the *Educational Screen* (some examples are referenced in Simonet, "George Kleine's Effort," 178–79.) As far as NAVI was concerned, during the Des Moines conference in 1921, fourteen of its members were party to

a resolution that stated that it should be a "distinct duty" of visual instruction departments at extension divisions "to secure from all sources possible, both commercial and non-commercial, the best of entertainment films for educational and community meetings" (see resolution adopted by fourteen NAVI members, July 4, 1921, GKP, box 40, file "Nontheatrical; Educational Use of Films, 1919–1922"). On Dudley's views specifically, see "Moving Pictures in Schools," *Stevens Point Daily Journal*, June 27, 1914, 15, cited in Kupfer, "Cinema and the Service Ideal"; and William H. Dudley, "Organization for Visual Instruction," Department of the Interior, Bureau of Education, Bulletin, 1921, no. 7 (Washington: Government Printing Office, 1921).

80. Dudley, "Organization for Visual Instruction," 16.

81. Dudley to Kleine, September 11, 1922, GKP, box 40, file "Nontheatrical; Dudley, W. H., and Reynolds, F. W., 1921–1923."

82. For Kleine's comments regarding Levey and his company, see, for example, Kleine to Dudley, August 22, 1922, GKP, box 42, file "Nontheatrical; University Propaganda, July 1922–1923 and undated"; and the correspondence between Kleine and W. C. Crosby (at the institutional exchange in North Carolina) found in GKP, box 40, file "Nontheatrical; Crosby, W. C. (N.C. State Dept. of Education and Carolina Film Corporation), 1921–1923," in particular Crosby to Kleine, August 26, 1922 and Kleine to Crosby, August 31, 1922.

83. Crosby to Kleine, August 26, 1922.

84. Kleine to Dudley, August 22, 1922. Antisemitic views were rampant in American culture at large around this time. With regard to the film industry specifically, John Trumpbour's book about American cinema's global expansion offers ample evidence of strong antisemitic currents in many pockets of what he calls the "early domestic mobilizers against Hollywood" (John Trumpbour, *Selling Hollywood to the World: U.S. and European Struggles for Mastery of the Global Film Industry, 1920–1950* [New York: Cambridge University Press, 2002], 21–22, 75–77).

85. See, for example, correspondence between Kleine and his associate at the North Carolina State Department of Education, W. C. Crosby, in GKP, box 40, file "Nontheatrical; Crosby, W. C. (N.C. State Dept. of Education and Carolina Film Corporation), 1921–1923."

86. Kleine to L. W. McChesney, August 11, 1922, GKP, box 17, file "Edison (Thomas A.), Inc., 1922–1924."

87. Dudley to Kleine, November 4, 1922; and Kleine to Dudley, November 6, 1922, both in GKP, box 40, file "Nontheatrical; Dudley, W. H., and Reynolds, F. W., 1921–1923."

88. See note 75 in this chapter.

89. The questionnaire and replies to it are in GKP, box 18, file "Educational Institutions, 1913–1930."

90. Kleine to Thomas A. Edison, April 20, 1921, GKP, box 18, file "Educational Films, 1916, 1920–1930."

91. W. T. Wilt, University of Minnesota–Minneapolis, to Kleine, March 8, 1924, GKP, box 18, file "Educational Institutions, 1913–1930."

92. Kleine to James A. Moyer, National University Extension Association, December 21, 1923, GKP, box 21, file "Finances; Expenses, 1917–1923."

93. Kleine's idea was to organize a corporation "to handle the non-theatrical field in a serious and businesslike manner," as he put it in a memo. He suggested that the new corporation would handle nontheatrical distribution for all leading manufacturers, based on a uniform price scale. Kleine would pay 30 percent of the gross receipts to the manufacturer for the privilege of making new prints, paying for the prints and their distribution himself. The memo was submitted to United Artists attorney Dennis F. O'Brien, and possibly also to other leading studios, but there are no indications that this led to further negotiations

("Memorandum—To Cover Non-Theatrical Distribution; A Proposition to United Artists," GKP, box 39, file "Nontheatrical; General, Sept 1921–1924 and undated").

94. The Kinereflex was developed for home and amateur use but could potentially also find a large market among a miscellany of nontheatrical customers. The launch of the Kinereflex in the United States and Canada was backed by a circle of people who were connected to the Joseph P. Day Industrial Department Inc., part of New York City real estate tycoon Joseph P. Day's business organization. Kleine helped produce a financial plan and a business prospectus and was the designated head of the proposed company, but the project ultimately failed to attract investors. For more details, see Kleine, "Memorandum to Mr. Bulkley," April 16, 1924, GKP, box 5, file "Bulkley, H. G. (Paper Film—Positype Film Corp. of America), 1924–1926." Drafts of the prospectus as well as the final version are located in the same file. Some sample strips of the actual paper film can be found in GKP, box 43, file "Paper Film, 1922 and undated."

95. Kleine acquired the rights to the Proctor projector as part of the fallout when the United Theatre Equipment Corporation, in which Kleine had been a major shareholder, went into bankruptcy in June 1923. A prospectus for "Corporation X" and other documents in the Kleine Papers show that Kleine intended to set up a new corporation that would acquire exclusive rights to market the Simplex and Powers projectors, the two brands that dominated the theatrical market, with the purpose of marketing these machines, as well as the Proctor projector, which Kleine regarded to be on par with the two market leaders. The venture was publicly (but anonymously) announced in *Motion Picture News* in December 1924 but aborted shortly thereafter, presumably because the attempt to combine with the Simplex and Powers interests fell through. Later, Kleine retooled his plans for a new equipment corporation, but the plans yet again failed to materialize beyond an initial trade advertisement (see "Contract between United Theatre Equipment Corp. and Kleine Optical Co., made and entered March 24, 1917," GKP, box 60, file "United Theatre Equipment Corp.; Contracts, 1916–1919" [on Kleine's acquisition of rights to the Proctor machine]; miscellaneous documents in GKP, boxes 59–61 [for additional information about UTE]; miscellaneous documents in GKP, box 47, files "Proctor Automatic Projectors, 1919–1924" and "Proctor Automatic Projectors, 1927–1929 and undated" [on the interrelated histories of the Proctor projector, Kleine, and UTE]; prospectus for "Corporation X," GKP, box 19, file "Equipment; Theater, 1916–1925"; agreement between George Kleine and Barton A. Proctor, September 10, 1924, GKP, box 47, file "Proctor Automatic Projectors, 1919–1924" [on the plans for marketing the Proctor machine]; advertisement, *Motion Picture News* 30, no. 26 (1924): 3375 [public announcement of the Proctor plan]). A great number of documents that relate to Kleine's subsequent attempts to market the Proctor are located in GKP, boxes 47–48.

96. Kleine to George Eastman, Eastman-Kodak, January 7, 1925, GKP, box 13, file "Eastman Kodak; General, 1908–1925."

97. See, for example, ad for George Kleine motion pictures, *Educational Screen* 3, no. 9 (1924): 369. See also Kleine to James S. Thomas, Extension Division, University of Alabama, December 10, 1924 [circular to institutional exchanges], GKP, box 18, file "Educational Institutions, 1913–1930."

98. Kleine to George Eastman, January 7, 1925.

99. Kleine to L. R. Abbott, September 5, 1924, GKP, box 52, file "Seabury and Binder, 1924 and undated." The Kleine Papers abound with similar complaints regarding missing reports, mishandling of prints and other offences that the institutional exchanges allegedly committed.

100. See, for example, Kleine to Dudley, March 1, 1924, and Kleine to the University of Wisconsin, December 17, 1924, both in George Kleine Collection, file "Wisconsin Documents 11/1920–12/1924," Museum of Modern Art (NYC), Film Study Center Special Collections.

101. Kleine to the University of Wisconsin, Extension Division, May 21, 1925, GKP, box 42, file "Nontheatrical; University of Wisconsin, 1922–1927."

102. Dudley to Kleine, June 5, 1925, GKP, box 42, file "Nontheatrical; University of Wisconsin, 1922–1927."

103. Dudley to Members of Film Committee [NUEA], "Subject: Distribution of the George Kleine films," August 25, 1925, GKP, box 42, file "Nontheatrical; University of Wisconsin, 1922–1927."

104. Russell F. Egner to Dudley, September 3, 1925, GKP, box 42, file "Nontheatrical; University of Wisconsin."

105. Kleine to Dudley, September 29, 1925, GKP, box 42, file "Nontheatrical; University of Wisconsin."

106. Kleine to Dudley, May 4, 1926, GKP, box 42, file "Nontheatrical; University of Wisconsin."

107. Kleine to Dudley, July 22, 1926, August 17, 1926, and May 11, 1927, all in GKP, box 42, file "Nontheatrical; University of Wisconsin"; Kleine to Dudley, June 8, 1927, GKP, box 68, file "Inventories and Lists; Educational Distribution; University of Wisconsin, 1921–1928."

108. Kleine to the Dean of the University of Wisconsin, August 11, 1927; Kleine to Dudley, October 14, 1927, both in GKP, box 42, file "Nontheatrical; University of Wisconsin." Nevertheless, Kleine's cooperation with University of Wisconsin continued well into 1929, when Dudley left Wisconsin for a position as regional director of the Yale University Film Service. On Dudley's career, and his tenure at University of Wisconsin from 1914 to 1929, see Kupfer, "Cinema and the Service Ideal."

109. "List of Institutional Exchanges Handling George Kleine Films, Dec 1, 1923 (Corrected To April 24, 1927)," GKP, box 39, file "Nontheatrical; General, Sept 1921–1924 and undated."

110. Kleine to H. B. Gislason, University of Minnesota, Minneapolis, October 21, 1927, GKP, box 74, file "Distribution File; States; Minnesota; University of Minnesota, 1922–1927."

111. Thomas Simonet's 1973 article in the *Educational Broadcast Review* scrutinizes Kleine's own views on the financial failure of the experiment and argues that he saw "commercial sabotage" and hardware problems as the two main causes but failed to recognize that there might have been problems with the content and style of his films. While not entirely misleading, I would argue that there is more nuance to Kleine's discourse (Simonet, "George Kleine's Effort," 174–82).

112. As mentioned earlier (see note 94 in this chapter), when it came to technical standards for the nontheatrical market, Kleine put his money on another horse—standard-width paper film—around the same time that Eastman-Kodak launched its 16 mm acetate safety film system for amateur and nontheatrical use, which became a kind of industry standard for these markets. In 1925, Kleine acknowledged that ideally, all films should be transferred to nonflammable film stock, but he argued that the meager income he had received from the institutional exchanges did not warrant the expense of "recall and replacement." A 16 mm version of *The Midnight Ride of Paul Revere* was issued in 1929 "as an experiment," and in 1930 he also released a 16 mm version of *Julius Caesar*, offering this film as well as *Paul Revere* for outright sale. Neither seems to have had wide circulation (Kleine to George Eastman, Eastman-Kodak, January 7, 1925, GKP, box 13, file "Eastman-Kodak; General, 1908–1925"; Kleine (by K. Nolan, secretary), Circular letter, August 28, 1929; Kleine to W. W. Withinghill, Detroit Public Schools, January 21, 1930; Kleine to Monongahela Township High School, March 3, 1930, all three in GKP, box 18, file "Educational Films, 1916, 1920–1930").

113. Sources in the Kleine Papers indicate a spirit of cooperation rather than conflict between the institutional exchanges and commercial film distributors in most states and make clear that

several of the institutional exchanges were supplied with entertainment films from theatrical exchanges after completion of their theatrical runs. See, for example, Ellsworth C. Dent, University of Kansas, Lawrence to Kleine, November 2, 1923; R. F. Egner, University of Utah, Salt Lake City, to Kleine, November 6, 1923; W. T. Wilt, University of Minnesota–Minneapolis to Kleine, November 9, 1923; and J. W. Shepherd, University of Oklahoma–Norman to Kleine, undated [1923], all in GKP, box 18, file "Educational Institutions, 1913–1930."

114. Kleine to George Eastman, January 7, 1925.

115. See Gaycken in this volume for further corroboration.

116. Arthur Edwin Krows, "Motion Pictures—Not for Theatres," *Educational Screen* 17, no. 9 (1938): 291.

117. This discussion draws on Kari Karppinen and Hallvard Moe, "What We Talk about When We Talk about 'The Market': Conceptual Contestation in Contemporary Media Policy Research," *Journal of Information Policy* 4 (2014): 327–41.

118. Kleine to F. W. Reynolds, November 18, 1921, GKP, box 41, file "Nontheatrical; University of Utah, 1921–1922."

119. See, for example, William Leach, *Land of Desire: Merchants, Power, and the Rise of a New American Culture* (New York: Pantheon Books, 1993).

120. Haidee Wasson, *Museum Movies: The Museum of Modern Art and the Birth of Art Cinema* (Berkeley: University of California Press, 2005), 65.

121. Ben Singer has argued that people who gathered for "non-theater modes of film consumption" could be considered "groups" in a sociological sense, each with a specific and homogenous identity. Singer, "Early Home Cinema and the Edison Home Projecting Kinetoscope," *Film History* 2, no. 1 (1988): 63n3.

122. Kupfer, "Cinema and the Service Ideal."

123. Ibid.

124. This is borrowed from Roman Lobato, who in turn draws on Franco Morretti's notion of the "slaughterhouse of literature" (Roman Lobato, *Shadow Economies of Cinema: Mapping Informal Film Distribution* [London: BFI, 2012], chapter 2).

125. A. P. Hollis, "Visual Education Departments in Educational Institutions," Department of the Interior, Bureau of Education, Bulletin, 1924, no. 8 (Washington: Government Printing Office, 1924), 1.

126. Ibid., 25.

127. For an analysis of Kleine's anti-Hollywood stance and how this informed his work in nontheatrical cinema, see Frykholm, *George Kleine and American Cinema*, chapter 5.

128. For a brief overview, see Dan Streible, Martina Roepke, and Anke Mebold, "Introduction: Nontheatrical Film," *Film History* 19 no. 4 (2007): 339–43.

129. Making a similar point, but with regard to the history of 16 mm film, Greg Waller argues that a "fuller history" needs to take into account the different roles played by various agents, including "commercial distributors, Hollywood studios, government agencies, non-profit film libraries, and foundations" (Gregory A. Waller, "Projecting the Promise of 16mm, 1935–45," in *Useful Cinema*, ed. Charles Acland and Haidee Wasson [Durham: Duke University Press, 2011], 144–45).

130. Ronald Walter Greene, "Pastoral Exhibition: The YMCA Motion Picture Bureau and the Transition to 16 mm, 1928–39," in Acland and Wasson, *Useful Cinema*, 205–29; Grieveson, "Work of Film in the Age of Fordist Mechanization," 25–51; Lee Grieveson, "Visualizing Industrial Citizenship," in *Learning with the Lights Off: Educational Film in the United States*, ed. Devin Orgeron, Marsha Orgeron, and Dan Streible (New York: Oxford University Press, 2011), 107–23; Streible, Roepke, and Mebold, "Introduction: Nontheatrical Film," 339–43; and Jennifer Zwarich, "The Bureaucratic Activist Federal Filmmakers and Social Change in the U.S.

Department of Agriculture's Tick Eradication Campaign," *Moving Image* 9 no. 1 (2009): 19–53. See also Slide, *Before Video.*

131. An achievement of studies in "useful cinema," as suggested by Charles Acland and Haidee Wasson, is precisely that they capture the diversity of cinema (Charles A. Acland and Haidee Wasson, "Introduction: Utility and Cinema," in *Useful Cinema*, ed. Charles R. Acland and Haidee Wasson [Durham, NC: Duke University Press, 2011], 13).

132. Kleine to Samuel Datlowe, July 3, 1929, GKP, box 10, file "Datlowe, Samuel, 1929."

Filmography

Antony and Cleopatra (*Marc'Antonio e Cleopatra*, Cines 1913).
The Apple Tree Girl (Edison, 1917).
The Awakening of Ruth (Edison, 1917).
Caring for Birds in Winter (Edison, 1917).
The Courage of the Commonplace (Edison, 1917).
Crystals in Formation (revised version of *Crystals: Their Making, Habits and Beauty*, Edison, 1914).
Curious Scenes in Far Off India (Edison, 1913).
The Customary Two Weeks (Edison, 1917).
Cy Whittaker's Ward (Edison, 1917).
Deliverance (Helen Keller Film Corporation, 1919).
For Napoleon and France (*Scuola d'eroi*, Cines, 1914).
Gold and Diamond Mines in South Africa (Edison, 1914).
He Couldn't Get Up in the Morning (Edison, 1917).
Julius Caesar (*Gaio Giulio Cesare*, Cines 1914).
Kidnapped (Edison, 1917).
Knights of the Square Table (Edison, 1917).
The Last Days of Pompeii (*Gli ultimi giorni di Pompei*, Ambrosio 1913).
Little Chevalier (Edison, 1917).
The Merchant of Venice (*Shylock, le marchand de Venise*, Eclipse, 1913).
A Message to Garcia (Edison, 1916).
Microscopic Pond Life (Edison, 1915).
The Midnight Ride of Paul Revere (one-reel version, first released as part of Conquest Program no. 12 in 1917, original two-reel version produced by Edison in 1914).
One Touch of Nature (Edison, 1917).
Othello (*Otello*, Ambrosio, 1914).
Pilgrim's Progress (*Il pellegrino*, Ambrosio, 1912).
Putting the Bee in Herbert (Edison, 1917).
Quaint Provincetown on Cape Cod (Edison, 1917).
Quo Vadis? (Cines, 1912).
The Royal Pauper (Edison, 1917).
Salt of the Earth (Edison, 1917).
Spartacus (*Spartaco*, Pasquali, 1913).
Star Spangled Banner (Edison, 1917).
Two Kentucky Boys (Edison, 1917).
The Unbeliever (Edison, 1918).
Vanity Fair (Edison, 1915).

Bibliography

Abel, Richard. *The Red Rooster Scare: Making Cinema American, 1900–1910*. Berkeley: University of California Press, 1999.

Acland, Charles A., and Haidee Wasson. "Introduction: Utility and Cinema." In *Useful Cinema*, edited by Charles R. Acland and Haidee Wasson, 1–14. Durham, NC: Duke University Press, 2011.

Dudley, William. "Moving Pictures in Schools." *Stevens Point Daily Journal*, June 27, 1914, 15.

Ford Educational Library advertisement. *Moving Picture Age* 3, no. 11 (1920): 6.

———. *Moving Picture Age* 3, no. 12 (1920): 6.

Frykholm, Joel. *George Kleine and American Cinema: The Movie Business and Film Culture in the Silent Era*. London: Palgrave Macmillan/BFI, 2015.

Grau, Robert. *The Business Man in the Amusement World: A Volume of Progress in the Field of the Theatre*. New York: Broadway Publishing Co., 1910.

Greene, Ronald Walter. "Pastoral Exhibition: The YMCA Motion Picture Bureau and the Transition to 16mm, 1928–39." In *Useful Cinema*, edited by Charles R. Acland and Haidee Wasson, 205–29. Durham: Duke University Press.

Greif, Avner. *Institutions and the Path to the Modern Economy: Lessons from Medieval Trade*. Cambridge, NY: Cambridge University Press, 2006.

Grieveson, Lee. "Visualizing Industrial Citizenship." In *Learning with the Lights Off: Educational Film in the United States*, edited by Devin Orgeron, Marsha Orgeron, and Dan Streible, 107–23. New York: Oxford University Press, 2011.

———. "The Work of Film in the Age of Fordist Mechanization." *Cinema Journal* 51, no. 3 (2012): 25–51.

Horne, Jennifer. "Nostalgia and Non-Fiction in Edison's 1917 *Conquest Program*." *Historical Journal of Film, Radio and Television* 22, no. 3 (2002): 315–31.

Karppinen, Kari, and Hallvard Moe. "What We Talk about When We Talk about 'The Market': Conceptual Contestation in Contemporary Media Policy Research." *Journal of Information Policy* 4 (2014): 327–41.

Keeler, Amanda R. "'Sugar Coat the Educational Pill': The Educational Aspirations of Emergent Film, Radio, and Television." PhD diss., Indiana University, 2011.

Krows, Arthur Edwin. "Motion Pictures—Not for Theatres." *Educational Screen* 17, no. 9 (1938): 291–294.

Kupfer, Alex. "Cinema and the Service Ideal: Nontheatrical Film Distribution and the University of Wisconsin Bureau of Visual Instruction, 1910–1930." Chapter from forthcoming PhD diss., New York University.

Leach, William. *Land of Desire: Merchants, Power, and the Rise of a New American Culture*. New York: Pantheon Books, 1993.

Lobato, Ramon. *Shadow Economies of Cinema: Mapping Informal Film Distribution*. London: BFI, 2012.

"New Educational Film Library." *Moving Picture Age* 3, no. 8 (1920): 22.

Peterson, Jennifer Lynn. *Education in the School of Dreams: Travelogues and Early Nonfiction Film*. Durham, NC: Duke University Press, 2013.

Simonet, Thomas. "George Kleine's Effort in Non-Theatrical Film Distribution, 1921–1928." *Educational Broadcasting Review* 7, no. 3 (1973): 174–82.

Singer, Ben. "Early Home Cinema and the Edison Home Projecting Kinetoscope." *Film History* 2, no. 1 (1988): 37–69.

Slide, Anthony. *Before Video: A History of the Non-Theatrical Film.* New York: Greenwood Press, 1992.

———. *Early American Cinema.* Rev. ed. Metuchen, NJ: Scarecrow Press, 1994; originally published 1970.

Streible, Dan, Martina Roepke, and Anke Mebold. "Introduction: Nontheatrical Film." *Film History* 19, no. 4 (2007): 339–43.

Trumpbour, John. *Selling Hollywood to the World: U.S. and European Struggles for Mastery of the Global Film Industry, 1920–1950.* New York: Cambridge University Press, 2002.

Waller, Gregory A. "Projecting the Promise of 16mm, 1935–45." In *Useful Cinema*, edited by Charles R. Acland and Haidee Wasson, 125–148. Durham, NC: Duke University Press, 2011.

Wasson, Haidee. *Museum Movies: The Museum of Modern Art and the Birth of Art Cinema.* Berkeley: University of California Press, 2005.

Zwarich, Jennifer. "The Bureaucratic Activist Federal Filmmakers and Social Change in the U.S. Department of Agriculture's Tick Eradication Campaign." *Moving Image* 9, no. 1 (2009): 19–53.

JOEL FRYKHOLM is Research Associate at Stockholm University, Department of Media Studies, Section for Cinema Studies. He is author of *George Kleine and American Cinema: The Movie Business and Film Culture in the Silent Era.*

9 Ford Films and Ford Viewers

Examining "Nontheatrical" Films in the Theaters and Beyond

Katy Peplin

Introduction

The Ford Motor company spent the first two decades of the twentieth century spearheading a revolution in affordable transportation for the American, and soon global, public. Model T cars showed up nearly immediately in photographs and motion pictures, and the car culture born in Detroit was quickly becoming national. Ford was revolutionary not only in its product but also in its practices, particularly regarding labor and operations. However, unlike other companies that were adopting the assembly line methods of production, the company was unique in capturing its practices on film. Beginning in 1908, Ford's Photography Department grew eventually to film, edit, and produce up to 200,000 feet of film a week to be distributed nationally in theaters.[1]

In "The Work of Film in the Age of Fordist Mechanization," Lee Grieveson draws clear connections between Ford's labor policies and methods of worker control and the ways in which film was used by the Ford Motor Company at the time. He presents the films as belonging to a group, often neglected by film studies, that he terms "non-theatrical" and specifically looks at their styles of narration and address as sites for emerging Fordist rhetoric.[2] He compellingly situates the filmic output of Ford squarely in the industrial and pedagogic genres to create a narrative of corporate engagement in civic life, using the word *Fordist* to encompass a much broader sense of the worker as mass-produced and politically manipulated. His argument uses many of the films as evidence to link the output to an overall project of Americanization that aimed to take poor, immigrant workers and make them into workers sympathetic with the company and its political causes. However, the Ford Motion Picture Laboratory produced films in a variety of modes, ranging from newsreel to self-contained pedagogical units, at a time when genres of films, and especially where they were screened and for whom, were in constant flux. Although the films certainly had a tremendous impact on the rise of industrial film, and were most certainly tied to questions of citizenship, scholars thus far have placed them squarely in the nontheatrical context, to the detriment of these complicated and nuanced examples of early commercial film.

This chapter examines the Ford Motion Picture Laboratory and its filmic output during this time of standardization and changing labor practices. The company was most widely known for the implementation of the "five-dollar-a-day" worker compensation plan, which provided a livable wage for workers on the assembly line. This rote, repetitive work often went to lower-class, ethnically diverse workers. The company policy of higher wages was part of a broader view of American life pushed by Ford that included car ownership, financial responsibility, and Americanization. Until now, the dominant understanding of Ford's motion picture output has been one in which its films were intended as a public service, with educational purposes at the heart of the project, fitting neatly into the larger narrative of a responsible, fair company.[3] This is the picture that Ford attempted to put forward, as seen in the rich trove of documents maintained by Ford on the history of the department's projects, organization, and rhetoric, as cataloged in its internal house organs and company archives. The narrative has been complicated by scholars like Grieveson, who focused on the economic and rhetorical gains the department afforded and how these aims related to larger projects of citizenship. However, a more complete history of Ford's Motion Picture Department can and should be told. This chapter will put the Ford-approved history in contact with the history of Ford's film output, as seen in the pages of popular and trade presses, to give a broader view of the Ford film project as educational and industrial both, shifting its mission nimbly in order to seek maximum profits and potent public relation effects. While these films were no doubt doing work to advance the Ford Company's aims of Americanization and its Taylorist notions of standardization, they also point to Ford's inability to enter an increasingly standardized educational cinema circuit by brute force.

The categorization of Ford films is important not only for reasons of historical accuracy but also as a window into how the public and industry alike understood films with educational or nonfiction content. During this time, the Ford Motor Company and its charismatic head, Henry Ford, were engaging in national debates about World War I and the US's role in foreign policy, and as the war continued, nonfiction films grew to include news updates about the war abroad and at home. The viewer during this period was no naive patron but instead was aware of the motivations of various film projects and objected when they were played in venues not fit for them. Exhibition companies were cognizant of the growing separation between subjects fit for movie palaces and those fit for the classroom, and Ford films often fell in the space between the two. Although Ford would claim that the films could "in no way be construed as advertising," exhibitors balked at being asked to pay to show "propaganda and advertising films."[4] While Ford may have conceived of its film output as a civic service, the classifications of viewers and exhibitors determined how the films actually functioned in public screening spaces.

Looking more closely at Ford thus allows for a better understanding of the multitude of elements latent in even seemingly benign educational films. Despite framing themselves as such, Ford's films were not simply benevolent educational films granted unto the American public but also advertisements, political propaganda, and moneymaking ventures. By teasing out where Ford films played, how they were handled by distributors and exhibitors, and how Ford internally conceived of the role these films were to play, this chapter aims to illustrate the shifting public and corporate understandings of the role of nontheatrical film in the larger field of film exhibition. Shifting the focus from the films' content to the context of their exhibition, I work to illustrate the changing priorities of the Ford Motion Picture Department, opening a window into the institutionalization of educational film: who produces it, where they exhibit it, and how audiences understand the films to be functioning.

The Motion Picture Department

The Motion Picture Department was established at the company's headquarters in Dearborn in 1913 after the Photography Department had seen tremendous success documenting the company's expansion, particularly the River Rouge plant.[5] Advised by Thomas Edison and W. K. L. Dickson, both old friends, Henry Ford indulged his personal interest in the new medium by challenging his staff to come up with creative uses for film in the decidedly standardized production of automobiles. As Grieveson notes, the original mandate for the department was to create films of workers on the assembly line: by filming the worker performing his single, discrete task, the camera could pick up subtle variations in form or movement that the eye cannot observe, which when corrected, would lead to a more productive worker.[6] These time-motion studies, an integral part of the Taylorist system of scientific management, were performed in many companies by contracting outside firms to film the workers. However, in keeping with Ford's well-known theories of vertical integration, a department was formed to streamline the process and control the costs by performing this work in house.

As the internal organ *Ford Weekly* was keen to point out, Ford spared no expense in making the Motion Picture Department competitive with the burgeoning studio system in Hollywood, California. One article in 1917 describes the twenty-four-person crew traveling the country looking for material to shoot and then returning to the photographic facilities built on the Dearborn campus. A stone's throw from the assembly line for the Model T, this facility could produce high-quality motion pictures, from shooting to distribution, without the need for any outside services.[7] Photographs show rows of men developing film, drying it on large wheels, and shooting tracking shots from the interior of a Model T rather than a dolly. Although the article gives technical specifications of the motion picture endeavor, the creative aspects of filmmaking are downplayed here. Thirteen sections composed the department: "Administration, Studio and Art, Stock, Enlarging Room, Developing Room for 8x10 still pictures, Laboratory, Title Making, Printing of Films, Perforating, Developing of Films, Drying Room, Assembly Room, Shipping."[8] These sources make clear that the department, like all others in the company, was organized to separate complex systems into singular, repeatable tasks, despite the more creative nature of the department's endeavors—no photographs of the scriptwriting team, for example, were published. Ford boasted that "discipline, order and system prevail everywhere [including the Photography Department] . . . an excellent example of modern industrial good housekeeping."[9]

By 1915, Ford was not only producing films for internal consumption but also filming, editing, and distributing a national newsreel called *Ford Animated Weekly*. Teams were sent in their Ford automobiles to picturesque American sights, breaking news stories in the Detroit area, and popular attractions nationwide to create news reels that were referred to as "a clever form of subtle advertising" by Ford executives.[10] They followed the form of other popular reels like *Pathé Weekly*, although with more shots of Ford cars driving down the street, and a very clear focus on midwestern news events, such as dignitary visits, most likely due to the limited range of the camera crew. At its height, Ford claims that the *Ford Animated Weekly* was being shown in two thousand theaters and seen by three million people weekly around the United States. By virtue of their self-distribution (using a network of dealerships as exchange points for the film material), the Ford Motor Company claimed to be the largest motion picture distributor in the country. When the political climate surrounding World War I grew more heated, Ford switched the format to feature more educational material rather than current events and renamed the newsreel the *Ford Educational Weekly*.[11] Ford sources claim that demand for these entertaining and enlightening shorts grew beyond their own distribution capabilities, and Goldwyn was recruited to expand their reach, distributing the material in 1919 to their highest number of theaters, well over five thousand.[12]

The department was active until roughly 1920 when production of new material was halted, and existing content was repackaged as pedagogical tools for public schooling. The *Ford Educational Library* was marketed to schools across the nation, as well as offered to other nontheatrical venues including prisons and churches.[13] This reconfiguration was a response to the broader company cutting costs in lean financial times that would presage such times for the entire country as well as a recognition that the demands of a weekly film distribution scheme were too burdensome for a company whose primary focus remained automobiles.

This narrative progresses neatly from Taylorist time-motion studies to the *Ford Educational Library*, framing the entire department as a public service producing various forms of educational material to a nation whose entertainment industry was quickly becoming dependent on narrative films. The rapid succession of products, from the newsreel-like model of the *Animated Weekly* to the less demanding *Educational Weekly* and the much more static and limited *Educational Library*, is explained by Ford as responses to a shifting public need, without any mention of financial or political pressures affecting the changes. The next section examines the same time period, 1913 to 1920, but through the lens of popular and trade press publications, with the goal of complicating Ford's teleological narrative and presenting one that exemplifies the shifting conception of nonfiction film, the role of advertising, and the concept of a citizen.

Ford Motion Picture Lab Redux

An editorial published in December 1920 in *Film Daily* and labeled "What is really needed" called for a "pictorially inclined Henry Ford" to "keep one eye on art and save the other for the box office."[14] The writer was concerned with the passing of production costs along through exhibitors to customers, but the turn of phrase reveals much about the way that Ford in all senses was viewed nearly three years after the introduction of the *Ford Animated Weekly*. Ford, both the person and the company, were indeed pictorially minded and producing film at a prolific rate, but the name is used here to indicate business savvy in manufacturing rather than creative prowess. This section examines the discussion in trade publications, namely *Film Daily* and *Moving Picture World*, of Ford Motion Pictures and its relationship to exhibitors and distributors. The narrative is more complex than the one told by internal Ford sources, complicating the "grass-roots" narrative found there, and also highlights the tensions developing among various modes of films and their place in exhibition and distribution schemes.

As discussed in the previous section, Ford Motion Picture Laboratory was presented as a seamless outgrowth of the Photography Department and its uses. However, several articles appeared in trade journals in 1915 reporting that Ford had contracted outside companies to advise or, in some cases, directly produce its growing film output. This was in the very first year of the *Animated Weekly*, which was just being established and still had very limited reach beyond the Michigan regional theater chains. In June of that year, the Duplex Machine Company, providers of motion picture equipment, was reported as visiting Ford Motor Company. Ford Motor Company "has applied picture advertising for the Fords" and invested in additional Duplex equipment in order to "double the output of Ford films," although the *Animated Weekly* was not explicitly named. Other companies accompanying Duplex Machine in visits to the company were the Industrial Moving Picture Company and the Selig Polyscope Company, placing Ford and their needs in the same league as other "motion picture studios," as the article names them.[15]

Ford Motion Picture Laboratory had been described an outgrowth of a Ford-centered interest in photographic technologies, inspired by Henry Ford's personal acquaintance with Thomas Edison and built organically from Ford's interest, intelligence, and thirst for innovation. This fits closely with the broader narrative told about Henry Ford and his company, built in one large room into which raw materials entered through one door and a Model T drove out the other. Film in this framework becomes just one more product whose production Ford had streamlined and profited from, accomplished strictly on the merits of one man's immense vision and curiosity. However, the trades portray the relationship between Edison Studios and Ford as a much more collaborative one. Rather than Ford producing all the material internally, a brief article in *Moving Picture World* from 1915 titled "Edison Company in Detroit" says that "the Edison Company makes weekly a short length of film on current events that the Ford Company distributes free to the exhibitor

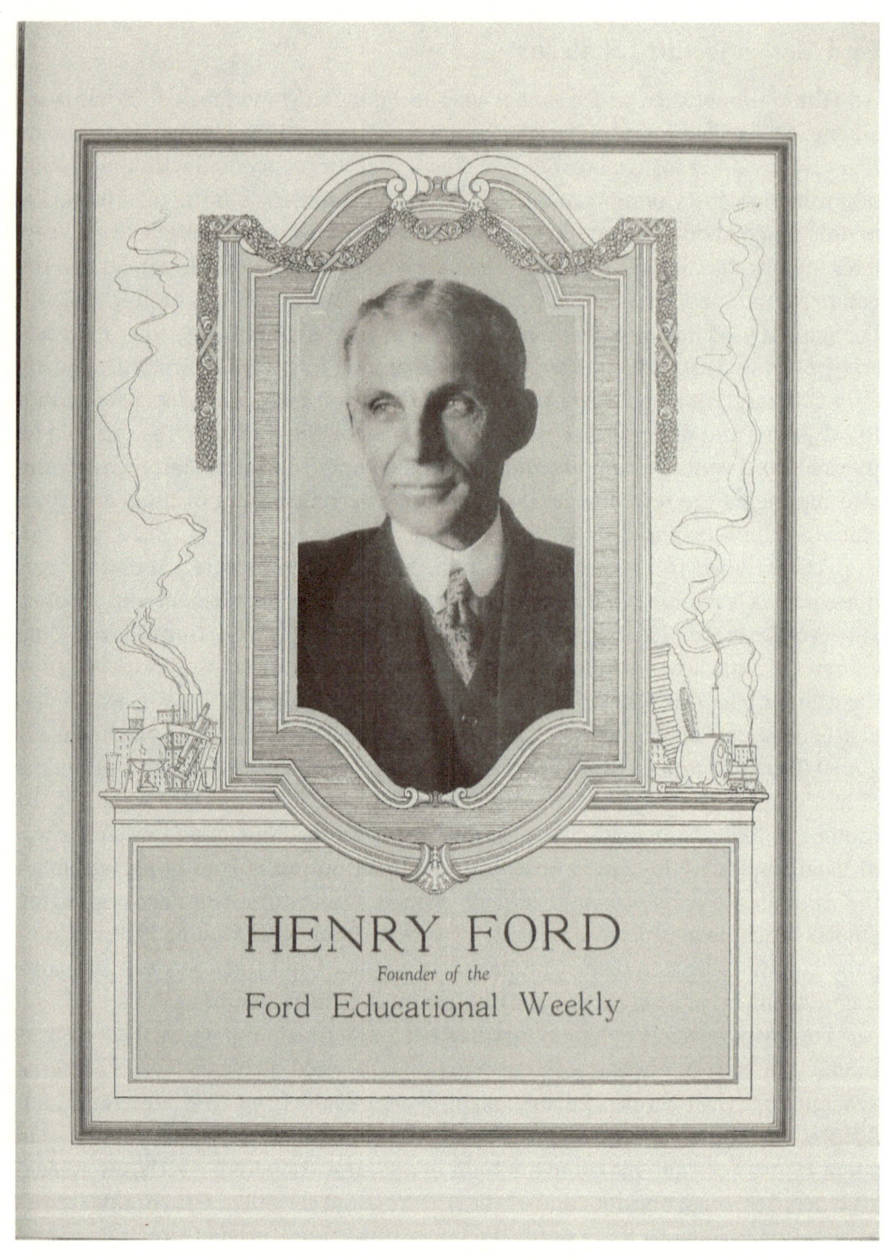

Fig. 9.1. Although Henry Ford had little, if anything, to do with the day-to-day management of the Motion Picture Department, his personality loomed large over the brand. *Motion Picture News*, July 12, 1919.

through the organization branch offices."[16] This suggests that despite descriptions to the contrary, Ford's Photography and later Motion Picture Departments at least began with significant help and labor from external, more experienced companies. At a time when the industry was rapidly professionalizing and becoming concentrated in centers of production on the two coasts of the United States, it is a sensible proposition that a company that makes automobiles may be reliant on outside experts in order to establish a sizable foothold in the motion picture industry, despite the company's interest in appearing to be self-contained. The article suggests that this was not simply advice being given from one mogul friend to another, not another inspired move of a genius businessman, but a network of interrelated efforts in both the wider Ford company and the motion picture industry.

The idea that Ford had created the "largest independent distribution system" in the country in order to distribute the company's films is one of the most frequently mentioned facets of the Ford Motion Picture Laboratory. This aspect of the laboratory was cited in several internal Ford sources, although those sources seem to suggest varying methods of distribution. Ford's preexisting "national network" is a phrase that occurs again and again and seems to suggest that the films were distributed through the dealerships around the country, sparing Ford the expense of contracting individual film exchanges in each region and relying on the local dealer to arrange for the films' transportation and screening.[17] An intriguing deviation from the standard film exchanges used to distribute most of the studio-produced films, which relied on regional offices to make contact with local chains on a theater-to-theater basis, this would account for Grieveson's observation that the Ford Motion Picture Laboratory penetrated into the rural areas of the country.[18] It also hews closely to the Ford mythology of novel uses for established networks of commerce, seen in their factory practices of building smelting plants, like the River Rouge plant in use at the time. The company built plants near existing ore shipping routes rather than transporting the material inland just to accommodate an existing factory, minimizing costs and streamlining production from raw material to final product.

Film Daily does name several regional distributors as assisting in the distribution of various Ford Motion Picture Laboratory products, including the Dawn Masterplay Company in Michigan, the Griever Distributing Corporation working with the Bee-Hive Exchange in the greater New York area, the Strand Film Service in Michigan, Regal films in Toronto, and the Federated Film Exchanges in New York between 1915 and 1918. It also directly contradicts the Ford sources when Griever Distribution Corporation is named as the "national distributors" of *Ford Educational Weekly* beginning in October 1918.[19] This runs counter to the idea that the Ford Motion Picture Laboratory was organizing or facilitating its production and distribution in house for the first majority of the early Ford Motion Picture Laboratory run. A later blurb in November 1918 reports that Griever Corp. had opened executive offices in Chicago and mentions *Ford Educational Weekly* as the sole property it represents through its twenty-two national branches.[20] These articles do not mention the novel use of the dealer network to distribute film. Further, the frequency of new or different exchanges being used suggests that Ford was constantly working to farm out distribution to other companies several years before the company acknowledged that this model was being used.

Less than three weeks later in December 1918, a *Film Daily* headline read: "Goldwyn to Run Ford Weekly." This switch to the much more prominent distributor was recorded internally at Ford, expanding from three thousand theaters to five thousand, with more than seven thousand showings a week nationwide and heralded as a large step forward for what was called "an unusual weekly booking." Internal Ford documents laud the increasing demand for the shorts, but given that a national distributor was named less than three weeks before the contract with Goldwyn was signed, it seems more likely that Ford was dissatisfied with the quality of Griever's work in distribution and sought out Goldwyn to gain a distribution schema that justified the "$600,000 annual cost" quoted in *Film Daily*.[21]

Working with Goldwyn appears to have stretched the thin operating budget of this automobile manufacturer turned film producer, and at some point during the first month of the Goldwyn-Ford contract, the company levied a fee of one dollar per week to all exhibitors, when previously no charge had been assessed for any iteration of the Ford Motion Picture Laboratory output. Exhibitors rebelled quickly and in no uncertain terms, with the story landing on the front page of *Film Daily* in an article entitled "After Ford: Rembusch Wants Exhibitors Paid for Showing Weekly—Goldwyn's Ideas." Rembusch, then secretary of the national organization Motion Picture Exhibitors of America, had filed protests, saying that exhibitors not only objected to the idea of being charged to show the *Educational Weekly* but also would like compensation for doing so. He categorized the *Weekly* as "industrial, propaganda and advertising films" and noted that other companies, such as Universal Film, were paying exhibitors for the ability to screen their films to the already established audience. By labeling the films this way, Ford films were put squarely on par with commercial, studio films. Clearly, exhibitors made distinctions between the various uses and motivations of the films they displayed. Rembusch's request for compensation flies in the face of the rhetoric Ford was using at the time to describe its output—that is, as almost solely a civic service or magnanimous gesture provided by the Ford Motor Company on behalf of the citizens of the United States, who may not have had access to educational materials of this type. The service orientation of the films is echoed by the comments given by Goldwyn for the article, which say that "in no way can [the *Weekly*] be construed as advertisement . . . and the return is negligible."[22]

Articles continued for the next month covering various other protests lodged against the new contract requiring payment from the exhibitors. The majority of the arguments against the new cost structure centered on the classification of *Ford Educational Weekly* as an "advertisement" rather than an educational film.[23] The classification is significant because, as later sections detail, the distinction affects not only how the film is distributed but in which places viewers and exhibitors alike

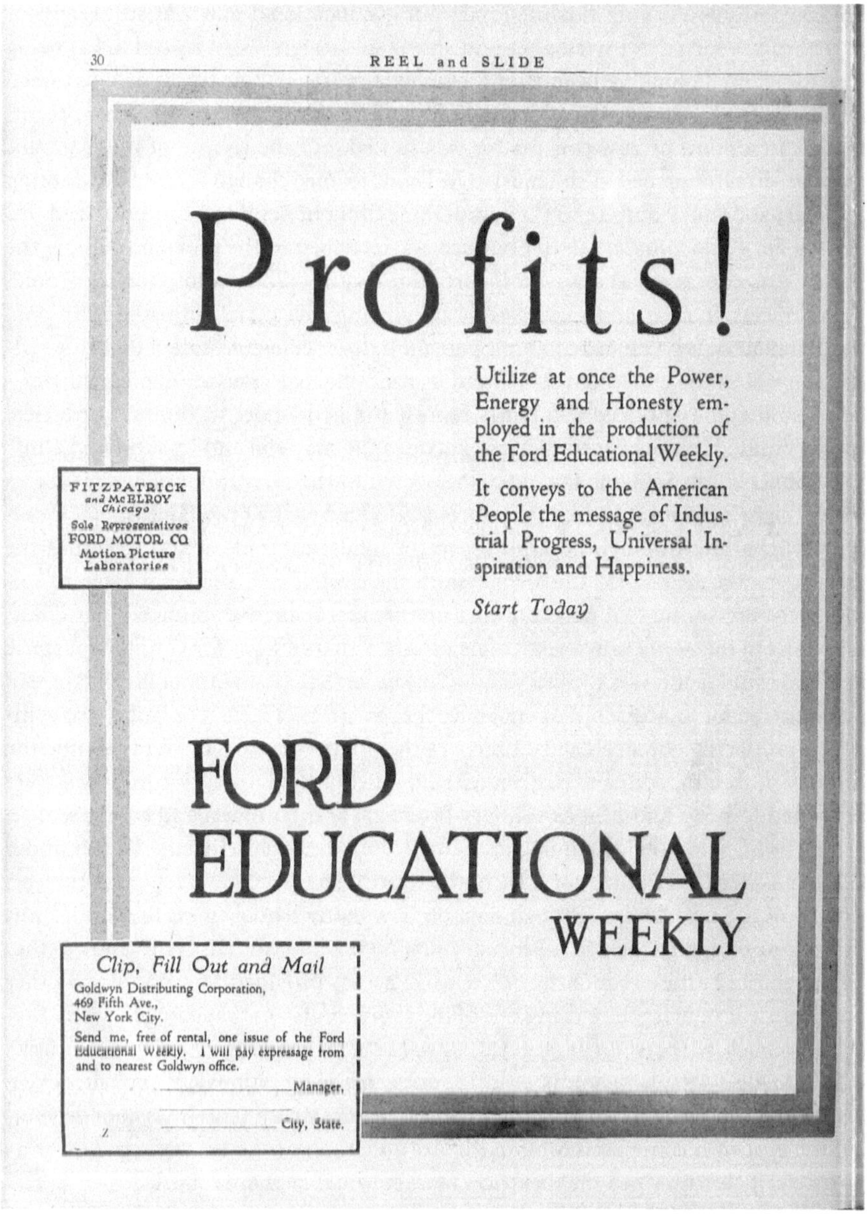

30 REEL and SLIDE

Profits!

Utilize at once the Power, Energy and Honesty employed in the production of the Ford Educational Weekly.

It conveys to the American People the message of Industrial Progress, Universal Inspiration and Happiness.

Start Today

FITZPATRICK
and McELROY
Chicago
Sole Representatives
FORD MOTOR CO.
Motion Picture
Laboratories

FORD EDUCATIONAL WEEKLY

Clip, Fill Out and Mail

Goldwyn Distributing Corporation,
469 Fifth Ave.,
New York City.

Send me, free of rental, one issue of the Ford Educational Weekly. I will pay expressage from and to nearest Goldwyn office.

________________ Manager,

____

________________ City, State.

Z

Fig. 9.2. Although the name change to *Ford Educational Weekly* sought to emphasize the pedagogical content of the films, the intended monetary boon for exhibitors and the Ford Motor Company was clear. *Reel and Slide*, July 1919.

are comfortable viewing this material. While educational material still regularly played in the forms of travelogues and shorts in theaters, Ford material was being judged not on its stated aims but on the understanding of how the films functioned in relation to the larger Ford Motor Company and its public image. There seems to be no mention of how this matter was settled, but the timing of the exhibitor protests directly preceded the most significant format change of the Ford Motion Picture Laboratory output, to the stand-alone film curriculum units packaged under the *Ford Educational Library* banner. As described in the previous section, the library was conceived as a way to incorporate motion pictures into the classroom, with subjects, like agriculture and geography, being covered in a film and additional written materials produced to accompany it. It does seem convenient that this sudden interest in the classroom space, and its presumably less astute adolescent viewers, would come after the exhibitors representing the more traditional theatrical spaces pointed out the contradictions between the material and its supposed aims.

Launched on September 1, 1920, the switch to the *Educational Library* follows within eight months of the exhibitor protests lodged against the *Educational Weekly*'s new charge. Although no Ford source or industrial trade article mentions the disputes as the reason for the format shift, the timing is at the least suggestive of the forces impacting that decision. In a market increasingly dominated by studios, especially in the nonfiction format of newsreels, it makes sense for Ford to repurpose material shot for the *Weekly* into stand-alone units that exist without the pressure of being current or topical. Ford did not have the resources of Hearst or Pathé, two companies producing newsreels at the time, to either follow the current events around the country or to film, edit, and distribute them quickly enough. Both companies were dedicated to news and film as primary products, and Ford was and would remain primarily an automobile manufacturer. The *Library* materials, like the *Weekly* under Goldwyn, were distributed for a fee and advertised as "specially prepared" subjects worthy of the investment. Though data on how many schools used the service was difficult to find, an article in a February 1921 *Film Daily* advertises the units to theatrical sources after six months of exclusive access provided to schools and other nontheatrical venues. The closing line of the article indicates that going forward, theatrical venues will have six months exclusive use of future units, after which the films will be made available to nontheatrical venues. While no rationale is explicitly given for this switch, it suggests that the market for nontheatrical rentals was not generating the type of income Ford Motion Picture Laboratory believed was capable for its products; it clearly hoped the theatrical market would be more robust.[24]

The narrative told by Ford internal sources spoke of a successful motion picture department growing out of a company that was primarily focused on other types of manufacturing, as well as the ways in which the Ford Motor Company was acting in a philanthropic way to make its products available across the country. However, comparing this narrative against the one told by the trade journals of the time reveals a more complicated story of balancing profit and exposure against the benefits of creating, or at least appearing to create, this material for the good of the country absent any commercial motive. The shift from the *Educational Weekly* to the *Educational Library* especially speaks to a growing concern on the part of Ford Motor Company about capitalizing on its investment in the motion picture industry. The adjustments it made to its products are likely not in response to changing company ideals but to criticism levied against it from within the industry itself. These criticisms take on extra weight when the public image of Ford, both the person and the company, are placed in the context of World War I, as the next section will demonstrate.

Ford and World War I: Public Relations and Public Image

The Ford Motion Picture Laboratory output was regularly accused of being mere advertisement for the company, but the role of the films in society was in reality more complex than either simple advertisement or altruistic educational film. Screening in theaters across the country weekly, they were a large part of the company's outward-facing image during a period in which the figurehead was actively involved in the politics of the nation. By the time the United States entered World War I, Henry Ford was a household name, having splashed onto the scene with his low-cost automobile and "progressive" campaign to raise factory worker wages to five dollars a day in 1914. He presented himself as a self-made man who wanted to make real the American dream for thousands of his workers. It was an image carefully cultivated throughout the 1910s after the launch of the Model T, when he had performed as the bumbling, self-effacing man who was reticent to speak in public for fear of sounding inarticulate.[25] By 1917, Ford was regularly interacting with local and national newspapers and was particularly outspoken about the US's role in the escalating violence in Europe and Central Asia. Gone were the days of stuttering speeches and humble suits, and in its place was a massive public relations effort centered on his media output.

Ford exerted editorial control over the contents of the internal organ the *Ford News* in addition to having influence over what was published in a local public paper, the *Dearborn Independent*, making the *Ford Animated Weekly* similar as a business model to the *Hearst Metrotone News*, which was established in its first form in 1914. Both companies had both a print and film presence under the same company banner, although, like Ford, Hearst was unable to launch a film operation alone and sought help first from Pathé and then from Selig in 1914–15.[26] Using his "in-house" media outlets, Ford vocally and frequently advocated against entering the fighting in Europe in editorials published in Dearborn, and the *Animated Weekly* was notably devoid of any footage of training exercises or troop mobilizations. After mounting an unsuccessful peace campaign, which involved several prominent men of industry and politics sailing across the Atlantic aboard a chartered yacht to try to broker peace, it was clear that Ford was out of step with the country at large, which would enter the war despite his opposition.[27] Although Ford would quickly reverse his position on war, describing himself as a "fighting pacifist" as soon as diplomatic relations with Germany were severed in February, the war was simply not part of the output of Ford films in the period leading up to the conflict.[28]

Although Ford was against becoming involved in the war, the *Animated Weekly* devoted considerable space to mobilization and training for World War I once war began.[29] Training entries ranged from "moments of relaxation" during basic training to navy swimming instruction, but it is in the footage classified under "World War I Mobilization" that a sense of the broader Ford ethos is at work.[30] It was important for Ford, as both a company and a public personality, to quickly and decisively change the conversation away from pacifism to full-throated support of the American participation in World War I, and this was attempted by devoting considerable industrial capability to creating military vehicles and then distributing that footage nationally. Ford executives said that the *Animated Weekly* was the best form of advertising the company ever engaged in, despite insisting publicly that the films were solely a civic enterprise, and the mobilization entries bear out the subtle inclusion of Ford as a patriotic, modern and technologically advanced company in reels that covered the news of the week. The catalog of film descriptions provided by the National Archives describes "men and women [at] work on the factory floor" as they "assemble airplanes," and the famous "flivver" tanks produced by Ford Motor Company but never brought to the front lines because of their propensity to become stuck, nose in the air, in trenches, are shown "being test-driven over rough field."[31] This footage was shown around the country as part of the *Animated Weekly*'s focus on current events but also functioned to bolster Ford's image as patriotic after the war he protested so heartily had begun.

Ford's emphasis on technology was part of a larger national discourse in 1917, promising the nation that home-grown industrial might would deliver airplanes, submarines, and battle carriers to the front lines, a fact covered prominently in newspapers around the country. This thinking insisted that the US's technological supremacy would break the stalemate rather than the addition of masses of bodies on the front lines.[32] The focus on technology allowed the company to minimize the presence of human bodies in its wartime rhetoric while engaging in patriotic displays of support, important for a company whose figurehead had railed so publicly against the potential loss of life by entering the war. The animated shorts fit into this pattern and worked both to show off Ford products and ingenuity and to demonstrate the company's patriotism. *Ford Animated Weekly* was almost entirely controlled by the Ford Motor Company, which conveniently erased any mention of earlier pacifist rhetoric in favor of a more aggressive, but technologically focused, mission for the country in wartime. Eventually, the demands for current images of a country at war outstripped Ford's ability to produce and distribute material effectively, and the format was switched to the *Educational Weekly*. This switch was described by Ford sources as an attempt to play to the company's strengths in educational short works but was in all likelihood also an admission that alongside newsreels like *Hearst Metrotone*, the *Animated Weekly* was even more clearly a public relations effort rather than a journalistic service.[33]

Coincident with the end of the war was the rise of an established and separate discourse from educational film as well as the first movement of Ford Motion

Picture Laboratory away from nonfiction film writ large and into a more focused effort in educational filmmaking. Film made for and screened in classrooms was becoming a larger market (with more frequent discussion in trade journals around how and when to use this.) However, the market for educational film was still developing, and Ford was not immune to the pressures of its shifting public and industrial definitions. By separating from the broader nonfiction genre in terms of classification, educational film needed to establish both a regular mode of content distribution as well as a consistent identity through exhibition. This double need manifested in the tension between content and exhibition as the split between entertainment and education came to an uneasy balance in the medium-wide discourse, as well as in the specific problems that arose in marketing and exhibiting Ford films. The next section considers the terrain of the nontheatrical market that the later products of Ford Motion Picture Laboratory are often placed into and how the term *educational* was subject to a variety of pressures, including technological shifts, historical conditions, and industrial organizations.

Ford Film Viewers

Educational film has traditionally been considered in relation to so-called entertainment films. Grieveson gives Ford Motion Picture Laboratory films the label "non-theatrical" largely because they encompass various types of pedagogical address and did not exist solely in the classroom context. However, Ford films played regularly in traditional theatrical venues and alongside fictional films in nearly every instance, until the switch to the *Educational Library* format in 1920. Ford films, and their unstable naming and formats, as discussed previously, mixed an orientation toward education with a theatrical exhibition, defying a simple understanding of educational films existing only in the classroom. By the time the *Educational Library* format was introduced, it was clear that the materials produced were not simply lessons on corn farming and road construction, but materials made for and produced by an automobile manufacturer. How then can Ford films help us complicate an overly schematic relationship between educational and entertainment films and theatrical and nontheatrical venues?

In their concise summation of the history of educational film, the editors of *Learning with the Lights Off*, write this: "While the first decades of educational film use most often found commentators urging educational filmmakers to avoid being too entertaining lest the patina of frivolity denigrate their product, by the 1940's most advocates realized that 'engaging films' . . . were potentially more educational by virtue of the attention given them by spectators."[34] This implies not only that the two forms of filmic address are different but also that a distinct shift between them occurred. Ford films, both implicitly in their address and explicitly in the written discourse produced about them, complicate this binary in content and in time frame. Rather than a simple relationship between educational films and those that entertain and a single shift between modes, educational film, in the Ford context as well as more generally, was conceived in a dual sense from nearly its inception: on the one hand, as a mode of film production geared specifically to an educational purpose and, on the other, as a mode of viewing that allowed latent educational content to be gleaned from otherwise noneducational films.

By looking at these two conceptions as coexisting, if not equally balanced, impulses in educational film, we can begin to unravel the connections between producer and consumer in a more complex way, opening up space for ambiguity and multiple motivations. The Ford Motion Picture Laboratory offers a rich case study in educational film and the rhetoric produced about it in trade press, specialized educational film journals, and public journalism. The output illuminates changing conceptions of both educational practice and film's role in the classroom. This section aims to place the rhetoric about Ford Motion Picture Laboratory, both that produced internally and that found in external sources, and the rhetoric of educational filmmaking at large in conversation with each other to better illustrate this dual sense of the term as well as complicate the past narratives of Ford films, and industrial films more generally, that have been told thus far.

Educational Film Magazine published its first issue in 1919 with a two-page editorial introducing the magazine and its aims. Running nearly concurrently with the rise of Ford's *Educational Weekly* to national prominence, it is a useful window on the rhetoric of educational film into which Ford was entering. *Educational Film Magazine*'s only appeal to exhibitors in commercial theaters was in its "co-operational and noncompetitive face," and from its first pages spoke directly to educators and makers of educational films, to whom it would be a "class magazine of a character that justifies the subheading 'A National Authority.'"[35] This clearly divides the two markets, educational and commercial, and in fact allows that commercial film is the established and reigning force in the film market at large by ceding from the outset its desire to compete. The magazine also catered to interested parties in religious or community contexts, including churches, YMCAs, and rural areas that might not be within reach of more traditional film exhibition circuits. *Educational film* means more here than just films played in schools but seems to function as a catch-all for films that do not fit the bill in more mainstream theaters, and screening these films can capitalize on the segments of the markets not being touched by the present theatrical distribution circuit. This broader mission makes sense from a marketing standpoint, as a wider possible readership would lead to a wider possible circulation. However, this expanded mission complicates our more pat definitions of educational film.

What then was the difference between educational and commercial film if not the venue of exhibition? Even at the time of the magazine's launch in 1919, the term *nontheatrical* would not have been apt to describe the variety of locations and audiences exposed to educational film. As demonstrated, Ford films played regularly as part of programs in theaters of all types rather than exclusively in church basements and school classrooms. Although the sense of educational film being defined through its site of exhibition became dominant, in the 1910s and much of the 1920s the means of projection (most notably without sound) were still available in roughly equal measure to theaters and other venues alike. What makes these films educational is not that they played in a school setting but that their content was believed to have pedagogical significance. It is important here to notice that the intended venue for Ford films did not switch to the school setting until the last iteration, the *Educational Library*. The *Educational Weekly* was intended to and did play alongside one- and two-reelers in major cities, as well as in smaller venues and nontraditional sites because of its free cost. However, this is not to say that both types of films were viewed as technically equivalent, and reviews never confused a Ford short on zinc with the latest swashbuckling adventure. Ford films were not able to match the increasing production value of studio films, and viewers were of course savvy enough to note the difference and begin to classify films not only in terms of content but also in execution of the content.

From the beginning, *Educational Film Magazine* often discussed how to become professionalized in the area of film, specifically in matters of projection, suggesting that producing and displaying films in a skillful way was key to legitimacy. Articles ranging from advice on setting up a film exhibition space safely (as most films were nitrate 35 mm prints and thus flammable under certain conditions) to how to best approach making an educational film on one's own, were run in nearly every issue.[36] While film was certainly an expensive medium in which to work, the publication seems to be a source of information for amateur filmmakers and exhibitors in many contexts. There was a "lack of caution outside theaters," one editorial proclaims, necessitating a law that prevents "amateur operators whose knowledge of projection matters is limited to the threading of the machine and the switching on of the current" from projecting "inflammable" or nitrate film without a fireproof booth enclosing the projector.[37] Production was still out of the reach of an amateur while it remained bound to the expensive 35 mm format, but exhibition practices were nevertheless promoted as a site of professionalization for nontheatrical venues to raise the caliber of their screenings and, concordantly, the level of respect the screening could command. Ford was already engaged in questions of professionalization, as earlier sections demonstrated, as it grappled with the conflicting desire to present its product as having grown organically out of the larger Ford mission and to contract outside, established companies in order to produce a product of quality. By working with outside companies, and later downplaying their role, Ford could project mastery of film production while still delivering a quality product that could play alongside a studio film.

This emphasis on quality follows in line with the growing professionalization trend present in the film industry at large; as film became an established medium with specialized venues, it seems only logical that the industry coalesces under a unified banner of "Hollywood films," aided in no small part by the growing power of the West Coast production houses, soon to be bastions of the studio system. This unification is significant not only because it relates to a medium-wide impulse toward professional standards but also because it establishes the main body of work with which educational film is continually contrasted. As Hollywood, and all the weight that the term carries, became common parlance, educational film had to work to establish itself against or alongside the dominant modes of production, distribution and exhibition. Theaters were for Hollywood, and educational film was out of place in the new landscape of features and serials. In order to play alongside these professional products, an educational film had to match the quality of the West Coast products. Ford of course was already well-positioned within a professional discourse and was able to transition to educational cinema not as a novice but as a leader in the field of utilitarian film. However, it was perhaps the burden of professionalization that most weighed down the automaker; in nearly every review of the films put out under the *Educational Weekly* banner, they were noted as well done for an educational film, as opposed to having the production values of a studio-produced product. Despite its efforts, Ford was simply unable to match the production values of dedicated filmmaking companies.

Advertising revenue simply could not sustain *Educational Film Magazine* financially. The magazine stopped publication in 1922 after the establishment of an editorial board and a raise in prices. The market imagined by the magazine as surpassing the theatrical circuit was in fact hampered by the very virtues the magazine extolled: schools, churches, and other nontheatrical venues simply did not have the resources, financial or otherwise, to compete with an ever-improving theatrical experience. The folding of the magazine coincides almost to the month with the point at which Ford stopped advertising the *Educational Library* in print, although it would be available through the 1950s. As the company backed away from active participation in national politics and moved into the educational film arena, it can be supposed that Ford expected to find a thriving market with lower costs and lower expectations of quality. However, as the *Educational Film Magazine*'s contents and ultimate shuttering demonstrates, the tension over how to define educational film meant that the new classification did little to ease tensions, and both magazine and film products would eventually cease to be profitable.

Conclusion

The case study of the *Ford Educational Film Library* is a fitting coda to the history of Ford Motion Picture Laboratories: it recycles previous footage to create a new product in a way that fits extremely neatly into the larger Ford narratives of economy and streamlined production but also demonstrates a shrewd understanding of market for educational film. What was originally filmed as a demonstration of the Fordson tractor as news in the *Animated Weekly* was recut into a unit on mechanized farming for the *Educational Library*. By replacing a title card that pushes the tractor as a solution to the food shortage in Great Britain during World War I with one that shows how efficiently the tractor tills the soil to prepare the field for planting, Ford took an advertisement for both its tractor and its patriotism and turned it into a model of mechanized farming for schoolchildren to study. As the rhetoric of *Educational Film Magazine* suggests, a polished product that fit viewer expectations for a quality film experience would succeed in the increasingly professionalized world of educational film, and its clear packaging of units with associated curriculum materials leaves no doubt that these films were meant for the classroom and not the downtown theater. Just as the viewer and exhibitor alike could see past the civic-minded rhetoric of the weekly Ford offerings and understand them as advertisements for the products and politics of the company at large, it is not surprising that a branded library was essentially abandoned in 1922 after less than a year of advertisements, when other more neutral projects to put film into classrooms succeeded. Effective as the assembly line model was for automobile manufacturing, film necessitates a more nuanced means of production; even early viewers were able to discern the complex roles film plays in an educational or commercial context.

It is remarkable that perhaps the world's most famous and innovative automotive company would have an interest in motion pictures at all, much less the kind of operation that produced, distributed, and exhibited at the volume that the Ford Motion Picture Laboratory claimed. Scholarship on this phenomenon has thus far focused on the ways in which film was used and conceptualized by the industrial companies who adopted the new technology alongside so many other markers of modernity. The work in this chapter aims to complicate pat distinctions between educational and commercial film to examine how different types of address functioned in theatrical and nontheatrical exhibition contexts. Too often historians relegate nontheatrical film to the margins of film history, assuming wrongly that it was less widely seen because its production and exhibition often went undocumented. Ford films were well-documented both internally by the company and by the industry at large, and the contradictions those narratives expose force a more complex understanding of the exhibition landscape of the time. The *Film Daily* and *Moving Picture World* coverage reveals, perhaps inadvertently, the complexities of film production and exhibition that Ford was, for practical and political reasons, willing to reduce to a larger narrative of self-reliance and streamlined manufacturing. Examining Ford films through more than an industrial lens destabilizes classification systems that place theatrical and nontheatrical films at odds with one another and unsettle the traditional understandings of the relationship between production and exhibition context in order to view these items in not only a broader historical context but a broader filmic context as well.

Notes

1. "The Motion Picture Department," *Ford Man*, September 20, 1917, accession 951, box 11, folder "1915?," Benson Ford Research Center.

2. Lee Grieveson, "The Work of Film in the Age of Fordist Mechanization," *Cinema Journal* 51, no. 3 (2012): 25–51, doi:10.1353/cj.2012.0042.

3. For example, see how the department is described in the finding aid to the collection at the Benson Research Center: "Henry Ford was intrigued by the possibilities of using motion picture film to train workers and to communicate to the public the news of the day and show them scenes of the world in which they lived—including the wonders of manufacturing at the Ford Motor Company" ("Ford Motor Company Photographic and Film Department," The

Henry Ford, accessed February 18. 2011, https://www.thehenryford.org/collections-and-research/digital-resources/popular-topics/photo-and-film-department/).

4. "After Ford," *Film Daily*, January 21, 1920.

5. "Motion Picture Department."

6. Grieveson, "Work of Film in the Age of Fordist Mechanization," 27.

7. "Motion Picture Department."

8. Ibid.

9. Ibid.

10. "Following the Ford Movie Man," *Ford Times* 10, no. 7 (February 1917), 301–5.

11. Unfortunately, documents detailing the thinking behind this change are sadly missing from the archives, if they existed at all.

12. David L. Lewis, "Henry Ford—Movie Producer," *Ford Times*, February 1971, vertical file, "Motion Picture and Photography Department," Benson Ford Research Center.

13. "Ford's Educational Library," *Ford News*, June 15, 1925, vertical file, "Motion Picture and Photography Department," Benson Ford Research Center.

14. "What Is Needed," *Film Daily*, December 9, 1920.

15. "Carelton Visits Coast," *Moving Picture World*, June 19, 1915.

16. "Edison Company in Detroit," *Moving Picture World* 25, no. 5 (1915): 769.

17. "The Silent Celluloid Salesman," *Ford Times*, July 1946, vertical file, "Motion Picture and Photography Department," Benson Ford Research Center; "Motion Picture Man"; Lewis, "Henry Ford—Movie Producer."

18. Grieveson, "Work of Film in the Age of Fordist Mechanization," 27.

19. "Griever Closes Contracts," *Film Daily*, October 15, 1918.

20. "Opens Executive Offices," *Film Daily*, November 10, 1918.

21. "Following the Ford Movie Man"; "Goldwyn to Run Ford Weekly," *Film Daily*, December 3, 1918.

22. "After Ford."

23. "Exhibitors Agree," *Film Daily*, April 7, 1921.

24. "For Exhibitor's Use," *Film Daily*, February 21, 1921.

25. David Lanier Lewis, *The Public Image of Henry Ford: An American Folk Hero and His Company* (Detroit: Wayne State University Press, 1976), 42.

26. Ibid., 51.

27. Ibid., 45.

28. Lewis, "Henry Ford—Movie Producer," 19.

29. Unfortunately, footage from the *Animated* and *Educational Weekly* was cut up and classified by subject matter when it was made part of the National Archives. This makes it impossible to determine when exactly any subject was screened and even complicates the matter of whether a particular segment belongs to the *Animated* or *Educational Weekly*. Using contextual clues, such as the limited production of the flivver tank, I have only included material here that I am sure was filmed and exhibited between the US entry into World War I and the conclusion of the conflict.

30. Mayfield Bray, *Guide to the Ford Film Collection in the National Archives* (National Archives and Record Service: Washington, DC, 1970), http://archive.org/details/guidetofordfilmcoobrayrich.

31. Ibid.

32. David Burgess-Wise, *Ford at Dagenham: The Rise and Fall of Detroit in Europe* (Derby: Breedon Books, 2001), 65.

33. Lewis, "Henry Ford—Movie Producer," 44.

34. Devin Orgeron, Marsha Orgeron, and Dan Streible, eds., *Learning with the Lights Off: Educational Film in the United States* (New York: Oxford University Press, 2012), 20.

35. "Editor's Letter," *Educational Film Magazine* 2, no. 3 (March 1919).

36. In just one issue, articles ranged from passionate defenses of using classrooms from elementary to university spaces, using educational film in the Catholic Church, equipping church spaces with projectors, and the continued economical uses of slide projectors (*Educational Film Magazine* 3, no. 1 [January 1920]).

37. "Safety First," *Educational Film Magazine* 3, no. 3 (March 1920).

Filmography

"Benjamin Franklin" and Modern Communication Systems, 1918 (Ford Motor Company Collection, ca. 1903– ca. 1954). Online version available through the Archival Research Catalog (ARC identifier 9707) at www.archives.gov.

Ford Animated Weekly, 1918 (Ford Motor Company Collection, ca. 1903– ca. 1954). Online version available through the Archival Research Catalog (ARC identifier 90579) at www.archives.gov.

Lumbering, 1925 (Ford Motor Company Collection, ca. 1903– ca. 1954). Online version available through the Archival Research Catalog (ARC identifier 91422) at www.archives.gov.

Making a Broach, 1925 (Ford Motor Company Collection, ca. 1903–ca. 1954). Online version available through the Archival Research Catalog (ARC identifier 91401) at www.archives.gov.

Meat Packing, 1921 (Ford Motor Company Collection, ca. 1903– ca. 1954). Online version available through the Archival Research Catalog (ARC identifier 90791) at www.archives.gov.

Bibliography

Bray, Mayfield. *Guide to the Ford Film Collection in the National Archives* (National Archives and Record Service: Washington, DC, 1970). http://archive.org/details/guidetofordfilmcoobrayrich.

Burgess-Wise, David. *Ford at Dagenham. The Rise and Fall of Detroit in Europe.* Derby: Breedon Books, 2001.

"Following the Ford Movie Man," *Ford Times* 10, no. 7 (February 1917), 301–5.

Grieveson, Lee. "The Work of Film in the Age of Fordist Mechanization." *Cinema Journal* 51, no. 3 (2012): 25–51. doi:10.1353/cj.2012.0042.

Lewis, David Lanier. *The Public Image of Henry Ford: An American Folk Hero and His Company.* Detroit: Wayne State University Press, 1976.

Orgeron, Devin, Marsha Orgeron, and Dan Streible, eds. *Learning with the Lights Off: Educational Film in the United States.* New York: Oxford University Press, 2012.

KATY PEPLIN holds a PhD in Screen Arts and Cultures from the University of Michigan. Her research focuses on nonfiction film.

10 Institutionalizing Educational Cinema in the United States during the Early 1920s

Gregory A. Waller

Well after the first flush of utopic enthusiasm for the pedagogical potential of moving pictures, and well before the full uptake of 16 mm as a viable alternative to 35 mm, the early 1920s saw cinema, theatrical and nontheatrical alike, widely screened and publicly debated in an America that was rife with particularly exacerbated racial, class, and political conflict in the wake of World War I. Americans were learning about the promise of radio as an even newer mass medium, while witnessing a wave of highly publicized Hollywood scandals. And it was likely hard not to notice the ramped-up public relations efforts of Will Hays and the newly created Motion Picture Producers and Distributors of America, a campaign that included a widely publicized address by Hays to the delegates at the National Education Association convention in July 1922. On that occasion, Hays's effusive praise for the visual education movement seemed to signal the commercial film industry's newfound respect for and ringing endorsement of motion pictures designed specifically for classroom use.[1] At this particular moment in the history of American cinema, what was entailed in the institutionalization of educational cinema?

That is a valid and potentially rewarding question, which for me begs or triggers other questions, including: What might institutionalization mean? What might it mean in relation to educational cinema or nontheatrical cinema more broadly? And, further, this line of inquiry generates certain other questions that would have been especially germane for the users and proponents of film for educational purposes in the early 1920s: why *educational* cinema rather than, say, *nontheatrical* cinema or *classroom* film or *visual instruction* aids? Should educational cinema be taken to include films originally produced for theatrical distribution as well as films designed specifically for use in churches or factories? Would the institutionalization of educational cinema somehow solve what was frequently deemed the major problem of the nontheatrical: how to manage distribution efficiently and effectively? These questions inform my discussion of several different takes on the institutionalization of educational cinema in the

United States during the early 1920s—institutionalization understood both as involving certain actions and practices (successful or unsuccessful) and also as discursively constructed as a necessity, opportunity, goal, or solution to particular problems.

The primary objects of my study are varied, though they all date from the same period: a state university department that distributed motion pictures (the Bureau of Visual Instruction at Indiana University), an organization with a national membership (the American Farm Bureau Federation), a national initiative led by professional educators (the National Academy for Visual Instruction), a minor federal agency (the US Bureau of Education), and a monograph (*Motion Pictures in Education: A Practical Handbook for Users of Visual Aids* [1923]). Rarely, if ever, do any of these organizations or publications use the words *institutionalize* or *institutionalization*. In fact, these terms appear infrequently during the early 1920s.

Institution, however, figured prominently in sociological studies such as Edward Cary Hayes's *An Introduction to the Study of Sociology* (1923) and John Mecklin Moffatt's *An Introduction to Social Ethics: The Social Conscience in a Democracy* (1920), books that are very much concerned with the etiology of institutions, their relation to government, and the "practical" and "desirable" results (Hayes) or the "deadening" and mechanizing effects (Moffatt) of living within societal institutions.[2] *Institution* also was more generally used in reference to certain specific sites (i.e., hospitals, museums, universities, orphanages, banks), time-honored activities or events or people (i.e., an annual public celebration, a long-running performance, an ensconced elected official), widely recognized, supposedly definitive features of American life (i.e., the family, the school, the press), and symbolically resonant forms of American popular culture (i.e., baseball, the circus).

It is particularly noteworthy, given the focus of this chapter, how various film periodicals in the early 1920s used *institution* as a way of underscoring the significance of motion pictures. "If there ever was a democratic institution," a *Photoplay* editorial from May 1922 declared, "it is the motion picture," a purported truism echoed by Cecil B. De Mille in an article for *Moving Picture Age*.[3] Not surprisingly, the trade press geared toward exhibitors located the institutional status of film quite specifically in the theater itself. "As an institution the motion picture theatre is and should be considered on a par with the bank, the library, the school and the newspaper," affirmed *Exhibitors Herald* in December 1920, while, the following September, *Exhibitors Trade Review* announced: "We regard the establishment of the theatre as an institution as the most important part of the exhibitor's activity."[4] For these periodicals, a theater achieved the status of an institution not when it turned a profit but when it achieved a certain level of prominence, was solidly established as a going concern, and was taken to be important (perhaps essential) to the life of the community. Against this theatrical backdrop, what might it have meant and how might it have been possible for educational cinema to become an institution or to undergo institutionalization?[5]

Exhibition as Institutionalization

To institutionalize educational cinema could mean, quite simply, making screenings of films that are in some fashion identified as "educational" a regular practice and not simply an intermittent novelty attraction in what we usually think of as public institutions—that is, in schools, colleges, and universities as well as hospitals, museums, veteran's homes, orphanages, churches, libraries, asylums, reformatories, and prisons.[6] Soon after the first wave of nickelodeons, the still-novel dispersion of cinema into institutional sites well beyond the movie theater was often highlighted in the motion picture trade press and local newspapers (particularly in smaller communities). By the early 1920s, such screenings were more commonplace and thus less likely to be noted as innovative—or simply odd—and hence newsworthy activities, though a quick search of digital archives of American newspapers for the early 1920s readily turns up examples of motion pictures explicitly labeled as "educational film" being exhibited in public institutions, like the "industrial subjects" screened weekly at the library in Hibbing, Minnesota, or a series of "educational films" shown to high school students at the Congregational Church in Mount Vernon, Ohio.[7] To these scattered instances we can add the testimonials and advertisements published in every issue of *Moving Picture Age* regarding successful film use in particular churches and social centers. Searchable digital archives of newspapers and periodicals—always an incomplete and random source of information—make possible at least a provisional mapping of the dispersion and saturation of institutionalized educational cinema understood as regular screenings in public institutions.

Incorporation as Institutionalization

The exhibition of educational films in libraries or schools does not necessarily have much to do with *institutionalization* as understood to mean the process of incorporating something into a well-defined organization or system. This usage is common in widely accessed online sources, but it was also in play in the early 1920s. For example, the chancellor of Kansas University declared in 1924 that "the goal of the University is to catch the genius of the University of hard knocks and institutionalize it," while Henry Ford, in a syndicated newspaper editorial from October 1920, bemoaned the debilitating effects of the government "institutionalizing the normal impulses of the people."[8]

Understanding institutionalization as the introduction, emplacement, deployment, and ongoing role of educational cinema within an identifiable organization or system brings a different set of questions to the fore: How was this process of incorporation initiated and justified in terms of the larger goals and strategies of the institution? What audiences did the institution seek to reach through the use of educational film? Did institutionalization entail the production as well as the distribution and exhibition of motion pictures?[9] Relevant examples of the incorporation of educational cinema from this period include, for instance, the US

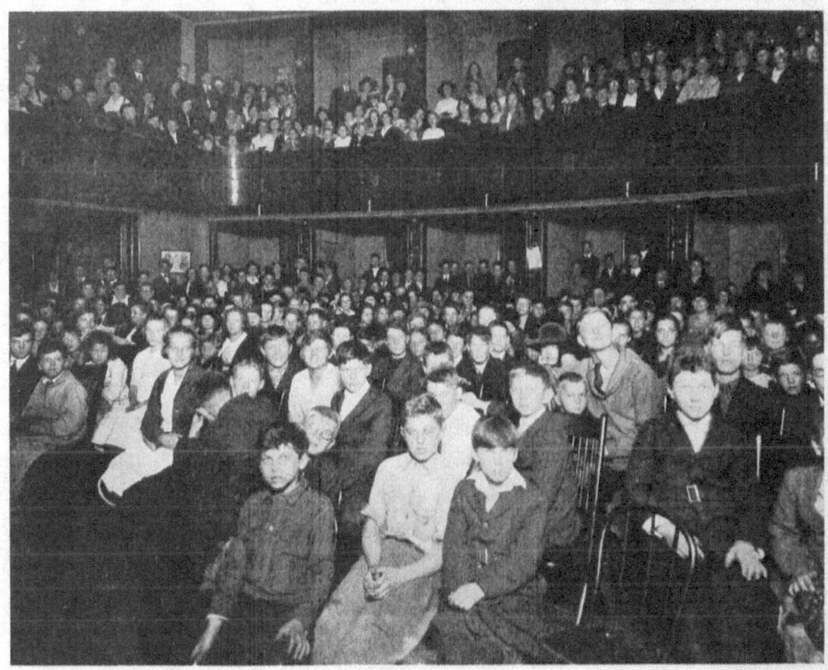

"Neighborhood Night" Comes Every Friday at Simpson

Simpson Methodist Church in Minneapolis keeps its children off the street through its Friday movie night. This is only about half of the crowd. Many evenings over 900 people attend. At times 200 children and some parents are waiting at 7:00 when the doors are opened a half hour before beginning the program. Another special show is given after school in the afternoon for the smaller children, as the church is not large enough to hold all at one show. Children, unattended, are seated on the main floor. How they are kept quiet is only one element of the well planned organization which takes care of these meetings. The work of the several committees is described in the article beginning on the opposite page

Fig. 10.1. Simpson Methodist Church, *Moving Picture Age* (January 1921).

Department of Agriculture, nonprofits like the American Red Cross and the Baptist Home Mission Society, and high-profile corporations like Ford, General Electric, and International Harvester.[10] Among the most visible examples of this process were the community outreach services of large land-grant universities, typically—though not exclusively—located in the American Midwest.[11] In addition to film distribution, many of these institutions contributed to the broader dissemination of educational cinema by producing films, making available projectors, holding teaching training sessions, or providing traveling exhibition services.[12]

For example, Indiana University (IU)—the state's flagship liberal arts university—added motion pictures to its Extension Division as early as 1914.[13] Encompassing correspondence courses, classes actually taught in other cities, a roster of available public speakers, efforts on behalf of public health and child welfare, and informational publications, the Extension Division (formally created in 1912) was a publicly prominent link between the university and the statewide citizenry it was mandated to serve.[14] The university's distribution of motion pictures was discontinued in 1917, but in 1919, with the acquisition of more than two hundred reels of government-produced war-related motion pictures, the Bureau of Visual Instruction (BVI) found a bureaucratic home as one of the seven units within the Public Welfare branch of the Extension Division.[15]

IU's student-run campus newspaper noted that as of July 1919, the Extension Division had "furnished 503 reels of film to 44 communities and 459 lantern slides to 121 communities. Over 35,712 persons attended these exhibitions."[16] This form of quantification remained a favored way to publicize the success and growth of the Bureau of Visual Instruction. (Another favored form of representation was a photograph of film cans filling shelves at the BVI.) Measured in feet, reels, even miles of film, and in the aggregate number of screenings, spectators, and communities, the numbers seem designed to convince Indiana residents and university officials that IU's delivery of educational film to sites statewide was not some trendy Progressive-era pedagogical experiment but a quite tangible and expanding public service: During the fiscal year ending in June 1921, with 197 "non-theatrical motion picture machines" across the state, "2,395 motion picture films were sent [by the bureau] to 137 communities. These films were shown from five to fifteen times with a total average attendance for each community of approximately 41,000."[17] By the summer of 1923, the BVI was reported to be serving more than 400 communities each year with a library of 1,000 "films for educational needs" and 17,000 lantern slides.[18]

What were these films? The official catalog, published in July 1925, of motion pictures available from the bureau listed 472 different titles, all bookable by in-state users for a nominal fee, except for 34 identified as "special rentals"—a mix of films (largely features) that had been released theatrically and were then available to rent for screenings that charged admission, provided that "the films are used in raising funds for school use or other worthy causes." (In small towns these fundraising screenings were sometimes held in movie theaters, which seemed to pose no problem for the BVI).[19] Among the special rentals were *Nanook of the North* (1922), a few contemporary dramas and comedies, literary adaptations like *A Hoosier Schoolmaster* (1914), George Kleine's *Quo Vadis* (1913) and *Julius Caesar* (1914), and *King Basketball* (1924), a one-reel instructional film actually produced by the bureau.[20] In a speech at the National Academy of Visual Instruction's 1923 conference (subsequently reprinted in full in the journal *Visual Education*), Hugh W. Norman, the head of the BVI, made no apologies for distributing what he called "entertainment

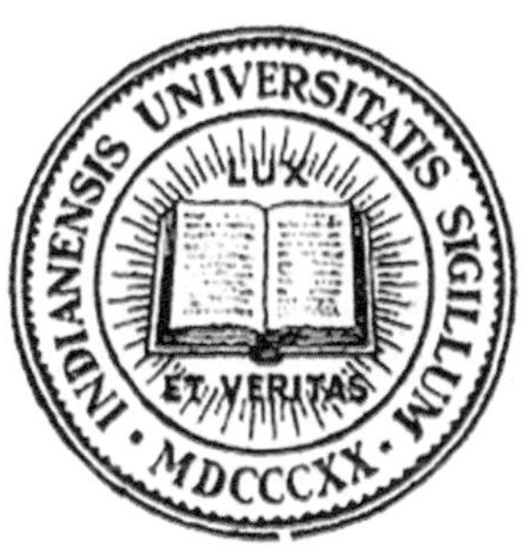

Fig. 10.2. Motion Pictures, Indiana University Bureau of Visual Instruction Bulletin (1925).

films," which, he affirmed, "have a place in school activities."[21] This logic allowed the bureau to offer the "special rentals" listed earlier as well as Kinogram newsreels, Harold Lloyd's *Take a Chance* (1918), and a host of Bray Studio's split-reel cartoons (featuring the likes of Bobby Bumps and Goodrich Dirt) in addition to titles that were grouped as "educational," including films from the USDA and the Bureau of Mines, travelogues, films promoting health or exploring nature, industrials, and government-produced war films.

The bureau's eclectic assortment of motion pictures made good sense—and not just because of the paucity of available nontheatrical titles in the early 1920s. Even before the founding of the BVI, the Extension Division had, in early 1919, announced that part of its statewide responsibility was "contributing to the growing tendency toward community provision for noncommercial entertainment."[22] To this end, the BVI fulfilled its mandate in part by circulating films well beyond the classroom or the school auditorium. Publications by or about the bureau often contained a quite expansive list of audiences and constituencies served: "churches, Christian associations, County agricultural agents, clubs and civic organizations"—to which at one time or another were added health officers, YMCAs, American Legion posts, orphan asylums, reformatories, women's clubs, hospitals, and farm bureaus.[23] Such lists, of course, are revealing instances of what counted for variety and breadth when it came to constructing nontheatrical cinema's audiences—and Indiana's public sphere as the state moved into the 1920s.

Efficiently dispatching motion pictures to a range of nontheatrical sites across the state was by no means the sole function of the BVI. Fulfilling its institutional charge also meant publishing in 1921 a circular entitled "Motion Pictures of Educational Value" and, more interestingly, acquiring production equipment in 1920, which seems to have been largely used to film football games and campus celebrations.[24] Soon thereafter, the BVI began offering extension courses and special classes in "visual education" for teachers attending IU's summer school program.[25] At the same time, the bureau continued to advance the cause of visual instruction by encouraging schools in Indiana to purchase projectors and by helping, in Norman's words, to "standardize and give stability to the comparatively new educational film service as a whole" and to provide "impetus to the task of producing genuine educational films."[26]

Institutionalizing educational cinema at Indiana University, then, went well beyond finding a space on campus and a home in the institution's bureaucratic structure. Acquiring (and producing) films in some sense set the parameters of what counted as educational film; systematizing the distribution of these films helped to realize the nontheatrical as a field that was both established and rapidly expanding; encouraging the screening of these film at certain sites and targeting certain users across the state created the vision of a vast potential viewership, not flattened into a mass of consumers but composed of many audiences with different demographics and different reasons for watching and making use of educational—which is to say, institutionally authorized—cinema.

The means and ends of institutionalization look considerably different when we move from a state university's visual instruction unit to a national organization with a much more tightly focused, well-articulated agenda, like the American Farm Bureau Federation (AFBF), which was created in 1919. The AFBF was designed to link the various state farm bureaus, which in turn were composed of local farm bureaus organized at the county level. (The first of these local bureaus had been formed in 1911.) The new national organization defined its mission as working "for the advancement of agriculture in the United States of America, economically, educationally, and socially." To this end, it encouraged cooperative marketing. It also monitored and sought to influence any relevant legislation and government regulations with any bearing on American agriculture, including policies related to transportation, taxation, and commerce—all the while avowing to "remain free from political entanglements." (The AFBF thus distanced itself from politically active groups during the 1910s that organized American farmers, like the Farmers' Union and the Nonpartisan League.[27]) At the same time, the AFBF mounted an extensive education campaign to attract new members, bring relevant information to farmers, and "keep the general public sympathetically informed as to the ideas and accomplishments of organized agriculture."[28] The "Motion Picture Division" (initially called the "Farm Film Service") figured as one of nine divisions in the

AFBF's Department of Information, along with other divisions tasked with creating a newsletter for local bureaus, regularly sending information and "bulletins" to newspapers and press syndicates, providing feature articles to magazines, printing pamphlets, creating cartoons and other visual material, and helping organize advertising and publicity campaigns in concert with state bureaus.

Even early in the history of this organization, the scale of the Department of Information's activity was vast. According to the AFBF's annual report for the year ending October 31, 1922, when membership totaled 772,634 across forty-six states (with the largest membership in Iowa, Illinois, and Indiana), the Department of Information—to cite only some of its work—produced and delivered to state and county bureaus 513,600 copies of a weekly newsletter, 24,000 posters, 90,500 stickers for automobiles, and multiple thousands of pamphlets, posters, and poster stamps. The department issued an average of one press release each day, circulated more than 49,500 copies of a weekly sheet of reprintable news items, provided 42 features articles, and distributed 3,050 cartoons. As part of its efforts that year, the Department of Information also "produced 25 new reels of Farm Bureau motion pictures" and "supplied motion pictures for 3,609 meetings, attended by 721,800 people."[29]

In many ways, the AFBF's investment in producing and distributing motion pictures made perfect sense. The 1910s had seen a surge of interest in agricultural education, greatly encouraged by the passage of the Smith-Lever Act (1914) that had provided funds for agricultural extension agents connected to state universities in every county of the United States. Not only these extension services but corporations like International Harvester (which began its own high-profile Agricultural Extension Department in 1912) had developed a range of successful strategies for delivering instruction directly to farmers, including one-day institutes, exhibits at fairs, trains with special "demonstration" cars, lectures using lantern slides and portable charts, and film screenings in community halls and rural schools.[30]

The "Movie Show Program" of "six reels of educational farm films" arranged by the Hancock County (Illinois) Farm Bureau in October 1922 gives a sense of the type of exhibition promoted by the AFBF. In this case, four titles were screened: *Horse Sense*, a two-reel film about horse training, *Farm for Sale*, which argues for the use of limestone for soil improvement; *Farming in One Lesson*, billed as a "comedy, which does not caricature the farmer in the usual unkind way" but shows the misadventures of a city couple who decide to have a go at farming; and *Chinch Bugs*, "a straight educational film showing the mode of life and destruction" of these insects. Screenings of the program were arranged in twenty-one different communities over a four-week period, with Farm Bureau exhibitions held in churches, high schools, opera houses, town halls, and even a few movie theaters—underscoring how the relation between theatrical and nontheatrical film exhibition was very much dependent on local conditions and the flexibility of independent theater owners, particularly in rural areas.[31]

Available evidence suggests that it was common for Farm Bureau agents to arrange and run such institutionally sanctioned screenings: freely provided to all

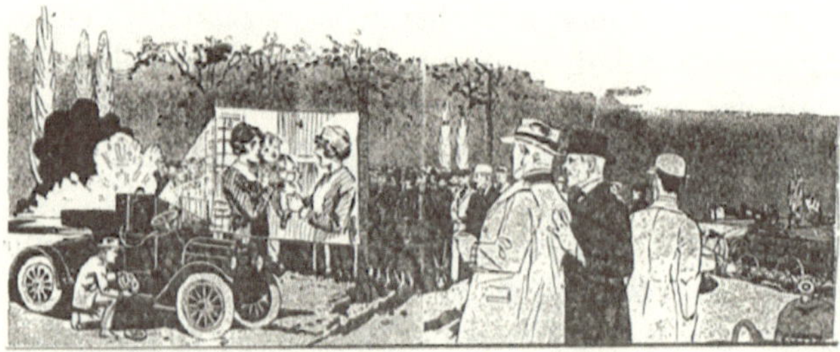

Fig. 10.3. De Vry ad *County Agent and Farm Bureau* (June 1921).

comers, scheduled with some degree of regularity, and mobile in that they moved from site to site within a specific territory. Preaching that "a projectorless farm bureau is a handicapped institution," *Moving Picture Age* included in virtually every issue in 1922 a first-person testimonial to the value of motion pictures for the work of county agents.[32] For example, having put on 178 programs in less than two years with his bureau's portable projector, the county agent from Cedar County, Iowa, was absolutely convinced of the appeal of agricultural films and comedies at Farm Bureau gatherings and was likewise committed to screenings attended by broader audiences at rural churches and schools, which offered the Farm Bureau the opportunity to use the "motion picture screen" to spread even more widely its "gospel of better farming and better living."[33]

These uses of film were in keeping with the advice offered in the monthly magazine, *County Agent and Farm Bureau*, which ran a section in each issue with news and editorial commentary from the AFBF. The magazine fully endorsed its policies but was not actually published by the national organization. In June 1921, this magazine began what it called a regular "motion picture service department" to provide information for those county agents "anxious to accomplish big things in the most efficient way known to our age"—that is, through motion pictures, as demonstrated dramatically by the government's deployment of film as part of the American war effort.[34]

Like IU's Bureau of Visual Instruction, *Country Agent and Farm Bureau* and the AFBF's Motion Picture Division campaigned strongly to convince potential exhibitors to invest in projectors—a necessary step to increase the demand for and hence the supply of a certain type of educational film. Unlike the school or church, however, the local Farm Bureau required a fully portable machine that could be powered by a standard 110-volt electrical source, automobile generator, or storage battery. Not surprisingly, with the introduction of *County Agent and Farm Bureau's* "Motion Picture Service Department," the magazine began to attract more regular advertising from manufacturers pitching projectors, most notably the DeVry

Portable Motion Picture Projector (a twenty-pound machine, "portable in every sense"); the American Projectiscope ("Take It Any Place Any Time"), and the Zenith ("A Professional Machine at a Non-Professional Price").[35] In fact, the potential of rural film exhibition likely gave significant impetus to the development and marketability of portable projectors, which, in turn, proved to be essential in shaping what I have elsewhere called multi-sited cinema in the United States.

If for the AFBF and the state university extension division, the wider dispersion of projectors meant the greater likelihood of films suitable for the classroom or the Farm Bureau meeting, the AFBF was much more fully committed than the Bureau of Visual Instruction to producing its own films. (In this way it was following the lead of corporations like International Harvester and Ford.) The AFBF announced in April 1922 that it had signed a contract covering both production and distribution with Homestead Films, run largely by men who had been associated with the Farm Bureau movement. Eleven films (produced by Homestead) that had already been screened under the auspices of the AFBF became part of what was formally called the American Farm Bureau Motion Picture Library and would be distributed nontheatrically to "county Farm Bureaus, agricultural schools, rural churches, community clubs, and other groups of farm people" through a new film exchange operated by Homestead in Chicago—the first in a planned network of exchanges. New productions would be "approved" by the Department of Information, produced by Homestead personnel, advertised and promoted by the AFBF, and exhibited both to the "Farm Bureau field" and also to "regular theatres." Any profits from theatrical and nontheatrical exhibition were to be shared by Homestead and the AFBF.[36]

The AFBF moved into film production at a time when the US Department of Agriculture was ramping up its motion picture production. By 1921, the USDA had over 130 titles available, mainly instructional films, though not all strictly related to agriculture, as the AFBF understood the term. (USDA films also dealt, for example, with home economy, national forests, the lumber industry, and road construction.) USDA films were distributed at no charge to agricultural extension agents—who could also be affiliated with a Farm Bureau—and to other users for only shipping costs.[37] Why wouldn't the AFBF have encouraged county agents to become exhibitors but left the actual film production to the USDA and put its resources into some other information medium? A look at the first batch of films that Homestead released points to AFBF's likely rationale for creating the American Farm Bureau Motion Picture Library.

Under the AFBF's auspices, Homestead in 1922 produced eight "real farm movies" that fell into two categories: "educational films" and "story films." Among the "educational films" was an instructional one-reeler, *Corn Root Rot*, and a film directly promoting membership in the Farm Bureau, *Forward, Farm Bureau*. The "story films" were largely multireel narratives, including *Farming in One Lesson*, the comedy I mentioned earlier, and the five-reel "rural romance," *Joe McGuire*, whose plot hinged on the personal benefits afforded by cooperative marketing, the linchpin of AFBF's strategy for improving economic conditions for farmers.[38] It is hardly surprising to find that some of the 1922 films added to the American Farm Bureau Motion Picture Library were designed for recruitment purposes and that all of the Homestead films were very likely informed—directly or indirectly—by the AFBF's particular take on what *County Agent and Farm Bureau* called "the true story of American agriculture."[39] Put simply, producing films allowed the AFBF to increase the number of screening opportunities for county agents and to bring its national message to local screens.

At the same time, the strategy of producing both "story" and also educational farm films made good sense, given that most accounts of Farm Bureau screenings underscored (1) that showing motion pictures was an effective way to boost attendance at meetings; and (2) that screenings were social events, with programs designed to be entertaining for the adults as well as for the children in the audience. A "well-balanced evening's program would consist of a three reel show [meaning a "recreational" feature film], a comedy or a scenic reel and three reels of educational movies," wrote a county agent from Montana. This type of screening was, he affirmed, a "morale builder," especially for often quite isolated farm families.[40]

Accounts like this indicate that county agents acting as film exhibitors, fully realizing the drawing power of motion pictures, acknowledged the tastes of their target audience and recognized the value of Farm Bureau screenings as social experiences for viewers who were by no means captive. The AFBF, in turn, encouraged film exhibition as an effective way to help recruit, engage, and retain members, an all-important task for a still-emerging national organization that depended on dues-paying farmers. The AFBF also viewed local film exhibition as an opportunity to screen its own institutional values and policies. Yet the national organization did not own the projectors in use by county agents and did not, it seems, have any way to control what was screened by these projectors. With these conditions and goals in mind, Homestead produced an assortment of motion pictures varied in genre if not in ideology, and the individual pictures in the American Farm Bureau Motion Picture Library seemed readily combinable into "well-balanced" all-AFBF programs, mixing (as did so many Farm Bureau screenings) the educational with the entertaining. In so doing, the AFBF moved beyond what E. L. Hill called "straight educational pictures on agriculture." For Hill, then "in charge of motion pictures" in the Department of Information, the "wonderful stories" of rural life being turned into films by the AFBF "visualize to the audience the possibilities and the brighter side of farm life, suggest solutions of problems, and inspire." These films allowed "the farm bureau to drive home lessons in a very effective manner" without being bound to a tightly circumscribed sense of what passed for "educational cinema."[41]

Professionalization as Institutionalization

Whatever indirect impact they might have had on nontheatrical cinema more generally, the American Farm Bureau Federation and Indiana University's Bureau of Visual Instruction did not attempt to institutionalize what we might call the field of educational cinema, which in this period figured as an important—and ambitious—goal, particularly for certain clusters of academics. Institutionalization, understood as the attempt to give structure, order, and direction to the field of educational cinema—typically through a process of centralization and professionalization—looks to be very much of a piece with what historian Robert H. Wiebe calls the "bureaucratic orientation" that in the United States "defined a basic part of the nation's discourse" in the years after World War I.[42]

Such an orientation would find expression in the efforts on behalf of the Society for Visual Education (1920) and the Visual Instruction Association of America (1922), and the example I will focus on, the National Academy for Visual Instruction (NAVI).[43] Founded in 1920, largely by employees of extension departments in state universities, NAVI lost a measure of independent identity when it first affiliated with the National Education Association (NEA) in 1922, then helped to create a new NEA Department of Visual Instruction in 1923, and eventually merged with this department in 1932.[44] However, particularly during its formative years, NAVI was quite visible as an organization, largely as a result of its annual conventions and its regular monthly presence in *Moving Picture Age* beginning in October 1921 and continuing after that magazine merged with *Educational Screen* in January 1923.

From its inception at a meeting at the University of Michigan in April 1920, NAVI aimed to assume an ongoing, permanent leadership role, bringing order and direction to the practice and the promise of visual instruction, with obvious implications for educational cinema and for nontheatrical film more generally.[45] Officially welcoming attendees to the well-publicized inaugural NAVI conference in July 1920 at the University of Wisconsin–Madison, William H. Dudley—the organization's first president and one of its founders—called on the participants to bring their expertise to bear in the service of active and wide-ranging governance: "It is for us, therefore, to preempt the field, to plan out standards, to set the pace. We must establish fundamental principles, must work out specific and constructive programs of procedures, must study the needs of schools and other educational groups and point out definite ways to meet such needs."[46] Standards and principles as well as programs and procedures—these are what NAVI deemed necessary to regularize and realize the full potential of the uneven and yet limitless field of visual instruction. "The thing to be explained is how institutions even start to stabilize," Mary Douglas observes in *How Institutions Think*.[47] NAVI clearly presented itself as an authoritative, professionalizing agent of stabilization.

To achieve its goals, in its formal constitution NAVI proposed to set policy and research goals, and to forge a centralized network "through which" schools, churches, welfare groups, and other stakeholders "engaged in educational or semi-educational work" could "co-operate in furthering better production of and a more systematic and intelligent use of visual aids." Essential to the identity and institutional aims of NAVI was the rigid hierarchical distinction it mandated between noncommercial voting members and commercial interests. The new organization's

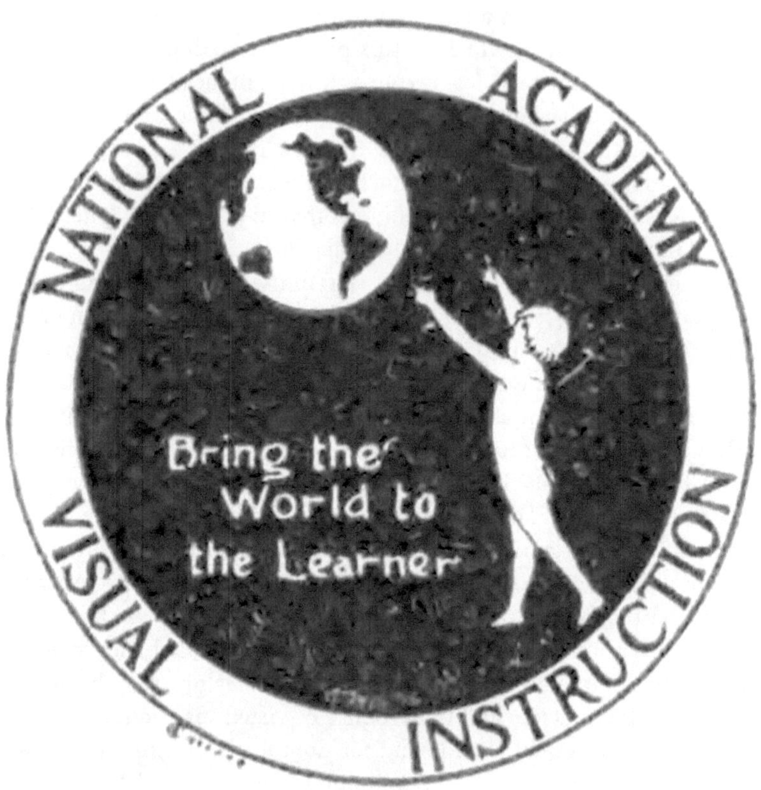

Fig. 10.4. NAVI logo *Educational Screen* (April 1923).

official bylaws explicitly barred "companies, dealers, agents, or persons financially interested in the sale of visual-instruction materials" from becoming active members with voting privileges.[48] Less explicitly articulated but evident to later commentators was NAVI's privileging of university extension programs over metropolitan public school districts and classroom teachers.

NAVI's widely publicized inaugural meeting, however, appeared to be inclusive, featuring displays by DeVry, Power, and other equipment manufacturers as well as film companies like Ford Educational Films and New Era Films (a commercial distributor based in Chicago specializing in motion pictures for schools, churches, and community associations). Initial announcements for the conference invited participation from a range of potential stakeholders, and the final program, much of which was later circulated as a volume of *Proceedings*, included presentations on rural exhibition, the YMCA motion picture service and its contributions to Americanization campaigns, the Red Cross Bureau of Pictures, the federal government's motion picture initiatives, agricultural extension, and the "desirability of establishing ideal standards" for the use of visual aids in the classroom.[49] In other words, the organization seemed interested in the manifold uses of motion pictures and other media across multiple sites, including but well beyond the classroom.

But NAVI was inflexible when it came to solving what Ernest L. Crandall at the first NAVI conference called the fundamental question (or opportunity) facing the field: "How will the problem of distribution of educational motion pictures be solved?" Then-director of the Department of Lectures and Visual Instruction for the New York City schools, and soon to be founding president of the Visual Instruction Association of America, Crandall reasoned that a "suitable method of distribution will evolve" once a financially powerful "commercial organization" entered the field.[50] The National Academy of Visual Instruction, however, was much more inclined to stake its faith in the academy than the market. Thus, the national map NAVI produced in 1921 of "distributing centers" indicates the solution to the problem of distribution by rendering the field of visual instruction in the United States as essentially a terrain strategically covered by state universities, with no commercial competition.[51]

This map in many ways literalized the centralized system, the institution that NAVI sought to establish. For all its claims of inclusiveness, the majority of NAVI's first elected officials and all but six of the forty vice presidents (each representing a different state) came from university extension programs or bureaus of visual instruction. By its second annual conference (held in Des Moines, Iowa, in July 1921), NAVI would in fact face criticism for being too focused on university extension programs and broader nontheatrical uses of motion pictures at the expense of public schools.[52] *Educational Screen* suggested that NAVI seek formal affiliation with the National Educational Association and elect a "more representative" leadership and then noted positively the increased role of public school professionals at the 1922 conference and the attention paid to "the concrete and practical aspects of the teaching problems of today" at NAVI's fourth annual meeting. By far the majority of presentations at the 1923 conference dealt with the use of films in the classroom, and extensive evening screening programs featured self-styled "school films" from a host of commercial and noncommercial producers, including the USDA, Atlas Educational Film, Ford, and Westinghouse.[53] When the NEA in July 1923 created its own Department of Visual Instruction—a year after Will Hays's speech about the glorious future of educational cinema—NAVI found its own institutional home. It scaled back its ambitious aspirations for institutionalizing educational cinema in the United States and officially defined itself—quite modestly, given its earliest statement of goals—as "an organization of men and women interested in a wider, more intelligent, and more systematic use of visual aids."[54]

Prescription as Institutionalization

Was there another strategy for improving and systematizing the use of educational cinema that did not hinge on the creation of a top-down professional organization?

Compare these images of institutionalized educational cinema: first, NAVI's map of the United States dotted with university distributors and second, the photograph of a classroom that appeared as the frontispiece of one of the first American book-length treatments of educational cinema, Don Carlos Ellis and Laura Thornborough's *Motion Pictures in Education: A Practical Handbook for Users of Visual Aids* (published in 1923 by Crowell, a major commercial press).[55] Captioned "the correct way to teach with motion pictures," this photograph locates the institutionalization of educational cinema not as a professional academic network but rather in a place—the generic classroom—and as a practice, teaching using a motion picture projector. The precise location and even the grade level of the class are never identified; the teacher is conspicuously out of the frame; and, most notably, nothing appears on the all-important screen. *Motion Pictures in Education* aims to fill in these blanks by offering practical tips for selecting specific films and purchasing equipment and, more tellingly, by establishing "the correct way to teach with motion pictures"—that is, by prescribing best practices. In so doing, Ellis and Thornborough attempt to secure for educational cinema what they take to be its deserved place in the mediated classroom and, more broadly, in the field of modern pedagogy.

Not surprisingly, like so many other proponents of educational cinema in this period, Ellis and Thornborough could not ignore the "troublesome problem" of distribution, going so far as to provide as an appendix to *Motion Pictures in Education* a "selected list" of some 125 distributors, including state university extension divisions as well as manufacturers, government agencies, and major theatrical distributors. The sheer number is impressive, but Ellis and Thornborough are quick to note that the national networks of theatrical exchanges have proven to be uninterested in servicing low-profit, high-maintenance nontheatrical clientele, while universities have tended to focus their distribution efforts on the needs of the community rather than the classroom.[56] The only viable solution to the problem of distribution, Ellis and Thornborough conclude, is that commercial companies "establish and maintain national systems of exchanges devoted exclusively to supplying films to the nontheatrical market," including "schools everywhere."[57] In this vision of nontheatrical cinema, efficient, specialized, profit-minded distribution conducted on a national basis would provide the necessary incentive for the equally profit-minded "small independent educational producer" to create "pedagogical" films specifically designed for the classroom.[58] While Ellis and Thornborough fully embrace the competitive marketplace, they do not trust Hollywood to create classroom films, no matter how many speeches Will Hays makes. Nor do they put their faith in the state, even after the successful motion picture activity of the USDA and the Committee on Public Information during World War I.[59]

That motion pictures do indeed belong in the classroom is a given in *Motion Pictures in Education*, though Ellis and Thornborough spend a chapter refuting, one-by-one, the seventeen "more important objections to the use of film in education."[60] This section of the book shares little with the utopian claims or pleas for legitimation that proponents of using moving images for educational purposes

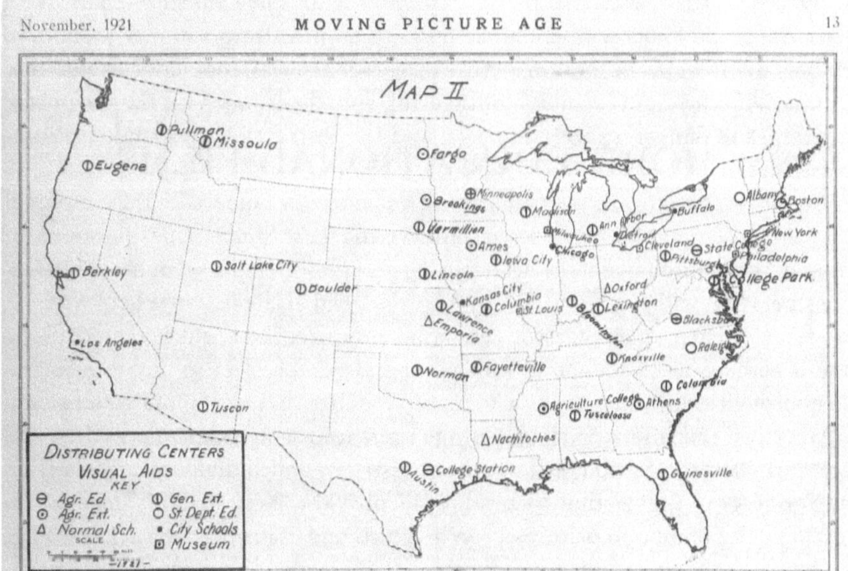

Fig. 10.5. NAVI map Moving Picture Age (November 1921).

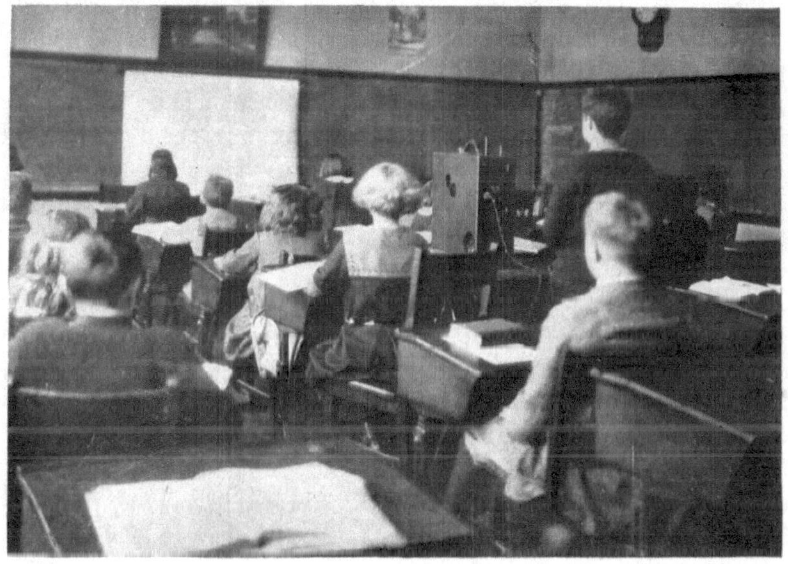

THE CORRECT WAY TO TEACH WITH MOTION PICTURES

Fig. 10.6. Frontispiece of Motion Pictures in Education (1923).

had offered a decade earlier.[61] In fact, *Motion Pictures in Education* reads like a functional guide for how to convince hesitant administrators and school board members to invest in the motion picture projector as a classroom tool, as Ellis and Thornborough lay out responses to lingering apprehension about the purported eye strain, fire danger, exorbitant costs, and the instructional capability of motion pictures.

But how to maximize the pedagogical value of this potentially rich resource? How to fill the empty classroom screen? Answering these fundamental questions for Ellis and Thornborough entails determining and prescribing a set of best practices for teachers that will help film "occupy its proper and ideal place in school work . . . as a valuable helper, making lessons easier here, simpler there, quicker, more pleasant and perhaps more economical for pupil and school."[62] In so doing, Ellis and Thornborough are, I argue, seeking to institutionalize the use of motion pictures in the American educational system. Citing expert testimony, academic studies, and successful efforts in various cities, school districts, and individual schools from New York City to Port Arthur, Texas, they identify the "best methods" for "the instructional use of motion pictures."[63] While Ellis and Thornborough acknowledge that "one of the great benefits of the films in school work is that they do make learning less of a drudgery and more pleasant and entertaining," the recommendations offered in *Motion Pictures in Education* often seem designed to create not simply a nontheatrical but what we might call an *antitheatrical* experience of film.[64] Unlike the screen programs offered by American Farm Bureau Motion Picture Library, the plan for classroom screenings in *Motion Pictures in Education* never attempts to mimic the movie theater's multireel, balanced (or at least varied) program or approximate its particular pleasures. Moreover, Ellis and Thornborough propose that motion pictures in the classroom—always understood to be "teaching aids"—be projected "practically in silence," with the projector stopped "one or two times during the course of a reel to ask questions" and the film shown "twice when possible" with a quiz between screenings. Screenings, they insist, should be followed directly by "class instruction," and under no circumstances should motion pictures "be shown as entertainment" in the classroom.[65]

Best practices in the classroom depend, of course, on choosing appropriate films, and *Motion Pictures in Education* includes a list of sample titles, classified largely by subject (e.g., civics, biology, US geography). But more fundamentally, optimal classroom use of film requires, for Ellis and Thornborough, being able to differentiate the "instructional motion picture" from other types of film that have been used outside of movie theaters.[66] (They also distinguish motion pictures from other "visual aids to instruction," like slides and stereoviews.) To this end, they break nontheatrical motion pictures down into six categories or genres:

- Theatrical films exhibited outside of theaters for "community" screenings and other entertainment purposes

- "Theatrical films suitable for school use," such as certain literary adaptations, historical films, and newsreels
- "Industrial films" made for "advertising purposes," which might be suitable for school use, depending on their "truthfulness" and lack of anything that smacks of the "rabid exaggerating press agent"
- "Informational films" originally "prepared for entertainment" and then edited to suit instructional purposes, like certain travelogues and nature pictures
- Purpose-made "strictly pedagogical" films "prepared from the teaching angle," that are accompanied by teacher's manuals[67]

Since "strictly pedagogical pictures" are currently produced "under the stress of rigid economy for a school market as yet meagerly financed," *Motion Pictures in Education*'s list of sample titles includes a number of films that "have been thoroughly correlated and edited for school use," like travelogues from Burton Holmes on Alaska and Hawaii that have been cut from six to two reels for classroom use.[68] Yet the purpose-made pedagogical film, for Ellis and Thornborough, stands not simply as one of five nontheatrical variants but rather as the decidedly preferable option, in that such films are tailored for classroom use and hence are "true pedagogic films."[69] Articulating these generic differences thus becomes another way of indicating best practices and a significant step in what Ellis and Thornborough take to be a process we could call the *purification* or (adapting the term from Rick Altman) the *genrification* of loosely understood "educational cinema," aiming toward a perfected "pedagogical film," correctly deployed and fully institutionalized as a valued and widely utilized classroom tool in the American educational system.[70]

Classification as Institutionalization

Writing not as the coauthor of *Motion Pictures in Education* but as the secretary of the Visual Instruction Association of America, Don Carlos Ellis explained in *Educational Screen* (January 1923) that the first action of this newly formed organization would be "to classify, list, evaluate and disseminate information concerning material of visual instruction valuable for school use."[71] This public gesture would no doubt have helped demonstrate that the field of visual instruction warranted an association that had national aspirations. The Visual Instruction Association of America's primary concern with information also seems fully in keeping with institutionalization understood as a process of regulation, integration, and standardization, a process that can involve setting parameters and identifying relevant "material." *Motion Pictures in Education* is in many ways an apt example of how gathering, collating, and circulating information could be put in the service of institutionalizing educational cinema—though for Ellis and Thornborough, listing distributors, films, or types of film is not an end in itself but a necessary step toward setting priorities and establishing best practices.

Consider, by way of contrast, the film-related activities of the Bureau of Education, a relatively minor part of the US Department of the Interior. Unlike the USDA, this bureau did not produce films, but for a brief time after World War I, it did play a prominent role in what could be seen as the federal government's efforts at encouraging the institutionalization of educational cinema in the United States.

Publicly charged with serving "as a clearing house through which pass educational data and statistics,"[72] the Bureau of Education was, in the beginning of the postwar period, home to more than eight million feet of film that had been received from "the departments of the government, of allied organizations and industrial companies." Well over half of this footage was being distributed by the bureau's Visual Instruction Section through forty-two state university extension departments.[73] According to its 1921 annual report, the Bureau of Education "is, therefore, principally engaged in the salvaging of educational and war film and in systematically distributing it throughout the country for as wide a use through educational and public organizations as can be secured."[74] This deployment of "systematic" distribution, which might have constituted a major step toward federal control of educational cinema in the United States, proved to be short-lived, ceasing when the bureau's appropriation for 1921 was cut.[75]

During the brief period it was receiving, storing, and distributing celluloid, the Bureau of Education—in keeping with its mandated role in the federal bureaucracy—also gathered and disseminated information about film, resulting in three publications issued in December 1919, authored by F. W. Reynolds, a former employee of the bureau then working for the extension division of the University of Utah.[76] The bureau's justification for preparing *Motion Pictures and Motion-Picture Equipment: A Handbook of General Information* (Bureau of Education Bulletin, 1919, No. 82) was the widespread "interest in motion pictures for purposes of education." Indeed, wrote Reynolds, "the time is near when no school will be without its motion-picture projection machine."[77] Accordingly, his eighteen-page pamphlet explained for "educators" how film should be handled and projectors should be installed and operated, in keeping with the relevant state and local laws and regulations devised by other federal agencies, like the Bureau of Standards and the Interstate Commerce Commission.

Complementing this bulletin were two visual instruction leaflets that described in quantitative terms the current state of educational cinema. *Educational Institutions Equipped with Motion-Picture Projection Machines* (Visual Instruction Leaflet No. 1) tabulated state by state and projector by projector the result of a survey designed to "locate the motion picture projection machines in use for purely educational purposes in the United States." While the data culled from written queries to such institutions was admittedly incomplete and would require continual updating, the Bureau of Education reasoned that circulating its findings was valuable since the lists "may mark progress, and more than that, may actually stimulate progress."[78] The unstated goal of this "progress" was, I propose, the institutionalization of educational cinema in America's schools, which at a minimum required readily available projectors and appropriate films.

To this end, Reynolds compiled what he deemed to be the relevant information about the dispersion of motion picture machines: the location of educational institutions that had a projector, the make of the projector, and the "capacity of auditorium" used for screenings. The data for seating capacity makes clear that film exhibition in schools virtually always took place in auditoria rather than classrooms, a point reinforced by the fact that portable machines accounted for only a small percentage of the projectors owned by schools. More interesting, the bureau's breakdown of its information privileged the 1,129 projectors actually installed in schools, even though 2,177 respondents to the initial survey reported "having arrangements with a local theater, public hall, library, club, or church by which educational pictures may be shown for the benefit of students" (6,761 respondents did not own, have access to, or plan to install a projector).[79] Rather than underscore the breadth of exhibition sites as a way of emphasizing the presence of "educational pictures" on American screens, the bureau's report measured—and actually saw—progress only in terms of the number of educational institutions that were equipped to project such pictures.[80]

By pinpointing the location of motion picture projectors, Visual Instruction Leaflet no. 1 provided distributors handling educational film with a potentially valuable list of likely exhibitors—thereby encouraging further investment in the production of usable films. "Educational pictures" currently available for projector-equipped schools—as well as for screening to "chambers of commerce, women's clubs, and other organizations"—was the subject of Visual Instruction Leaflet no. 2, *Motion Picture Films of Educational Value in the Possession of Associations and Commercial and Manufacturing Companies* (coauthored by Reynolds and Carl Anderson). In effect, this leaflet is a filmography of sponsored films, primarily industrials. Organized by company, this list is clearly weighted toward corporate sources like Ford, Canadian Pacific Railway, US Steel, and General Electric.

Most significant, for my purposes, is that all of these films merit inclusion because of their "educational value," a criteria that is never explained in the leaflet.[81] Presumably, either all industrials were deemed to have "educational value" or—more likely—there were motion pictures distributed by manufacturers and corporations that did not have such value, in which case the Bureau of Education as a federal agency assumed responsibility to adjudicate the "value" of individual films not produced by the government, based on some undefined sense of what counts as "educational." Either way, the result is that the Bureau of Education encouraged the screening in schools of sponsored films, giving its stamp of approval to films produced by "associations and commercial and manufacturing companies."

The Bureau of Education's efforts at gathering and disseminating information encouraged the progress of educational cinema within particular parameters: the school auditorium as exhibition site ready to make use of motion pictures of "educational value" produced by American manufacturers, business associations, and corporations. Unlike Ellis and Thornborough's *Motion Pictures in Education*, there is no sense in the Bureau of Education material that these sponsored films should or will give way to the purer genre of the classroom instructional film or that the classroom, in fact, should be the privileged site for educational cinema.

It is also worth noting, even if only in passing here, that the early 1920s saw other examples of what we might call "filmographical" efforts to organize and encourage the development of educational cinema as a field—or a market. Particular noteworthy in this regard is the annually updated *1001 Films: A Reference Book for Non-Theatrical Film Users*, which endorses a view of nontheatrical cinema not as institutionally "pure" or limited to the educational but as inclusive, heterogeneous, decentered, and rapidly expanding. This sense, too, readily emerges from the advertisements for producers and distributors that filled every issue of a journal like *Moving Picture Age*, advertisements that conjure up the nontheatrical as a multi-sited enterprise zone filled with innumerable niche audiences far beyond the classroom, a film field remarkably unlike the oligopolistic Hollywood motion picture industry.

Conclusion

Much of the discourse and practice I have examined in this essay was informed by or was responding to the material conditions relevant to educational cinema in the United States in the early 1920s. By the late 1930s, not to mention the late 1950s, these conditions would change dramatically—for example, in terms of the shift from 35 mm to 16 mm, the number of films in circulation, the funding available for renting or purchasing these films, and the type, cost, and ubiquity of motion picture projectors.[82] And yet what we might think of as the work of institutionalization continued. Motion pictures deemed educational continued to be exhibited in all types of institutional settings and to be formally incorporated into the bureaucratic structure of all manner of commercial, noncommercial, and governmental organizations and agencies. Various professional associations continued to attempt to shape and reshape the field. The work of classification continued, as did efforts to demarcate, regulate, and systematize the production and presentation of educational films. In short, none of the modes of and strategies for institutionalization that I have surveyed here were unique to the period I have been considering.

It would appear, then, that the institutionalization of educational cinema in the United States was an ongoing process, not something realized once and for all during the early 1920s. But how to gauge what counts as full or partial realization—or what signifies, in Mary Douglas's words, the "stabilization" of institutions "as organizers of information"?[83] By tabulating what the *Moving Picture Age* claimed were the "hundreds of American institutions [in which] the moving picture has a particular department with its particular appropriation"?[84] By assessing the success or failure of initiatives like the National Academy of Visual Instruction, the extension services of state universities, and the motion picture division of the

American Farm Bureau Federation? Or, more generally, by determining the extent to which educational cinema came under the control of a single or a handful of aligned agencies or corporations? Or perhaps by analyzing policy decisions and print discourse to determine whether something commonly understood to be educational cinema was perceived as having stability, prominence, and value in the eyes of certain beholders—professional educators, funding agencies, elected officials, even Hollywood insiders?

These questions about how to gauge the process and the progress of the institutionalization of educational cinema during the early 1920s become even more resonant in the context of certain powerful—and now quite familiar—claims about the institutionalization of cinema more generally, including those put forward so compellingly by André Gaudreault in *Film and Attraction: From Kinematography to Cinema*.[85] There was no "cinema," Gaudreault asserts, until cinema became institutionalized and was thereby distinguished unequivocally from what came before—"kinematography" or "kino-attractography" or what has been known in English-language studies as "early cinema." For Gaudreault, even though the dividing line between these two "paradigms" is clear, institutionalization is not an event, but a "slow process" that begins in 1907–8, moves through a "proto-institutional" period during 1908–14, and is fully realized by around 1915. It requires both "objective" conditions—the introduction of trade magazines, trade organizations, film exchanges—and "subjective" conditions, meaning the efforts of certain practitioners, notably working for Pathé.

The institutionalization of cinema, for Gaudreault, had nothing directly to do with attaining some level of cultural visibility, with the everyday ubiquity of Hollywood across North American communities large and small, or with what *Exhibitors Trade Review* meant when it counseled exhibitors to make the movie theater a local institution. Institutionalization, Gaudreault argues, establishes and is defined by "rules, constraints, exclusions, and procedure," as certain ways of producing meaning by filmmakers and viewers alike become "regulated and sanctioned." In and through this process of "normalization and codification," cinema gains "stability, specificity, and legitimacy."

Although Gaudreault does not take up nontheatrical film or devote much attention to how exhibition practices might figure in the changes during the 1910s, it would be well worth exploring whether educational cinema in some fashion replicated the historical trajectory he proposes for cinema. Or perhaps educational cinema was prompted or bullied into its own efforts at institutionalization when confronted with the overarching fact of motion pictures becoming Institutional Cinema (or what we might simply call *the movies*)? Of the practices and publications I have examined in this essay, only *Motion Pictures in Education* could readily be seen as an attempt to push educational cinema down the institutional path of medium specificity and regulated meaning production, in that Ellis and Thornborough set out to codify best practices for the production and teaching of the classroom film as an autonomous and pedagogically legitimate genre. By way of contrast, an organization with institutionalizing aims like the National Academy of Visual Instruction aimed to stabilize the field of educational cinema by regulating and sanctioning film circulation rather than the production and reception of motion pictures.

Whether or not there is in fact a master historical narrative of educational cinema in the United States, what the examples I have examined most emphatically demonstrate are the varied imperatives, trajectories, and velocities of institutionalization as a historically specific set of practices and discourses—concerned in the early 1920s with putting motion pictures to use, incorporating them into organizations, professionalizing a field, prescribing best practices, and disseminating information. That institutionalization, so understood, is richly multivalent and multipurpose makes it, to my mind, a valuable heuristic for thinking about the history of educational cinema and, more broadly, the history of multi-sited cinema in the United States.

Notes

1. See, especially, Hays's much-publicized address to the National Educational Association convention in Boston on July 6, 1922, which is quoted at length in "Wants Aid of N.E.A.," *Film Daily* 21, no. 6 (July 7, 1922), 1–2. For a broader chronological history of educational film in the United States, see Devin Orgeron, Marsha Orgeron, and Dan Streible, "A History of Learning with the Lights Off," in *Learning with the Lights Off: Educational Film in the United States*, ed. Devon Orgeron, Marsha Orgeron, and Dan Streible (New York: Oxford University Press, 2012), 15–66.

2. Edward Cary Hayes, *An Introduction to the Study of Sociology* (New York: Appleton, 1923), 405–9; John Mecklin Moffatt, *An Introduction to Social Ethics: The Social Conscience in a Democracy* (New York: Harcourt, Brace and Howe, 1920), 207–9.

3. "What Do You Want?" *Photoplay* 21, no. 6 (May 1922), 1; Cecil B. De Mille, "The Screen Considered in Relation to the Social Fabric," *Moving Picture Age* 3, no. 2 (February 1920), 17–18.

4. "The Importance of Importance," *Exhibitors Herald* 10, no. 25 (1920): 45; "An Announcement," *Exhibitors Trade Review* 10, no. 14 (1921): 21.

5. Whatever else institutionalization might have meant in relation to educational cinema in the period under consideration, it did not refer to the familiar contemporary use of the term as meaning committing and confining someone to an institution, sometimes against his or her will. (Although, motion pictures were screened in what Ernest Goffman called "total institutions" like hospitals, penitentiaries, and orphanages.) Nothing I have seen from the early 1920s, at least, posits that institutionalizing educational cinema might be a form of confinement, incarceration, health management, or debilitating punishment. If anything, this meaning of institutionalization echoes more clearly with an abiding anxiety about commercial cinema, which, like those deemed dangerous, unmanageable, or infectious enough to need professional care, supervision, and sequestering from society at large, might be reformed, made well (or at least less dangerous to society), nurtured, turned into a good citizen if housed in the right institutional home—say, under the watchful eye of a federal censorship board.

6. Even a simple search for "educational film" also quickly and quite dramatically reveals the range of motion pictures that in 1922 were identified (and often advertised) as examples

of "educational film": industrials, USDA and Bureau of Mines films, advertisements for corsets or Fords, American Farm Bureau films, travelogues, historical dramas. Many of the titles designated as "educational films" were being shown in movie theaters as part of regular programming or as specially scheduled screenings.

7. The Hibbing screening is reported in the *Duluth (MN) News-Tribune*, September 25, 1922, 6; the Mount Vernon screening in *Democratic Banner* (Mount Vernon, OH), February 3, 1922, 1.

8. *Lawrence (KA) Journal World*, June 19, 1924, 1; *Holbrook (AZ) News*, October 1, 1920, 2. See also William Allen White's claim that "America is an attempt to institutionalize the Puritan ideal . . . basically an economic aspiration. It hopes for the greatest good for the greatest number" (reprinted from *Collier's Weekly* by the *Denver Post*, July 11, 1922, 12).

9. In thinking through the notion of institutionalization as incorporation, I am indebted to a wave of excellent research on the public institutional settings for nontheatrical cinema during the 1910s–20s, including Alison Griffiths, "A Portal to the Outside World: Motion Pictures in the Penitentiary," *Film History* 25, no. 4 (2013): 1–35; essays in *Learning with the Lights Off* by Miriam Posner (on the Red Cross), Alison Griffiths (on the Natural History Museum), and Kristin Ostherr (on the American College of Surgeons); and essays in *Useful Cinema*, ed. Charles R. Acland and Haidee Wasson (Durham, NC: Duke University Press, 2011) by Jennifer Horne (on libraries) and Haidee Wasson (on art museums).

10. On the USDA, see, for example, John L. Cobbs Jr., "Playing the Farmer's Game," *Moving Picture Age* 4, no. 10 (1921): 9–10; on Ford, see Lee Grieveson, "Visualizing Industrial Citizenship," in *Learning with the Lights Off*, ed. Devin Orgeron, Marsha Orgeron, and Dan Streible (New York: Oxford University Press, 2011), 107–23; and "The Work of Film in the Age of Fordist Mechanization," *Cinema Journal* 51, no. 2 (2012): 25–51.

11. See, for example, the listing in Don Carlos Ellis and Laura Thornborough, *Motion Pictures in Education* (New York: Thomas Y. Crowell, 1923), 266–67. Will Hays in his address to the NEA referred to "28 colleges and universities which have organized departments for the distribution of film" (2).

12. For information on Iowa State College, see Charles Roach, "Visual Instruction in the School Room: I. The Part Pictures Play in Instruction," *Moving Picture Age* 4, no. 3 (1921): 11–12; for Kansas State, see W. O. Starks, "Visual Education in Kansas," *Moving Picture Age* 4, no. 19 (1921): 18, 42; for the University of Oklahoma, see "Visual Instruction in Oklahoma," *Moving Picture Age* 4, no. 3 (1921): 32.

13. For a period discussion fully endorsing the work of extension divisions of state universities, see W. S. Bittner, *The University Extension Movement*, Bulletin 84 (Bureau of Education 1919). Bittner was at this time associate director of IU's Extension Division.

14. The Extension Division's promotional efforts never flagged. See, for instance, "University Extension—What It Is," *Bulletin of the Extension Division, Indiana University* 6, no. 6 (1924).

15. "Visual Instruction," *Bulletin of the Extension Division, Indiana University* 4, no. 7 (1919): 4–5.

16. "Scope of Extension Work Reaches over Entire State," *Bloomington Daily Student*, July 20, 1919, 4.

17. "Expert Will Demonstrate Visual Education on Campus, July 25–26," *Bloomington Daily Student*, July 14, 1921, 1.

18. "University Bureau of Visual Instruction Serves More than 400 Communities in a Year," *Indiana Summer Student*, June 15, 1923, 4. Of course, when it came to numbers, the Bureau of Visual Instruction had nothing on Will Hays, who in his speech to the National Education Association in July 1922 described the motion picture as "one of the greatest industries in America having an investment of $1,250,000,000 with $75,000,000 paid annually in salaries

and wages, and $520,000,000 taken in annually for admissions" quoted in *That Marvel—The Movie* (1923), 23.

19. For instance, the *Batesville (IN) Tribune*, January 5, 1922, 1, reported that *A Hoosier Romance* (booked through the BVI) would be the first of a series of ten films shown at a local theater under the auspices of local schools. Similarly with *The Mill on the Floss* in Middlebury (*Middlebury [IN] Independent*, May 12, 1922, 4).

20. A pamphlet by A. P. Hollis published in 1924 by the Department of the Interior's Bureau of Education includes both the number of films held by visual education departments in state universities and also "the chief sources" of these film holdings, headed by the US government agencies, Ford, George Kleine, the Bureau of Commercial Economics, and various "industrial firms." Hollis notes that the "wide use" of Kleine's films by "State institutions" is "an index of their tendency to attempt to cover the entertainment field in churches and schools as well as the strictly educational and religious" (25).

21. H. W. Norman, "A Program for State-Wide Film Instruction," *Visual Education* 4, no. 5 (1923): 145. Norman had been directing the Bureau for Visual Instruction while still an undergraduate at the university. In January 1921, he completed his BA thesis in the Department of Economics and Social Science, entitled "Visual Instruction through Motion Pictures." Much of the material in Norman's "Stimulative Visual Work at Indiana University," *Educational Film Magazine* 4, no. 6 (1920): 8–9, 24, appears in his thesis.

22. "Visual Instruction," *Bulletin of the Extension Division, Indiana University* 4, no. 7 (1919): 4.

23. See, for instance, "Sixteen New Films Swell Collection," *Bloomington Daily Student*, October 21, 1920, 1; "Extension Film Service Meets Heavy Demand," *Bloomington Daily Student*, June 21, 1921, 3; "Motion Pictures: Bureau of Visual Instruction," *Bulletin of the Extension Service of Indiana University* 10, no. 11 (1925), which has for its cover page a list of fifteen "Groups Using Films."

24. *Bulletin of the Extension Division, Indiana University* 6, no. 5 (January 1921): 30. Norman, in "Stimulative Visual Work," mentions the purchase of production equipment (8).

25. "Offer Extension Course in Visual Instruction," *Bloomington Daily Student*, March 29, 1921, 3.

26. Norman, "Stimulative Visual Work," 8. Much of the information from this article by Norman also appears in "Two Hundred Schools Show Films Says Bureau Report," *Exhibitors Herald* 11, no. 21 (1920): 34.

27. A contemporary account of the AFBF in relation to previous farmer organizations is Orville Merton Kile, *The Farm Bureau Movement* (New York: Macmillan, 1921).

28. The AFBF's initial policies and objectives were spelled out most directly in the pamphlet, *American Farm Bureau Federation—What Is It?* which was reprinted in full as part of the congressional hearings in the volume, *Farm Organizations: Hearings before the Committee on Banking and Currency in the House of Representatives, February 1, 1921* (Washington: Government Printing Office, 1921), 59–64. Robert H. Wiebe argues that with the formation of the AFBF "the firm business values, the new vocabulary of marketing and chemistry, and the exaggerated repudiation of the Populist heritage emerged most clearly, an official declaration of these farmers as agricultural businessmen" (*The Search for Order: 1877–1920* [New York: Hill and Want, 1967], 127).

29. American Farm Bureau Federation, *Annual Report* 3 (1922): 53.

30. See Kile, *Farm Bureau Movement*, 62–93. Before the founding of the AFBF, at least some local Farm Bureaus (often in collaboration with county extension agents) had screened films. See, for instance, "Salt Lake County Will Use Films to Educate Farmers," *Exhibitors Herald* 6, no. 13 (October 23, 1918): 36.

31. "Movie Show Program," *Hancock County Farm Bureau Bulletin* 3, no. 3 (1922): 8.
32. *Moving Picture Age* 5, no. 5 (1922): 13.
33. Charles H. Obye," Results Count!" *Moving Picture Age* 5, no. 8 (1922): 12. See also, for example, W. H. Williamson, "Farm Bureau Work with Moving Pictures in Iowa," *Moving Picture Age* 3, no. 2 (1920): 16; I. R. Bradshaw, "Rural Showings," *Moving Picture Age* 4, no. 10 (1921): 16, 39; "Farmers and Film" *Visual Education*, October–November 1922, 371–72. C. M. Yerrington, "Enhancing Farm-Bureau Results," *Moving Picture Age* 5, no. 1 (1922): 15–16, 12; Charles A. Rehling, "More Power Through Pictures," *Moving Picture Age* 5, no. 3 (1922): 10; Murray E. Stebbins, "Rural Exhibitions in Montana," *Moving Picture Age* 5, no. 4 (19122): 15; E. M. Phillips, "Logical Appeals to Interest," *Moving Picture Age* 5, no. 5 (1922): 13–4; G. F. Baumeister, "Bringing Them Out," *Moving Picture Age* 5, no. 6 (1922): 11, 19; Alfred Raut, "A Spur to Thought," *Moving Picture Age* 5, no. 7 (1922).
34. "Motion Picture Service Department," *County Agent and Farm Bureau* 9, no. 6 (1912): 24–26.
35. See, for instance, "Motion Picture Service Department," *County Agent and Farm Bureau* 9, no. 9 (September 1921): 18–21; W. R. Rutledge, "The County Agent and Film Projection," *County Agent and Farm Bureau* 9, no. 12 (December 1921): 18; Raymond Cavanaugh, "Retroscope Overcomes 'Rewind' Problems," *County Agent and Farm Bureau* 10, no. 3 (1922): 17–18; "What the 'Movies' Are Doing for the Farmer," *County Agent and Farm Bureau* 10, no. 3 (1922): 18–19.
36. "Farm Bureau Federation Sponsors Extensive Motion Picture Undertaking," *County Agent and Farm Bureau Magazine* 10, no. 4 (April 1922):25; American Farm Bureau Federation, *Annual Report* 3 (1922): 55.
37. See Cobbs, "Playing the Farmer's Game," 9–10. New USDA releases were announced in virtually every issue of *Moving Picture Age* and other visual education periodicals in this period.
38. See Homestead ad for *Joe McGuire, Moving Picture Age*, October 1922, 23; for information about screenings: *Wyoming (IL) Post Herald*, September 6, 1922, 7; *Princeton (IL) Daily Democrat*, January 39, 1923, 1.
39. "Farm Bureau Federation Sponsors Extensive Motion Picture Undertaking," *County Agent and Farm Bureau Magazine* 10, no. 4 (April 1922): 25.
40. M. A. Thorfinnson, "Movies Valuable in Extension Work," *County Agent and Farm Bureau* 10, no. 4 (April 1922): 24–25.
41. E. L. Bill, "Filming the Home Acres," *Moving Picture Age* 5, no. 2 (February 1922): 15.
42. Wiebe, *Search for Order*, xiv, 295.
43. Orgeron, Orgeron, and Streible, *Learning with the Lights Off*, 26–28.
44. Dudley Grant Hays, "The New Department of the N.E.A.," *Educational Screen* 2, no. 6 (June 1923): 281–83; Ellsworth C. Dent, "The Washington Meeting," *Educational Screen* 11, no. 3 (March 1932), 66–67, 84.
45. For early endorsements of NAVI's aspirations to institutionalizing the field, see *Visual Education* 1, no. 5 (September–October 1920): 39; "An Academy of Visual Instruction," *Educational Film Magazine* 3, no. 6 (1920): 7.
46. *Proceedings of the Annual Meeting of the National Academy of Visual Instruction* (Madison, Wisconsin, 1922), 10. For an example of the syndicated coverage in local newspapers, see "Movies as Educational Enterprise to be Considered," *Connorsville (IN) News Examiner*, July 7, 1920, 6, which foregrounds the conference's attention to a range of "educational" movies produced for "home, farm, church, industry and school." William H. Dudley (1868–1941) was then directing the Bureau of Visual Instruction at the University of Wisconsin–Madison, a

position he held from 1913 to 1928. Another way of approaching the history of educational film in the United States would, in fact, be tracking the career of a figure like Dudley, who in addition to his efforts on behalf of NAVI and for the University of Wisconsin also served on the editorial board of *Reel and Slide* and *Moving Picture Age*; wrote the Bureau of Education pamphlet, *Organization for Visual Instruction* (GPO 1921); worked with Yale University Press in developing the *Chronicles of America* series of films (1928); continued to lecture and publish in *Educational Screen* in the 1930s; and from 1929 to 1938 ran his own distribution company, the William H. Dudley Visual Educational Service, based in Chicago.

47. Mary Douglas, *How Institutions Think* (Syracuse: Syracuse University Press, 1986), 111.

48. "Constitution of the Academy," reprinted in *Moving Picture Age* 4, no. 10 (October 1921): 17.

49. *Proceedings of the Annual Meeting of the National Academy of Visual Instruction* (Madison, Wisconsin, 1922).

50. *Proceedings of the Annual Meeting of the National Academy of Visual Instruction* (Madison, Wisconsin, 1922), 13–14. Founded by Crandall in 1922, the Visual Instruction Association of America quite explicitly aimed to "bring producers, distributors, and users of instructional films together for co-operation on an equal footing for the advancement of visual instruction." The initial officers included representatives from the commercial companies, Pathé and National Non-Theatrical Motion Pictures. See "The Visual Instruction Association of America," *American Cinematographer* 3, no. 1 (1922): 30.

51. *Moving Picture Age* 4, no. 11 (November 1921): 13.

52. "The National Academy of Visual Instruction," *Educational Film Magazine* 7, nos. 2–3 (1922): 4–5.

53. J. W. Shepherd, "Are More Organizations Needed?" *Educational Screen* 1, no. 4 (1922): 107–8; J. W. Shepherd, "The Meeting of the National Academy of Visual Instruction," *Educational Screen* 1, no. 5 (1922): 131–34; Editorial, *Educational Screen* 2, no. 3 (1923): 101. For material on the fourth NAVI conference, see "The Fourth Annual Meeting," *Educational Screen* 2, no. 2 (1923): 83–84; "Evening Film Showings," *Educational Screen* 2, no. 4 (1923): 164–65.

54. "What the Academy Is," *Educational Screen* 2, no. 9 (1923): 439.

55. Laura Thornborough (1885–1973) had apparently worked on scenarios for the USDA before becoming a professional writer (her *Etiquette for Everybody* appeared in 1924, with *Interior Decorating for Everybody* a year later). Thornborough taught a summer course called "Visual Aids in Education" at George Washington in July 1924 "Visual Aids in Education," *New York Times*, June 15, 1924, x.2. Don Carlos Ellis had headed the Education Section of the US Forest Service, before organizing and directing the USDA motion picture section. He resigned in 1920 to enter the private sector, first as director of Educational Production at Universal Studio, then soon thereafter as a cofounder of the Harry Levey Service Corporation ("Producers and Distributors of Industrial-Educational Film" announced a June 1920 ad). With Levey, Ellis in November 1923 formed National Non-Theatrical Motion Pictures, a distribution company, and then Ellis helped to found General Vision Company, which specialized in religious and educational motion pictures. He published articles about film production at the USDA—including one in the fan magazine, *Motion Picture Story*—and became secretary of the Visual Instruction Association of America in 1922. For information on Ellis, see the introduction to *Motion Pictures in Education* by Philander P. Claxton, former US commissioner of education; *Educational Film Magazine* 3, no. 6 (June 1920): 11; Harry Levey Service Corporation ad, *Wid's Daily* 13, no. 4 (1920): 6; *Moving Picture Age* 3, no. 3 (1920): 48; "The Visual Instruction Association of America," *American Cinematographer* 3, no. 1 (1922): 30; *Exhibitors Herald* 17,

no. 22 (1923): 38; *Educational Screen* 3, no. 7 (1924): 291. Ellis's articles on the USDA motion picture program include "Movies on Husbandry at State Fairs," *Reel and Slide* 2, no. 2 (February 1919): 11; ad announcing the founding of National Non-Theatrical Motion Pictures Inc. *Moving Picture Age* 4, no. 6 (June 1921): 38; and "Starring Nature," *Motion Picture Magazine* 20, no. 12 (January 1921): 38–39, 103.

56. *Motion Pictures in Education*, 28.

57. "Another Forward Step," *Educational Screen* 3, no. 7 (September 1924): 291.

58. *Motion Pictures in Education*, 25.

59. Ibid., 21.

60. Ibid., 40.

61. See Amanda R. Keeler, "'Sugar Coat the Educational Pill': The Early Educational Aspirations of Film, Radio, and Television" (PhD diss., Indiana University, 2011).

62. *Motion Pictures in Education*, 256.

63. Ibid., 159–61.

64. Ibid., 165.

65. Ibid., 202, 167–69, 165, 170.

66. Ibid., 17.

67. Ibid., 33, 117, 129, 135.

68. Ibid., 129, 134, 139.

69. Ibid., 135.

70. Ibid., 258. On "genrification," see Rick Altman, *Film/Genre* (London: British Film Institute, 1999).

71. Don Carlos Ellis, "What the Association Proposes to Do," *Educational Screen* 2, no. 1 (1923): 36–37.

72. See the Department of the Interior's "illustration" of its activities, "Exhibition Week May, 1919," (Washington, DC: GPO, 1919), 8. Here visual instruction is listed under "Educational Extension," which has the responsibility "to make available to university extension divisions the visual instruction material collected by the Federal Government for the purpose of individual and mass education."

73. Quoted in Fred F. Perkins, "Film Service Uncle Sam Can Give You," *Moving Picture Age* 3, no. 9 (1920): 9. All the accounts I have found of the footage from the Bureau of Education that was distributed through extension departments only mention the government's war films and not any motion pictures that came from private companies. There is some indication that the Bureau of Education's Visual Instruction Department distributed at least a few films, like *Our Wings of Victory*, about airplane production and use, mentioned in *Visual Education* 1, no. 5 (1920): 55.

74. Quoted in Perkins, "Film Service Uncle Sam Can Give You," 9.

75. *Moving Picture Age* 4, no. 5 (1921): 3. The *Washington Post*'s detailed description of the activities and personnel of the Bureau of Education in 1921 made no mention at all of Visual Instruction or motion pictures ("Half Hours with the Government Departments: Bureau of Education," *Washington Post*, March 6, 1921, 50). The *Report of the Commissioner of Education for the Year Ended June, 20, 1921* only mentioned "Visual Education" as one of several "recommendations" should funding become available.

76. The Bureau of Education published ninety-one bulletins in 1919, including one explaining the university extension movement and several titles concerning the role of education in the process of Americanization.

77. *Motion Pictures and Motion-Picture Equipment: A Handbook of General Information* (Bureau of Education Bulletin, 1919, No. 82), 4.

78. *Educational Institutions Equipped with Motion-Picture Projection Machines* (Visual Instruction Leaflet no. 1), 2.

79. *Educational Institutions Equipped with Motion-Picture Projection Machines* (Visual Instruction Leaflet no. 1), 1.

80. F. R. Egner, who was identified as "formerly in Charge of Visual Instruction Section, Bureau of Education" made use of the information compiled by these questionnaires in his article, "A Suggestion for a National Educational Film Service for Educational Institutions," *Visual Education* 2, no. 2 (1921): 27–31. Extrapolating from the percentage of questionnaires returned, Egner concluded that that there are sixty-four hundred projectors in American educational institutions. He also explains that of the schools that depended on screening facilities located elsewhere, 62 percent used theaters, 30 percent used halls or lodges, and 8 percent used churches.

81. Commenting on the sort of films covered in this leaflet, Egner pointed out that films produced by manufacturers are very often "of a publicity nature" and will serve, at best, for "recreational and community purposes and . . . as fillers in pedagogical film programs" ("A Suggestion for a National Educational Film Service for Educational Institutions," 30–31).

82. *Learning with the Lights Off* offers a comprehensive overview of the history of educational film (15–66).

83. Douglas, *How Institutions Think*, 47.

84. Milton Ford Baldwin, "Introducing a Vital Asset," *County Agent and Farm Bureau Magazine* 9, no. 9 (1921): 6.

85. The following summary and all direct quotations are drawn from André Gaudreault, *Film and Attraction: From Kinematography to Cinema* [2008], trans. Timothy Bernard (Urbana: University of Illinois Press, 2011), 55–71, 83–84.

Filmography

A Hoosier Schoolmaster (dir. Edwin August & Max Figman, Masterpiece Film Manufacturing Company, 1914).
Cajus Julius Caesar (dir. Enrico Guazzoni, Società Italiana, 1914).
Chinch Bugs and How to Control Them (Homestead Films, c. 1922).
Farming in One Lesson (Homestead Films, c. 1922).
Horse Sense (Homestead Films, c. 1922).
Joe McGuire (Homestead Films).
King Basketball (Indiana University Bureau of Visual Instruction, 1924).
Nanook of the North (dir. Robert J. Flaherty, Les Frères Revillon & Pathé Exchange, 1922).
Spring Valley (Homestead Films c. 1921).
Quo Vadis (dir. Enrico Guazzoni, Società Italiana Cines, 1913).
Take a Chance (dir. Alfred J. Goulding, Rolin Films, 1918).

Bibliography

Acland, Charles R., and Haidee Wasson, eds. *Useful Cinema*. Durham, NC: Duke University Press, 2011.
Altman, Rick. *Film/Genre*. London: British Film Institute, 1999.

"An Announcement." *Exhibitors Trade Review* 10, no. 14 (1921): 21.
Baumeister, G. F. "Bringing Them Out." *Moving Picture Age* 5, no. 6 (1922): 11, 19.
Bradshaw, I. R. "Rural Showings." *Moving Picture Age* 4, no. 10 (1921): 16, 39.
Cobbs Jr., John L. "Playing the Farmer's Game." *Moving Picture Age* 4, no. 10 (1921): 9–10.
De Mille, Cecil B. "The Screen Considered in Relation to the Social Fabric." *Moving Picture Age* 3, no. 2 (February 1920): 17–18.
Dent, Ellsworth C. "The Washington Meeting." *Educational Screen* 11, no. 3 (March 1932): 66–67, 84.
Douglas, Mary. *How Institutions Think*. Syracuse: Syracuse University Press, 1986.
Ellis, Don Carlos, and Laura Thornborough. *Motion Pictures in Education*. New York: Thomas Y. Crowell, 1923.
"Farmers and Film." *Visual Education*, October–November 1922, 371–72.
Gaudreault, André. *Film and Attraction: From Kinematography to Cinema*. Translated by Timothy Bernard. Urbana: University of Illinois Press, 2011.
Grieveson, Lee. "Visualizing Industrial Citizenship." In *Learning with the Lights Off: Educational Film in the United States*, edited by Devin Orgeron, Marsha Orgeron, and Dan Streible, 107–23. New York: Oxford University Press, 2011.
———. "The Work of Film in the Age of Fordist Mechanization." *Cinema Journal* 51, no. 3 (Spring 2012): 25–51.
Griffiths, Alison. "A Portal to the Outside World: Motion Pictures in the Penitentiary." *Film History* 25, no. 4 (2013): 1–35.
Hayes, Edward Cary. *An Introduction to the Study of Sociology*. New York: Appleton, 1923.
"The Importance of Importance." *Exhibitors Herald* 10, no. 25 (1920): 45.
Keeler, Amanda R. "'Sugar Coat the Educational Pill': The Early Educational Aspirations of Film, Radio, and Television." PhD diss., Indiana University, 2011.
Kile, Merton. *The Farm Bureau Movement*. New York: Macmillan, 1921.
Moffatt, John Mecklin. *An Introduction to Social Ethics: The Social Conscience in a Democracy*. New York: Harcourt, Brace and Howe, 1920.
Obye, Charles H. "Results Count!" *Moving Picture Age* 5, no. 8 (1922): 12.
Orgeron, Devin, Marsha Orgeron, and Dan Streible. "A History of Learning with the Lights Off." In *Learning with the Lights Off: Educational Film in the United States*, edited by Devon Orgeron, Marsha Orgeron, and Dan Streible, 15–66. New York: Oxford University Press, 2012.
———, eds. *Learning with the Lights Off: Educational Film in the United States*. New York: Oxford University Press, 2012.
Phillips, E. M. "Logical Appeals to Interest." *Moving Picture Age* 5, no. 5 (1922): 13–14.
Proceedings of the Annual Meeting of the National Academy of Visual Instruction. Madison, Wisconsin, 1922.
Raut, Alfred. "A Spur to Thought." *Moving Picture Age* 5, no. 7 (1922).
Rehling, Charles A. "More Power Through Pictures." *Moving Picture Age* 5, no. 3 (1922): 10.
Roach, Charles. "Visual Instruction in the School Room: I. The Part Pictures Play in Instruction." *Moving Picture Age* 4, no. 3 (1921): 11–12.
Starks, W. O. "Visual Education in Kansas." *Moving Picture Age* 4, no. 19 (1921): 18, 42.
Stebbins, Murray E. "Rural Exhibitions in Montana." *Moving Picture Age* 5, no. 4 (1922): 15.
"Visual Instruction in Oklahoma." *Moving Picture Age* 4, no. 3 (1921): 32.
"Wants Aid of N.E.A." *Film Daily* 21, no. 6 (July 7, 1922): 1–2.
"What Do You Want?" *Photoplay* 21, no. 6 (May 1922): 1.
Wiebe, Robert H. *The Search for Order: 1877–1920*. New York: Hill and Want, 1967.

Williamson, W. H. "Farm Bureau Work with Moving Pictures in Iowa." *Moving Picture Age* 3, no. 2 (1920): 16.
C. M. Yerrington. "Enhancing Farm-Bureau Results." *Moving Picture Age* 5, no. 1 (1922): 15–16, 12.

GREGORY A. WALLER is Provost Professor and Director of Cinema and Media Studies in the Media School at Indiana University. He is author of *Main Street Amusements: Movies and Commercial Entertainment in a Southern City, 1896–1930*, and editor of *Film History*.

Index

Page numbers in italics refer to figures.

www.ingramcontent.com/pod-product-compliance
Lightning Source LLC
LaVergne TN
LVHW090755070826
844660LV00024B/1143

* 9 7 8 0 2 5 3 0 4 5 2 0 1 *